THE

EXISTING CONFLICT

BETWEEN

REPUBLICAN GOVERNMENT

AND

Southern Oligarchy

BY

GREEN B. RAUM

NEGRO UNIVERSITIES PRESS
NEW YORK

Originally published in 1884
by The Charles M. Greene Printing Co., Washington, D.C.

Reprinted 1969 by
Negro Universities Press
A DIVISION OF GREENWOOD PUBLISHING CORP.
NEW YORK

SBN 8371-1618-X

PRINTED IN UNITED STATES OF AMERICA

TO

ALL LOVERS OF REPUBLICAN LIBERTY

WHO

WISH TO MAINTAIN AND PRESERVE THE

BASIS ON WHICH IT RESTS,

NAMELY:

"A FREE BALLOT, AN HONEST COUNT AND CORRECT RETURNS,"

THIS BOOK IS

FRATERNALLY DEDICATED

BY THE AUTHOR.

> *I am in blood*
> *Stepp'd in so far, that, should I wade no more*
> *Returning were as tedious as go o'er.*
>
> —SHAKESPEARE, Macbeth, Act 3, Sc. iv.

> *May one be pardoned and retain the offence?*
> *   *   *   *   *   *
> *In the corrupted currents of this world*
> *Offence's gilded hand may shove by justice,*
> *And oft 'tis seen, the wicked prize itself*
>   *Buys out the law.*
>
> —SHAKESPEARE, Hamlet, Act 3, Sc. iii.

TABLE OF CONTENTS.

CHAPTER I.

CHAPTER II.

CHAPTER III.

CHAPTER XX.

CHAPTER XXI.

CHAPTER XXII.

CHAPTER XXIII.

CHAPTER XXIV.

CHAPTER XXV.

CHAPTER XXVI.

THE EXISTING CONFLICT.

CHAPTER I.

INTRODUCTORY.

Free Speech and a Free Ballot the Corner-stones of Republican Government—Thomas Jefferson's Opinions—The People will not long Tolerate Abuses in Government—Relations of Duties of Electors and Advantages of Good Government—Grounds for Division in Politics stated—Progressive Influence of Liberty and Equality upon Politics—Suppression of Free Speech and a Free Ballot a Crime against Republican Government—The Victims entitled to Universal Sympathy—Accusation of National Republican Convention against Democratic Party—It must be Met—False Step of Southern People in 1865—Aim of this Work to trace Political Events in Southern States since 1865, and to show how the South was made Solid for the Democracy.

THE pride and boast of the American citizen is the free representative republican form of government under which we live. This system is founded upon the principle that governments derive their just powers from the consent of the governed.

The corner-stones of the structure are the right of Free Speech and the right of a Free Ballot.

The success and permanence of the system unquestionably depends upon the maintenance of these rights.

In laying down a creed of political faith, Thomas Jefferson insisted upon a jealous care of the right of election by the people, and absolute acquiescence in the decisions of the majority; he declared in favor of the diffusion of information and the arraignment of all abuses at the bar of public reason.

The interests of the masses of the people of each State and of the Nation are so indissolubly connected with the laws, the administration of justice, and the general conduct of public affairs, that they will not long tolerate abuses either in the character of the laws or of their administration if the abuses are " arraigned at the bar of public reason."

The natural relation between duties well performed by the elector and the advantages of good government under honest and competent public servants, is so intimate, that majorities, although sometimes falling into error, may be relied upon to secure to all equal rights under just laws.

The free, unrestrained interchange of opinions among the people upon public questions has a permanent healthful influence in the interest of good government. If this be not so, then are all our hopes vain for maintaining good government founded upon the will of the people. Observation and experience have shown that where the rights of the educated and intelligent are identical with those of the illiterate and ignorant, the difference in attainment will not be the line of party division between them, unless those of superior education choose to have it so. Men divide in politics upon issues involving individual rights and liberties, and pecuniary interests. Particular classes of persons will act together in politics when they find their rights invaded; they will unite with and cling to a party which promises relief, and oppose with their utmost power a party which seeks to deprive them of their rights or to destroy their financial interests.

The Spirit of Progress, born of Liberty and Equality, animates the people in all the avenues of thought and action. Its influence has been highly beneficial in bringing the people into more direct relations with public affairs.

While our form of government is now practically the same as when our forefathers made it, the influence and control of the people over it is immeasurably greater to-day than when it was formed. Originally the people had very little to do in selecting candidates for office, or in determining the principles which were to control them when elected.

In his first inaugural address as President, Thomas Jefferson laid down a political code, which was accepted by his adherents as a permanent platform of principles. *He* made a platform for his *party ;* now *parties* make platforms for their candidates.

Now the people, acting through their political parties, call conventions, select delegates to represent them, in a popular assemblage not provided for by law—an assemblage which possesses neither legislative, executive, nor judicial powers; they announce principles and policies for the Government, and select candidates to be voted for to fill the various offices required for making and enforcing laws.

These are the methods which have been adopted by the people as a means of giving general direction to the movements of the State and Nation, and of maintaining a proper accountability of public officers. Add to these free and voluntary proceedings the public discussion of the relative merits of parties and candidates, a free and fair election, and an honest declaration of the result, followed by the peaceful acquiescence of the minority, and you have the highest type of civil government by the people. This system grows more and more in favor with mankind the world over with each revolving year.

The great body of the people expressing their opinions through these conventions and ballot-boxes are animated by a desire to secure the passage of wholesome laws, the honest and economical administration of the government, the promotion of the general welfare of the people, and especially the protection of every citizen in his equal and just rights. So long as the ballot is free, and every elector can freely and voluntarily vote for the candidate of his choice, and have his ballot honestly counted and declared, so long will our rights of life, liberty, and property be secured. It must never be forgotten that the right of free discussion is inseparable from, and essential to, the exercise of the right of a free ballot.

When free speech shall be effectually denied to the majority of the people, and the ballot shall no longer register their will, the rights of the people will be already gone, and life, liberty, and property will be at the mercy of the usurper.

The suppression of free speech and a free ballot is a crime against republican government: it saps and mines the very foundation of the system. It is a crime so black and damnable that the perpetrators of it deserve the execration and condemnation of all liberty-loving people.

The victims of such a usurpation are entitled to universal sympathy: their cause should be made the cause of every right-minded citizen; the public press should agitate for their relief, and all constitutional means should be exhausted by every department of the Government in their behalf.

The Republican Party in National Convention assembled at Chicago, Ill., June 3, 1884, adopted as a part of its platform the following resolution:

"The perpetuity of our institutions rests upon the maintenance of a free ballot, an honest count, and correct returns. We denounce the fraud and violence practised by the Democracy in Southern States, by which the will of the voter is defeated, as dangerous to the preservation of free institutions; and we solemnly arraign the Democratic Party as being the guilty recipient of the fruits of such fraud and violence.

"We extend to the Republicans of the South, regardless of their former party affiliations, our cordial sympathy, and pledge to them our most earnest efforts to promote the passage of such legislation as will secure to every citizen, of whatever race and color, the full and complete recognition, possession, and exercise of all civil and political rights."

The charge here preferred against the Democratic Party is of immense gravity. If true, the law-abiding people of this country should in the most signal manner express their abhorrence and utter condemnation of its conduct by its overwhelming defeat in the Presidential and Congressional elections. If this charge is untrue—is not capable of being proven by satisfactory testimony, it should react upon the heads of those who make it.

This accusation cannot be treated lightly; it cannot be thrust aside as meaningless, and unworthy of consideration; it must form one of the issues in the Presidential contest of 1884. The conflict of opinion between the Republican and Democratic parties upon all the questions which grew out of the Rebellion was radical and uncompromising. The giving of freedom, citizenship, and the ballot to the negro race was resisted at every point by the entire strength of the Democratic Party; and these questions constituted the line of party division between the old slaveholders and the freedmen. If, when President Johnson in 1865 placed the reorganization of the Southern States solely in the hands of white men, they had enacted laws securing to the colored people equal rights, and encouraged and protected them in the right to acquire property, to work and receive wages, and to enjoy the fruits of their labor, and for the education of their children, had treated them with humanity, and had manifested a disposition to aid in their elevation, their advancement and prosperity, such relations of interest and sympathy would have been established between them that no cause would have existed for political divisions: the two races would have gone forward in peace and harmony, in building up the places laid waste by the war, and in the development of their country.

This, however, was not done: it was not done because the white people elected that it should not be done. The colored people had no voice in deciding this question: their old masters were to consider, were to weigh, were to decide, whether this course, which seemed to be dictated by the logic of the situation, should be adopted and carried out in an enlightened, humane, and Christian spirit.

The object of these pages is to trace the course of political events since the close of the civil war as they relate to the Southern States; to recall to the public mind the manner in which the Republican Party was overthrown in some of those States; and to point out the means by which the South is made *solid* for the Democratic Party.

CHAPTER II.

THE BLACK CODES OF 1865.

South Carolina—Contracts for Service—Regulation of Labor on Farms—Causes of Discharge of a Servant—Regulation of House Servants—Form of Contract—Colored Mechanics, Artisans, and Shopkeepers to be Licensed—Servants forbidden to acquire Homes —Servants forbidden to sell the Products of Labor without Permit —Arms forbidden to Colored Men—Migration of Colored People, except under Bond, forbidden—Mississippi—The Vagrant Act— Every Colored Man to be Licensed—Contracts for Labor—Deserters from Employment to be Arrested and Returned—Harboring Deserters—Perils of Colored Men complaining against Whites—Arms forbidden to Colored Men and Extraordinary Offences created—Testimony of Governor Orr and General Gordon to the Docility and Good Behavior of the Negro during and since the War—A Summary Statement of the Black Codes.

As soon as the master class of the South at the close of the war had partially recovered from the stupefaction incident to the total defeat of their cause and the overthrow of their cherished system of slavery, they began to devise methods by which they might recover their lost power over the subject race. Under the proclamations of President Johnson in 1865 for the reorganization of the governments of the rebellious States the Legislatures were elected by this class.

South Carolina and Mississippi, ever foremost as champions of slavery, were among the first to try to rebuild the fallen fabric of their power, by a system of laws known as the Black Codes. Most, if not all, of the late rebellious States followed the example with codes of greater or less severity, but the laws of the States named are believed to be the most characteristic, and to most clearly reveal the Southern purpose.

How they proposed to treat the newly emancipated race the ample extracts which follow will fully show.

SOUTH CAROLINA.

Extracts from an Act to Establish and Regulate the Domestic Relations of Persons of Color. [Approved December 21, 1865.]

CONTRACTS FOR SERVICE.

Sec. 35. All persons of color who make contracts for service or labor shall be known as servants, and those with whom they contract shall be known as masters.

Sec. 36. Contracts between masters and servants for one month or more shall be in writing, be attested by one white person, and be approved by the judge of the district court or by a magistrate.

Sec. 37. The period of service shall be expressed in the contract; but if it be not expressed, it shall be until the 25th day of December next after the commencement of the service.

Sec. 38. If the rate of wages be not stipulated by the parties to the contract, it shall be fixed by the district judge or a magistrate, on application by one of the parties and notice to the other.

Sec. 42. Contracts for one month or more shall not be binding on the servant, unless they are in writing and have been presented for approval within the time aforesaid.

Sec. 43. For any neglect of the duty to make a contract as herein directed, or the evasion of that duty by the repeated employment of the same persons for periods less than one month, the party offending shall be guilty of a misdemeanor, and be liable on conviction to pay a sum not exceeding fifty dollars, and not less than five dollars, for each person so employed. No written contract shall be required when the servant voluntarily receives no remuneration except food and clothing.

REGULATION OF LABOR ON FARMS.

Sec. 45. On farms or in out-door service, the hours of labor, except on Sunday, shall be from sunrise to sunset, with a reasonable interval for breakfast and dinner. Servants shall rise at the dawn in the morning, feed, water, and care for the animals on the farm, do the usual and needful work about the premises, prepare their meals for the day, if required by the master, and begin the farm-work or other work by sunrise. The servant shall be careful of all the animals and property of his master, and especially of the animals and implements used by him, shall protect the same from injury by other persons, and shall be answerable for all property lost, destroyed, or injured by his negligence, dishonesty, or bad faith.

Sec. 46. All lost time, not caused by the act of the master, and all losses occasioned by neglect of the duties hereinbefore prescribed, may be deducted from the wages of the servant; and food, nursing, and other necessaries for the servant, whilst he is absent from work on account of sickness or other cause, may also be deducted from his wages. Servants shall be quiet and orderly in their quarters, at their work, and on the premises; shall extinguish their lights and fires, and retire to rest at seasonable hours. Work at night, and out-door work in inclement weather, shall not be exacted, unless in case of necessity. Servants shall not be kept at home on Sunday, unless to take care of the premises, or animals there, upon, or for work of daily necessity, or on unusual occasions; and in such cases only so many shall be kept at home as are necessary for these purposes. Sunday work shall be done by the servants in turn, except in cases of sickness or other disability, when it may be assigned to them out of their regular turn. Absentees on Sunday shall return to their homes by sunset.

Sec. 47. The master may give to a servant a task at work about the business of the farm which shall be reasonable. If the servant complain of the task, the district judge or a magistrate shall have power to reduce or increase it. Failure to do a task shall be deemed evidence of indolence, but a single failure shall not be conclusive. When a servant is entering into a contract he may be required to rate himself as a full hand, three-fourths, half, or one-fourth hand, and according to this rate, inserted in the contract, shall be the task, and of course the wages.

Sec. 48. Visitors or other persons shall not be invited or allowed by the servant to come or remain upon the premises of the master without his express permission.

Sec. 49. Servants shall not be absent from the premises without the permission of the master.

Sec. 50. When the servant shall depart from the service of the master without good cause, he shall forfeit the wages due him. The servant shall obey all lawful orders of the master or his agent, and shall be honest, truthful, sober, civil, and diligent in his business. The master may moderately correct servants who have made contracts, and are under eighteen years of age. He shall not be liable to pay for any additional or extraordinary services or labor of his servant, the same being necessary, unless by his express agreement.

CAUSES OF DISCHARGE OF A SERVANT.

Sec. 51. The master may discharge his servant for wilful disobedience of the lawful order of himself or his agent; habitual negligence or indolence in business; drunkenness, gross moral or legal misconduct; want of respect and civility to himself, his family, guests, or agents; or for prolonged absence from the premises, or absence on two or more occasions without permission.

Sec. 52. For any acts or things herein declared to be causes for the discharge of a servant, or for any breach of contract or duty by him, instead of discharging the servant, the master may complain to the district judge or one of the magistrates, who shall have power, on being satisfied of the misconduct complained of, to inflict, or cause to be inflicted, on the servant, suitable corporal punishment, or impose upon him such pecuniary fine as may be thought fit, and immediately to remand him to his work; which fine shall be deducted from his wages, if not otherwise paid.

Sec. 53. If a master has made a valid contract with a servant the district judge or magistrate may compel such servant to observe his contract by ordering infliction of the punishment, or imposition of the fine hereinbefore authorized.

Sec. 56. The master may command his servant to aid him in the defence of his own person, family, premises, or property; or of the person or property of any servant on the premises of the master; and it shall be the duty of the servant promptly to obey such command.

Sec. 57. The master shall not be bound to furnish medicine or medical assistance for his servant, without his express engagement.

Sec. 58. A master may give the character of one who has been in his service to a person who may make inquiry of him; which shall be a privileged communication, unless it be falsely and maliciously given. And no servant shall have the power to make a new contract without the production of the discharge of his former master, district judge or magistrate.

REGULATION OF HOUSE SERVANTS.

Sec. 68. The rules and regulations prescribed for master and servant apply to persons in service as household servants, conferring the same rights and imposing the same duties, with the following modifications:

Sec. 69. Servants and apprentices employed as house servants in the various duties of the household, and in all the domestic duties of the family, shall, at all hours of the day and night, and on all days of the week, promptly answer all calls and obey and execute all lawful orders and commands of the family in whose service they are employed.

Sec. 70. It is the duty of this class of servants to be especially civil and polite to their masters, their families and guests, and they shall receive gentle and kind treatment.

FORM OF CONTRACT.

Sec. 71. In all contracts between master and servant for service, the foregoing regulations shall be stipulations, unless it shall be otherwise provided in the contract, and the following form shall be a sufficient contract, unless some special agreement be made between the parties:

I [name of servant] do hereby agree with [name of master] to be his [here insert the words "household servant" or "servant in husbandry," as the case may be] from the date hereof, at the wages of [herein insert the wages, to be paid by the year or month]; and in consideration thereof, I [name of master] agree to receive the said [name of servant] as such servant, and to pay him the said wages, this   day of   , 186 .

A. B.

Witness: E. F.   C. D.

I approve the above contract this   day of   ,
186 .   G. H.

[Judge of the District Court or Magistrate].

After the words "servant in husbandry" may be inserted, if it be required, the words "to be rated as [full hand, three-fourths hand, half hand, or one-fourth hand," as the case may be].

COLORED MECHANICS, ARTISANS, AND SHOPKEEPERS TO BE LICENSED.

Sec. 72. No person of color shall pursue or practise the art, trade, or business of an artisan, mechanic, or shopkeeper, or any other trade, employment, or business (besides that of husbandry, or that of a servant under a contract for service or labor), on his own account and for his own benefit, or in partnership with a white person or as agent or servant of any person, until he shall have obtained a license therefor from the judge of the district court, which license shall be good for one year only. This license the judge may grant upon petition of the applicant, and upon being satisfied of his skill and fitness and of his good moral character, and upon payment by the applicant to the clerk of the district court of one hundred dollars, if a shopkeeper or pedler, to be paid annually, and ten dollars if a mechanic, artisan, or to engage in any other trade, also to be paid annually: Provided, however, that upon complaint being made and proved to the district judge of an abuse of such license he shall revoke the same; and provided also that no person of color shall practise any mechanical art or trade unless he shows that he has served an apprenticeship in such trade or art, or is now practising such trade or art.

Sec. 73. For violation of the prohibition contained in the section next preceding, the offender upon conviction thereof before the judge of the district court shall pay for each offence a fine of double the amount of such license; one half whereof shall go to the informer, who shall be a competent witness.

SERVANTS FORBIDDEN TO ACQUIRE HOMES.

Sec. 78. During the term of service the house occupied by any servant is the master's; and, on the expiration of the term of service or the discharge of a servant, he shall no longer remain on the premises of the master; and it shall be the duty of the judge of the district court, or a magistrate, on complaint of any person interested, and due proof made, to cause such servant to be immediately removed from such premises.

Sec. 79. Leases of a house or land to a person of color shall be in writing. If there be no written lease, or the term of lease shall have expired, a person of color in possession shall be a tenant at will, and shall not be entitled to notice; and on complaint by any person interested to the judge of the district or a magistrate, such person of color shall be instantly ejected by order or warrant, unless he produce a written lease authorizing his possession, or prove that such writing existed and was lost.

Extracts from an Act to Amend the Criminal Law of South Carolina, December 19, 1865.

SERVANTS FORBIDDEN TO SELL THE PRODUCTS OF LABOR WITHOUT PERMIT.

Sec. 10 provides that a person of color who is in the employment of a master engaged in husbandry shall not have the right to sell any corn, rice, peas, wheat or other grain, any flour, cotton, fodder, hay, bacon, fresh meat of any kind, poultry of any kind, animals of any kind, or any other product of a farm, without having written evidence from such master or some person authorized by him, or from the district judge or a magistrate, that he has the right to sell such product; and if any person shall directly or indirectly purchase any such product from such person of color without such written evidence, the purchaser and seller shall each be guilty of a misdemeanor.

Sec. 11 provides that it shall be a misdemeanor for any person not authorized to write or give a person of color a writing which professes to show evidence of the right of that person of color to sell any product of a farm which by the section last preceding he is forbidden to sell without written evidence, and any person convicted of this misdemeanor shall be liable to the same extent as the purchaser in the section last preceding is made liable; and it shall be a misdemeanor for a person of color to exhibit as evidence of his right to sell any product a writing which he knows to be false or counterfeited, or to have been written or given by any person not authorized.

ARMS FORBIDDEN TO COLORED MEN.

Sec. 13 states that persons of color constitute no part of the militia of the State, and no one of them shall without permission in writing from the district judge or magistrate be allowed to keep a fire-arm, sword, or other military weapon except that one of them who is the owner of a farm may keep a shot-gun or rifle, such as is ordinarily used in hunting, but not a pistol, musket, or other fire-arm or weapon appropriate for purposes of war. The district judge or magistrate may give an order, under which any weapon unlawfully kept may be seized and sold, the proceeds of sale to go into the district court fund. The possession of a weapon in violation of this act shall be a misdemeanor, which shall be tried before a district court or a magistrate, and in case of conviction shall be punished by a fine equal to twice the value of the weapon so unlawfully kept, and if that be not immediately paid, by corporeal punishment.

MIGRATION OF COLORED PEOPLE FORBIDDEN EXCEPT UNDER BOND.

Sec. 22 provides that no person of color shall migrate into and reside in this State unless within twenty days after his arrival within the same he shall enter into a bond with two freeholders as sureties to be approved by the judge of the district court or a magistrate in a penalty of one thousand dollars, conditioned for his good behavior and for his support if he should become unable to support himself.

Sec. 30 provides that, upon view of a misdemeanor committed by a person of color, any person present may

arrest the offender and take him before a magistrate, to
be dealt with as the case may require. In case of a misdemeanor committed by a white towards a person of
color, any person may complain to a magistrate, who
shall cause the offender to be arrested and, according to
the nature of the case, to be brought before himself or
be taken for trial in the district court.

MISSISSIPPI.

Extract from the Vagrant Act, November 24, 1865.

Sec. 2 provides that all freedmen, free negroes, and
mulattoes in this State over the age of eighteen years,
found on the second Monday in January, 1866, or thereafter, with no lawful employment or business, or found
unlawfully assembling themselves together, either in the
day or night time, and all white persons so assembling
with freedmen, free negroes, or mulattoes, or usually asso-
ciating with freedmen, free negroes or mulattoes, on terms
of equality, or living in adultery or fornication with a
freed-woman, free negro, or mulatto, shall be deemed
vagrants, and on conviction thereof shall be fined in the
sum of not exceeding, in the case of a freedman, free
negro, or mulatto, fifty dollars, and a white man two
hundred dollars, and imprisoned, at the discretion of the
court, the free negro not exceeding ten days, and the
white man not exceeding six months.

Sec. 3 gives all justices of the peace, mayors, and aldermen jurisdiction to try all questions of vagrancy, and
it is made their duty to arrest parties violating any provisions of this act, investigate the charges, and, on conviction, punish as provided. It is made the duty of all
sheriffs, constables, town constables, city marshals, and
all like officers to report to some officer having jurisdic-

tion all violations of any of the provisions of this act, and it is made the duty of the county courts to inquire if any officer has neglected any of these duties, and if guilty, to fine him not exceeding one hundred dollars, to be paid into the county treasury.

Sec. 5 provides that all fines and forfeitures collected under the provisions of this act shall be paid into the county treasury for general county purposes; and in case any freedman, free negro, or mulatto shall fail for five days after the imposition of any fine or forfeiture upon him or her for violations of any of the provisions of this act to pay the same, that it shall be, and is hereby made, the duty of the sheriff of the proper county to hire out said freedman, free negro, or mulatto to any person who will, for the shortest period of service, pay said fine or forfeiture and all costs: Provided, a preference shall be given to the employer, if there be one, in which case the employer shall be entitled to deduct and retain the amount so paid from the wages of such freedman, free negro, or mulatto then due or to become due; and in case such freedman, free negro, or mulatto cannot be hired out, he or she may be dealt with as a pauper.

Sec. 6 provides that the same duties and liabilities existing among white persons of this State shall attach to freedmen, free negroes, and mulattoes to support their indigent families and all colored paupers; and that in order to secure a support for such indigent freedmen, free negroes, and mulattoes, it shall be lawful, and it is hereby made the duty of the boards of county police of each county in this State, to levy a poll or capitation tax on each and every freedman, free negro, or mulatto between the ages of eighteen and sixty years, not to exceed the sum of one dollar annually to each person so taxed, which tax when collected shall be paid into the county treasurer's hands, and constitute a fund to be called the freedmen's pauper fund, which shall be applied by the commissioners of the poor for the maintenance of the poor of the freedmen, free negroes, and mulattoes of this State, under such regulations as may be established by the boards of the county police in the respective counties of this State.

Sec. 7 provides that if any freedman, free negro, or mulatto shall fail or refuse to pay any tax levied according to the provisions of the sixth section of this act, it shall be prima-facie evidence of vagrancy, and it shall be the duty of the sheriff to arrest such freedman, free negro, or mulatto, or such persons refusing or neglecting to pay such tax, and proceed at once to hire for the shortest time such delinquent taxpayer to any one who will pay the said tax with the accruing costs, giving preference to the employer if there be one.

Extracts from an Act to Confer Civil Rights on Freedmen, and for other Purposes, November 25, 1865.

EVERY COLORED MAN TO BE LICENSED.

Sec. 5 provides that every freedman, free negro, and mulatto shall, on the second Monday of January, 1866, and annually thereafter, have a lawful home or employment, and shall have written evidence thereof as follows, to wit: if living in any incorporated city, town, or village, a license from the mayor thereof, and if living outside of any incorporated city, town, or village, from the member of the board of police of his beat, authorizing him or her to do irregular and job work, or a written contract as provided in section six of this act, which licenses may be revoked for cause at any time by the authority granting the same.

CONTRACTS FOR LABOR.

Sec. 6 provides that all contracts for labor made with freedmen, free negroes, and mulattoes, for a longer period than one month, shall be in writing and in duplicate, attested and read to said freedman, free negro, or mulatto, by a beat, city, or county officer, or two disinterested white persons of the county in which the labor is to be performed, of which each party shall have one; and said contracts shall be taken and held as entire contracts, and if the laborer shall quit the service of the employer before the expiration of his term of service without good cause, he shall forfeit his wages for that year up to the time of quitting.

DESERTERS FROM EMPLOYMENT TO BE ARRESTED AND RETURNED.

Sec. 7 provides that every civil officer shall, and every person may, arrest and carry back to his or her legal employer any freedman, free negro, or mulatto who shall have quit the service of his or her employer before the expiration of his or her term of service without good cause; and said officer and said persons shall be entitled to receive for arresting and carrying back every deserting employee aforesaid the sum of five dollars and ten cents per mile from the place of arrest to the place of delivery, and the same shall be paid by the employer and held as a set-off for so much against the wages of said deserting employee; provided, that said arrested party after being so returned may appeal to a justice of the peace or member of the board of police of the county, who, on notice to the alleged employer, shall try summarily whether said appellant is legally employed by the alleged employer, and had good cause to quit said employer; either party shall have the right of appeal to the county court, pending which the alleged deserter shall be remanded to the alleged employer, or otherwise disposed of as shall be right and just; and the decision of the county court shall be final.

Sec. 8 provides that upon affidavit made by the employer of any freedman, free negro, or mulatto, or other credible person, before any justice of the peace or member of the board of police, that any freedman, free negro, or mulatto legally employed by said employer has illegally deserted said employment, such justice of the peace or member of the board of the police shall issue his warrant or warrants, returnable before himself or other such officer, directed to any sheriff, constable, or special deputy, commanding him to arrest said deserter, and return him or her to said employer, and the like proceedings shall be had as provided in the preceding section; and it shall be lawful for any officer to whom such warrant shall be directed to execute said warrant in any county of this State, and that said warrant may be transmitted without endorsement to any like officer of another county to be executed and returned as aforesaid, and the said employer shall pay the cost of said warrants and arrest and return, which shall be set off for so much against the wages of said deserter.

HARBORING DESERTERS.

Sec. 9 provides that if any person shall persuade, or attempt to persuade, entice, or cause any freedman, free negro, or mulatto to desert from the legal employment of any person before the expiration of his or her term of service, or shall knowingly employ any such deserting freedman, free negro, or mulatto, or shall knowingly deal or sell to any such deserting freedman, free negro, or mulatto, any food, raiment, or other things, he or she shall be guilty of a misdemeanor, and upon conviction shall be fined not less than twenty-five dollars and not more than two hundred dollars and costs; and if said fine and costs shall not be immediately paid, the court shall sentence said convict to not exceeding two months' imprisonment in the county jail, and he or she shall moreover be liable to the party injured in damages: provided if any person shall or shall attempt to persuade, entice, or cause any freedman, free negro, or mulatto to desert from any legal employment of any person with the view to employ said freedman, free negro, or mulatto without the limits of this State, such person, on conviction, shall be fined not less than fifty dollars and not more than five hundred dollars and costs; and if said fine and costs shall not be immediately paid, the court shall sentence said convict to not exceeding six months' imprisonment in the county jail.

Sec. 10 provides that it shall be lawful for any freedman, free negro, or mulatto, to charge any white person, freedman, free negro, or mulatto, by affidavit, with any criminal offence against his or her person or property, and upon such affidavit the proper process shall be issued and executed as if said affidavit was made by a white person; and it shall be lawful for any freedman, free negro, or mulatto, in any action, suit, or controversy pending or about to be instituted in any court of law or equity in this State, to make all needful and lawful affidavits as shall be necessary for the institution, prosecution, or defence of such suit or controversy.

PERILS OF COLORED PERSONS COMPLAINING AGAINST WHITE.

An Act supplementary to "An Act to Confer Civil Rights upon Freedmen," and for other purposes, December 2, 1865:

Sec. 1 provides that in every case where any white person has been arrested and brought to trial by virtue of the provisions of the tenth section of the above recited act, in any court in this State, upon sufficient proof being made to the court or jury upon the trial before said court, that any freedman, free negro, or mulatto has falsely and maliciously caused the arrest and trial of said white person or persons, the court shall render up a judgment against said freedman, free negro, or mulatto, for all costs of the case, and impose a fine, not to exceed fifty dollars, and imprisonment in the county jail, not to exceed twenty days; and for a failure of said freedman, free negro, or mulatto to pay, or cause to be paid, all costs, fines, and jail fees, the sheriff of the county is hereby authorized and required, after giving ten days' public notice, to proceed to hire out at public outcry, at the court-house of the county, said freedman, free negro, or mulatto, for the shortest time to raise the amount necessary to discharge said freedman, free negro, or mulatto, from all costs, fines, and jail fees aforesaid.

ARMS FORBIDDEN TO COLORED MEN, AND EXTRAORDINARY
OFFENCES CREATED.

An Act to Punish Certain Offences therein Named, and for other purposes, November 29, 1865:

Sec. 1. Be it enacted, etc., that no freedman, free negro, or mulatto, not in the military service of the United

States Government and not licensed to do so by the board of police of his or her county, shall keep or carry fire-arms of any kind, or any ammunition, dirk, or bowie-knife; and on conviction thereof in the county court shall be punished by fine not exceeding ten dollars, and pay costs of such proceedings, and all such arms or ammunition shall be forfeited to the informer; and it shall be the duty of every civil and military officer to arrest any freedman, free negro, or mulatto found with any such arms or ammunition, and cause him to be committed for trial in default of bail.

Sec. 2. That any freedman, free negro, or mulatto committing riots, routs, affrays, trespasses, malicious mischief, and cruel treatment to animals, seditious speeches, *insulting gestures*, language, or acts, or assaults on any person, disturbance of the peace, exercising the functions of a minister of the gospel without a license from some regularly organized church, vending spirituous or intoxicating liquors, or committing any other misdemeanor the punishment of which is not specifically provided by law, shall, upon conviction thereof in the county court, be fined not less than ten dollars and not more than one hundred dollars, and may be imprisoned at the discretion of the court, not exceeding thirty days.

Sec. 3. That if any white person shall sell, lend, or give to any freedman, free negro, or mulatto, any fire-arms, dirk, or bowie-knife, or ammunition, or any spirituous or intoxicating liquors, such person or persons so offending, upon conviction thereof in the county court of his or her county, shall be fined not exceeding fifty dollars, and may be imprisoned at the discretion of the court, not exceeding thirty days.

Sec. 4. That all the penal and criminal laws now in force in this State, defining offences and prescribing the

mode of punishment for crimes and misdemeanors committed by slaves, free negroes, or mulattoes, be, and the
same are hereby, re-enacted, and declared to be in full
force and effect against freedmen, free negroes, and free
mulattoes, except so far as the mode and manner of trial
and punishment have been changed or altered by law.

Sec. 5. That if any freedman, free negro, or mulatto,
convicted of any of the misdemeanors provided in this
act, shall fail or refuse for the space of five days after
conviction to pay the fine and costs imposed, such person shall be hired out by the sheriff or other officer, at
public outcry, to any white person who will pay said fine
and all costs, and take such convict for the shortest time.

An examination of these laws clearly demonstrates
the fact that their entire end and aim was to reduce to
the most abject servitude the four millions of negroes
who had been made free by Lincoln's Proclamation of
Emancipation and the Thirteenth Amendment of the
Constitution of the United States. This unfortunate
race of people, whose ancestors had been brought hither
more than two hundred years ago as slaves, were now
about to have all their bright hopes of freedom dashed
to the ground. While they were slaves their masters
were interested in providing them with food, shelter, and
raiment, so that they would have such health and
strength as would enable them to perform their daily
toil. As they represented a money value to their masters,
it was to *their* interest to protect them in their lives and
health; and while they were deprived by law and custom
of all the rights and privileges held sacred and dear by
free men, their condition was every way more tolerable
as slaves than it was proposed to make them as a free
people. While the civil war raged, the fact dawned

upon them that their interests were in some way mixed
up with the bloody struggle; and at last they realized
the fact that freedom and slavery were the contending
forces in the contest; that if the Union was saved they
would be made free, and that if the Union was destroyed
their fetters would be more securely riveted. This feeling spread amongst all the colored people in the revolted
States, until the entire colored population regarded the
soldiers of the Union as instruments in the hands of
Heaven to set them free.

Wherever the Union army appeared they found the
negroes to be their friends. Whenever a Union soldier
escaped from a prison pen and bent his steps towards
the north star, he never feared to enter the lowly cabin
of the negro for food and protection: the negro was his
friend, not simply because he was unfortunate and fleeing for his life, but because as a soldier of the Union he
was a representative of that mighty and benign National
Government which had declared its purpose that the
black man as well as the white man should be free.

At last the men of the North recognized the necessity
of inviting the colored man to aid in the preservation of
the Union. Hundreds of thousands of them gladly took
up arms to fight for the Union cause, and rendered efficient and valiant service; and so when the war closed and
it was made known throughout the entire land that the
chains of slavery were broken and that the colored people were free, they were filled with inexpressible joy and
hope. They felt, and had a right to feel, that the mighty
and victorious people who had given them their freedom
would fully protect them in the enjoyment of it; and
now when their old masters undertook by State legislation to deprive them of every right which makes life
worth living, every right which is enjoyed by the hum-

blest white man in any portion of the country, every feeling of their nature rose against this terrible proposition.

Nothing can more fully bring to view the cause of the political antagonism between a majority of the white people of the Southern States on the one side and the colored population on the other, than the testimony of Hon. James L. Orr of South Carolina, given before the Poland Investigating Committee in 1871. Mr. Orr said:

"Freedom was considered by the negro a great boon, and he naturally was very grateful to that particular party that he supposed had given him his freedom.

"From the very outset he was made to believe that the Republican Party as a party had done that for him; that Mr. Lincoln, in September, 1862, issued a proclamation providing for their freedom on the 1st of January, 1863. Then there was a legislation of Congress afterwards, the civil-rights bill and the Freedmen's Bureau Bill; then the constitutional amendments, etc. That was all explained to him; and it required a very short argument to be addressed to the most ignorant negro in the State to satisfy him that his attachment to the Republican Party should be greater than to the Democratic Party.

"It was charged publicly by his orators, those whom he had confidence in, that the Democratic Party had resisted all that legislation; that the Democratic Party had declared that the reconstruction was unconstitutional, revolutionary, and void; and that if the Democrats were reinstated in power very many of these privileges would be taken away from the colored people. I thought at the time that it was very unreasonable to imagine for a moment that the colored population could be induced to vote for a party from whom they apprehended such results, and against a party that had done them such service. I have no doubt in the world that if the white element of the South would turn Republicans, would consent to support the Republican Party instead of the Democratic Party,—although in the Republican Party there has been a very pernicious element, there is no doubt of it,—I have no doubt if they should support the Republican Party instead of the Democratic Party, then the white population of the South would obtain absolute control of the affairs there.

"Q. As I understand you, the reason the colored men in a body have gone for the Republican Party is not their antagonism to the old white citizens as such, but their opposition to the Democratic Party?

"A. The very moment that the colored man could have been satisfied that it was not the purpose of his old master to put him back into slavery, the old master would have obtained influence over him. And as conclusive proof of the correctness of my statement, I think if you will deem it worth while to put the question to every gentleman of the South who may come before you, you will be told that in everything outside of politics the white population, the Democratic population, the slaveholder, the man of most intelligence in the community, has just as much influence over the negro and his conduct and the management of him as they ever had. He goes to them for advice, and takes their advice on everything except on the subject of voting.

"Q. Were not the negroes very quiet before the war, and during the war, as a class, orderly and docile?

"A. Yes, sir; I think they are a very docile race.

"Q. According to your knowledge of the negro race, is it not the most docile of all races?

"A. I cannot tell about some of the Eastern races. I think the negro race is a very controllable and manage-

able race. While they have not the very highest sense
of right of property (and that could not be expected of
them), yet I do not think that they are wanting in gratitude upon all proper occasions. But when you consider
a sudden change wrought in the condition of the slave
from 1865 to the present time, the matter of surprise is
that the negro has not become much more insulting, ex-
acting, and domineering than he has.

"Q. Is it not true that the negro, during the war and
since the war, has behaved rather better than was expected of him by his old master?

"A. Infinitely better. In some parts of my State during the war, towards the close of the war, I suppose
there were some communities in which the proportion
of white men to colored men was about five to one hundred. I do not think that there was more negro violence
during the war than preceding the war. Yes, sir; it was
very astonishing.

"Q. Did they not understand that their freedom de-
pended upon the issue of the war?

"A. I have no doubt that they did, though I did not
suppose so then. I have no doubt that they understood
it better than we supposed they did. I found that whenever any Federal soldiers who were imprisoned there
made their escape they were always taken care of in
some way or other."

This testimony throws a flood of light upon the conduct of the negro, not only since the war but during the
war. Governor Orr shows that the motives that animated the colored population in uniting themselves with
the Republican Party were entirely consistent with the
natural impulse of self-preservation. The negro knew
that after the passage of these odious black laws by the
State Legislatures that the Republicans in Congress had

passed a law to secure them in their civil rights, and also a law creating a bureau for their special protection; and that these measures were violently opposed by the Democrats in Congress and by their old masters at home.

Governor Orr in his testimony puts on record his recognition of the historical fact that, while almost the entire able-bodied population of the Southern States was absent from home in the Confederate army, fighting to destroy the Union and to perpetuate slavery, the negroes remained upon the plantations, labored faithfully, were orderly and obedient, and took care of and protected the families of their masters. The testimony, taken by the same committee, of Gen. J. B. Gordon of Georgia, who commanded the left wing of Lee's army at Appomattox, and who was afterwards a Senator of the United States from Georgia, fully corroborates the statements of Mr. Orr.

General Gordon testified as follows:

"Q. Have the negroes, as a general thing, behaved well since the war?

"A. They have behaved so well that the remark is not uncommon in Georgia, that no race on earth, relieved from servitude under such circumstances as they were, would have behaved so well.

"Q. How did they behave during the war when the white men went off to fight and left them at home?

"A. Well, sir, I had occasion to refer just now to a little speech which I made at Montgomery, Alabama, when General Clanton also spoke. He and I both struck on that train of thought. I went so far as to say that the citizens of the South owed it to the negroes to educate them. One of the things which I mentioned, and which General Clanton also mentioned, was the behavior of the negroes during the war: the fact that when almost the entire white male population, old enough to bear arms, was in the army, and large plantations were left to be managed by the women and children, not a single insurrection had occurred, not a life had been taken; and that, too, when the Federal armies were marching through the country with freedom, as was understood, upon their banners.

"Q. Scarcely an outrage occurred on the part of the negroes at that time ?

A. Scarcely an outrage. When I made that speech at Montgomery, I may say, without intending to compliment myself, that, when I referred to the handsome behavior of the negro during our absence in the army, and his protection of our families at that time, my remarks were heartily responded to and with a great deal of feeling by every man in the convention."

But in vain had they and their ancestors for two hundred years labored patiently for their masters; in vain had they, during the dreadful four years of civil war, by their industry, fidelity, and obedience, elicited the gratitude of the white people of the South: their old masters, acting towards them as did Pharoah of old towards the Israelites, would not let them go. Four millions of slaves made free, and turned out under the sky without a roof of their own, were now to be deprived of the right of purchasing a home.

They were prohibited from cultivating the soil on their own account.

They were required to pay an onerous license for the privileges of pursuing the business of an artisan, mechanic, or shopkeeper.

They were required to become employed as "husbandmen" or "house-servants;" their employers were to be known as "masters" and they as "servants."

Contracts for services, in case of disagreement between master and servant, were to be regulated and the rate of wages fixed by the district judge or magistrate.

They were subject to arrest and imprisonment if they abandoned their contracts of labor.

They were prohibited from making new contracts without having the discharges of their former masters.

The law fixed their time of rising and retiring, their hours of labor, and regulated their social intercourse.

The responsibilities of self-support were imposed by their condition of freedom; but by these laws they were to be deprived of the right of choosing the means by which this end was to be secured.

In fact they were hedged around by so many legal disabilities and regulations, that they possessed none of the ordinary rights of free men.

They were to be controlled by the most odious and tyrannical customs of the old slave system, now for the first time stereotyped into law.

This legislation possessed one merit—it was not insidious: it was a frank and open movement of the old master class to maintain their hold upon the negro by a system of restrictions and limitations which would reduce him to a state of servitude more abject, degrading, and pitiable than the slavery from which he had been just relieved. Is it to be wondered at that the entire negro population of the Southern States rose up in political opposition to their former masters? Is it surprising that they united with the Republican Party? They knew that that party had made them free, and was then engaged in a great political struggle with its old antagonist, the Democratic Party, over measures in Congress and Constitutional amendments designed to make them citizens and invest them with civil rights and protect them in their exercise and enjoyment. Had they joined the party of their old masters, who sought to re-enslave them, in opposition to the Republican Party, which proposed to protect them in their freedom, they would have been guilty of an act of black ingratitude inconsistent with every impulse of the human heart. They would have demonstrated to the world their total unfitness to be free. But they were true to human nature; they were true to themselves.

CHAPTER III.

THE RECONSTRUCTION ACTS—MASSACRE OF REPUB-LICANS AT MECHANICS INSTITUTE, NEW ORLEANS.

Action of President Johnson—Conflict of Opinion between the President and Congress—Fourteenth Amendment Proposed—Congress Sustained by Election of 1866—Reconstruction Acts passed—Attitude of the Rebel White Population of the South towards these Acts—Testimony of Governor Orr of South Carolina—The Classes in the South who sustained these Acts—Situation in Louisiana at the close of the War—Proposed Reassembling of the Constitutional Convention in 1866 at Mechanics Institute, New Orleans—Bloody Massacre and Dispersal of the Convention—Report of the Committee of Congress who investigated the Facts—Details of the Massacre—No one ever Punished for the Murders—Its Result in Emboldening the Perpetrators to further Crimes.

WHEN Congress met in December, 1865, the Provisional Governments organized under the proclamations of President Johnson in the Southern States, but recently in rebellion, were exercising legislative, executive, and judicial powers, and some of the legislatures had already enacted their Black Codes. Congress was not in session when the war closed, nor was it convened in extra session by proclamation of the President, so that the law-making power might consider all the important questions which arose from the abnormal condition in which the country was placed, and enact laws that might be deemed necessary to restore the people of those States to their proper relations in the Union.

What had been done by the President was by virtue of his authority as Commander-in-Chief of the Army

and Navy of the United States; and not under or by
virtue of any laws which had been enacted by Congress
to meet the new and trying state of affairs which would
necessarily grow out of a civil war.

The first and highest duty, therefore, devolving upon
Congress when it assembled was to consider these important questions.

The theory upon which the President seemed to proceed was that the State Governments might be reorganized, and the powers of the States fully re-established
without any Congressional legislation whatever; that
the right of the people of those States to representation
in Congress had not been impaired by the fact that the
great body of the electors had actually made war upon
the Government; and had placed their State Governments in the same position.

The majority in Congress had very different views of
the case. They took into account the momentous
changes wrought by the war—the creation of a moun-
tain of public debt, and the wisdom and necessity of
taking measures to preserve the public credit. They
recognized the great obligation the country was under
to provide suitable pensions to the wounded and dis-
abled soldiers who had assisted in saving the Union,
and their widows and orphans. They also recognized
the duty of the Government to confer citizenship and
equal civil rights upon the four millions of slaves but
recently made free. The Fourteenth Amendment to
the Constitution was adopted and referred to the various State Legislatures for their action, and a number of
statutes were enacted to secure the above-named ends.
All of these measures were violently opposed by President Johnson. He separated himself politically from
the men who elected him to office; and in public

speeches denounced in unmeasured terms some of their most trusted leaders. The result of this conflict of opinion was to bring the Democrats North and South to the support of the President; and they were reinforced by a handful of Republicans. The issues were carried before the people in the Congressional contest of 1866; and the Republicans were sustained by the election of more than two-thirds majority in Congress from the loyal States; elections were also held in the seceded States for members of Congress; and their various Legislatures chose United States Senators. Upon the organization of the Fortieth Congress the Senators and members from the disloyal States were refused admission upon the ground that the State Governments had not been recognized by Congress as Governments legally existing; and that the people of those States were not entitled to representation except upon such terms as Congress by law might prescribe. And so it came to pass that the Democracy of the South who precipitated the Rebellion found themselves side by side with the Democrats of the North who had opposed the war for the Union; and these men joined hands in antagonizing every measure enacted by the Republican Congress for the reconstruction of the Southern States, and were aided by the whole power of President Johnson's administration.

It seems proper to note as a remarkable incident in politics, that almost every measure which was then opposed by the Democrats, both North and South, have since been repeatedly approved in their political conventions.

The legislation in behalf of the negro race was met with the most bitter animadversion. To give them freedom, to give them equal rights with the whites, and the right to work for themselves, to acquire and hold property, and to the equal protection of the laws, and the right to vote, was so repugnant to the Democratic judgment, that no denunciations were too fierce to be uttered against such measures and the political party which would enact them.

It now became obvious that while the conflict of arms was ended, the antagonism of opinion between the political parties was so great that there could be no compromise, and that the responsibility of deciding upon the principles and measures for the reconstruction of the Southern States would devolve entirely upon the Republican Party. The Fortieth Congress was convened by law March 4, 1867, and was sworn in immediately after the Thirty-ninth Congress adjourned.

On March 2, 1867, a law was passed entitled "An act to provide for the more efficient government of the Rebel States," and on the 23d of the same month a supplementary act was passed for the same purpose; these acts divided the States in question into five military districts, and directed the President to assign to the command of each of said districts an officer of the army not below the rank of brigadier-general, and to detail a sufficient military force to enable such officer to perform his duties and enforce his authority within the district to which he was assigned; and it was made his duty to suppress insurrection, disorder, and violence, and to punish or cause to be punished all disturbers of the public peace and criminals either through the local civil tribunals or military commissions organized for that purpose; and this act declared that all interference under color of State authority should be null and void. These acts provided for the calling of constitutional conventions to frame new constitutions for those States, and to that end provided for a registration of voters; and all male citizens were declared to be electors who were twenty-one years of age, of whatever race, color, or previous condition, who had been resident in the State for one year previous to the election, except such as were disfranchised for participation in the rebellion, or for felony at common law. The elections were to be held under military authority and protection. The first act above named fixed the conditions upon which the States were to become entitled to representation in Congress, the most important of which were, 1st, that the new constitutions should secure the elective franchise to such persons as were qualified electors under said act; and, 2d, that the State Legislatures should ratify the Fourteenth Amendment of the Constitution. The Democrats everywhere denounced these acts as unconstitutional and void. The great majority of the white men of the Southern States sullenly declined to participate in these elections, but two or three men of National standing and influence who had taken part in the rebellion separated from the great body of their old party friends and took part in this work.

The Charleston *Courier* of November 20, 1867, speaking of the election for delegates to the State Reconstruction Convention, said, "From the opening to the closing of the polls they were crowded by the newly enfranchised citizens eager to exercise their recently acquired right; but very few white people, as the annexed table of the result shows, participated at all. . . .

"The general feeling amongst all classes of white people was averse to countenancing the affair at all. Only one ticket was run, and that was nominated by the Radical Republicans."

Speaking of the managers of the election, the paper

states that there were "fourteen colored to seven white managers. The discrepancy is owing to the fact that other white men could not be found to serve."

The result of the first day's voting (the election lasted two days) in the eight wards of the city was, whites, 12; colored, 2427. In the Fifth and Seventh Wards no white persons voted, while there were 381 colored votes cast.

The attitude of the white population of South Carolina in regard to the Reconstruction laws, and their utter indifference in reference to the result of the election under these laws, are clearly shown by the statement of Mr. Orr upon this subject, taken by the Poland Investigating Committee, hereafter mentioned.

The question of the committee and his answer thereto are as follows:

"Q. Is it not true that upon the commencement of reconstruction the old white population to a great degree refrained from taking part in the elections?

"A. Yes, sir. I stated that in the early part of my examination, according to my recollection—I may be mistaken in some of the figures, but my recollection is that in the vote for a convention there were but three thousand white votes cast in the entire State."

In several of the States there were many old Union men who fully endorsed these measures; and there were also many men who fought in the Rebel army with gallantry who now felt it to be their duty to acquiesce in the results of the war, and in such legislation as Congress might enact for the restoration of the Southern States.

Many men who had served in the Union army, and others of the Northern States who were desirous of changing their locations, settled in the South. These three classes uniting, constituted the white element, which supported the Reconstruction measures of Congress, and with the colored voters controlled the elections in those States.

After the capture of New Orleans and the opening of the Mississippi River by the Union arms in 1863, Mr. Lincoln was anxious to have civil government established in that State by the people.

In 1864, under the auspices of General Banks, commanding the Department, a convention had been chosen looking to the formation of a State Government.

It met April 6, 1864, and remained in session until July 23, 1864.

It prepared a constitution and submitted the same to the people for ratification. The constitution was adopted by a large majority of the votes cast, and a State Government was organized thereunder.

The convention adjourned, subject to the call of its president. Congress had not recognized the new State Government, and in the summer of 1866 the vice-president of the convention issued a call for the convention to reassemble in the city of New Orleans. The president of the convention had refused to sign this call.

Great opposition was manifested to the reassembling of the convention by the Democracy. It was claimed that the convention would possess no legal powers, and that any action taken by it would be void.

It had been arranged that the convention should meet at Mechanics Institute July 30, 1866. That day and that place have been made memorable by the first notable outburst of the pent-up wrath of the Southern Democracy against Republicans and negroes, in the long and still undetermined struggle for liberty of thought, speech, and political action in the South. The events of that day were generally spoken of at the time as a "massacre;" outside of Louisiana they were not justified by any Democratic newspaper; and scarcely an effort was made to extenuate or palliate them, or to attribute them to local or personal causes not political. The committee of the Thirty-ninth Congress who investigated the facts only voiced the general opinion of the loyal States when they declared—

"There has been no occasiond uring our national history when a riot has occurred so destitute of justifiable cause, resulting in a massacre so inhuman and fiend-like, as that which took place at New Orleans on the 30th of July last. The character and position of the gentlemen— members of the convention which had originally assembled in 1864—who were the subjects of the attack in common with the unoffending negroes, whose political condition, claims, and rights it was their ultimate purpose to consider and determine, give to the events of July significance and national importance. The massacre was begun and finished in mid-day ; and such proofs of preparation were disclosed that we are constrained to say that an intention, existing somewhere, to disperse and to slaughter the members of the convention, and those persons, white and black, who were present and were friendly to its purposes, was mercilessly carried into full effect."

There seemed to be a well-settled determination on the part of its opponents that the convention should not be allowed to assemble, and if it did assemble that it should be dispersed. The Mayor of the city of New Orleans acted upon the assumption that the duty devolved upon him to prevent the convention from transacting any business. About noon a large body of armed police were massed at the hall where the convention was attempting to meet. A mob of private citizens joined them, and an organized attack was made upon those in the hall. It was supposed that this movement was intended to forcibly disperse, under color of recognized authority, an assemblage which was believed by the mayor to be an illegal body. The attack, however, became an indiscriminate butchery of Republicans and colored men, the horrors of which are thus described by a committee of Congress (Report No. 16, 39th Cong., p. 11):

"It is in evidence that men who were in the hall, terrified by the merciless attacks of the armed police, sought safety by jumping from the windows, a distance of twenty feet, to the ground, and as they jumped were shot by police or citizens. Some, disfigured by wounds, fought their way down-stairs to the street, to be shot or beaten to death on the pavement. Colored persons, at distant points in the city, peaceably pursuing their lawful business, were attacked by the police, shot, and cruelly beaten. Men of character and position, some of whom were members and some spectators of the convention, escaped from the hall covered with wounds and blood, and were preserved almost by miracle from death. Scores of colored citizens bear frightful scars, more numerous than many soldiers of a dozen well-fought fields can show—proofs of fearful danger and strange escape; men were shot while waving handkerchiefs in token of surrender and submission; white men and black, with arms uplifted praying for life, were answered by shot and blow from knife and club; the bodies of some were 'pounded to a jelly;' a colored man was dragged from under a street-crossing, and killed at a blow; men concealed in outhouses and among piles of lumber were eagerly sought for and slaughtered or maimed without remorse; the dead bodies upon the street were violated

by shot, kick, and stab; .the face of a man 'just breath-
ing his last' was gashed by a knife or razor in the hands
of a woman; 'an old, gray-haired man,' peaceably walking the street at a distance from the Institute, was shot
through the head; negroes were taken out of their
houses and shot; a policeman riding in a buggy deliberately fired his revolver from the carriage into a crowd
of colored men; a colored man two miles away from the
convention hall was taken from his shop by the police,
at about four o'clock on the afternoon of the riot, and
shot and wounded in side, hip, and back; one man was
wounded by fourteen blows, shots, and stabs; the body
of another received seven pistol balls. After the slaughter had measurably ceased, carts, wagons, and drays,
driven through the streets, gathered the dead, the dying,
and the wounded in 'promiscuous loads,' a policeman,
in some cases, riding in the wagon, seated upon the living men beneath him.

*   *   *   *   *   *

"For several hours, the police and mob, in mutual and
bloody emulation, continued the butchery in the hall
and on the street, until nearly two hundred people were
killed and wounded. The number was probably much
larger than this; but of that number the names and residences are known. Some were injured whose friends
conveyed them at once quietly away. There is evidence
tending to show that some who were killed were privately carried away and buried. One witness testified:
'I saw a dray taking five or six of those who were
wounded away. I heard a drayman say, " Where will I
take them to?" And a policeman said, "Throw them in
the river."' Several witnesses testify that the killed and
wounded exceed two hundred. One witness says that
he saw from forty to fifty killed. Another states that

he saw from twenty to thirty carriage-loads of killed and wounded. Dr. Harris, of the Freedmen's Hospital, shows that one hundred and eight were brought wounded to his hospital, of whom fourteen died there and one died after removal. A. V. Ward saw twenty-seven dead bodies taken from the workhouse. How many were killed will never be known. But we cannot doubt there were many more than are set down in the official list in evidence."

Most of the victims were colored men, but Dr. Dostie and several other of the white leaders in the movement were also murdered.

The massacre at Mechanics Institute gave these men a taste of blood. They found that while their acts were condemned at the North, and but faintly justified in their own State, the strong arm of the law was not brought to bear against them. The killing of a few white Republicans and two hundred negroes, more or less, was simply one of those things that people regretted as a necessary means of preserving a white-man's government in the hands of Democrats.

CHAPTER IV.

RISE OF THE KU KLUX KLAN—THE ELECTION MURDERS IN LOUISIANA IN 1868.

Origin of the Ku Klux Klan—Its Spread from Virginia to Texas—
Its Organization—An Ally of the Democratic Party in Opposing
the Reconstruction Acts—Nomination of Seymour and Blair—
Letter of General F. P. Blair to Colonel James O. Brodhead,
announcing the Overthrow of the Reconstruction Acts as the Real
Purpose of the Democrats—Innumerable Outrages of the Klan all
over the South—The Presidential Election of 1868 in Louisiana—
Investigation by a Congressional Committee—What the Testimony
Showed—Startling Number of Killed and Wounded for Political
Reasons throughout the State—The Republican Vote effectually
Suppressed—Massacre of Republicans at St. Landry Parish—De-
tails of the Shocking Crimes committed—Massacre of Negroes in
St. Bernard Parish—A Democratic Senator's Ideal of a Peaceable
and Quiet Election—The State goes for Seymour and Blair by a
" Large Majority."

SOMETIME during the progress of the events narrated
in the preceding chapter, probably in the year 1866, a
secret political association, which is claimed to have
originated in the State of Tennessee, was organized. It
soon spread over the States extending from Virginia to
Texas, and was known by different names in various
parts of the country. It has gone into history, however,
as the Ku Klux Klan. In an article published in the
Century Magazine for July, 1884, from the pen of Mr. D.
L. Wilson, who claims to be in possession of accurate
information upon the subject, it is stated that the Klan
was reorganized, in the spring of 1867, by a convention of
delegates sent from the different " Dens," which secretly

met at Nashville, Tenn. The article states that "At this convention the territory covered by the Klan was designated as 'The Invisible Empire.' This was subdivided into 'realms,' coterminous with the boundaries of States. The 'realms' were divided into 'dominions,' corresponding to Congressional districts; the 'dominions' into 'provinces,' coterminous with counties; and the 'provinces' into 'dens.'

"To each of these departments officers were assigned. Except in the case of the supreme officer, the duties of each were minutely specified. These officers were:

"The Grand Wizard of the Invisible Empire and his ten Genii. The powers of this officer were almost autocratic.

"The Grand Dragon of the Realm and his eight Hydras.

"The Grand Titan of the Dominion and his six Furies.

"The Grand Giant of the Province and his four Goblins.

"The Grand Cyclops of the Den and his two Night Hawks.

"A Grand Monk.

"A Grand Scribe.

"A Grand Exchequer.

"A Grand Turk.

"A Grand Sentinel.

"One of the most important things done by this Nashville convention was to make a positive and emphatic statement of the principles of the order. It was in the following terms:

"'We recognize our relation to the United States Government; the supremacy of the Constitution; the constitutional laws thereof; and the union of States thereunder.'

" This Nashville convention also set forth the peculiar objects of the order, as follows:

"(1) To protect the weak, the innocent, and the defenceless from the indignities, wrongs, and outrages of the lawless, the violent, and the brutal; to relieve the injured and the oppressed; to succor the suffering, and especially the widows and orphans of Confederate soldiers. (2) To protect and defend the Constitution of the United States, and all laws passed in conformity thereto, and to protect the States and people thereof from all invasion from any source whatever. (3) To aid and assist in the execution of all constitutional laws, and to protect the people from unlawful seizure, and from trial except by their peers in conformity to the laws of the land."

This statement as to the organization of the Klan is fully sustained by voluminous evidence taken in 1871 before the Joint Committee of Congress for the investigation of Ku Klux outrages. This reorganization of the Klan at Nashville occurred no doubt after the passage of the Reconstruction acts of March, 1867. The declarations of the convention as to the objects of the order must therefore be construed in the light of the opinions which were entertained by its members in regard to the validity of those acts. This organization was pledged to defend the Constitution of the United States, and *all laws passed in conformity thereto ;* and to protect the States and people thereof from all invasion, from *any source* whatever; and to assist in the execution of all *constitutional laws.* The entire Democratic Party North and South had in the most emphatic manner declared the Reconstruction laws to be unconstitutional. President Johnson in his messages vetoing those laws expressed a decided opinion that they were unconstitutional. If these laws were unconstitutional their enforcement would have been an invasion of the rights of the people. The Klan was composed of ex-Confederate soldiers, and was in full sympathy with the Democratic Party. It is fair to assume, therefore, that it was violently opposed to the Reconstruction acts and to their enforcement.

The Klan was probably at the height of its power in 1868, when the Democratic Party nominated Seymour and Blair as candidates for President and Vice-President. The Democratic platform declared "that we regard the Reconstruction acts (so-called) of Congress, as suoh, as usurpations, and unconstitutional, revolutionary, and void." General Frank P. Blair, the Democratic nominee for Vice-President, in his notable letter of June 30th, 1868, to Colonel James O. Brodhead, said "there is but one way to restore the Government and the Constitution, and that is for the President-elect to declare these acts (the Reconstruction act) null and void, compel the army to undo its usurpations at the South, disperse the carpet-bag State Governments, allow the white people to reorganize their own governments, and elect senators and representatives." Mr. Seymour fully endorsed the resolutions of the Convention which nominated him, in a speech delivered July 10th, 1868, accepting the nomination. Thus it appears that the Democratic Party was committed to the proposition that if their candidate was elected President, he would use the army to prevent the enforcement of the Reconstruction acts, and by military authority secure to the white people *alone* the right of forming State constitutions and the election of Senators and Members to Congress.

These questions were carried before the country in

the election of 1868, and the measures adopted by the Republican Party were again triumphantly endorsed by the people.

During this political campaign the Ku Klux Klan perpetrated innumerable outrages in various parts of the Southern States. It became a terror to Republicans especially, whenever it made its appearance. Its dark and inhuman crimes were usually committed under such circumstances as to prevent detection; in other cases where some of the parties became known the apprehension of danger was so great that persons cognizant of the crimes were deterred from giving information.

Prominent and influential Democrats who were not members of the Klan, and whose instincts were opposed to such outrage and violence, were powerless to arouse a public sentiment to resist the madness and fury of the times. While it was true that the Klan had turned its mailed hand against society, and might justly have been extirpated as a public enemy, no one rose up as a leader to sound the alarm, and arouse the people against this unlawful and lawless organization.

It was the opinion of some that it was beyond the reach of a remedy, and that it would be necessary to allow it to spend its fury, like a tornado.

The secret political organization in Louisiana, although known by another name, had the same objects to accomplish in 1868 that the Ku Klux were so vigorously laboring for in other States, but less effort was made for concealment and secrecy.

In the spring of 1868 an election was held in Louisiana for governor and other State officers and a Legislature. The registration and the election were conducted under the military supervision of the United States, thus insuring the right of every man to cast his ballot as he pleased and the certainty of having his ballot counted as cast. The Republican State officers were elected by overwhelming majorities. The Democracy decided that there should not be a repetition of such a result, and that the State of Louisiana should be carried at all hazards for Seymour and Blair. Soldiers were not to be stationed near all the polls, to see that every elector should be allowed to cast a free ballot. The conditions were all favorable for carrying the election by force, and after all was the contest not being made upon the platform that "we regard the Reconstruction acts (so called) of Congress, as such, as usurpations, and unconstitutional, revolutionary, and void"? And had not General Blair said, "There is but one way to restore the Government and Constitution, and that is for the President-elect to declare these acts null and void, compel the army to undo its usurpations at the South, disperse the carpet-bag State Governments, allow the white people to reorganize their own governments, and elect senators and representatives"?

How could this be done without electing Seymour and Blair? How could they be elected more certainly than by suppressing the Republican carpet-bag negro vote?

And so the Democracy entered upon this work. How well they did it is best described by the report of a committee of Congress who investigated the matter.

The testimony taken by it fills nearly fifteen hundred pages of close print. Two hundred witnesses were examined,—fully one half of them on behalf of the Democratic Party,—their testimony covering the leading incidents of the campaign in thirty-six parishes of the State and in the city of New Orleans. The conclusions arrived at by that committee are thus summarized in the report of the majority of the committee:

"The testimony shows that over 2000 persons were killed, wounded, and otherwise injured in that State within a few weeks prior to the Presidential election; that half of the State was overrun by violence. Midnight raids, secret murders, and open riot kept the people in constant terror until the Republicans surrendered all claims, and then the election was carried by the Democracy. The parish of Orleans contained 29,910 voters— 15,020 black. In the spring of 1868 that parish gave 13,973 Republican votes; in the fall of 1868 it gave Grant 1178, a falling off of 12,795 votes. Riots prevailed for weeks, sweeping the city of New Orleans, and filling it with scenes of blood, and Ku Klux notices were scattered through the city warning the colored men not to vote. In Caddo there were 2987 Republicans. In the spring of 1868 they carried the parish. In the fall they gave Grant one vote. Here also were bloody riots. But the most remarkable case is that of St. Landry, a planting parish on the river Teche. Here the Republicans had a registered majority of 1071 voters. In the spring of 1868 they carried the parish by 678. In the fall they gave Grant no vote—not one, while the Democrats cast 4787, the full vote of the parish, for Seymour and Blair.

"Here occurred one of the bloodiest riots on record, in which the Ku Klux killed and wounded over two hundred Republicans, hunting and chasing them for two days and nights through fields and swamps. Thirteen captives were taken from jail and shot. A pile of twenty-five dead bodies was found half buried in the woods. Having conquered the Republicans, killed and driven off the white leaders, the Ku Klux captured the masses, marked them with badges of red flannel, enrolled them in clubs, led them to the polls, made them vote the

Democratic ticket, and then gave them certificates of the fact."

From the testimony on which this report is based quotations may be taken almost at random. It is so full of uncontroverted facts that any selection is difficult. Open the ponderous volume at almost any page, and a record of shameless murder stands out, bald, naked, and inexcusable.

Colonel and Brevet Major-General Edward Hatch of the 9th U. S. Cavalry, in charge of the Freedmen's Bureau, with headquarters at New Orleans, testified (Mis. Doc. No. 154, 41st Congress, 2d session, p. 32):

"Q. From the time you first saw the riot on Canal Street [which riot was simply an unprovoked attack upon an unarmed Republican procession by armed Democrats in the interests of "peace and quiet"] up to the time of the election, what number of men were killed in the city of New Orleans, to the best of your knowledge and estimation?

"A. My estimation might be different from others. I think there were three white men and a hundred negroes. I know of three white men being killed; and the reason I speak of a hundred negroes being killed is because connected with our office was an institution for paying bounty [some of these colored men, it seemed, supplemented the offence of being radicals by the additional crime of being ex-Union soldiers], and there are some twenty or thirty cases which have totally disappeared. My estimate may be light; I don't know that my official report gives more than thirty or forty killed.

"Q. How would the list of wounded compare with the killed?

"A. I think the wounded would bear a very small proportion to the killed. I will give you an instance: In front of my boarding-house, corner of St. Andrews and Coliseum Streets, I saw some men kill a negro; they wounded him two or three times, and finally finished him. It was done in the presence of ladies. There were no arrests made and nothing done in the matter. It is very seldom a negro is simply wounded. If he is hit at all he is finished. When a negro made himself obnoxious enough to engender attack he was generally killed. If they made up their minds to injure a negro, they made up their minds to kill him.

"Q. Do you recognize this report?

" *Report of Brevet Major-General Hatch, Assistant Commissioner of the Freedmen's Bureau.*

Killed..	297
Wounded by gunshot............................	50
Maltreated....................................	142
Total.....................	489

" A. Yes, sir; these are less than the numbers. No case was reported unless it was thoroughly investigated and substantiated. We reported sixteen killed at St. Landry. This was considered an exaggeration by General Rousseau, who sent his inspector, Captain Hooker, down to investigate matters, and Captain Hooker reported five times as many killed as I did.

"Q. What color were the two hundred and ninety-seven killed and fifty wounded included in this report?

" A. Black.

"Q. What period of time does that embrace?

" A. Probably one month.

"Q. For the whole State?

" A. No, sir; just the parishes adjacent to New Orleans."

It appears from the evidence, and was uncontradicted, that during the three or four weeks preceding the election the gun-stores in the city of New Orleans were crowded by people purchasing arms, and no negro or known white Republican was allowed to purchase a weapon at any price. The ward club-rooms of the Republicans throughout the city, almost without exception, were sacked and gutted by armed Democratic mobs. Some of the most outrageous of these acts of violence have since been made the subjects of suits at law, and heavy damages have been awarded against the city in consequence thereof, in courts presided over by Democratic judges. Domiciliary visits were made in dead of night to the houses of prominent Republicans, ostensibly in search of arms, by bodies of men who themselves were armed to the teeth. In every assassination it was always a Republican that was the victim; in every so-called riot it was Republicans alone who were found among the killed and wounded. One possible exception in all this sickening history of carnage and wrong should perhaps in fairness be noted. An attack on a colored procession, in the parish of St. Bernard, was followed by an excited gathering of negroes from the neighboring plantations, and the burning of the house and the killing of a white Democrat, one of a peculiar race of mixed Spaniards and Italians, known in Louisiana as *dagoes*, who as a class were prominent at this time in all the outrages perpetrated upon the colored men. For this one solitary act of reprisal (if such it was) a terrible revenge was extorted. For three days an indiscriminate massacre of colored people was kept up in the parish of St. Bernard, over one hundred falling victims, while sixty supposed ringleaders were thrown into prison, and were kept there for months without trial, subject to brutal ill-usage, and were finally discharged under writ of habeas corpus, not one particle of evidence being found against them.

In the three days preceding the election, the two Democratic coroners of the city of New Orleans made official return to the Board of Health of sixteen inquests held on colored men, whose names, ages, and residences are given, each of whom appears to have "peacefully" died of gunshot wounds, inflicted by unknown persons.

Such, in brief, is the history of the Presidential election in Louisiana in 1868. One of the Democratic Senators from Louisiana, in a speech delivered in the Senate July 22, 1879, said: "Although the State was at that time full of troops, yet on that single occasion they were not used for the purpose of controlling the elections. Under the policy of Mr. Johnson and of the military commanders then in that section, the troops were held to the performance of their proper duties, and the polls were unmolested and undisturbed by their presence; and the Republican Party, which had carried the election for the convention, the State ticket, and the Legislature in the June previous by the aid of the military authorities, seeing that it was impossible to carry the election in the fall without them, adopted a different policy, called off their voters from the polls, and *in the midst of perfect peace and quiet* they alleged that there was intimidation and force employed against them, that they could not go to the polls and cast a free ballot, and therefore they abstained in a large degree from voting; and instead of our carrying the State by twelve or fifteen thousand majority, we carried it by forty thousand because of Republican abstention."

The picture of a "peaceful and quiet election unmolested and undisturbed by United States troops," as drawn by the committee, is in singular contrast to the one presented by the Honorable Senator from Louisiana. The State went for Seymour and Blair by a large majority.

CHAPTER V.

OPERATIONS OF THE KU KLUX KLAN—INVESTIGATION
BY CONGRESS—TESTIMONY OF A PRESIDING ELDER
OF THE METHODIST EPISCOPAL CHURCH IN ALA-
BAMA.

Tennessee enacts Laws against the Ku Klux Klan—The Klan becomes More Desperate, and its Outrages More Numerous and Terrible—Congress takes the Subject in hand—The Law of May 31,
1870, called the Enforcement Act—Investigation by a Joint Select
Committee of Congress, composed of Twenty-one Members—Tes-
timony of General Forrest as to Numbers of the Klan—Testimony
of Hon. James L. Orr, of South Carolina, in regard to Ku Klux
Outrages—Inability of Colored People to defend themselves—
Speech of Hon. Reverdy Johnson expressing his "Unmixed Horror"
of Outrages proved on Trial—Testimony of Elder Lakin—His
Account of the Killing, Whipping, and Driving Out of Methodist
Preachers—The Burning of Churches and Schoolhouses—Details of
Many Murders and Outrages, all in Alabama—Account of Horrible
Ku Klux Birthmarks.

THE Legislature of the State of Tennessee was first in
the enactment of laws to break up the Ku Klux Klan.
Governor Brownlow advocated the most stringent measures. The laws were of unusual severity; they were
designed to meet an emergency of the most extraordinary character, but utterly failed of their purpose. They
were violently opposed as being unconstitutional. The
Klan became more desperate in the presence of a law
which proposed to punish them for past offences, and for
a time outrages were more numerous and terrible than
ever before. It, however, was not until Congress took
the subject in hand and enacted the law of May 31, 1870,

to enforce the right of citizens of the United States to vote in the several States of the Union, and turned the machinery of the United States courts against the Klan, that the power of the "Invisible Empire" began to wane.

Finally it was deemed advisable to let the light of day in upon the subject. On the 20th of March, 1871, the House of Representatives passed a resolution, which was concurred in by the Senate on the 7th of April following, that authorized the appointment of a joint committee, consisting of seven Senators and fourteen Representatives, "whose duty it shall be to inquire into the condition of the late insurrectionary States, so far as regards the execution of the laws and the safety of the lives and property of the citizens of the United States."

The committee consisted of the following-named Senators :

John Scott, of Pennsylvania; Zachariah Chandler, of Michigan; Benjamin F. Rice, of Arkansas; Thomas F. Bayard, of Delaware; Frank P. Blair, of Missouri; John Pool, of North Carolina; D. D. Pratt, of Indiana;

And members of the House of Representatives:

Luke P. Poland, of Vermont; Horace Maynard, of Tennessee; Glenni W. Schofield, of Pennsylvania; Burton C. Cook, of Illinois; John Coburn, of Indiana; Job E. Stevenson, of Ohio; Chas. W. Buckley, of Alabama; William E. Lansing, of New York; Samuel S. Cox, of New York; James B. Beck, of Kentucky; Daniel W. Voorhees, of Indiana; Philadelph Van Trump, of Ohio; Alfred M. Waddell, of North Carolina; James C. Robinson, of Illinois.

The committee examined a number of witnesses in the city of Washington, and also sent sub-committees to several of the States to take testimony. The report and testimony are contained in thirteen large volumes of printed matter. Innumerable witnesses were examined, including many of the most prominent citizens of the Southern States. The majority of the committee reported that the following facts were established by the testimony: First. The existence of the Ku Klux. Second. That it was opposed to the Thirteenth and Fourteenth Amendments to the Constitution. Third. That it was a political organization, based upon the Democratic platform of 1868. Fourth. That it was either perverted by those who controlled it, or they deceived those whom they took into it, for it became a fearful conspiracy against society, committing atrocities and crimes that richly deserved punishment. Fifth. That it demoralized society, and held men silent by the terror of its acts, and by its powers for evil. Sixth. That relief has come through the instrumentality of the Act of Congress and its enforcement, aided by a better public sentiment.

It is impracticable within the compass of this volume to give anything more than a brief survey of the evidence taken by the committee.

The sickening details of murders and outrages are found in every volume. Cruelties unheard of except in the annals of Indian warfare were perpetrated in every State where the Klan held sway, and it is confidently stated as a fact that not one of the offenders was ever punished by the sentence of a State court.

It is a remarkable proof of the objects for which these terrible wrongs were perpetrated to state the fact that these disguised raiders disbanded and slunk away when a law to enforce the right of suffrage was directed against them. The crimes which could be punished under this Act of Congress were. those which were committed after its passage. The perpetrators of the mighty catalogue of outrage and crime, from the Mechanics Institute massacre, July 30, 1866, to the date of the Act of Congress of May, 1870, go unwhipt of justice.

The Klan was thoroughly organized, officered, and armed; its operations were conducted almost exclusively in the night-time, and the men were invariably concealed by the most hideous disguises. The Invisible Empire was directed against the Republican Party; it was particularly vindictive against the white leaders, and influential colored Republicans were maltreated in the most cruel manner, and often killed without remorse. The Klan would not brook the slightest opposition. If any show of resistance was made and any of their men were killed or injured the most fearful retribution was visited, not only upon the persons guilty of the act, but relentlessly upon whole neighborhoods. Alabama, Georgia, Mississippi, North Carolina, South Carolina, Florida, Tennessee, and Louisiana and other States were overawed by its outrageous acts.

The Ku Klux Klan set all law at defiance, took the law into its own hands, and by military array terrorized whole communities, killed thousands of persons by shooting, hanging, cutting, drowning, burning, and by every barbarous means by which human life could be overcome. It whipped, beat, and abused thousands of others in the most cruel and heartless manner.

The following extracts from the testimony taken by the above-named Investigating Committee will give some idea of the terrible magnitude and character of this organization, and the dangers to which men were subjected who were in favor of freedom and equal rights, and who proposed to exercise the right of free speech and a free ballot.

General N. B. Forrest, late of the Confederate Army, was examined as a witness.

He stated that it was reported that the Ku Klux Klan had numbered 40,000 members in Tennessee; that he believed the report, and believed the organization stronger in other States.

Hon. James L. Orr of South Carolina, testifying in regard to the action of the Klan towards public officers in his State, stated:

"It seems that in almost every single instance where they have given notice to persons in advance in these various counties, the persons notified have been those holding office in their respective county, such as auditors, treasurers, county commissioners, school commissioners, and so forth. In many instances I have no doubt such officials are incompetent. In some instances they are certainly sufficiently competent not to be disturbed in the performance of their duties. If they are incompetent there is a legal method of getting rid of them."

Question by Mr. Van Trump: Are they colored men?

A. Most of them, though some whites have been waited upon, particularly in Fairfield, Union, and York Counties. I think none in Newberry County have been waited upon.

Q. Do these men parade the neighborhood in disguise at night, or have they been in the habit of doing so?

A. I think they have made their appearance at Fairfield twice to notify certain officers that if they did not resign within a given time they would come in and attend to them.

Q. Does that produce a state of terror among the citizens?

A. I suppose that a band of from fifty to five hundred men armed and in disguise appearing in that way would be very well calculated to terrify them.

Q. Is there any reluctance on the part of witnesses to go before the tribunals?

A. They never had any chance to go before the tribunals ; *there never has been a prosecution.*

Q. In those counties which you have named, where these acts of violence have been committed by bands of disguised and armed men, has the law in any instance that you are aware of been executed against them?

A. No, sir ; the trouble is to find out who they are. If persons know, they are afraid to disclose their knowledge.

Q. In other parts of the State can justice be administered in all ordinary cases, civil or criminal, arising between man and man?

A. Yes, sir, I think so—all violations of the right of persons and property.

The operations of the Klan were conducted with such secrecy and their conduct produced such terror that the committee recognized the difficulty in dealing with such desperadoes. Mr. Orr also testified in regard to that point, and while the acts of these men were such as to warrant the passage of a law declaring them public enemies, he felt it would even then be difficult to bring them to justice. He testified as follows :

Q. Assuming that these organizations exist, and that the persons who ride in armed bands are members of them for the purpose of inflicting these injuries upon citizens, is not the plain way of looking at the matter to treat them as a public enemy in armed resistance to the State and General Government?

A. I would be prepared to go to that extent. But then you have the very same difficulty—you have to find out who those parties are before you can inflict any punishment upon them.

In regard to the ability of the colored people to defend themselves against these outrages, Mr. Orr also testified:

Q. I would like to have your opinion on a question that has been somewhat mooted, and that is why, in a State like South Carolina, where the negroes are largely in the majority, they have not resisted and retaliated when outraged? Why have they not done somewhat as the white race would do if attacked in the same way?

A. I think the moral power of the white race over the colored—it was acquired during two hundred years of slavery—exists to a very great extent yet. I think you may take colored men and train them and make good soldiers of them, if you have officers who will lead them. But if you trust to their individuality in resisting aggression and outrage upon them, it would be an exceptional case where the white race would be resisted.

Q. Do you believe that having the numerical majority, as they have there, if they would make an organized and determined effort at resistance and retaliation they would be successful?

A. No, sir; I do not.

Q. Why not?

A. For the very reason that I have assigned to you. Nearly all of the white element of South Carolina, from twenty to sixty years of age, was, more or less, during the war trained to bear arms; they are familiar with the use of arms, and have always been. And when you put, what it would practically be, an organized mass against an unorganized mob, you will at once perceive what the result would be. I have no doubt that great damage would be done by them.

Q. You mean the whites would be organized and the negroes unorganized?

A. Yes, sir; and they could not be organized to such an extent as to accomplish the end you seem to indicate.

Hon. Reverdy Johnson, in a speech made December 18, 1871, in defence of certain persons indicted under this Act of Congress, in the State of South Carolina, while admitting the existence of the Klan, spoke of the outrages shown to have been committed in a manner that entitles his remarks to a place here. Mr. Johnson said:

"But Mr. Attorney-General has remarked, and would have you suppose, that my friend and myself are here to defend, to justify, or to palliate the outrages that may have been perpetrated in your State by this association of Ku Klux.

"He makes a great mistake as to both of us. I have listened with unmixed horror to some of the testimony which has been brought before you. The outrages proved are shocking to humanity; they admit of neither excuse nor justification; they violate every obligation which law and nature impose upon men; they show that the parties engaged were brutes, insensible to the obligations of humanity and religion.

"The day will come, however, if it has not already arrived, when they will deeply lament it. Even if justice shall not overtake them, there is one tribunal from which there is no escape.

"It is their own judgment: that tribunal which sits in the breast of every living man; that small still voice that thrills through the heart, the soul of the mind, and as it speaks gives happiness or torture—the voice of conscience, the voice of God.

"If it has not already spoken to them in tones which have startled them to the enormity of their conduct, I trust, in the mercy of Heaven, that that voice will speak before they shall be called above to account for the transactions of this world ; that it will so speak as to make them penitent ; and that, trusting in the dispensations of Heaven, whose justice is dispensed with mercy, when they shall be brought before the bar of their great tribunal, so to speak,—that incomprehensible tribunal,—there will be found in the fact of their penitence or in their previous lives some grounds upon which God may say, Pardon."

Rev. A. S. Lakin, a member of the Methodist Episcopal Church, and Presiding Elder of the Huntsville, Ala. District at the time of giving his testimony, June 13, 1871, and who had also been Presiding Elder of the Montgomery District, had ample opportunity while engaged upon his work of becoming informed in regard to the condition of society, and especially in reference to the numerous outrages committed upon unoffending citizens in a number of counties in Northern Alabama.

Huntsville is one of the most beautiful places in the South; its homes are elegant, and its people intelligent, educated, and refined. It is situated in Madison, a large and wealthy county.

Mr. Lakin's testimony shows that numerous frightful outrages had been committed in that and adjoining counties, many persons killed, others frightfully mangled; and further, that the Ku Klux made it a special point to abuse and drive Methodist preachers out of the country, and burn churches and schoolhouses. His testimony, as will be seen, is most thrilling in its details of frightful acts of barbarism and cruelty.

By the Chairman:

Q. You say that cut and that article appeared in the Tuscaloosa paper?

A. Yes, sir; two days after I left that city.

Q. Do you desire to have that incorporated into your testimony?

A. Yes, sir; I do.   The person represented in the cut, hanging from the limb of a tree, with a carpet-bag in his hand, on which is the word "Ohio," is intended to represent myself: a mule, with the letters "K. K. K." on its side, is walking away from under me.   The tall man represented as hanging there with me is intended for Mr. Cloud.   And there is space on the limb for all Ohioans after the 4th of March.

By Mr. Van Trump:

Q. How do you know that is intended for you?

A. The reading so represents.

The following are the extracts referred to by the witness:

[From the *Independent Monitor*, Tuscaloosa, Ala., Sept. 1, 1868.]

A PROSPECTIVE SCENE IN THE CITY OF OAKS, 4TH OF MARCH, 1869.

" Hang, curs, hang! * * * *Their* complexion is perfect gallows.   Stand fast, good fate, to *their* hanging!* * If they be not born to be hanged, our case is miserable."

"The above cut represents the fate in store for those pests of Southern society—the carpet-bagger and scalawag—if found in Dixie's land after the break of day on the 4th of March next.

"The *genus* carpet-bagger is a man with a lank head of dry hair, a lank stomach, and long legs, club knees, and splay feet, dried legs, and lank jaws, with eyes like a fish and mouth like a shark. Add to this a habit of sneaking and dodging about in unknown places, habiting with negroes in dark dens and back streets, a look like a hound, and the smell of a polecat.

"Words are wanting to do full justice to the *genus* scalawag. He is a cur with a contracted head, downward look, slinking and uneasy gait ; sleeps in the woods, like old Crosslands, at the bare idea of a Ku Klux raid.

"Our scalawag is the local leper of the community. Unlike the carpet-bagger, he is native, which is so much the worse. Once he was respected in his circle, his head was level, and he would look his neighbor in the face. Now, possessed of the itch of office and the salt rheum of radicalism, he is a mangy dog, slinking through the alleys, hunting the governor's office, defiling with tobacco-juice the steps of the capitol, stretching his lazy carcass in the sun on the square or the benches of the mayor's court.

"He waiteth for the troubling of the political waters, to the end that he may step in and be healed of the itch by the ointment of office. For years he "bums," as a toper "bums," for the satisfying dram. For office, yet in prospective, he hath bartered respectability ; he hath abandoned business and ceased to labor with his hands, but employs his feet kicking out boot-heels against lamp-post and corner-curb while discussing the question of office.

"It requires no seer to foretell the inevitable events that are to result from the coming fall election throughout the Southern States.

"The unprecedented reaction is moving onward with the swiftness of a velocipede, with the violence of a tornado, and with the crash of an avalanche, sweeping negroism from the face of the earth.

"Woe, woe, woe to the inhabitants of Alabama who have recently become squatter sovereigns, carpet-bags in hand, and they filled with dirty electioneering documents! And twenty times woe to those so-called southrons who have turned their narrow heads, infinitesimal hearts, and filthy hands against the land of their nativity!

"Hereafter, when future generations shall contemplate the fate that these white-skinned wretches had in store for us, they will wonder at the extraordinary degree of forbearance manifested by us of the present dark day.

"But the happy day of reckoning with these white-cuticled scoundrels approacheth rapidly. Each and every one who has so unblushingly essayed to lower the Caucasian to a degree even beneath the African race will be regarded as *hostis sui generis*, and be dealt with accordingly if found hereabouts when the time is ripe for action.

"The carpet-bagger already begins to snuff the coming ill-wind, and is sneaking out of the country, *à la* Harrington, of Mobile. But we hope some boreal stragglers may be left from their "hums," to swing alongside of their meridional coadjutors in infamy.

"We candidly believe that the picture, given to our readers *ut supra*, correctly represents the attitude and altitude of all foreign and domestic foes of our land who shall have the folly to remain "down South" after the

ides of March. The contract for hanging will be given
to the negro, who, having mounted the carpet-bagger
and scalawag on the mule that he *didn't* draw at the
elections, will tie them to a limb, and, leading the said
mule from under them, over the *forty acres of ground* that
he also didn't get, will leave the vagabonds high in mid-
air, a feast for anthropophagous vermin.

"P. S.—It will be seen that there is room left on the
limb for the suspension of any bad Grant negro who
may be found at the propitious moment."

[From the *Independent Monitor*, Tuscaloosa, Ala., September 1, 1868.]

"Scalawag Cloud, of Montgomery, and Carpet-bagger
Lakin, of Nowhere, arrived here Thursday. Cloud, the
radical jockey, comes as trainer of Lakin, the negro-lov-
ing jackass. The one is a long, slim creature of the
natrix kind ; the other is a stout, pursy reptile of the
genus *batrachia*. Both would make first-rate hemp-
stretchers. For further information, they may regard
the wood-cut elsewhere. Next week we will give a
more elaborate description of the *varmints*. We would
not take a good deal for this fresh game.

"LATER.—On Friday afternoon Lakin incontinently
departed, by way of the Huntsville road. On Saturday
morning Cloud also "made tracks," in direction of
Montgomery. It seems that these fellows had come
here to take formal possession of the university
premises. Professor Wyman, however, who is the real
president of the institution, so far objected to their proposed impudent procedure as to positively refuse to
give up the keys. The two pretenders then opened
their peepers as big as saucers, in wonder, and were
sorely perplexed. We think Professor Wyman did exactly right in pursuing this bold course; for he has thus

saved the university from the everlasting stigma of having once been polluted by the obnoxious presence of
a nigger-worshipping faculty, and of black-and-white-
spotted animals."

Rev. A. S. Lakin continued his testimony:

By the Chairman :

Q. In what part of Alabama do you reside, and how
long have you resided there?

A. I reside in Huntsville, in the northern part of Alabama ; I have resided there five years and about eight
months.

Q. What is your profession?

A. I am a minister of the Gospel.

Q. Of what denomination?

A. Of the Methodist Episcopal Church.

Q. Will you now proceed to give us your knowledge
and observation of the organization and operations of
what is known as the Ku Klux Klan in Alabama during
your residence there? Give us as distinct a statement
as you can of such occurrences as have fallen under
your own observation.

A. In the fall of 1867 I was appointed to the Montgomery District.

Q. As a preacher or as a presiding elder?

A. As presiding elder.

Q. In travelling through the State of Alabama, and
supervising the interests of your church there, have you
made any examination into the number of your
preachers who have been visited by these bands of disguised men, and the number of persons who have been
whipped and outraged in the different counties through
which you have passed? If you have, state what was
the result of that examination.

A. (Referring to memorandum-book.) Rev. Mr. Hill,

of Eutaw, was whipped and driven from the State in 1867, and is now in Illinois.

By Mr. Van Trump:

Q. Did you commence making that record in 1867?

A. No, sir.

Q. When did you commence that memorandum-book?

A. I drew up this from a former scrap-book.

Q. You kept a scrap-book, then?

A. Yes, sir.

Q. Did you commence it in 1867?

A. Yes, sir.

By Mr. Stevenson:

Q. Who was Mr. Hill, and where was he from?

A. He was a native Alabamian. We have not had a Northern preacher there, except one to assist me, for about three months. I have raised all these men on the ground—native Alabamians.

Q. Was the Mr. Sullivan, to whom you have referred, a Southern man?

A. Yes, sir.

By Mr. Van Trump:

Q. How many preachers have you under your charge?

A. In the conference?

Q. In your Alabama organization; do you not preside over the Alabama organization?

A. No, sir. I preside over only one district; we have six districts.

Q. You are a presiding elder, as known in the Methodist Church?

A. Yes, sir; but I have had the supervision of the whole work.

Q. Then where you speak of all your preachers but one being native Alabamians, do you mean that remark to apply to your district only, or to the entire State?

A. I mean that to apply to the whole conference in the State.

Q. How many preachers are there of that sort?

A. Who have been maltreated?

Q. No; who are native Alabamians.

A. They are all native Alabamians.

Q. How many are there?

A. Seventy.

By Mr. Coburn:

Q. Native Alabamians or resident Alabamians?

A. Resident Alabamians, and I suppose all native Alabamians, and there are one hundred and fifty local preachers. The first I named who was maltreated was a Mr. Hill : he has some three initials to his name,—F. B. L., I think,—but I do not now remember exactly what they are. The parties who whipped him were arrested, and tried by General Shepperd, by military commission, adjudged to have their heads shaved, and sent to the Dry Tortugas, one class for one year, and the other class for two years, at hard labor. Mr. President Johnson pardoned them all. J. A. McCutcheon, presiding elder, was driven from the Demopolis District in 1868.

By Mr. Stevenson:

Q. Who was he?

A. A native Alabamian, and subsequently chaplain of the Senate; he was chaplain for two years. James Buchanan was driven from the Tuscaloosa Circuit; he was fired upon in his house and upon the highway, and notified to leave on pain of death. He has gone to Texas.

Q. Who was he?

A. He was a native Alabamian—born and raised in Blount County, Alabama. John W. Talley, a native Alabamian, an old travelling minister in the Methodist

Episcopal Church before the division, fell into the Southern division; but when the Methodist Church came there he came to her. He was Presiding Elder of the Talladega District, but is now in Missouri. Moses B. Sullivan, as I have already stated, was whipped, and is now in Florida, sent out of the State.

By Mr. Coburn:

Q. Who is Moses B. Sullivan?

A. The man who was whipped, whom I named before, and whose affidavit I presented.

By the Chairman:

Q. When was that?

A. It was in 1868. I do not remember the exact time. I sent him over the river to take charge of the colored people on those large Tennessee cotton plantations. Jesse Knight, local preacher, shot in his own house in Morgan County in 1869, and died in a few days after.

By Mr. Stevenson:

Q. Who was he?

A. A native Alabamian; had lived all his life in that place, and owned a grist-mill and a saw-mill there. He was a steady, sedate, virtuous, intelligent man. I held a quarterly-meeting in his neighborhood and stopped at his house.

By Mr. Coburn:

Q. How long was it after you held a quarterly-meeting there and stopped at his house that that outrage was committed?

A. About fifteen months. Rev. Mr. Johnson, local preacher, of Fayetteville, shot dead in the pulpit while preaching, in 1869.

By Mr. Stevenson:

Q. Who was he?

A. A native Alabamian, living in the place ; a local preacher.

Q. Do you know anything about the circumstances of that case ?

A. Not particularly ; only that a man from the congregation shot him while he was preaching.

By Mr. Van Trump:

Q. A single man ?

A. No, sir ; he was a man of family.

Q. I mean the man who shot him was not supported by others around him. You say a man rose in the congregation and shot him.

A. He was sitting in the congregation, and drew his pistol and shot him.

By Mr. Stevenson:

Q. Was there any punishment for that that you have heard of ?

A. I have never heard of a man in Alabama being punished for any outrage of the kind.

Q. Were the military there then ?

A. They were in Huntsville.

By the Chairman:

Q. When was that ?

A. In 1869.

Q. The State Government was organized then ?

A. Yes, sir.

By Mr. Coburn:

Q. At what time in 1869 ?

A. In the summer of 1869. James Dorman, a member of the conference, at Wetumpka, was brutally whipped on Sunday, after service, and run from the circuit in 1870.

By Mr. Stevenson :

Q. Who was he ?

A. A native Alabamian; a nephew of the celebrated and distinguished Dr. Dorman, of the Georgia Conference—the presiding elder of that conference. I failed to look over the minutes. I was secretary of the conference, and have not here the name of a man who joined the conference last fall, at our session, and in a few weeks after he and his son were shot dead on the line of the West Point and Montgomery road.

Q. Was he a preacher?

A. He was a member of the conference; a colored man. He joined the conference, went to his circuit, and a few days after reaching the place he was shot. It was between West Point and Opelika, on the line of that road. His presiding elder, Dr. Franklin, wrote me the facts of the case. George Taylor, local preacher, in 1869, in the county that was taken off Florence and Lawrence. It was in Tuscumbia, Colbert County. I was in the neighborhood and know the facts. He was taken from his bed by a band of disguised men and whipped; laid upon his face, with men upon his arms and legs, and whipped till his back was scarified; he was punched in the head with their pistols until his hair was clotted with coagulated blood; and then, with a knife, his body and legs and thighs were punctured all over, and then they would slit them out with the knife. They ordered him to leave; his wife carried him out and fed him; he was taken to one of my travelling preachers there.

Q. Did you see him?

A. Yes, sir; at old Uncle George Merrill's; he was kept concealed in their loft for about three months and then he was able to travel when he left.

By Mr. Pool:

Q. Was he stripped when they whipped him?

A. I did not ascertain ; he had nothing but his night-clothes on when they whipped him.

By Mr. Stevenson:

Q. Who was he ?

A. A colored man, born and raised in that neighborhood ; one of the most meek, humble, devoted boys I have ever known among the colored people. About the same time they hung three men from the bridge.

By the Chairman:

Q. Three colored men?

A. Yes, sir ; from a bridge across a large creek. The leading man's name was Johnson, a member of the Methodist church. Two others were hung by him from the bridge by disguised men.

By Mr. Blair:

Q. Was that at Tuscumbia?

A. Yes, sir. I have another case that I wish to present, and then I will submit the whole of their affidavits.

By Mr. Coburn:

Q. In regard to the men hung from a bridge, do you mean that they were hung until they were dead ?

A. Yes, sir ; and they were taken down and buried by the colored people.

By Mr. Stevenson:

Q. You were going on to make a statement in the case of Blair.

A. Yes, sir. Here is the affidavit in that case. He was taken from his house—from his father, mother, brother, and sisters—and whipped ; his legs were slit open on three sides on his thighs ; the calves of his legs were slit open on two sides ; the bottoms of his feet were slit open; and then there were cuts made across both legs.

By Mr. Pool:

Q. Cuts with a knife?

A. With some sharp-cutting instrument.

By Mr. Blair:

Q. Where did he live?

A. In Madison County, near the little town of Vienna, on the Tennessee River. It was done by disguised men.

Q. Was he a preacher?

A. No, sir; he was a laboring man. He was thrown into spasms. He was brought into Huntsville on a stretcher, carried into the grand-jury room, and exhibited to the grand jury. He was subject to violent spasms, and about three months after he died in one of those spasms.

By Mr. Stevenson:

Q. Have they been tried yet?

A. No, sir; there never has been one of them tried in that court. I think there were some thirty-three indictments, as I learned from the foreman of the grand jury, and from one of his colleagues; and seven of those indictments were for manslaughter and murder in the first degree. Judge Charlton, the foreman of the grand jury, came to Huntsville to investigate, and told me he would go to the bottom of the affair, as but two had been arrested, and they were illicit distillers.

Mr. Lakin also stated that Judge Charlton was a short time afterwards murdered, and that he saw the murderer and talked with the people who buried the judge, who had been shot to death, seven buckshot entering the body.

Mr. Lakin spoke of a number of cases which had been brought to his knowledge of persons who had been whipped. He said:

"Here are two cases that occurred on one plantation. I had the statement from the gentleman himself, two mornings after they were whipped, and I saw one of the men. Seven were whipped in one night on the plantation of Mr. David Bush ; seven were whipped, three were shot, and one was murdered. I was taken to see him ; he was lacerated all over, and his body punctured with some four or five bullets He was living when I saw him, but died a few days after."

By the Chairman:

Q. Taking the various counties, give us a summary of what you have so recorded ; you need not give the names.

A. I have taken down Madison, Jackson, Limestone, Morgan, Blount, and Marshall counties.

Q. Give a summary of the result of your examination, beginning first with Madison County.

A. At the time I was getting out of the way, I got into the creek and got my book wet, so that the entries are somewhat blurred; in Madison County there were sixty-one cases.

Q. Between what dates ?

A. From 1868 to 1871.

By Mr. Coburn:

Q. Do you mean including 1871 up to this time ?

A. Yes, sir.

By Mr. Pool:

Q. Have there been any in 1871 ?

A. Yes, sir; they are going on now, or were when I left home. They were raiding constantly. In Jackson County there were forty cases.

By the Chairman:

Q. Between the same dates ?

A. Yes, sir; there were seven killed in Madison among the sixty-one cases. In Limestone County there were thirty-six cases, of whom six were killed.

Q. The six were included in the thirty-six ?

A. Yes, sir.

By Mr. Pool:

Q. How about Jackson?

A. There were thirty-one punished and six killed there. In Blount County seventy-one were punished, six killed; in Marshall County there were seventy-six punished and seven killed; in Morgan County fifty-seven were punished and eight killed.

By Mr. Blair:

Q. Have you the names in that memorandum-book?

A. Not all in all the counties; some have been blurred or obliterated so that I have been compelled to transfer them.

By Mr. Van Trump:

Q. How came you to state a while ago that there were forty cases in Jackson County?

A. I made a mistake.

By Mr. Van Trump:

Q. It does not come up to the facts, then?

A. I think it is a very moderate estimate, for these reasons: I heard of whippings and hangings in different places—many that I have not recorded there.

Q. In these special counties?

A. Oh yes, sir.

Q. Murders which you have not recorded?

A. Yes, sir; one man hung by the name of Smith.

Q. How many more murders?

A. There was a Mr. Francis, a school-teacher, and a blacksmith, and several others.

Q. Why did you not put them down in this record?

A. I could not testify to them, and by some means or other they escaped me, and I would not make any fresh entry.

*   *   *   *   *   *

At the time I ceased my labors, when I made my last tour around my district, I was in more peril than in any other I have ever made there.

Q. That was how long ago?

A. I closed out in April. I wish to name three other circumstances that escaped me. I have been very ill. I have not been so ill before for twenty years as I have been since I have been here, and my memory does not serve me as readily as it would under other circumstances. I may get things a little out of place. In the month of August, 1869, I was travelling through a long piece of woods when a rifle-bullet passed by my ear, cutting through my whiskers, which were a little longer than they are now. I saw the smoke of a gun from behind a large oak-tree. I wheeled my horse and rode up, and found a man there who was trembling and shaking.

Q. Were you alone?

A. Yes, sir.

Q. Unarmed?

A. Yes, sir. I came rapidly on him as he was trying to reload his gun. He thought he was going to be killed. He knew that he deserved it, and begged piteously for life. I made him go down to the road. I will state one fact more. There have been six churches burned in my district by incendiaries, and four of them —three colored and one white—within the space of four weeks preceding the Congressional election last summer.

The following additional testimony of Rev. Mr. Lakin will show to what extent the people were terrorized by the outrageous conduct of the Klan; the facts occurred while he was holding a camp-meeting in his district.

"A lady, whose father, mother, brothers, and sisters

were attending on the ground, the father a local preacher, and all of them members of our church—

By Mr. Van Trump:

Q. White persons?

A. Yes, sir; they were all white; there were no colored persons on the ground at all—were not during the meeting, that I now remember of. This lady, on Sunday morning, gave birth to a child that was a perfect representation and fac-simile of a disguised Ku Klux.

Q. In a tent, on the ground?

A. No, sir; at her home about a mile and a half from the ground. The head of the child was about three times as large as an ordinary child's head, with a soft, spongy fungous growth over the skull.

Q. Are you describing now from your own observation?

A. Yes, sir. I examined the child very carefully and very minutely. The forehead was flat and square, and about perpendicular, about three times the height of an ordinary child. In a straight line from the crown of the head to the front of the forehead, commencing at each cheek-bone, there was a sort of fringe, flaring very little to near the top, and then full around the top. It was about an inch wide and about half an inch thick at the base; a gristly fringe, of dark-purple color. At two points near the temples there were two gristly horns of the same consistency, about an inch and a half or an inch and three quarters long, projecting from the forehead.

Q. Fleshy horns?

A. Gristly. The eyes and mouth were about one third smaller than those of an ordinary child. The face was nearly flat, with but little nose. The eyes and mouth were of a scarlet-red. The chin sloped off on a plane with its body. Around the neck was a scarlet-red band, and from the point of each shoulder, extending down each side, to about the centre of the abdomen, was all a scarlet-red. The child was brought on the camp-ground and exhibited to from a thousand to fifteen hundred persons.

Q. By the mother?

A. No, sir; by the friends of the family. It was demanded by the people; they seemed to clamor for it to be seen.

By the Chairman:

Q. Was it living?

A. No; dead.

By Mr. Van Trump:

Q. Dead then?

A. Yes, sir. The mother was a member of our church, a very delicate, pious lady, of very strong sensibilities. Her husband was an outspoken man, and the Ku Klux had visited them. They had forced her husband into the Ku-Klux ranks, and they had stopped there at an improper time. And she, fearing for the safety of her husband, the child was marked in that way.

* * * * * * *

There were persons present from different counties, and within the knowledge of persons on the camp-ground there were other cases as they represented. They spoke of some six or seven—some seven instances of such marking. They were nearly all living, but not marked to the extent of this one. This was the most marked of any that had been born.

CHAPTER VI.

THE KU KLUX KLAN IN NORTH AND SOUTH CAROLINA.

The Stevens Murder in North Carolina—Details of one of the Most Atrocious Political Murders on Record—Testimony of Essic Harris (Colored) of Chatham County, N. C.—How the Ku Klux visited his House and Shot him nearly to Pieces—William H. Howle's Testimony—Contractor on a Railroad in North Carolina visited by Ku Klux—No Protection to be obtained from a Magistrate—Testimony of Edwin A. Hull, Foreman to Contractor Howle, corroborating him—Outrages on Colored Men and White Women —Testimony of James M. Justice, Attorney-at-Law, Rutherford-ton, N. C.—Outrages on Aaron Biggerstaff, an Aged White Citizen —Justice dragged from his Bed at Dead of Night by Disguised Men—Description of the Band—Details of the Outrage upon him—Charlotte Fowler (Colored) describes the Killing of her Husband by a Band of Murderers in Spartanburg County, S. C. —Commodore Perry Price, an Elderly White Farmer of Spartanburg County, S. C., testifies to the Savage Scourging he received for not Voting the Democratic Ticket.

In the latter part of April, 1870, the Democrats held a public meeting in the court-house at Yanceyville, N. C. Judge Carr was one of the speakers. Hon. Mr. Stevens, a member of the State Senate, a prominent Republican, and a white man, attended the meeting. While engaged in taking notes of the speech some one beckoned to him, and he left the court-room and went down-stairs. After the meeting was over inquiry was made for Mr. Stevens, but no one seemed to know his whereabouts; some one suggested that he had been seen on a horse riding out of town. As the evening wore away his friends became uneasy in consequence of his absence;

diligent inquiry was made as to his movements, but no trace could be found of him after he left the court-room during the speaking. He was last seen in the hall of the court-house on the lower floor. All the rooms in the court house were entered and examined, except one which was locked; the person who usually carried the key to the door was unable to produce it. By this time night came on and the excitement ran high as to Stevens' whereabouts.

A guard was placed to watch the room in the court-house which could not be entered. The next morning the door was forced open, and there lay the dead body of Stevens. It was evident that he had been decoyed into the room, where a rope had been placed about his neck, and that he had been choked so he could not give an alarm. His murderers deliberately cut his throat and stabbed him, and caught the blood in a bucket. When he was dead the assassins passed out of the room and locked the door. The circumstances of this case were afterwards investigated by an employee of the Department of Justice, who learned enough of the facts to satisfy him that at least twelve men were engaged in this murder, all of whom were well acquainted with Stevens; that they belonged to the Ku Klux, and had been ordered by their den to kill Stevens.

Senator Stevens was killed within sight of his home. It transpired that the murderers permitted him, before cutting his throat, to approach the window to take a last look at his little ones as they were playing in the front yard at his home.

The following additional statements taken here and there from the eight thousand pages of testimony in regard to Ku-Klux outrages will give some idea of the fiendish character of that organization. It must be borne in mind that the men and women who were dragged from their houses and shot, cut, and scourged were Republicans, and that the disguised bands of men who perpetrated these inhuman, atrocious crimes were Democrats. Their malignant acts were directed against white as well as black men. The gray hairs of age were no protection. Women were terrorized, often beaten, and sometimes subjected to still greater outrage. To speak or work for the Republican Party, and to vote its ticket, were offences which merited punishment.

Essic Harris (colored) sworn and examined. Resident of Chatham County, N. C.

"I had been cutting new ground that day, working very hard, and I was sitting by the fire; I had not lain down, but was nodding. I could sleep sitting as well as lying down, if I had been working hard. My wife woke me, and said, "Essic, you had better go to bed instead of sitting here by the fire in this way." I went to bed. Stirring up the fire I got sort of awake; I was lying in the bed awake. After a while she came and laid down. As she laid down she thought I was asleep. I have got a dog that hardly ever barks at anybody; but he has barked every time these men came: he don't bark at anything else. He made about three barks. She said, "Essic, the Ku Klux is coming." I never said anything, but bounced out of the bed and went to the door. I took my bar down to see what was the matter. They cried "Hello!" I peeped out and saw that my yard was full of men. I jumped against my door and fastened it. I had a bucket of water sitting beside the door on the pavement. As soon as I shut the door I took the bucket of water and poured it on the fire and put it out. My gun was at the head of my bed. As soon as I put my fire out I went back to the head of my bed and got my gun. By the time I had got my gun they had knocked my window open. I had to fall on my knees then to keep from getting shot. My wife was lying in bed. After they got the window open they commenced firing in the window. Some of them said they were going to come in at the window and get me out. As soon as they came, or by the time I could shut my door, Mr. Ned Finch, the man I stay with, a white gentleman, came out among them. Said he, "Gentlemen, what do you all want?"

Q. He came from his house?

A. Yes, sir; I heard him; I did not see him from my door. He said, "Gentlemen, what do you want? What are you going to do? Let this negro alone. He is a negro that I have here to work my land. He has a family, and is a hard-working nigger, and don't bother anybody. Please let him alone." He kept on talking, and going around pleading, and begging them to let me alone. He went all around the house. They were all around my house. After awhile they got sort of vexed, and ran him back into his own house, and told that as soon as they got through with me they would fix him. He got very much scared then. He went back and just stood in the door and looked at my house all the time they were there. He was about to leave the house; he was afraid they were going to rob him after they had killed me. Miss Sallie begged him not to leave the house.

Q. Who was she?

A. She is his sister. They never married; they are both single. He never left. They kept on knocking at my door, saying that they had killed me. It was half an hour before they knocked the door down, I reckon, but as soon as they got the door down so that they could shoot in, they commenced firing in the door, though they had been shooting in at the window all the time. I don't reckon there were five minutes' time when they were not shooting. I was sitting very close by the window. I have two doors in my house; and if I sat in front of the door there was danger of my being shot.

I sat very close to the window. When they put pistols in at the window I could see them and prevent them from hitting me. They stayed so long that the moon turned over; and that gave light in my house, like the sun when it turns and comes into the window when it is going down.

Q. The moon had got around so that it shone in?

A. Yes, sir; I moved away from that place. When the moon began to give such an amount of light they commenced shooting right at me. Miss Sallie kept walking among them, and begged them not to bother me; that I was a hard-working man, and she did not know of anybody having anything against me. After they had run the old man back so that he could not talk any more, she came out among them, and walked among them until they left. She was all the time begging them to let me alone. She thought I was dead, that my wife and all my children were dead. I thought at the same time they were all dead. They said that they had killed me. I was then shot almost to pieces. My wife has got six children. Two of them were gone to school. I only had four children in there of my own; two of them were away at school. I had there with me a little boy twelve or thirteen years old, my sister's son. I had him there to help me work. There were five children in the house. I never had time to see what they were all doing; but they all got out of the way. I thought they were all dead. My wife had got between the bed-ticking and the mat; my children were in another bed; they had got in a pile, right on top of one another, like a parcel of pigs.

Q. Under the bed?

A. In the bed. The shots were flying all over where they were. The men poked their guns so as to make the range of the balls as nigh all over the house as they could. One thing that prevented them from killing my wife and children was, I reckon, this—I had four bushels of corn in my house, and I put them against the door, and also a little meal in a bag. When the door fell, it did not fall flat down.

Q. The corn held it up?

A. Yes, sir; when the door fell the top was two or three feet from the floor.

Q. It leaned over on the door?

A. Yes, sir. They kept shooting, and saying, "We have killed the old man; let us go in and fetch them out," etc., etc. "Boys, let's go in; I have killed him; I saw him fall; he is dead." One had said that I was dead. They came to my window and pulled off their caps. Some of them I knew, and some of them I would not know if I was to see them in the day-time.

Q. Did you shoot back?

A. They were there I reckon an hour and a half. They said they had killed me. I felt it to be life and death anyhow. I thought my wife and children all dead; I did not expect anything else. The shot just rained like rain. I raised my gun once to shoot; when I raised it I saw Miss Sallie, Mr. Finch's sister, come along, and I laid my gun right down. I had my axe; it was lying on my right hand; my arm was shot so I could hardly use it; I drew it to me, and when Miss Sallie passed I got my axe to me after a while; I took aim at Clark's head.

Q. Where was he standing?

A. At my door. The door was partly down; any two men could have come in at the door side by side at the same time. Clark was cutting at the door, and I raised my gun to shoot his head. They always said that a man in my country could not kill a Ku Klux; they said that they could not be hit; that if they were, the ball would bounce back and kill you. I thought, though, that I would try it, and see if my gun would hit one. It had no load in it to kill a man. I never loaded it to kill any-thing except squirrels, etc. It only had a common load with one or two big shot, such as I always put in. If I had put in a load to kill a man I could have killed him, because I was very close to him. I shot this man, Joe Clark, and Mr. Burgess.

Q. You fired?

A. Yes, sir. When I fired I hallooed for a boy I had to give me hold of my five-shooter. They caught this shot-fellow and carried him off round the chimney. I expected they were going to come in. I never had any five-shooter. I had bought one, but had not fetched it home. I thought I would fetch it home after a while; it had to be fixed a little. But I called for it as if I had it. They thought I did have it, I reckon.

Q. You shot only one load with a single-barrelled gun?

A. Yes, sir, only one load; I was the last man that shot a gun at my house. They said they were going to set my house on fire; that they did not intend to leave there until they had done it. I thought they were going to do it. I was just as certain they were as that I was in there. I had some shot. I have often heard of people talk about a man being so scared that he could not shoot people; but they had been there so long my fear was over; I had no fear at all by that time—not a bit. I went to my little wallet where I kept my shot and powder. The men were standing behind the chimney waiting for them to carry off this shot one, I reckon. He had time to get half a mile or a quarter of a mile before they left. Some eight or ten of them stayed after the rest had started, saying that they were going to set my house on fire.

Q. A part of them went off?

A. Yes, sir, carrying off the shot one. I loaded my gun again; I put in an uncommon load in it—a dangerous load. I was expecting them to come back to the door and maybe shoot me. They could hear me cramming the wadding in the gun. After I got it almost loaded I said, "Give me my five-shooter." They said, "Boys, the old man is calling for his five-shooter, and loading his gun; let us leave." Upon that they went off.

William R. Howle testified as a witness:

Q. Have you lived in the State of North Carolina within the last year?

A. Yes, sir.

Q. In what business were you engaged?

A. In railroad contracting.

Q. How long were you occupied in Chatham County?

A. About nine months.

Q. Were you visited by armed men in disguise, during that time, and if so, what did they do?

A. In November, after the election of member of Congress between Manning and young Holden, I was threatened by the Ku-Klux organization several times; told that I had better leave the State, and not interfere with North Carolina politics. I paid no attention to it; thought it was only gotten up for a show or brag. In fact, I had a good force of hands there, and was not afraid of molestation, knowing that I was in the right.

Q. In what manner were the threats made?

A. To my men, not to me : they told them that if I interfered in North Carolina politics they would Ku-Klux
me.

Q. To whom did they tell this?

A. I don't know, but principally negroes notified me
that I would be Ku-Kluxed.

Q. Had you any authentic information from anybody
upon which you placed reliance?

A. Yes, sir ; I got it also from one or two whites—
Gunter and Kelley. They said they would not be surprised if I was driven off the work for being suspected
in my political principles.

Q. Did you take any part in North Carolina politics?
If so, what?

A. I had gone through the country to get votes for
Holden in opposition to Manning, the Democratic candidate. I did not regard their threats, however ; but on
a return from a visit to Virginia my foreman told me
that the Ku Klux had been there.

Q. Who was your foreman?

A. Mr. Hull. When I got back I found my hands
very much disturbed and alarmed ; I could not get
them to work. I had had twenty-five or thirty at work,
but the number was reduced to six or seven. I told
them not to be alarmed ; that I was back with them. I
supposed it was mere fright. On the night of the 29th
of April, about three o'clock in the morning, I was
aroused by heavy firing about a quarter or half a mile
from the shanty where I slept. I had been sleeping in
the woods previously, in consequence of these apprehensions. . . . Mr. Kelley had been sent for by the foreman to assist in keeping off the Ku Klux. He told me
it would be unsafe for me to sleep in the house. So

from that time until the 29th I slept out; but on the 29th I ventured to sleep in the shanty. When I heard the firing I remarked to my foreman, who slept with me, that the Ku Klux must have come. We got up, went across the railroad, and found our hands scattered about in the woods, lying in the underbrush that had been cleared from the track. There was a deep cut just there, and we got around on the side nearest to where the firing was.

We heard the tramping of horses, and went off among the bushes and lay down, not wishing to be seen by the Ku Klux. They came on hurrahing and yelling, forty or fifty of them, in disguise. They said they had just cleaned out one house; that this was a Ku-Klux country, and they would be damned if the Ku Klux would not control it. All they wanted now was to drive the damned Yankee contractors off their work, and then they would have possession; that if they caught them they would hang them to the nearest tree they could find, and their stock should be killed. From their yelling and carrying on in this way I thought they must have been intoxicated.

Q. Where were you at this time?

A. I was just beyond the cut, some two or three hundred yards, lying down in the woods, about twenty feet from them.

Q. What further was done?

A. After they struck the railroad cut they turned down the track and took a road that ran off into the woods. I saw no more of them that night. The next morning I went over to where the firing was heard. There I found that two negroes had been whipped, one white man and three women, and that a negro had been shot. They told me that it was done by this party of

Ku Klux that I saw coming away. There seemed to have been three divisions of them : one party went toward Jonesboro', one toward Egypt, and the other toward my shanties, in the direction of Harnett County. My track was near the junction of three counties, Chatham, Moore, and Harnett, about a mile from the Moore line and five or six from the Harnett line. The next day was Sunday, the 30th. I went to Locksville and reported the circumstance to J. T. Moffet, magistrate, and asked for protection for my property. He told me that he could not give it to me. I have his certificate of the fact at my room.

Edwin A. Hull sworn and examined :

Q. Are you the foreman employed by Mr. Howle on the railroad in North Carolina in April last ?

A. Yes, sir.

Q. Go on and state what you saw and heard on the 29th of April last.

A. I saw the company of disguised men on horseback. I heard the firing, and supposed it was something of the kind. In the morning Mr. Howle and myself went and got the statement of facts. The old widow lady about sixty years of age, stated that they took her out of bed, threw her on the floor, and whipped her. I saw the marks where she said she had been beaten, and had been shot by a pistol ball in the right limb. While prostrate on the floor she said one of them kicked her in the head, and I saw blood on the floor that she said came from the wound. They also took her daughter and served her pretty much in the same manner. Another young widow lady there was whipped, and also some colored men on the premises. Two of them were whipped, and one, I understand, was mortally wounded.

I saw him, and afterward heard that he died from the effects of the wound.

Q. What kind of a wound?

A. A shot in about the centre of the back. It appeared to have come nearly through his body. I asked them if they knew any of the parties, and they said they recognized a few that they could positively swear to. Her son about eighteen or nineteen was also whipped. He went to Raleigh and swore out a warrant against these parties that the different members of the family said they could positively identify. I assisted to make the arrest of three of the men. They were brought before the United States Commissioner at Raleigh, and sent to the Circuit Court or held to bail in the sum of $2000 or $3000 each. Since then I have understood that the balance whose names were on the warrant have been arrested.

TESTIMONY OF JAMES M. JUSTICE, ATTORNEY-AT-LAW, RUTHERFORDTON, N. C.

Testifying as to the acts of the Ku Klux in his county, amongst many other things he stated as follows:

Q. Did you hear that the sheriff was waylaid?

A. The sheriff stated to me that he heard that a party was out that night looking for him. One of the jurors who was summoned, a colored man, who has served on the jury once or twice,—I remember to have seen him on a traverse jury once—I do not know, but what he has served on a grand jury; he sent word to the court that he was afraid to come; that the Ku Klux were very numerous in his neighborhood, and that they had sent him word by some colored people—by some that they had whipped and by others that they had not whipped

—that if he went to court they would kill him; that he was a good fellow, and that if he stayed at home they would not trouble him. He did not come, and a fine was entered against him.

Q. After the court adjourned you returned to Raleigh?

A. Yes, sir; and the Legislature adjourned a few days after my return. I went home immediately, and arrived at home Saturday night. The Legislature adjourned on Thursday night the 6th of April, and I arrived at home on Saturday the 8th. On Sunday morning I received news of a very shocking outrage in the lower part of the county, about ten miles from the village, on Mr. Aaron Biggerstaff.

Q. State the substance of that transaction.

A. Well, sir, Judge Logan had started to go to Cleveland County to hold court there: Monday the 10th of April was to be the first day of the term. He was met at the edge of the county by the daughter of Biggerstaff, who told him that she thought that her father had been murdered, that he would die of his wound, and she asked the judge to come back to town. He turned back. She made a statement, which caused him to issue a warrant and send for the sheriff to summon quite a number of men. I was summoned among others. I went to Mr. Biggerstaff's on Monday. He is a man sixty or sixty-five years of age.

Q. Is he a white man?

A. Yes, sir; he is quite an aged man, and his hair is very white; he is a farmer; I found him the most abused piece of flesh I ever saw. * * *

We gave up keeping guard in consequence of the lull which we thought had taken place by reason of the arrests that had been made, and also, in consequence of the assurances of those gentlemen, we had done no guarding for two or three weeks ; we had not been out at all during that time. Each of us went home and put our arms where we could readily get hold of them and use them—at least I did ; I thought I was very well prepared to make a defence. On Sunday evening about sundown I heard the discharge of two guns, or very large pistols, out east of the town, in the direction the Ku Klux usually come from. I remarked to my wife that it was strange that persons should be shooting on Sunday. She said the boys had been shooting so much about there of late, that they did not care anything about Sabbath—or something of the kind. I did not think of any trouble. Presently about twilight I saw some young men living in the village coming from that direction, and I supposed they had done the shooting I heard ; I never dreamed that the firing done was a signal of a meeting ; I do not say that it was, but I have understood that firing off a gun at night was a signal for a meeting of these men. I retired to bed very early that night, soon after dark, and as it was quite warm I left the windows of my bedroom hoisted. During the night I woke up, and it was raining very hard ; I got up and let down the windows. Everything was perfectly still at that time. I saw no light and heard no noise, except that made by the falling water. I laid down and went to sleep at once—almost instantly, I suppose. I just remember getting up and letting down the windows ; I do not remember lying there awake at any time. The next thing I recollect was being aroused by a violent crash at the door, and also a regular discharge of guns and pistols—a perfect volley, making a tremendous noise. The idea with me just as I woke up was this : my door is a panel door, with a thick frame and thin panels ; my impression was that they were firing their balls through the panels. I instantly knew it was an attack from these men ; I had no doubt about that. My impression was that they were firing through the panels of the door, and that there was a regular volley of balls passing through the entry.

But for that impression, which I now think was an erroneous one, I might have made my escape from the house. But believing there was a regular volley of balls being fired through the entry, of course I could not go through there. I told my wife to remain quiet ; that was all I said to her. I got out of bed with the intention of crossing the room and get my gun and make the best defence I could. My door was locked with a very good lock, such as are commonly put on doors ; and in addition to that it was very securely propped : I had placed a long piece of timber, nearly as long as the door, up under the top part of the frame of the door, and under it I had put a piece of something—raised it with a brick so as to make it operate upon the principle of a lever. Their custom is to rush against a door and burst it in ; and I had intended that that plan would prevent them from doing so. But it turned out that they split the panels of the door with an axe ; the axe was struck through the panel right against the prop, and of course knocked it away. One panel was knocked entirely out and the other was split a great deal, and the piece that received the bolt of the lock was broken off. Just as I got out of bed some men came into my room and passed between me and where my gun was. I thought of jumping out of the window, but I did not know what the result would be ; my room was in the second story, and I did not know how many men I might find around there. Instantly a man said, "Strike a match; where is the man with the matches?" At that matches were lighted making the room perfectly light, as matches will. I think two or three were lighted. They stood there in the room, several of them looking more like a man would imagine that devils would look, than you ever suppose human beings would fix themselves to look.

Q. Were they disguised?

A. Some wore disguises and strange fixings over their bodies. Some had horns which were erect; others had horns which lopped over like a mule's ears, and their caps ran up to a point with tassels. One had a red suit out and out—a great deal like those I have seen on clowns in circuses. There was something on the breast of one of them, something round, of a circular form; he stood full in view of me, right before me.

Q. Was there any elegance in the manner in which he was gotten up?

A. Yes, sir; it appeared to be a neat concern—much neater than ever I supposed a Ku-Klux disguise would be got up. I could do nothing else but look at them as they all stood there, after the matches were lit. Two of them came forward and said, "You damned rascal, come out." I began begging them to let me alone. They said, "Don't say a word; your time has come." They pulled me right where my bedroom leads into the entry, and there I was right in the midst of a gang of them. The entry seemed to be crowded full of them. All seemed to be trying to hit me. I screamed as loud as I could in order to wake up some persons about me. One person sleeps right on the ground floor of my building; I can go into his room without stepping on the ground. The first floor of my building is rented for

a store; I can go down on to my portico and step right
on the door-steps of the gentleman that sleeps in the
saloon. A little farther off is another neighbor. And
then below me and above me and on the opposite side
of the street are persons in every house; stores and
offices and dwellings all about there. One of my nearest neighbors was roused; his wife was very much
frightened, and they took their child out of bed, and,
the lady in her night-clothes, went up town to her
brother's—a quarter of a mile, I suppose.

As I learned afterwards, they went up there and said
there was a great insurrection of some kind; they did
not know what it was, but they thought the parties
were after me. When I hollered they struck me with a
pistol; I saw the pistol in the man's hands; it was a very
large pistol. You will see the scar on my forehead
made by the blow; it is very nearly healed now. I did
not know what part of the pistol hit me. I fell down
and became insensible. At the same time I think I said
"I give up." I then felt a pounding and beating in my
side; I did not know what it was. But my side is very
badly bruised, from near the armpit down to the hip,
down to the lowest ribs.

Q. That was after you had fallen down?

A. Yes, sir; after receiving the blows in my side I
suppose I was dragged; I have no remembrance of getting down my stairs; I say I was dragged, because I
found skin bruises on my legs.

Q. How were you dressed.

A. I had nothing in the world on except a .oose shirt
that I wear at night; I had no drawers on, only a shirt
that came down about to my knees.

Q. An ordinary night-shirt?

A. Yes, sir.

Q. Nothing on your feet?

A. Nothing at all on, except my night-shirt. Some time, either about the time I was down-stairs, or somewhere along there, I cannot describe it exactly, I have a remembrance of being asked where my pistol was, and I remember I stated it was perhaps in a drawer in my bedroom. The first that I remember after that distinctly, and I continued to recollect everything very well after that, I was in the street opposite my gate. The men seemed to be formed on both sides of me, and a man had hold of each arm. They commenced firing their pistols again, they commenced a regular discharge of pistols, and fairly lighted up the street with the pistols; a continuous firing all the way down the street. They commenced yelling—all yelled, I suppose. They made the most hideous screams of exultation, and said they had got me at last, and that they were a-going to kill me—a damned scoundrel. They asked, "Where is Logan?" That was the first word I heard them speak after I was knocked down by the blow with the pistol. Judge Logan was not at home at that time; young Logan, one of the editors of the *Star*, was at home. I said, "I suppose he is in his room." They told me to run, and they started forward in a run, pulling me and compelling me to go along with them. I said it hurt my feet so much I wished they would not do that. They said I would not need my feet long, that it would make no difference. I was carried down the street until I came in front of the court-house. The *Rutherford Star* office is in rear of the court-house. Some of the party turned across, and passed along just before the court-house, exactly in the direction of the *Star* office, crying out, "This is the way." A large majority of the crowd turned off in that direction. A number that I cannot state positively, not more than ten or twelve, went forward with me, two holding me by the arms, some before me and some on each side of me. At the foot of the hill I examined as well as I could with a view to escape ; I thought possibly I could jerk loose from these fellows and get away, but I saw I was surrounded by those men. It was raining very hard. They ran with me to a branch, a distance of four or three hundred yards. Across the branch they commenced walking up the road and began to converse quite freely. They had said very little up to that point.

Q. That was out of town.

A. Yes, sir, or rather at the edge of the town, where we consider it a road instead of a street. They commenced talking to me about my political course, and first about the trials. I was first asked what my profession was ; I said I was a lawyer. One said, "What kind of cases have you been having lately ; what cases have you on hand ;" I said, "Almost all kinds—from murder down to assault and battery." Said he, "What kind of cases have you been trying lately?" I said, "We have been trying some cases against the Ku Klux." "Yes," said he, "you are fond of that kind of practice ;" I said, "No, not especially so ; but I was appointed by the Commissioner to discharge a duty of that kind, and I have attempted to do it as I understand it to be right." "Yes," said he, "we know something about that; and you have been making some very strong speeches lately; you are in favor of hanging our leaders. Our party proposes to rid this country of this damned, infamous nigger government, and you propose to defeat us by hanging our leaders. You damned rascal, you are in favor of hanging leaders and letting ploughboys go. Now, you are a leader on the other side, and what objection can

you make to your being hung, as you advocate the doctrine of hanging leaders?" Well, I thought he was getting in on me pretty close, sure enough. I knew from
that they had heard what I had said ; but I replied that
I had never advised anybody to do wrong, whether I
was a leader or not. They said I had done some good
things. Said they, "You have done some good things,
which we appreciate ; you had Carson discharged when
he was wrongfully arrested."

Q. One of their men?

A. Yes, sir.

Q. He had been arrested?

A. Yes, sir, by mistake, by the marshal who was arresting men in the Biggerstaff case. The marshal had a
warrant for the arrest of one of the Carsons, but not for
this one ; and when I got to the camp I told him this
was the wrong man, and he let him go. They said I
was very good in some things, but they were going to
kill me, and if I had any preparation to make for another
world I had better make it then, and I believed it ; I
had no hope for my life, unless by some desperate means ;
I talked, and talked what I could : I asked them if they
could point out an act of my life in which I had wronged
them or any one else to the bigness of a pin, or had done
a disreputable act, or anything that any man could condemn me for, except my politics. I said if they came to
that I would agree that their treatment was just. He
said they made no such charge against me; that I was a
man they liked in everything except my politics, which
was most infamous and troublesome to them ; that I
supported negro suffrage and negro supremacy. In
reply to that I told them I thought they ought not to
kill me for that—that it was not my act; that the negroes
received their enfranchisement at the hands of our Gov-

ernment, and that I had supported it as I desired to
support all the laws of the country in which I lived.
They said, "Damn such an infamous Government, that
would put ignorant negroes to rule over and control
white men." And said he, "You are a white man, and
are you not ashamed of yourself? You know that you
have advocated and supported negroes being put in
office over white men, and you cannot deny it. And are
you not ashamed of yourself?" I told them that I had
never supported a negro for office only where I thought
he was qualified for it. They said, "Oh yes, damn you,
you know that a negro is not fit to rule over white men."
I cannot state all the conversation that took place.
There was considerable conversation on that subject and
in that way; I disclaiming any intention to violate any
law or to do any wrong. I said, "My course may be wrong;
but if I have done wrong I do not want to die for it; I
want to live; I don't want to be killed for any politics;
if I am wrong convince me of it, and let me live; don't
kill me." They said, "No, there are no such terms for
you; we know you too well; you have done too much;
you need not make any such overtures to us, for there
is nothing but death in store for you, and that very soon."
This conversation occurred after we had gone up the
road where the horses were. We were first halted by a
voice, and the man who had hold of my right arm
answered in some strange way, so that I could not tell
what he said. The other voice called out, "Who have
you?" The man turned to me and told me to tell my
name. He tried to talk all the time as if he were an
Irishman.

Q. Tried to disguise his voice?

A. Yes, sir. He told me to tell my name or he would
shoot me instantly; he told me to speak it out loud,

which I did.   The whole crowd then raised another yell.
A little above where this person halted us we found a
parcel of men—I cannot say how many.   There were
quite a number of men there, and most of them were
holding horses.   They seemed to turn the heads of four
or five horses together, and then one man would hold all
the bridles, and so on up the road for a considerable
distance.   I did not go as far as there were horses; there
were some still beyond me, but I was carried past a great
many horses.   I saw a great many men with pistols.   I
did not notice any with guns; some I noticed had belts
around them.

Q. Were all these men disguised?

A. I saw two or three who were not in disguise at all,
but while we were in town I saw none but what had
their faces covered.   When we arrived where the horses
were and had this talk, I became very sick; I felt that I
should faint, and I really think that I would have fainted
had I not been allowed to sit down.   I asked the fellow
to let me sit down; I said that I felt very sick, and
thought that I should faint.   He cursed me, and said
that I was putting it on.   I said no, my head was bleeding very much.   He said, "It's the damned negro-equal-
ity blood that is running out, and it will do you good."
When he saw that I was getting weak he allowed me to
sit down, and he squatted down and still held my arm.
They continued their talk.   One man approached me
while I was standing up; he had a covering over his face,
but nothing over his body.   He said to me, "Oh! you
damned rascal, will you believe a nigger's testimony to-
night as quick as you would a white man's?"   And then
I knew who the man was, for in one of the trials this
same man, in the same voice and in the same way, had
said to me that I would believe a nigger quicker than a

white man; and I said no, that I would believe him only when he was telling the truth.

Q. Who was he?

A. John Goode. But when they asked me if I knew them, I told them I did not, and I appealed to my Maker to witness the fact that I did not know them, although I did know some of them.

Q. Why did you do that?

A. Because I knew it would cut off my chance to escape if I said I knew any of them. This abuse and conversation was kept, I would say, thirty minutes; I judge that from the length of the time I was gone from home, more than I do from any exact remembrance of the time. I could occasionally hear shouts and screams from men over in town, and the firing of a great number of pistols. Presently they all came up who had remained over in town and had gone in the direction of the *Star* office. When they came up to the crowd a voice called for the prisoner. This man bade me get up, and I rose, and they led me to a little man, who had one of those things on his head, and he had an India-rubber riding-coat. It was raining all the time I was out, raining very hard, and it was very dark, but I had then been out in the dark until I could see very well. The little man told me that he was the chief of that command, and I think the first thing he said to me after telling me that, was, "Where did you say Judge Logan was?" I said, "I did not speak of Judge Logan; he is not at home." He said, "You are a damned liar; you said he was in his room." I said, "No, sir; I meant to say that Robert Logan was in his room. Judge Logan is not at home; he is down at Cabarras, at his court." Speaking of the Constitution, he said, "It will not be lawful long; we are going to break up that damned, infamous thing, and we are going to kill all men like you who advocate and support any such Government or Constitution." I said, "You will have a big task; the Government is very strong; I have been supporting it with a great deal of respect, but I may be wrong in it." He said, "We know all about that; we know our duty and we will perform it. I have come here to-night with positive orders to take your life ; it has been decreed in camp. We can get rid of you to-night, and we know how to get rid of just such men as you." He talked some minutes about that subject, and then said, "Who are traitors to our interest in this county? There are seven traitors. Who are they?"

Q. Did he seem to be a man of intelligence ?

A. Yes, sir. He seemed to be a sensible man, and asked questions and made answers like a man of good sense.

Q. Did he appear to be an educated man ?

A. I think he was: he appeared to be a man of fair education.

Q. Did you know him

A. I did not, and do not now.

At this point Mr. Justice recounts a colloquy he had with the chief of the band relating to certain parties who were suspected by the Ku Klux of having betrayed them.—Mr. Justice having been active in prosecuting the Ku Klux in his county, it appears was suspected of being in communication with several traitors to the Klan.—Mr. Justice then continued:

He said, "Were you not a member of the Union League?" I said, "I was." He said, "Now state what oath you took?" I said, "It has been so long since I have repeated it that I do not think I can state it verbatim ; but I will give you the substance of the oath as I remember it to-night." He said, "We have got you

on that point ; now state it correctly, for we are posted;
we have got it; and if you don't state it correctly we will
catch you." I went on to state the oath as I remem-
bered it—in substance, not in the exact form of it; what
I understood to be the oath in the Union League. He
said, "Very well; that is all right." He then said,
"What will you give if I discharge you without further
injury?" I said, "I will give you anything I have in the
world; I have nothing out here, as you see—nothing but
my shirt."

After much talk, the little man said, "I am sparing
your life, and you must promise me not to interfere in
this campaign." And I did promise him. He said they
could get along very well if Judge Logan, Mr. Carpen-
ter, and myself would quit our course, and that if we
did not do it we all certainly would be killed. They
then told me that I had to meet them on Saturday night.
I said, "Men, I am afraid to go out there; I am afraid if
I go out there you will kill me." He said, "Can't we
kill you to-night?" I said, "Of course, but I am afraid
some of those other fellows will go back on their promise
and kill me." They said, "No, if you will keep this
promise you are all right, and you need have no fears."
I said, "Well, then, tell me how I can be received into
your meeting that night; give me some words to say
when I am halted, at the point where I am to meet
you." He said, "When a voice calls out to you to
'Halt,' you will say 'Number one;' then you will be
asked 'Who are you?' and you will reply, 'A friend;'
you will then be asked, 'A friend to what?' The answer
you will give will be, 'A friend to my country.' You
will then be asked, 'How can you prove that?' and you
will reply, 'I s, a, y.' That is not our pass-word; I want
you to understand that, but you will get through with

that.   Don't forget what I have told you."   And he repeated it a second time, and then said, "I assure you you
will be treated all right that night."   After we had some
words in a friendly manner, I expressed my gratitude
not only to him, but to the men that stood around me,
for discharging me.   I shook hands with each of them
in a friendly way, and told them "Good-by," and they
let me go, and I ran home as rapidly as possible.

Charlotte Fowler (colored) testified as follows: Resided with her husband in Spartanburg County, South
Carolina.

Q.   How long ago is it since your husband was killed?

A.   It was the first of May.

Q.   What was his name?

A.   Wallace Fowler.

Q.   Tell how he was killed.

A.   The night he was killed—I was taken sick on Wednesday morning, and I laid on my bed Wednesday and
Thursday.   I didn't eat a mouthful; I couldn't do it, I
was so sick; so he went out working on his farm.   We
still had a little grandchild living with me—my daughter's child.   He had two little children living with him
on the farm, but still that little child stayed with me.   He
kept coming backward and forward to the house to see
how I got on and what he could do for me.   I never ate
nothing until Thursday night.   When he came home he
cooked something for me to eat, and said, "Old woman,
if you don't eat something you will die;" says I, "I can't
eat;" says he, "Then I will eat and feed the little baby."
That is the grandchild he meant.   I says, "You take
that little child and sleep in the bed; I think I have got
the fever, and I don't want you to get it."   He says,
"No, I don't want to get the fever, for I have too much
to do."   He got up and pulled off his clothes and got in

bed. He came and called to the grandchild, Tody,—
she is Sophia,—and he says, 'Tody, when you are ready
to come to bed, come, and grandmother will open your
frock, and you can go to bed." So he lay there for about
a half an hour, and then I heard the dogs. I was only
by myself now, for the children was all abed. Then I
got up and went into the room to my bed. I reckon I
did not lay in bed a half an hour before I heard somebody at the door; it was not one person, but two—ram!
ram! ram! at the door. Immediately I was going to
call him to open the door; but he heard it as quick as
lightning, and he said to them, "Gentlemen, do not
break the door down: I will open the door;" and just as
he said that they said, "God damn you, I have got you
now." I was awake, and I started and got out of bed,
and fell down on the floor. I was very much scared.
The little child followed its grandfather to the door—you
know in the night it is hard to direct a child. When he
said, "G—d d—n you, I have got you now," and he
said, "Don't you run," and just then I heard the report
of a pistol and they shot him down; and this little child
ran back to me before I could get out, and says, "O
grandma, they have killed my poor grandpappy!" He
was such an old gentleman that I thought they just shot
over him to scare him; but sure enough, as quick as I
got to the door, I raised my right hand and said, "Gentlemen, you have killed a poor, innocent man. My poor
old man." Says he, "Shut up." I never saw but two
of them, for by that time the others had vanished.

Commodore Perry Price sworn and examined:

Q. Where do you live?

A. My native place is in Spartanburg, South Carolina.

Q. How old are you?

A. I will be sixty-three about the 6th of next month.

Q. Were you born in Spartanburg County.

A. Yes, sir.

Q. What is your occupation?

A. Farming by trade, before the war.

Q. What portion of the county did you live?

A. Sixteen miles from the town of Spartanburg.

Q. Were you visited at any time by men in disguise who inflicted violence upon you? If so, tell when it was, how many there were of them, and what they did and said.

A. Yes, sir; it was the 26th of November, if my memory serves me aright.

Q. In what year?

A. In 1870; it was last fall.

Q. Go on and tell the whole story without particular question?

A. About midnight I was awakened by horses' feet tramping about the yard. About the time I awoke the order was given, "Close up, men; close up!" and about that time they ordered me to open my door. I rose up off the side of my bed and did not know what to do, and hesitated for a minute and then I straightened up and stepped out on the floor. They commenced lamming the door and striking the shutter with something. I suppose from the marks left afterward that it was with the muzzle or butt of a musket. The shutter was made with just plain plank, with two strips across the back, and it burst open.

It was pinned with an iron bolt, and they burst the front plank off next to the bolt, and the balance fell inside of the house. They arrested me at the orders—no, the order was, "Don't shoot in there; wait till he shoots." I told them I had nothing to shoot with. They ordered me out to the door. I advanced about half way. I had an iron poker about as broad as my two fingers, and about as long as my arm, and as I started I concluded to take that. I thought then I would kill one of them if I could. I advanced to where I could see the door. It was starlight and about midnight. I saw there were six or seven right before the door, as close up to the door as they could get. There was a box had some cotton-seed in it. I just dropped the poker right down there, and went to the door; it was opened, and as I went to the door two of them grabbed me, one by each hand. They were at the step—the rock for a step to come up into the house. They took me out, and as soon as they got me out, tied a cloth over my face, and took me three or four steps from the door. In the yard I saw six or seven men, but I only had an instant to look at them. As soon as they had me fast they blindfolded me, as I said, and they left me in possession of two of them. I could hear them coming up, and could hear the horses walking about the house. They left me some time in the possession of these two, and the others went in and rummaged the house.

They tore up the cotton and they tore up some cloth. I had taken off my pantaloons before I went to bed, and hung them up. They got them. I had a little money in my pocket, and I heard one of them say, "Here is his money, the damned old son of a bitch." Another said, "Give that here; nothing shall be taken from here to-night."

They rummaged the house as long as they wanted to, and then came out of doors, while the two still held me. They brought up the horses and mounted, and the crowd put out. They took me half a mile or a little over. They went along talking to me some. They said they were Ku Klux just from hell. They asked me if I did

not want to join them. I told them I knew nothing
about them or Ku Klux. They said, "By God, we are
Ku Klux just from hell." I told them to go back there
if they wanted to; that I did not want to go just that
night. There was a good deal just like that. We got
on the ground, where they stopped to beat me. They
got down, as I supposed, for they still had hold of me,
and I was blindfolded all the time. They said first,
"We are not going to do like Radicals; we are not going
to do anything until we have a trial." They asked what
I had taught the negroes. I said I had never taught
them anything. They asked what I had said to them.
I said, "I don't recollect that I have ever said anything,
without it was for all folks to work and make an honest
living, and for every man in the community to live by
his own labor, and be peaceable." They said I ought not
to have said anything. They then asked me if I had an
office. I said, "I have a constable's office." Another from
some portion of the crowd said, "Yes, God damn your old
soul," and he struck me in my breast and knocked me
down. I caught on my knees and one hand. One of
them as I fell had let my hand loose and I fell on it.
The one that struck me said, "Don't you intend to obey
law nor order?" Says he, "If you are going to kill the
man, kill him." That stopped the affray among them.
That blow knocked the breath out of me when he struck
me in my breast. Then they pulled me up, and one
came and ordered me to pull off my shirt. I would not
do it. I don't know whether it was him or another one
ran at me. I had on such a shirt as I have on—a common coarse shirt. He ran at me and caught me right
at the collar, and tore it open, and split the shirt clean
to the tail, stripping off everything. My shoes and
drawers I had on. Then they jerked me down on my

face, and called for Number One. He came and struck his lick; then for Number Two, and he struck two licks; then Three, and he struck three licks; and Number Four striking four licks, etc., each one striking his licks according to his number.

Q. Striking with what?

A. With brush, a hickory, a whip.

Q. Where did they strike you?

A. All the way from the hams to the back of the neck. Each struck his number. Number One struck one, Number Two struck two, and so on until they got to Number ten. Then they called for Number Twenty. He came with a whip. I could not see it, but I could hear it crack. I can show you a little item of gashes they left on me (baring his arm), from my elbow down. That was split open with a whip thong.

Q. How long is the large scar on the left lower arm?

A. Four inches long at least—more than that.

He struck me six or seven licks with that whip that split the hide, and some man in the crowd ordered him not to hit so hard. Then the balance of the whipping was whipped out of his number twenty, and it come chiefly on this left arm, for the arm was close to this side, and the licks cut my side some, but not very much. When they got done beating me I was just like a log or a stump. I had no feeling at all. They beat me until I could not tell the hurt when they beat me. When they got done they raised me up, and some of them slipped my gallowses back on my shoulders. They asked me then if I would vote the Democratic ticket. I told them, "I don't know that I ever will vote any more at all." They ordered me then to double-quick. Said I, "I cannot double-quick. You know it." They said, "Try." They told me to go home. I said, "I don't know which

way to go. How can I go home, coming here blindfolded and the blindfold still on me." Two of them took
me by each arm and went back forty or fifty yards from
the whipping-ground; and took off the blindfold and
gave me a push, and one of them started with that, and
it appeared to me that they gave me a shove, and as they
pulled off the cloth said, "God damn you, if you look
back I will shoot you down." As soon as they took off
the cloth I knew the road and fence—I almost knew the
saplings, you might say—and I went home.

CHAPTER VII.

THE KU KLUX KLAN IN GEORGIA AND ALABAMA.

George P. Burnett, of Atlanta, Ga., Merchant and Planter, testifies
—Warned out of the Country by Ku Klux, for making Republican
Speeches—Terrible Condition of Affairs in Georgia, induced by Ku-
Klux Outrages—Killings and Whippings—Terror of the Negroes—
No Prosecutions—No Redress—Good Behavior of Colored People
—Testimony of A. B. Martin, Haralson County, Ga., an Aged
White Citizen, Brutally Whipped for being a Union Man—Testi-
mony of John L. Coley, a Farmer of Haralson County, Ga.,
Whipped and Hung to a Tree for being a Radical—Testimony of
Joseph Addison, Union Man, same County, Hunted, Beaten, and
Driven from the Country for his Opinions—Testimony of Jasper
Carter (Colored)—Describes the Brutal Murder of Jasper Walthall
(also Colored)—Carter almost Beaten to Death—Obliged to Hide in
the Woods—All for Voting the Union Ticket—Caroline Smith of
Walton County (Colored), Ga., testifies to the Whipping of herself
and Husband and Sister-in-Law by the Ku-Klux Wretches—General
Terrorism among the Colored People—Driven from their Homes
and Crops—Alfred Richardson (Colored), of Clarke County, Ga.,
tells a Horrible Story of Outrages committed on himself and the
Defenceless Blacks in his Neighborhood—Testimony of Z. B. Har-
grove, of Rome, Ga., Attorney-at-Law, late Officer of the Confederate Army—Object of the Ku Klux to prevent Negroes and Whites
from Voting the Republican Ticket—Testimony of Augustus Blair,
of Limestone County, Ala.—Tells how the Inhuman Monsters
dragged his Son from his Bed and Killed him by the Infliction of
the most Savage Wounds, cutting him with Knives.

George P. Burnett sworn and examined:

Questioned by the Chairman, Mr. Poland, Mr. Burnett
stated:

"My home is at present in Atlanta, Georgia; have
lived in Atlanta about eighteen months; resided be-

fore that time in Rome, Georgia; was born in Tennessee; have lived in Georgia about thirty-one years. Occupation has been that of a merchant and planter; that is my occupation now, but have not been merchandising for two years. I do not hold any official position in the State; I have held some little offices; I was mayor of the city of Rome; and since the war I have held some positions. I was a member of the constitutional convention that framed our present constitution. Was a Union man during the war; was engaged during that period looking after my planting interests. I was not connected with the army. Have acted with the Republican Party since the war. I presume it would be considered that I have been active as a Republican, though I have not taken a great deal of interest in it. I was a Republican candidate for Congress at the last election, in my district. I canvassed the district pretty well—almost all the counties; cannot say that I found any obstacle or hindrance in doing so.

"I went from Rome to Summerville, where I was raised. I did not go for the purpose of making a speech; I intended and expected to have gone in company with General Young, the Democratic candidate, but he got away without me. I went over there and got there about six o'clock in the evening, I believe; I met a good number of citizens; about twelve o'clock that night, some disguised men, known as Ku Klux in that country, made their appearance, but they did not do me any harm at all; they sent me a note asking me to leave the place, stating that I could not travel through that country; that I could not be allowed to make a speech there, and that I must leave by a certain time. They came within about thirty yards of me. I saw only about six of them. They also stated in the note that I had to leave by eight o'clock the next day; that if I did so and returned the way I came, I should not be harmed; and that in the event I remained, I should be dealt with very severely.

"I do not think it is prudent or safe for a man to express his opinions fully in some localities in Georgia, especially if he is a Republican, and has been in the United States army, or connected with it.

"I am pretty well satisfied that there have been a number of outrages committed in my part of the country—principally upon negroes, although I have never witnessed anything of that sort. A few months ago there was a negro killed in or near Rome; I believe it was right in the town. There was also a negro named Jourdan Ware killed. The particulars of the attack on Ware, as I heard them, are as follows: A body of about twenty-five or thirty disguised men went one night and met him on the road. I am not certain that they went to his house. I believe that they met him on the road somewhere or other, and demanded of him his arms and his watch. I believe he gave up his arms, and they shot him upon his refusal to surrender the watch, and he died a day or two afterward.

"It is considered impudence for a negro not to be polite to a white man—not to pull off his hat and bow and scrape to a white man, as was always done formerly.

"A short time ago there was a negro killed at Marietta, Georgia, a short distance above Atlanta. These things occur so frequently that really I never pay much attention to them. If I hear of a negro being killed, I pay very little attention to it unless I happen to know him personally.

"The Ku Klux appeared in my part of the State about three years ago or a little over. About a month ago I heard of a band of armed men in disguise going about in the neighborhood. Do not think that these organizations have ceased or disbanded.

"In my part of the State of Georgia there have been a good many colored men whipped severely and some killed—a good many more whipped than killed. Have heard of white men being whipped and killed by these disguised bands in other parts of the State; think they have killed a good many more colored than white men Think the operations of these bands have been more generally directed against colored than white men. I think, from what I have heard, that these organizations are entirely political in their character, because the parties who have been maltreated by these men are generally Republicans. I have never known a Democrat to be assaulted. I do not think that any Republicans belong to these bands; think the Republicans throughout my State universally condemn this organization; the Republican papers in my State have universally denounced them.

"My opinion is that the purpose of keeping up the Ku-Klux organization, and operating it as they do, is to break down the Reconstruction acts; that they were dissatisfied with negro suffrage and the Reconstruction acts, and with everybody who was in favor of them.

"I think that this organization was intended to neutralize the votes of the negroes after suffrage had been extended to them, by intimidating them, and making them afraid to exercise the right of suffrage, and that the organization has in fact produced that result to some extent.

"In my section of the country the colored people generally are afraid now, and have been for some time, to turn out at an election. They are afraid to say much, or to have anything to do with public affairs. I own a plantation on Coosa River, upon which I have perhaps about forty negroes, and some of them have been pretty badly alarmed, afraid to say much. Some have lain out in the woods, afraid to stay at home, for fear of these attacks. I have told the negroes on my place that I thought their alarm was entirely unnecessary; that I did not think they would be hurt; but they have got scared.

"A good many negroes living in the country have been frightened to such an extent by the operations of this organization, that they have left and gone into the towns in order to be safe.

"This movement of the negroes has not been beneficial in its effects; their labor is needed in the country, on the land; and in the towns there are generally more of this class of people than are needed, and than can be usefully employed.

"So far as I know or have heard, there have been no prosecutions or punishment for any of these outrages (killings, whippings, or whatever else they may have been) committed by these armed bands, except in a few cases.

"I think the reasons why these cases have not been prosecuted and punished have been, in the first place, because it is a hard matter to find out who these persons are who commit these depredations and outrages, because they go about in the night and in disguise. In the next place, the parties who really believe that they know the criminals are afraid to say anything about it. They are afraid some evil will happen to them, if they give information or testify, or take any measures to prosecute. Also, I think there is is no doubt that some portion of the white community sympathized with the offenders, and did not wish to bring them to justice.

"The colored people have behaved themselves very well; as a general thing, they have been quiet and peaceable.

"Since the colored people have become free there has been, in my judgment, no just ground of apprehension that the white people were in danger from them, as respects person or property, and that there has been no necessity for organizing these Ku-Klux bands, or other bands of white men, for the purpose of affording protection to the white people against the colored people.

"So far as my knowledge goes, the expression of political opinion by members of the Democratic Party has been free and unrestricted."

Testimony of A. B. Martin:

"I will be seventy-one years old the 17th day of next January; I was born in Carolina, and now live in Haralson County, Georgia; I keep a shop there, and farm it, too. Have lived in Georgia since the day of Polk's election. I have been a Union man from my boyhood.

"There are a set of men in my county there that are disguised people. They disguise themselves with calico or anything; I do not know what all. I have seen some of them in the night that were disguised. On the 7th of last May they were at my house. I lay in one room and my sister-in-law in another; I had just got to sleeping soundly, so I had to be shaken two or three times to wake me up. The first I knew she was shaking me, and said, 'Mr. Martin, get up; there are a hundred men coming here, I think.' I jumped up, and ran out and opened the front door. I peeped out, and it looked to me like a heap of women.

"Thought it was another runaway set wanting to get married. The Alabama line is close by, and they run over on our side to be married. I said I would put on my clothes and be out in a minute. When I went out they presented their guns at me. They took me and my step-son out and whipped us a plenty. They whipped me so that I had to tote my drawers and pants in my hands to the house, and they whipped my step-son pretty considerably. Some of them are close neighbors to me. They are mighty rigid Democrats, and I was as much the other way. I had my undershirt and overshirt on, and my drawers and pants on. My suspenders were held with horn-buttons, and they whipped me until they cut the buttons all to pieces, and I had to carry my clothes in my hands. They struck me until I had no feeling.

"If they had whipped me on until yet it would not have made much odds; my sense of feeling was entirely gone.

"They got up, and put a rope around my neck, and tried to draw me up to a post-oak sapling. And then they whipped me about the legs. My neck is swelled yet, and it was black for two months.

"They had some negroes along with them, prisoners. They said they whipped the negroes powerfully, and kept whipping them; and they are afraid to come here. A great many of them are actually afraid to tell what they know.

"I think that the Ku Klux have a majority in my county.

"I and my wife have not slept in my house three nights since then. I am not going back, because I am afraid to go among them now. I know of some Democrats who do not belong to the Ku Klux, but who encourage them. Duncan Monroe is one. I heard him tell a man there about a man in the neighborhood, ' If he don't leave in three days, I will have him Ku-

Kluxed;' and they went and did it. His name was Thomas Powell. They went and whipped him and his wife, and scared her nearly to death.

"Duncan Monroe is a good man, as to property; he lives in a brick house, within a mile of me.

"If a man was to shoot another there, and I was to issue a warrant, I could not get a man to arrest him.

"I have seen the sheriff arrest one myself, and he and his father came and shot him."

TESTIMONY OF WILLIAM WILLINGHAM.

I am going on nineteen years old. I was born in Randolph County, Alabama, and I now live in Haralson County. I am farming there. I am a step-son of Mr. Martin, the last witness examined by this committee. He married my mother when she was a widow. I have lived with Mr. Martin between six and seven years. I was at home the night that disguised men came there and whipped my step-father. One of my aunts lived there with us. When they were coming up, she got up and waked me and the old man up. They told the old man to come out, and I think he went out. They came in the house, and in a few minutes took me out. They took the old man off from the house and made me follow him. I was standing right there when they whipped my step-father. George Carter, a negro there, said he counted the blows, and that they hit him seventy-five licks. I should think they gave him between fifty and one hundred licks.

They gave me about thirty blows. They pulled my shirt up and gave the blows on my bare back with a hickory; they tied me and drew me up to a tree, and whipped me standing up.

They made the old man lie down, and hit him fifteen or twenty licks, and then they took him and tied him and drew him up to a tree, and whipped him there.

They whipped the old man because he was a Radical, and whipped me because I lived with the old man.

They had three negroes with them. They hit one of them, Joe Ray, five licks. They said they whipped the negroes more. Their backs were cut very bad; blood and water was running out of their backs two days after that; I saw that myself.

They hit mother over the head with a gun. She told them she was going to follow me and Mr. Martin, and they cursed her and hit her over the head with a gun, and said that if she did, they would shoot her. Every man had his arms ready cocked for firing.

I have not laid in my house but two nights since the 7th of May last. I lay around watching for them. I slept in the bushes when I did sleep; they said they would kill me, and I was afraid to stay in the house.

They have been going about in the neighborhood since they whipped me; they killed a negro since that.

I think the men that were there accounted themselves respectable. They lived in common, weather-boarded houses. There are no fine houses there; some of them live in log-houses.

TESTIMONY OF JOHN L. COLEY.

Was born in South Carolina, in 1821. I now live in Haralson County, Georgia, and my occupation is that of a farmer.

On the 25th of February last a band of disguised men came to my dwelling between ten and eleven o'clock at night.

I had worked pretty hard all day, and had laid down and gone to sleep.

They hallooed, "Open your door, old man;" and I opened the door, according to their direction. As I bent myself to look out, two men seized me by the left arm and tried to jerk me out of doors.

They jerked me so hastily, that they got the door up against the point of my right shoulder. After stabbing at me with a knife, spear, or some sharp cutting instrument, and pointing guns at me, threatening to shoot, they took me out. My wife was scared almost to death, and also the young man's wife who was staying there; she sank right down.

They took me about seventy-five yards, and put a rope around my neck. They took me to the west end of my plantation, and stopped and whipped me.

They then took me out by the side of the road to a shade-tree, where they hanged me up by the neck —pulled me up clear from the earth. The last I knew about my actions I was trying to hold on to the rope.

When I came to, I was standing on the ground with my hands by my side. I could not say how long I had been there, because they deadened me so that I did not know anything.

I felt something pass from my neck way down to my extremities, like sometimes when you hit your elbow.

They asked me if I was a Radical, and how I voted. They next whipped me, giving me probably about seventy-five licks altogether.

The commander led me to the middle of the road, and said, "Don't you think you can find a home away from here?"

I said, "I cannot go. This is my place; I have earned it with my hands."

He said, "If you don't do it we will kill you."

TESTIMONY OF JOSEPH ADDISON.

Am about twenty-four years old; was born in Muscogee County, and now live in Haralson County. Have been living there ever since I was a little bit of a boy. I am a farmer. I was not in the Rebel army. I was what you call a Union man then. My opinions were well known. I know of people in our county called Ku Klux.

They came on a neighbor of mine, a brother in-law, who lived right close to me. They took both him and his son out and whipped them. They sent me word to leave where I was living. I said I should not do it. They said that if I did not leave they intended to shoot me. I laid out then about three weeks. I then went into the house and laid there I believe two nights. The third night they came on to me, and took me out and hit me some ten or twelve licks with a hickory. They then told me they would give me ten days to get away in. I begged them to let me stay until I had made my crop. They said I should not do it. Three or four of them kept saying, "He's not going." I said, "If I am obliged to go, I will go." They said, "You would rather go than to die, wouldn't you?" I said, "Yes, I would rather do anything than to die." They just went off and left me there. That was in the last of March, the first time they came on me. I laid out then, and the next time they came on me was the last day in May, on a dark rainy evening, about a half an hour by sun. I had been to the store to sell some wheat and corn so as to get some little things I wanted.

I did not sell it but brought it back home. I got back

about two or three o'clock in the evening. My wife had been hoeing cotton, and asked me if I wanted dinner. I ate a cold snack. We then went on and hoed until it came up to rain. My wife got supper, and I went in and sat down to supper. I got about half done eating when one of the dogs broke out barking powerfully.

I said, "What is that dog barking at?" My wife looked out and said, "Lord have mercy! Joe, it is the Ku Klux." I jumped out of the door and ran. One of them was right in the back yard, and he jabbed the top of his six-shooter almost against my head and said, "Halt, G—d d—n you." I said, "I will give up." I asked them what they were doing that for. They said that I had been stealing. I said, "You men here know I have not." They said, "We gave you time once to get away, and G—d d—n you, you have not gone. Now, G—d d—n you, you shall not go, for we allow to kill you." I said, "If you do not abuse me or whip me I will go next morning." They said they would not abuse me or whip me, but they would kill me. I said, "Let me go and see my wife and children." They said, "No, G—d d—n you." I turned away from the man; he jammed his pistol in my face, and said, "G—d d—n you, go on or I will kill you." They took me about eighty or ninety yards from there into a little thicket. The man on my right was a high, tall man; the one on my left was a low, chunky fellow. The man on my right stepped back and said to the little fellow on my left, "Old man, we have got him here now; do as you please with him." There were some little hickories near him; he looked at them but did not take them. They were all standing right around me with their guns pointing at me. Just as he turned around I wheeled and ran; but before I had run ten yards I heard half a dozen caps bursted at me. Just as I made a turn to go behind some buildings and little bushes I heard two guns fired. I must have gone seventy or eighty yards, and then I heard what I thought was a pistol fired. I heard a bullet hit a tree. I ran on eight or ten steps further, and then I heard a bullet hit a tree just in front of me. Every one of them took after me and run me for a hundred and fifty yards. I ran down a little bluff and ran across a branch. When I got across there I could not run any further, for my shoes were all muddy. I cut the strings of my old shoes and left them there. I stopped to listen, but I never saw anything more of them. That was the last I heard of them that night.

My wife would not stay there by herself, but went to her sister-in-law's. They came in on them on Sunday night, or about two hours and a half before day Monday morning. They abused her and cursed her, and tried to make her tell where I was. They said that if she did not tell them they would shoot her G—d-d—n brains out. I was laying out close by there, and I stood there and heard them. They shot five or six shots in the yard. Some of them said they shot into the house. They scared my wife and sister-in-law so bad that they took the children and went into the woods and stayed all night.

That was last month. They then told my wife that if they ever caught her or her sister-in-law, Milton Powell's wife, back there again, they would kill the last G—d d—n one of them.

I moved off and left my hogs and my crop and everything there—what little I made. I did not make much crop this year, for I was afraid to work, and now I am afraid to go back there to save anything. My brother-in-law left and went over into the valley.

It has been over a year since I heard of the Ku-Klux riding around in Haralson County. They have been riding about there a great deal this summer, doing right smart of whipping; they have beat up lots of people powerfully, and they killed a black man named John Walthall there not long ago.

It was just before the election that they made all these raids. I never heard of anybody, black or white, being raided on or molested or disturbed in any way, except those that are called Radicals.

They whipped my brother-in-law the time they sent me word to leave.

TESTIMONY OF JASPER CARTER (COLORED).

I recollect about John Walthall being killed. It was done on a Monday night.

They all came to my house first, and knocked the doors down and came in, and told me to kindle a light. They came in with pistols and guns, and trained them on each side of me. One had one right at my head. They struck me above the eye with a pistol; the scar is there yet. They ask me if I was John Walthall. I said, "No, sir." They said, "Where is he?" I said, "Up to the other house," which was about fifty yards off. They said I had to go with them up there. One had hold of my arm, one had hold of my clothes, and another had hold of my shirt. We went up there.

John Walthall, when he heard them knocking the doors down at my house, raised up a plank, went under the house, aiming to get out at the back end of the house; but he got under the house and got fastened there. They ran around the house and knocked his doors down, went in there, jerked his wife out of bed, and beat and knocked and stamped her about on the floor, and beat her over the head with guns and pistols. There is a great scar on the back of her head half as big as the palm of my hand.

They had a big light and were looking about in the house; they jerked up a plank, and happened to get a glimpse of his shirt or something white. They ran out into the garden and jerked up a plank there, and one of them had a rifle and ran it down close to him, and shot him in the small of the back. After they shot him, they pulled him out and hit him three hundred licks, and made her hug him; and then they beat them both; they beat their heads together. They beat them with a great big stick, and with their fists.

He was just sitting up when they beat him. They would stand on each side of him, and one of them would knock him nearly over, and the man on the other side would knock him back.

They beat them both there, knocked and kicked, and stamped them about just as long as they wanted to, and then went off and left them there.

They then took me about a quarter from the house, and whipped me. One stood on my head and the others beat me. After they had all done beating me as much as they wanted to, one of them made some of the rest go and stand on my head, and let him beat me.

They had me laying on my face, and one of them stood on my head.

There are welts on my back now as big as your finger and as black as a man's hat. They hit me one hundred and fifty blows. There were about twenty-six of them altogether. They were all mounted.

John Walthall lived until the next day about sundown. No attempt was ever made to find out who had done this or to punish them in any way. Some of the men I saw there are men of property. Some are well off. Walthall and I voted the Union ticket at the election, a short time before. These men I saw there voted right the other way.

I wanted to go to school some; there was a school going on close by. But they said that if I went to school they would hang me. Monroe said that if I went off to school with the other negroes, the first thing I knew the Ku Klux would have me. I never went; I was afraid.

The Ku Klux disturbed some of them that went to school. They got after my brother. They took him off, and told him to stay at home and not go any more, and to serve the master and mistress, and to do everything that white people told him to do; that he was not free yet, and should not vote for such and such a man.

The Ku Klux commenced in that part of the country last year. They have got the people about there, so that half of them are afraid to stay in the house.

I have not stayed in my house one night since corn-planting time; I stay in the woods. I do not know how my wife and children are getting on; I cannot tell anything about it. A great many of the colored people are in that condition.

TESTIMONY OF CAROLINE SMITH (COLORED).

I left home over two weeks ago. I left because the Ku Klux came there. They came to my house on Thursday night and took us out and whipped us. There were twenty-five or thirty of them, perhaps more; ten of them whipped me.

It was late in the night. I sat up very late that night for they had been there once before, and we never laid, down early in the night at all. Some of us sat up the better part of the night.

They had on some kind of false face. They caught my husband and beat him as much as they wanted to, and then they came in and made me go out and get down on my knees. One of them named Felker then said, "Take off this," pointing to my dress, "and fasten it around you." They made me fasten it to my waist. He whipped me some and then made me take my body off, which I wore under my dress. He gave me fifty more with hickories.

They beat Sarah Ann, my sister-in-law, and kicked her in her back, and she has not got over it yet. They hit her on the head with a pistol.

They beat my husband with rocks and pistols and sticks, and then they whipped him with hickories. They gave no reason why they whipped my husband. He said, "Just hold on a minute, please; what are you whipping me for?" They said, "Never mind that, so we whip you."

They never said anything particularly as to what they whipped Sarah Ann or me for; only just told us not to have any big talk, or sass any white ladies.

They made a scatterment of the darkies when they came through there the first time. After that we were all scared and uneasy, and watching for them. My husband went off, but I sent for him and told him that Mr. Moore had said that if we stayed there and worked his land we should not be pestered any more, and he came back. And just as we got our crop done and pulled all the upland fodder, and were going over the cotton the first time, they came. We then had to leave anyhow. I could not stand it any longer. Our crop is there now and they are gathering it.

In March, when they scattered the darkies, they said we should not have any schools; and that white people should not countenance us, and they intended to whip the last one.

They went to a colored man there, whose son had been teaching school, and they took every book they had and threw them into the fire; and they said they would just dare any other nigger to have a book in his house. We allowed last fall that we would have a schoolhouse in every district, and the colored men started them; but the Ku Klux said they would whip every man who sent a scholar there. There is a schoolhouse there, but no scholars. The colored people dare not dress up themselves, and fix up, as if they thought anything of themselves, for fear they would whip us.

I have been humble and obedient to them—a heap more so than I was to my master who raised me.

TESTIMONY OF ALFRED RICHARDSON (COLORED).

I live in Clarke County, Georgia; am about thirty-four years of age. Was born a slave; remained a slave until the general emancipation. Have been a house-carpenter since I became a free man. Have a wife and three children. Have voted with the Republican Party. I have been attacked twice. The first time was just before last Christmas. There was a set of men came down to about a quarter of a mile of where I live. They were all disguised. They had taken out an old man by the name of Charles Watson, and beat him. His wife and children all ran out, and hallooed and screamed for help to stop the men from beating him to death. We went out to see what was the matter, and heard a great parcel of men talking beside the fence. It was the Ku Klux, who had this old man down in the corner of the fence, knocking him, and telling him that he had to tell where Alfred Richardson was. A crowd of boys came up behind me, and we all ran up toward them. They all ran, carrying the old man with them. I ran up to see which way they went, but could not see any one for some time. After a while I saw one fellow slipping alongside the fence, holding a pistol in his hand as if to shoot me.

When I saw him doing that, I took my pistol and shot at him. Just then three or four men shot me through the fence. They shot about twenty shots into my leg and hip. On the 18th of January a white man named John O. Thrasher came to me and said to me, "There are some men about here that have something against you. They intend to kill you or break you up. They say you are making too much money; that they do not allow any nigger to rise that way; that you can control all the colored votes; and they intend to break you up, and then they can rule the balance of the niggers when they get you off."

That same night these men came, between twelve and one o'clock. There were about twenty or twenty-five of them. About eight or ten of them got abreast and ran against my door. I expected them, and had my door barred very tight. They cut the door down with an axe. I went up into the garret, thinking they might not find me. My wife opened the window to call out for help, and a fellow shot at her some twelve or fifteen times.

When they saw the window open, they said, "He has jumped out of the window," and they hallooed to the fellows on the ground to shoot on top of the house. They all went down-stairs except one man. He looked in the cuddy-hole where I was, and saw me. He commenced firing and shot me three times, two balls lodging in my side and one in my right arm. After he had shot his loads all out, he said to the rest of them, " Come back up here; I have got him, and I have shot him, but he is not quite dead yet; let us go up and finish him." I crept from the door of the little room where I was to the stairway; they came up-stairs with their pistols in their hands, and a man behind with a light. I shot one of them as he got on the top step. They gathered him up by the legs, and then they all ran and left me. I have not seen them since. I have heard talk of them, and they say they will have me, they don't care where I go.

After that they attacked a man named James Ponder five miles from the town. I think he was killed dead.

They got hold of a man named Hilliard Polo down about Farmington. They broke his door down, jumped in, and commenced beating him. He rushed through the door and ran. They shot after him, and shot him through a leader in the foot. They again caught him and beat him.

A great many whippings down there are never reported. Thousands of things are never published, and no one gets to know anything about them.

What I am telling is what people have come to me and told me.

A colored man named Jim Elder was living with Dr. Elder (white). His case happened two nights before mine—that is, on the 16th of January. Jim and one or two of Dr. Elder's sons were hanging up meat in the meat-house, about the 14th of January. This black man's little daughter went to the shuck-house to get some shucks to feed the cows. When she got there she found some disguise clothing—doughface, and long caps and gowns, and one thing or another. She got scared, and ran into the house and told about it. The little child's mother went and got the things and brought them in. The old man of the plantation, Dr. Elder, grabbed them, and took them away from the woman and carried them into the house.

Jim said, "They are some of your boys' clothes; I thought it was some of you that were Ku-Kluxing around here all the time; and here are the clothes you have been putting on in the shuck-house. I thought it was you and now I know it." He had been raised with them, and talked as he pleased.

They said, "Now, Jim, you have got to take that back, if you accuse us of Ku-Kluxing." Jim said, "I will not do it; I believe it is true," talking in a kind of joking way. They said, "We'll be damned if you had not better take it back, Jim." Nothing more was said. A night or two afterward they came and took him, and gave him two or three hundred lashes.

The men who took him were disguised. He then moved to the city of Athens. People who get scared at others being beaten go to the cities; many are afraid to stay at home.

Not a week passes now but what somebody is whipped. The week before I came up here Noah Thrasher, a black man, was whipped; also whipped his wife and child.

A blacksmith by the name of Jake Dannons was shot dead about ten miles from where I live. He had done some work for a man named Kemp. Kemp had been having his work done there for about a year or two, and had never paid the black man. Kemp, toward the last, brought a buggy there to fix. Dannons refused to work auy more for him until they settled up. Kemp said, "G—d d—n you, I will kill you." In a night or two about fifteen or twenty men came down there, and called him to the door. He saw the men standing there in disguise, and turned and ran into the house. As he turned back, they shot him in the back of the head. They ran in and shot five or six shots more into him, and then went away.

TESTIMONY OF Z. B. HARGROVE.

I reside at Rome, Georgia. I am an attorney by profession. I was an officer in the Confederate army for two years and a half.

Speaking of the acts of the Ku Klux, he said:

Just preceding the election, some forty in number disguised themselves, and rode around to the different farms, where there were a great many colored people and some white people. They went there and notified them both in writing and verbally that they must not leave their homes on the day of the election. That if they did they would suffer a very severe penalty. Some of them were very severely whipped; two of them showed themselves to me with their backs very much lacerated. They were colored men, and their names were William Garrett and William Bradham. Those two were whipped after the election.

There were some 850 colored registered voters, and some 500 white persons who acted with the Republican Party; and about 700 or 800 of them did not vote in the election at all.

There is now or was, up to a very few days ago, a band of disguised men who were going through the country.

There was a colored man that they whipped, living on the plantation of one Mr. Bryant, about four miles from Rome. Then there was one there by the name of

Patrick King, who was very severely beaten by them; and another named Hilliard Johnson.

Some women were badly abused by them: their names, if I remember correctly, were Adelia Horton, Anna Bryant, and another girl whose name I have forgotten; they were violated by these same men, as testified to by parties who saw the act committed.

There are some two or three whites who have been very badly used in my immediate county, whose names I have forgotten.

A short time ago an outrage was committed on an old negro named Ellison, employed on the plantation of one Mr. Foster, whom I have known for a number of years, a Democrat and a clever man. Some men went there to see him during the day while he was ploughing in the field, and tried to get him to enter into an agreement with them against the Ku Klux. He told them he did not like to have anything to do with anything away from home. Those men went to him without disguises. They finally prevailed on him to give them some feed for their horses, which he did. He said on his death-bed that he told them he had not voted at any election, that he did not think he had any chance in the country, and all he wanted to do was to make a living for himself, wife, and children. Some two nights afterwards they went back in disguise, some fifteen or sixteen of them, and called him out to the gate. He saw that they wanted to do some violence to him, and he broke and got away from them, and was about getting into the woods when he fell down. Before he could get up and go away they struck him over the head three blows with a sabre, and cut him to the brain, and then they went back to his house.

After a time he got up, and undertook to get back to

the house by creeping along, holding to the fence; as he turned the corner he was met by them, and they shot him in both arms and both breasts.

About three months ago a band of men went around within eight or ten miles of Rome, whipping a great many colored men, and driving them away from their homes, breaking up their little farming operations, taking their horses away, etc. Besides the colored persons whipped, two white persons—a gentleman and a lady— were abused in one way and another, but not whipped. On these occasions the guns of the colored people were taken away from them by these bands in their expeditions, and on some occasions other property was taken.

A very short time ago a colored man by the name of Wash Calhoun was working in a rolling-mill in Rome. Three parties came into Rome, and inquired where he lived and where he went to at night. Succeeding in this, they went and stationed themselves on a corner to be ready for him as he passed by. As he went home, about eight o'clock at night, these three men shot him five times. They did not kill him, but crippled and ruined him for life.

In all this class of cases in my county, where disguised men have gone out and perpetrated any of these acts, nobody has yet been prosecuted for any of them. Nobody has been arrested for them, and no attempt at arrest has been made, except men I am now trying to have arrested. I am the only man who has sworn out a warrant against them.

The difficulty of bringing these men to punishment is increased by the sympathy of a large part of the population in their favor, and in many instances from fear of being assassinated. I have been given facts by parties who exacted a promise from me not to give their names, for their lives would not be worth a cent to them in the neighborhood if it was known.

This state of things exists in all the counties about me, but not so much in Cass County, as in Polk, Floyd, Chattooga, Walker, Murray, and Gordon counties. Their plan of operations seems to be about the same everywhere I have seen them.

The general purpose of the organization is to prevent people from voting, especially colored people. There is no doubt about it in my county, and I presume what transpired in my own immediate county was the same as transpired in every other county where they had any existence at all.

The organization has the effect of intimidating and preventing colored people from voting—not only colored men, but a great many good white men. I could give you the names of some of the best white men in the county who were absolutely afraid to go to the election.

There is no feeling of intimidation which would prevent the people from voting the Democratic ticket. They have no trouble—none at all.

I was in Atlanta with a gentleman friend of mine, Robert Thornton, who lives in Cherokee County, Alabama, just over the line. He is a wealthy planter of Alabama. He was there trying to get help to go down to his plantation. He said the Ku Klux had driven the labor out of the county. He wanted me to aid him, and he said that he had found that the labor had been driven away from that section of the State also. I then got to inquiring around about the matter, and I found that a great many persons had been driven off from the country there.

The following testimony of Augustus Blair tells how the Ku Klux came to his house in Limestone County,

Alabama, in December, 1868, and dragged his son from his bed, and in the most savage manner inflicted wounds from which he afterwards died:

I had a son killed about that time—December, 1868. He was my only son, about eighteen years of age, well grown. They came in the night and knocked at the door. I got up and opened the door very quietly, and they came in. They ordered me to light a candle, which I did. Only one of the men, Jack Hinds, had a disguise on. They broke the door down in the room where my boy was, and said, "Here he is, by G—d; here he is." I walked in, and says to my daughter, "Where is William?" (my son,) and she said, "There he is: see the blood running!" and I stepped out on the platform, and held up the candle and looked at them, and two of them had his head drawn back in this way [illustrating], and two others were beating him in the face with a pistol. They finally took him off a quarter of a mile. When they started, this man went to me and said, "Do you know me? Don't you tell me no lie." I said, "No." This was Dick Hinds. He said, "No, G—d d—n you; you had better not know me."

I stepped in and put on my boots to get out through my stable, and as they went through the yard I went through the orchard, and got over where there were hog-weeds as high as my head, and came up and heard their conversation as they were going up the hill with my boy. On the hill there was some cotton, and I got on my knees there and crawled up to see what they would do; for if they killed him, I wanted to find him. There they stripped him naked. I was close enough to hear him, as they were going up, when he told them, "O gentlemen! you all carrying me along, and here are two men stabbing me with a knife." They said, "It's a damned lie; nobody is sticking you." He says, "Oh yes; I feel the blood running down my pants." They said, "Go on, G—d d—n you; you will have no use for no blood, no-how, mighty soon."

He went up the hill with them, and they were punching and cutting him. When they got up there they took him down and beat him on his head.

I was not further from them than twenty yards. I crept right around a patch of briers and laid there. He never hollered but once, but I could hear him (imitating the wheezing, rattling sound in the throat) as they were choking him, and others were cutting him with a knife as they held him there, and some of the rest of them were going ·backward and forward to the other company.

The night was very cold and they made up a fire, and they would pass backward and forward; and one of them says by and by, when they were cutting at him, "The captain says you have done enough." They said to the boy, "You feel here, and see how you like these gashes. Do you reckon they will do you?" He went back to the captain and told him, and the captain hollered, "I told you to spare life," and then one says, "Get up, get up, G—d d—n you;" and I looked up and the boy was so weak, that when he went to get up he was staggering, and one of them catched him by the shoulders and held him, and just then one hauled off and struck at him. He had staggered, I reckon through weakness, for the road was bloody all the way up the hill. This man hauled off and struck him, and then jumped on to him and stamped him, and they shot off their pistols then, and got on their horses and went away.

I went to take the boy on to the house. I was scrambling in the bushes and around, trying to find him, when I heard the girls a quarter of a mile from me, crying out, "O Lord, Lord! here's Billy cut to pieces with a knife! Come, sister, help me put him in the house." And I struck and ran home; and there he was standing, with nothing on him but his shirt, and trembling all over, and bloody, and I says, "Oh! what's the matter? Can't you tell me nothing, my boy?" and he says, "No, no;" and they took him in, and I drew the bed before the fire in my room, and sent the little boy off for the doctor, but the doctor sent word that he was going to Huntsville and couldn't come. I sent again the next morning before day. Dr. Frank Blair sent word he could not come, but would send his father, old Dr. John Blair. He did not come until eight or nine that morning; then he walked in and looked at the boy, and said, "I don't think I can do him any good." Says I, "Are you going without trying to do him any good, doctor?"

Then he turned in and made a poultice, salve, and dressed his wounds.

You couldn't touch him anywhere, from his shoulders down to the tips of his big toes. There was no place on his legs or his feet that you could touch, because it was cut to pieces with a knife.

The calves of his legs were split up and cut across, and his thighs were split open and cut across, and his knee looked as if they had tried to take the cap off his knee, and his hands and arms were all cut and slit up too. The bottoms of his feet were split open, and the bottom of his heel was split. He lived a year. He got so he could get about a little.

I hired a wagon and fetched him here, but directly he came here he was taken down with a hemorrhage that came from stamping him on the stomach and breast. They stamped him all over the stomach and breast.

In two weeks after he was examined in the court-room there, he died. Everybody that saw him said that he couldn't live, and they were surprised that he lived so long.

The same night my son was taken out, these men, when they came back to my house, asked, "Where is Gus?" She said she didn't know, and they knocked her down and stamped her, and choked her on the bed. They told my wife, "Tell Gus he has been here two years, and it is as long as we intend he shall be here. White folks wants to work this land." I rented out part of my land there to a white man named Mr. Wallace.

He told my wife to tell me that inside of two weeks I must not be caught there. He said, "He has got to get away, crop or no crop."

CHAPTER VIII.

CONSTITUTION OF THE KU KLUX KLAN.

Damnant quod——non intelligunt.

PRESCRIPT OF THE * *

What may this mean,
That thou, dead corse, again, in complete steel,
Revisit'st thus the glimpses of the moon,
Making night hideous, and we fools of nature
So horribly to shake our disposition
With thoughts beyond the reaches of our souls?

An' now auld Cloots, I ken ye're thinkin'
A certain *Ghoul* is rantin', drinkin';
Some luckless wight will send him linkin'
       To your black pit;
But, faith! he'll turn a corner jinkin',
       An' cheat you yet.

Amici humani generis.

CREED.

We, the * * , reverently acknowledge the majesty and supremacy of the Divine Being, and recognize the goodness and providence of the same.

PREAMBLE.

We recognize our relations to the United States Government, and acknowledge the supremacy of its laws.

APPELLATION.

ARTICLE I. This organization shall be styled and denominated the * * .

TITLES.

ART. II. The officers of this * shall consist of a Grand Wizard of the Empire and his ten Genii; a Grand Dragon of

BAND OF KU KLUX—FROM A PHOTOGRAPH OF THE DISGUISES OF A BAND OF KU KLUX ARRESTED AND TAKEN TO RALEIGH, N. C.

the Realm and his eight Hydras; a Grand Titan of the Dominion and his six Furies; a Grand Giant of the Province and his four Goblins; a Grand Cyclops of the Den and his two Night Hawks; a Grand Magi, a Grand Monk, a Grand Exchequer, a Grand Turk, a Grand Scribe, a Grand Sentinel, and a Grand Ensign.

SEC. 2. The body-politic of this * shall be designated and known as "Ghouls."

DIVISIONS.

ART. III. This * shall be divided into five departments, all combined constituting the Grand * of the Empire; the second department to be called the Grand * of the Realm; the third, the Grand * of the Dominion; the fourth, the Grand * of the Province; the fifth, the * of the Den.

Magna est veritas, et prævalebit.

Nec scire fas est omnia.

DUTIES OF OFFICERS.

Grand Wizard.

ART. IV, SEC. 1. It shall be the duty of the Grand Wizard, who is the supreme officer of the empire, to communicate with and receive reports from the Grand Dragons of Realms as to the condition, strength, efficiency, and progress of the *s within their respective realms; and he shall communicate from time to time to all subordinate *s, through the Grand Dragons, the condition, strength, efficiency, and progress of the *s, throughout his vast empire, and such other information as he may deem expedient to impart. And it shall further be his duty to keep by his G. Scribe a list of the names (without any caption or explanation whatever) of the Grand Dragons of the different realms of his empire, and shall number such realms with the Arabic numerals, 1, 2, 3, etc., *ad finem*. And he shall instruct his Grand Exchequer as to the appropriation and disbursement which he shall make of the revenue of the * that comes to his hands. He shall have the sole power to issue copies of this prescript, through his subalterns and deputies, for the organization and establishment of subordinate *s. And he shall have the further power to appoint his Genii, also a Grand Scribe and a Grand Exchequer for his department, and to appoint and ordain Special Deputy Grand Wizards to assist him in the more rapid and effectual dissemination and establishment of the * throughout his empire. He is further empowered to appoint and instruct deputies to organize and control realms, dominions, provinces, and dens, until the same shall elect a Grand Dragon, a Grand Titan, a Grand Giant, and a Grand Cyclops, in the manner hereinafter provided.

Ne vile fano.

Ars est celare artem.

And when a question of paramount importance to the interest or prosperity of the * arises not provided for in this prescript, he shall have power to determine such question, and his decision shall be final until the same shall be provided for by amendment, as hereinafter provided.

Grand Dragon.

SEC. 2. It shall be the duty of the Grand Dragon, who is the chief officer of the realm, to report to the Grand Wizard, when required by that officer, the condition, strength, efficiency, and progress of the * within his realm, and to transmit through the Grand Titan to the subordinate *s of his realm, all information or intelligence conveyed to him by the Grand Wizard for that purpose, and all such other information or instruction as he may think will promote the interests of the *. He shall keep by his G. Scribe a list of the names (without any caption) of the Grand Titans of the different dominions of his realm, and shall report the same to the Grand Wizard when required; and shall number the dominions of his realm with the Arabic numerals, 1, 2, 3, etc., *ad finem*. He shall instruct his Grand Exchequer as to the appropriation and disbursement of the revenue of the * that comes to his hands. He shall have the ,power to appoint his Hydras; also, a Grand Scribe and a Grand Exchequer for his department, and to appoint and ordain Special Deputy Grand Dragons to assist him in the more rapid and effectual dissemination and establishment of the * throughout his realm. He is further empowered to appoint and instruct deputies to organize and control dominions, provinces, and dens, until the same shall elect a Grand Titan, a Grand Giant, and Grand Cyclops in the manner hereinafter provided.

Nusquam tuta fides.

Quid faciendum ?

Grand Titan.

SEC. 3. It shall be the duty of the Grand Titan, who is the chief officer of the dominion, to report to the Grand Dragon, when required by that officer, the condition, strength, efficiency, and progress of the * within his dominion, and to transmit through the Grand Giants to the subordinate *s of his dominion, all information or intelligence conveyed to him by the Grand Dragon for that purpose, and all such other information or instruction as he may think will enhance the interests of the *. He shall keep, by his G. Scribe, a list of the names (without caption) of the Grand Giants of the different provinces of his dominion, and shall report the same to the Grand Dragon when required; and he shall number the provinces of his dominion with the Arabic numerals, 1, 2, 3, etc., *ad finem*. And he shall instruct and direct his Grand Exchequer as to the appropriation and disbursement of the revenue of the * that comes to his hands. He shall have power to appoint his Furies; also to appoint a Grand Scribe and a Grand Exchequer of his department, and appoint and ordain Special Deputy Grand Titans to assist him in the more rapid and effectual dissemination and establishment of the * throughout his dominion. He shall have further power to appoint and instruct deputies to organize and control provinces and dens until the same shall elect a Grand Giant and a Grand Cyclops, in the manner hereinafter provided.

Grand Giant.

SEC. 4. It shall be the duty of the Grand Giant, who is the chief officer of the province, to supervise and administer general and special instruction in the formation and establishment of *s within his province, and to report to the Grand Titan, when required by that officer, the condition, strength, progress,

Fide non armis.

Fiat justitia.

and efficiency of the * throughout his province, and to transmit through the Grand Cyclops to the subordinate *s of his province, all information or intelligence conveyed to him by the Grand Titan for that purpose and such other information and instruction as he may think will advance the interest of the *. He shall keep, by his G. Scribe, a list of the names (without caption) of the Grand Cyclops of the various dens of his province, and shall report the same to the Grand Titan when required, and shall number the dens of his province with the Arabic numerals, 1, 2, 3, etc., *ad finem*; and shall determine and limit the number of dens to be organized in his province; and he shall instruct the Grand Exchequer as to what appropriation and disbursement he shall make of the revenue of the * that comes to his hands. He shall have power to appoint his Goblins; also, a Grand Scribe and a Grand Exchequer for his department, and to appoint and ordain Special Deputy Grand Giants to assist him in the more rapid and effectual dissemination and establishment of the * throughout his province. He shall have the further power to appoint and instruct deputies to organize and control dens until the same shall elect a Grand Cyclops, in the manner hereinafter provided. And in all cases he shall preside at and conduct the Grand Council of Yahoos.

Grand Cyclops.

SEC. 5. It shall be the duty of the Grand Cyclops to take charge of the * of his den after his election, under the direction and with the assistance (when practicable) of the Grand Giant, and in accordance with, and in conformity to, the provisions of this prescript, a copy of which shall in all cases be obtained before the formation of a * begins. It shall further

Hic manent vestigia, morientis libertatis.

Curæ leves loquuntur, ingentes stupent.

be his duty to appoint all regular meetings of his *, and to preside at the same; to appoint irregular meetings when he deems it expedient; to preserve order in his den, and to impose fines for irregularities or disobedience of orders, and to receive and initiate candidates for admission into the *, after the same shall have been pronounced competent and worthy to become members by the investigating committee. He shall make a quarterly report to the Grand Giant of the condition, strength, and efficiency of the * of his den, and shall convey to the Ghouls of his den all information or intelligence conveyed to him by the Grand Giant for that purpose, and all such other information or instruction as he may think will conduce to the interests and welfare of the *. He shall preside at and conduct the Grand Council of Centaurs. He shall have power to appoint his Night Hawks, his Grand Scribe, his Grand Turk, his Grand Sentinel, and his Grand Ensign. And he shall instruct and direct the Grand Exchequer of his den as to what appropriation and disbursement he shall make of the revenue of the * that comes to his hands. And for any small offence he may punish any member by fine, and may reprimand him for the same. And he may admonish and reprimand the * of his den for any imprudence, irregularity, or transgression, when he is convinced or advised that the interests, welfare, and safety of the * demand it.

Dat Deus his quoque finem.

Cessante causa, cessat effectus.

Grand Magi.

SEC. 6. It shall be the duty of the Grand Magi, who is the second officer in authority of the den, to assist the Grand Cyclops, and to obey all the proper orders of that officer; to preside at all meetings in the den in the absence of the Grand Cyclops; and to exercise during his absence all the powers and authority conferred upon that officer.

Grand Monk.

SEC. 7. It shall be the duty of the Grand Monk, who is the third officer in authority of the den, to assist and obey all the proper orders of the Grand Cyclops and the Grand Magi. And in the absence of these officers, he shall preside at and conduct the meetings in the den, and shall exercise all the powers and authority of the Grand Cyclops.

Grand Exchequer.

SEC. 8. It shall be the duty of the Grand Exchequers of the different departments of the * to keep a correct account of all the revenue of the * that shall come to their hands, and shall make no appropriation or disbursement of the same except under the orders and direction of the chief officer of their respective departments. And it shall further be the duty of the Grand Exchequer of the dens to collect the initiation fees and all fines imposed by the Grand Cyclops.

Grand Turk.

SEC. 9. It shall be the duty of the Grand Turk, who is the executive officer of the Grand Cyclops, to notify the Ghouls of the den of all informal or irregular meetings appointed by the Grand Cyclops, and to obey and execute all the lawful orders

Droit et avant.

Cave quid dicis, quando, et cui.

of that officer in the control and government in his den. It shall further be his duty to receive and question at the outposts all candidates for admission into the *, and shall *there* administer the preliminary obligation required, and then conduct such candidate or candidates to the Grand Cyclops at his den, and to assist him in the initiation of the same ; and it shall further be his duty to act as the executive officer of the Grand Council of Centaurs.

Grand Scribe.

SEC. 10. It shall be the duty of the Grand Scribes of the different departments to conduct the correspondence, and to write the orders of the chiefs of their departments when required. And it shall further be the duty of the Grand Scribes of the den to keep a list of the names (without caption) of the Ghouls of the den, to call the roll at all regular meetings, and to make the quarterly report under the direction of the Grand Cyclops.

Grand Sentinel.

SEC. 11. It shall be the duty of the Grand Sentinel to detail, take charge of, post and instruct the grand guard, under the direction and orders of the Grand Cyclops, and to relieve and dismiss the same when directed by that officer.

Grand Ensign.

SEC. 12. It shall be the duty of the Grand Ensign to take charge of the grand banner of the *, to preserve it sacredly, and protect it carefully, and to bear it on all occasions of parade or ceremony, and on such other occasions as the Grand Cyclops may direct it to be flung to the night-breeze.

ELECTION OF OFFICERS.

ART. V, SEC. 1. The Grand Cyclops, the Grand Magi, the

Dormitur aliquando jus, moritur numquam.

Deo adjuvante, non timendum.

Grand Monk, and the Grand Exchequer of Dens shall be elected semi-annually by the Ghouls of Dens. And the first election of these officers may take place as soon as seven Ghouls have been initiated for that purpose.

SEC. 2. The Grand Wizard of the Empire, the Grand Dragons of Realms, the Grand Titans of•Dominions, and the Grand Giants of Provinces shall be elected biennially, and in the following manner, to wit: The Grand Wizard by a majority vote of the Grand Dragons of his empire; the Grand Dragon by a like vote of the Grand Titans of his realm; the Grand Titan by a like vote of the Grand Giants of his dominion; and the Grand Giant by a like vote of the Grand Cyclops of his province.

The first election for Grand Dragon may take place as soon as three dominions have been organized in a realm; but all subsequent elections shall be by a majority vote of the Grand Titans throughout the realm, and biennially as aforesaid.

The first election for Grand Titan may take place as soon as three provinces have been organized in a dominion, but all subsequent elections shall be by a majority vote of all the Grand Giants throughout the dominion, and biennially as aforesaid. The first election for Grand Giant may take place as soon as three dens have been organized in a province, but all subsequent elections shall be by a majority vote of the Grand Cyclops throughout the province, and biennially as aforesaid.

The Grand Wizard of the Empire is hereby created, to serve three years from the first Monday in May, 1867; after the expiration of which time biennial elections shall be held for that office as aforesaid, and the incumbent Grand Wizard shall

Spectemur agendo.

notify the Grand Dragons, at least six months before said election, at what time and place the same will be held.

*   *

JUDICIARY.

ART. VI, SEC. 1. The tribunal of justice of this * shall consist of a Grand Council of Yahoos, and a Grand Council of Centaurs.

SEC. 2. The Grand Council of Yahoos shall be the tribunal for the trial of elected officers, and shall be composed of officers of equal rank with the accused, and shall be appointed and presided over by an officer of the next rank above, and sworn by him to administer even-handed justice. The tribunal for the trial of the Grand Wizard shall be composed of all the Grand Dragons of the Empire, and shall be presided over and sworn by the Senior Grand Dragon. They shall have power to summon the accused, and witnesses for and against him; and if found guilty they shall prescribe the penalty and execute the same. And they shall have power to appoint an executive officer to attend said council while in session.

Nemo nos impune lacessit.

SEC. 3. The Grand Council of Centaurs shall be the tribunal for the trial of Ghouls and non-elective officers, and shall be composed of six judges appointed by the Grand Cyclops from the Ghouls of his den, presided over and sworn by him to give the accused a fair and impartial trial. They shall have power to summon the accused, and witnesses for and against him; and if found guilty they shall prescribe the penalty and execute the same. Said judges shall be selected by the Grand Cyclops

Patra cara, carior libertas.

with reference to their intelligence, integrity, and fairmindedness, and shall render their verdict without prejudice or partiality.

REVENUE.

ART. VII, SEC. 1. The revenue of this * shall be derived as follows: For every copy of this prescript issued to the *s of dens, ten dollars will be required; two dollars of which shall go into the hands of the Grand Exchequer of the Grand Giant; two into the hands of the Grand Exchequer of the Grand Titan; two into the hands of the Grand Exchequer of the Grand Dragon, and the remaining four into the hands of the Grand Exchequer of the Grand Wizard.

SEC. 2. A further source of revenue to the empire shall be ten per cent of all the revenue of the realms, and a tax upon realms when the Grand Wizard shall deem it necessary and indispensable to levy the same.

SEC. 3. A further source of revenue to the realms shall be ten per cent of all revenue of dominions; and a tax upon dominions when the Grand Dragon shall deem such tax necessary and indispensable.

SEC. 4. A further source of revenue to dominions shall be ten per cent of all revenue of provinces, and a tax upon prov-

Ad unum omnes.

inces when the Grand Titan shall deem such tax necessary and indispensable.

SEC. 5. A further source of revenue to provinces shall be ten per cent on all the revenue of dens, and a tax upon the dens when the Grand Giant shall deem such tax necessary and indispensable.

SEC. 6. The source of revenue to dens shall be the initiation fees, fines, and a per capita tax, whenever the Grand Cyclops shall deem such tax indispensable to the interests and purposes of the *.

SEC. 7. All of the revenue obtained in the manner herein aforesaid shall be for the exclusive benefit of the *, and shall be appropriated to the dissemination of the same, and to the creation of a fund to meet any disbursement that it may become necessary to make to accomplish the objects of the *, and to secure the protection of the same.

OBLIGATION.

ART. VIII. No one shall be a member of this * unless he shall take the following oath or obligation :

I, ———, of my own free will and accord, and in the presence of Almighty God, do solemnly swear (or affirm) that I will never reveal to any one not a member of the * *, by any intimation, sign, symbol, word, or act, or in any other manner whatever, any of the secrets, signs, grips, passwords, mysteries, or purposes of the * *, or that I am a member of the same, or that I know of any one who is a member, and that I will abide by the prescript and edicts of the * *. So help me God.

SEC. 2. The preliminary obligation to be administered before

Deo duce, ferro comitante.

the candidate for admission is taken to the Grand Cyclops for examination shall be as follows :

I do solemnly swear (or affirm) that I will never reveal anything that I may this day (or night) learn concerning the * *. So help me God.

ADMISSION.

ART. IX, SEC. 1. No one shall be presented for admission into this order until he shall have been recommended by some friend or intimate, who *is* a member, to the investigating committee, which shall be composed of the Grand Cyclops, the Grand Magi, and the Grand Monk ; and who shall investigate his antecedents, and his past and present standing and connections ; and if, after such investigation, they pronounce him competent and worthy to become a member, he may be ad-

mitted upon taking the obligation required, and passing
through the ceremonies of initiation: *Provided*, That no one
shall be admitted into this * who shall not have attained the
age of eighteen years.

SEC. 2. No one shall become a member of a distant * when
there is a * established and in operation in his own immediate
vicinity ; nor shall any one become a member of any * after he
shall have been rejected by another *.

ENSIGN.

ART. X. The grand banner of this * shall be in the form of
an isosceles triangle, five feet long and three feet wide at the
staff. The material shall be yellow, with a red scalloped bor-

(Tempora mutantur, et nos mutamen in illis, ad utrumque paratus.)

der, about three inches in width. There shall be painted upon
it, in black, a *Draco volens*, or Flying Dragon,† with the following motto inscribed above the Dragon: "Quod semper, quod
ubique, quod ab omnibus." ‡

AMENDMENTS.

ART. XI. This prescript, or any part, or edicts thereof, shall
never be changed except by a two-thirds vote of the Grand
Dragons of the Realms, in convention assembled, and at which
convention the Grand Wizard shall preside and be entitled to
a vote. And upon the application of a majority of the Grand
Dragons, for the purpose, the Grand Wizard shall appoint the
time and place for said convention ; which, when assembled,
shall proceed to make such modification and amendment as it
may think will advance the interest, enlarge the utility, and
more thoroughly effect the purposes of the *.

INTERDICTION.

ART. XII. The origin, designs, mysteries, and ritual of this *
shall never be written, but the same shall be communicated
orally.

(O tempora ! O mores !)

---

† See Webster's Unabridged Pictorial.
‡ "What always, what everywhere, what by all is held to be true."

REGISTER.

I.—1st. Dismal. 2d. Dark. 3d. Furious. 4th. Portentous. 5th. Wonderful. 6th. Alarming. 7th. Dreadful. 8th. Terrible. 9th. Horrible. 10th. Melancholy. 11th. Mournful. 12th. Dying.

II.—I. White. II. Green. III. Blue. IV. Black. V. Yellow. VI. Crimson, VII. ———.

III.—1. Fearful. 2. Startling. 3. Awful. 4. Woful. 5. Horrid. 6. Bloody. 7. Doleful. 8. Sorrowful. 9. Hideous. 10. Frightful. 11. Appalling. 12. Lost.

EDICTS.

I. The initiation fee of this * shall be one dollar, to be paid when the candidate is initiated and received into the *.

II. No member shall be allowed to take any intoxicating spirits to any meeting of the *, nor shall any member be allowed to attend a meeting when intoxicated; and for every appearance at a meeting in such a condition he shall be fined not less than one nor more than five dollars, to go into the revenue of the *.

III. Any member may be expelled from the * by a majority vote of the officers and Ghouls of the den to which he belongs,

Cavendo tutus.

Astra castra, numen lumen.

and if after expulsion such member shall assume any of the duties, regalia, or insignia of the *, or in any way claim to be a member of the same, he shall be severely punished. His obligation of secrecy shall be as binding upon him after expulsion as before, and for any revelation made by him thereafter he shall be held accountable in the same manner as if he were then a member.

IV. Every Grand Cyclops shall read, or cause to be read, this prescript and these edicts to the †s of his den at least once in every three months; and shall read them to each new member when he is initiated, or present the same to him for personal perusal.

V. Each den may provide itself with the grand banner of the *.

VI. The †s of dens may make such additional edicts for their control and government as they shall deem requisite and necessary : *Provided*, No edict shall be made to conflict with any of the provisions or edicts of this prescript.

VII. The strictest and most rigid secrecy concerning any and every thing that relates to the * shall at all times be maintained.

VIII. Any member who shall reveal or betray the secrets or purposes of this * shall suffer the extreme penalty of the law.

Hush, thou art not to utter what I am. Bethink thee ; it was our covenant. I said that I would see thee once again.

Ne quid detrimenti respublica capiat.   Amici neque ad aras.

L'ENVOI.

To the lovers of law and order, peace and justice, we send you greeting ; and to the shades of the venerated dead we affectionately dedicate the † †.

Nos ducit amor libertatis.

CHAPTER IX.

REVIEW OF THE KU-KLUX CONSPIRACY.

Spirit of the Southern Leaders—Violent Speech of Ben Hill at Atlanta, Ga.—Origin of the Terms "Carpet-bagger" and "Scalawag"—The Murders and Outrages Denied—Incredulity of Northern Republicans—Heroism of Southern Republicans—Eight Southern States carried for Grant in 1872—Disbandment of the Klan caused by Prosecutions in United States Courts—On Assurances of Future Peace and Good Order President Grant discontinues the Prosecutions—The "Invisible Empire" is Dissolved—Its Place in History.

IT is highly improbable that the names of the master-spirits of the Ku Klux Klan will ever be made known to the public.

It is obvious that it was organized, controlled, and directed by persons of great influence and power—persons who were the embodiment of the intense opposition which was waged against the measures of the Republican Party.

Southern newspapers were filled from day to day with denunciations of the most bitter character against the Republican Party. Prominent men spoke and wrote in a manner to excite the worst passions of those who adhered to the Lost Cause.

Hon. B. H. Hill, of Georgia, was probably the most conspicuous and able of those who pursued this course. His speech delivered at Atlanta, Ga., in July, 1867, had a powerful influence in arousing his friends and followers to the most earnest opposition to the measures proposed by Congress.

He told the people of the South that the military bills violated the Constitution, and that if they carried them out they aided in its violation. "If you vote for the Convention you are perjured." To the Republican Party he said, "On, on, with your work of ruin, ye hell-born rioters in sacred things! but remember the people will call you to judgment;" and to the Union men of Georgia, "You are but cowards and knaves, and the time will come when you will call on the rocks and mountains to fall on you, and the darkness to hide you from an outraged people." And to his Rebel friends he cried, "Do not abandon your rights. Defend them, talk for them, and if need be, before God and the country, fight and die for them!" He informed the negroes that the Republicans were their worst friends, and intended their extermination.

His words were the passionate expression of opinions which had full possession of every faculty of his mind; he was wrought up to a pitch which, had it found expression in acts, would have been quite as terrible as the fiercest doings of the Klan. The Klan gave visible expression in deeds to the opinions entertained and freely expressed by leading men all over the South.

Freedom, equal rights, and the ballot for the negro were regarded by them as an invasion of their rights, which was to be resisted to the bitter end.

To have a proper understanding of the condition of things in the States overrun by the Ku Klux, it must be kept in mind that the courts in each State were open for the redress of all grievances and controversies arising between individuals, and also for the prosecution of all offenders against the laws, except the crimes of these midnight raiders. This is shown to have been the case by the testimony of judges and other prominent persons of unimpeachable character, and whose testimony to that effect, taken by the committee, was entirely uncontradicted. Hon. James L. Orr, of South Carolina, testified fully to this effect as heartofore quoted.

The foundations of society were not broken up. The States were not without laws, nor the means of enforcing them. The people were not thrown upon their own resources and prowess for the defence of their lives, property, reputation, and other rights, nor were there combinations of men to deprive them, by force or fraud, of any of these rights. There was therefore no justification or excuse for the establishment of this great unlawful military organization, which spread over so many of the Southern States, and had for its membership some of their most prominent citizens. No good end was to be or could have been accomplished by such a political association.

There is not a generous or noble act recorded of it: it professed, as one of its purposes, the defence of the weak and oppressed; it does not appear that any of the dens ever sent out a body of its disguised members upon an errand of mercy or charity. Wherever *they* moved it was either to terrorize a community by their numbers and hideous appearance, or else to drive some citizen from his home, to inflict upon him some grievous bodily punishment, or actually to take his life. These outrages, too, were directed against Republicans, white and black; and a thoroughly organized and well-directed effort, in all the States lately in rebellion, was made to overthrow and deprive them of the just political power to which their numbers would entitle them. The newspaper press poured out a continual stream of abuse against Republicans. White men who dared to express an opinion in favor of giving the negroes equal political and civil rights with the white man were bitterly denounced as enemies of the white race. If native to the South, they were called "scalawags;" if born in the North, they were called "carpet-baggers." In the great majority of cases they were socially ostracized and proscribed—they and their wives and children. Leading men in speeches and leading newspapers in editorials would advise Democrats to have nothing whatever to do, socially or in a business way, with Republicans. When grievous outrages were perpetrated upon their persons and property without any cause or provocation, the unlawful acts were denied, or it was alleged that the Republicans were in the wrong. It came to be charged by the Democratic papers South and North that Republicans manufactured stories of murder and outrage for political purposes, and although the evidence taken by every investigating committee clearly demonstrated that the murders and outrages not only existed in numbers greatly exceeding what had been alleged, but were the work of Democrats, inaugurated for the express purpose of intimidating Republican voters and preventing them from voting at the elections, it came to pass that Republicans in the Northern States were ready to give greater credence to the newspaper editorials of their political opponents than to the sworn statements of their political friends. It was under circumstances thus discouraging that the Republicans of the Southern States participated in the Presidential elections of 1868 and of 1872. They encountered and braved social and business ostracism, the vituperation of public speakers and the press, in addition to the outrages and wrongs inflicted by the Ku Klux. In them burned the sacred fire of freedom and equal rights; for these they suffered, for these they contended, and aiding their brethren in the

North, twice helped to elect the great Soldier Statesman to the presidential office.

The election of 1872 found the Republican Party victorious in eight of the Southern States by majorities as follows: Alabama, 10,828; South Carolina, 49,587; Arkansas, 3446; Florida, 2336; Mississippi, 34,887; North Carolina, 24,675; Louisiana, 14,634; Virginia, 1814.

The Klan as a disguised organization was now upon its last legs. The light thrown upon it by the Congressional investigation caused leading and prominent persons to abandon it. The prosecutions in the United States courts finally broke it up. Thousands of persons were indicted in North Carolina and South Carolina, and a number were brought to trial and convicted, while others pleaded guilty, and these were all sent to the penitentiary. The punishment of these persons caused great consternation in the entire Klan.

Prominent citizens were induced to make an earnest appeal to President Grant for clemency. After due consideration he accepted assurances that lawlessness would cease, and finally directed the discontinuance of the prosecutions.

In North Carolina the Legislature passed an "act of oblivion," relieving certain classes of murderers and other offenders from prosecution.

And so the "Invisible Empire" ceased to exist; its dens were closed, never again to be reopened. Republicans all over the South felt that relief had at last come, and hoped that thereafter they would be able to exercise the rights of free men, with no one to molest or make them afraid.

In concluding this review of the grand Ku-Klux conspiracy, it should be said that while history has many pages steeped in blood and crime, yet for inexcusable and wanton cruelty no chapter can ever exceed the record of these midnight raiders visiting the humble cabins of peaceful and inoffensive citizens on their errands of outrage and murder; and these crimes, to the disgrace of the civilization of the nineteenth century, men of intelligence and virtue have been found to palliate or altogether excuse.

CHAPTER X.

THE POLITICAL SITUATION AFTER THE ELECTION OF 1872.

Apparent Agreement of both Parties as to the Validity of the Thirteenth, Fourteenth, and Fifteenth Amendments—Opinions of Southern Leaders Unchanged—The Democratic Platform of 1872 a Mere Device to catch Votes—Organization of the Southern Historical Society—General Wade Hampton explains its Objects in a Speech at Richmond, Va.—Hon. B. H. Hill's Speech at Atlanta, Ga.—The Rehabilitation of the "Lost Cause" the Burden of both Speeches—Preparations for the Political Contest of 1876.

THE election of 1872 was regarded by many as fixing the status of parties for many years to come, and as definitely settling the negro question as far as it could be considered a political issue.

Both parties had agreed to the validity, justice, and humanity of the three great war amendments to the Constitution. The victory of the Republican Party in that and the preceding election had been so overwhelming, that many Democrats began to feel that there was but little encouragement for them to hope for success either in a Presidential or Congressional election.

All the Southern States sent delegates to the National Democratic Convention of 1872, and they exercised a strong influence in settling the policy of that party. The platform contained the following resolutions:

" 1. We recognize the equality of all men before the law, and hold that it is the duty of Government in its dealings with the people to mete out equal and exact justice to all, of whatever nativity, race, color, or persuasion, religious or political.

"2. We pledge ourselves to maintain the union of these States, emancipation, and enfranchisement, and to oppose any reopening of the questions settled by the Thirteenth, Fourteenth, and Fifteenth Amendments to the Constitution."

These resolutions met with no opposition whatever in the Convention from any quarter; they were adopted as settled doctrines of the Democratic Party, South as well as North. The enfranchisement of the negro was accepted apparently in good faith, and the entire Democratic Party was pledged to oppose any reopening of the question. The Democratic leaders in the South accepted these resolutions, and became bound in honor to use their influence to see that they were carried out in good faith, and that a correct public opinion upon this subject should be encouraged by the Democratic press and public speakers.

The opinions of the Southern leaders, however, experienced no change by reason of the adoption of the party platform of 1872. With them its adoption seemed to have been simply an expedient to quiet Northern opposition, and to secure Republican votes for the Democratic candidates.

Their spirits were unbroken and their passions uncooled. They were determined to keep alive the issues of the war, and professed to look forward to a time in the near future when the cause which seemed lost would be regained forever.

In August, 1873, a large number of the most prominent officers of the Confederacy met at Montgomery Springs, Va., where they organized the Southern Historical Society. Two months later General Wade Hampton delivered a speech at Richmond, Va., in explanation of the objects of the society, in which he said:

"As it was the duty of every man to devote himself to the service of his country in the great struggle which has just ended so disastrously, not only to the South, but to the cause of constitutional government under republican institutions in the New World; so now, when that country is prostrate in the dust, weeping for her dead who died in vain to save her liberties, every patriotic impulse should urge her surviving children to vindicate the great principles for which she fought. . . . These are the imperative duties imposed upon us of the South; and the chief peril of the times is, that, in our despair at the evil that has fallen on us, we forget those obligations to the eternal principles for which we fought; to the martyred dead who gave up .their lives for their principles; . . . and to our children who should be taught to cling to them with unswerving fidelity. If those who are to come after us, and to whose hands the destinies of our country are soon to be committed, are properly instructed in the theory and practice of Republican institutions; if they are *made* to comprehend the origin, progress, and culmination of that great controversy between the antagonistic sections of this continent, which began in the convention of 1787, and ended, for the time being, at Appomattox in 1865, they cannot fail to see that truth, right, justice, were on the side of their fathers, and they will surely strive to bring back to the Republic those cardinal principles on which it was founded, and on which alone it can exist. . . .

"Our care should be to bring her (the Republic) back to her old and safe anchorage. . . .

"It is amid these gloomy surroundings and sad forebodings, gentlemen of the Historical Society, that we who have not lost all hope and faith are met to take counsel together. We may be able, it is true, to save but little from the general wreck, but we can, at least, leave to future generations the true record of our struggle in a righteous cause. . . .

"This society proposes to publish regularly and systematically all contributions which elucidate the truth, reflect the glory, and maintain the principles involved in the late war, and it calls upon all who are not lost to honor to aid in this laudable undertaking. It wishes to enroll not only every true man but every true woman in its ranks. . . .

"Maid, mother, wife, gave freely to that country the most cherished objects of their affections. . . . It was wisely done, therefore, to invoke their aid in behalf of our society. . . . It is theirs to teach our children that their fathers were neither traitors nor rebels; that we believed as firmly as in the eternal word of God that we were in the right; and that we have a settled faith which no trials can shake that in His own good time the right will be made manifest.

"These are the lessons our children should learn from their mothers. Nor are these the only ones which should be inculcated, for the pages of history furnish many which should not be overlooked. These teach in the clearest and most emphatic manner that there is always hope for a people who cherish the spirit of freedom, who will not tamely give up their rights, and who, amid all the changes of time, the trials of adversity, remain steadfast to their convictions that liberty is their birthright. . . . When Napoleon, in that wonderful campaign of Jena, struck down in a few weeks the whole military strength of Prussia, destroyed that army with which the great Frederick had held at bay the combined forces of Europe, and crushed out, apparently forever, the liberties, seemingly the very existence, of that great State, but one hope of her disenthralment and regeneration was left her—the unconquered and unconquerable patriotism of her sons. As far as human foresight could penetrate the future this hope appeared but a vain and delusive one; yet only a few years passed before her troops turned the scale to victory at Waterloo, and the Treaty of Paris atoned in part for the mortification of that of Tilsit. . . . She educated her children by a system which made them good citizens in peace and formidable soldiers in war; she kindled and kept alive the sacred fire of patriotism; she woke the slumbering spirit of the Fatherland; and what has been the result of this self-devotion of a whole people for half a century? Single-handed she has just met her old antagonist; the shame of her defeats of yore has been wiped out by glorious victories; the contributions extorted from her have been more than repaid; her insults have been avenged, and her victorious eagles sweeping over the broken lilies of her enemy waved in triumph from the walls of conquered Paris, while she dictated peace to prostrate and humbled France. Is not the moral to be drawn from this noble dedication of a people to the interests and honor of their country worth remembering? . . .

"Hungary in her recent struggle to throw off the yoke of Austria was crushed to the earth, and yet to-day the Hungarians, as citizens of Austria, exercise a controlling power in that great empire. . . .

"Mr. President and gentlemen of the Society, the task assigned to me by your partial kindness has been discharged. . . . It seemed to me not inappropriate, while explaining the purposes of the Society, to show to you how important are the objects it contemplates, how vital to the future condition of our people, and how vast the influence it may exercise if properly directed. History repeats itself, and history is philosophy, teaching by examples. If the examples presented to you have kindled any zeal in behalf of your suffering country, if they have inspired in your hearts any ray of hope for its redemption, my efforts have not been in vain."

At a meeting held at Atlanta, Ga., for the purpose of organizing a branch of the Southern Historical Society, Hon. B. H. Hill delivered an address, in which he said:

"Secession was a mistake, a terrible mistake; but secession was no crime. [Great applause.] It violated no oaths; it trampled upon no individual rights. . . . It sought to shed no blood! Radicalism is no mistake. It is deliberate, intentional, wicked, ever increasing crime. [Applause.] It has trampled upon ten thousand oaths to support the Constitution. It defied the Union as a fact, that it might destroy the Union as a principle, under the pretence of reconstructing the States. I arraign Radicalism to-night before the bar of this outraged country as the only real, intentional rebel in American history. [Applause.] It is a rebel against the Constitution of our fathers. It is a rebel against the sovereignty of States. . . . It is a rebel against every principle of justice, and a rebel against every blessing of liberty. [Tremendous applause.] . . .

"The great and final struggle to settle the question whether constitutional liberty on this continent shall be continued or not is to be fought in 1876. Can it be successfully fought at the ballot-box? . . .

"I want the mind of the American people directed to one inquiry; it is a great inquiry, a glorious inquiry! Oh! I look forward to the discussion with real rapture!

Who in American history is a rebel? Is it a man who tramples upon the Constitution, or a man who simply resents such infidelity by seeking to get away from such a party? . . .

"Fellow-citizens: I look to the contest of 1876 not only as the most important that ever occurred in American history, but as the most important in the history of the world. . . . If we fail with the ballot-box in 1876 by reason of force, a startling question will present itself to the American people. I trust we will not fail. . . . The indications are in our favor. . . . The great question, and the only question behind for the thought is the one that must be propounded, and for which there is no escape. The question is, Is the Constitution of our fathers worth blood? Will you have war or despotism? Will you have blood or empire? That is the question. . . . I tell you, my friends, there is no peace for this country until Radicalism is crushed; not only crushed, but despised; not only despised, but made infamous forever throughout America. [Tremendous applause and cheers.] . . . Let us now everywhere in the South habitually speak of the Constitution and the Union under it with that old reverence and love that distinguished us in the days that are past and gone. I say to-night, there was not a single hour in American history when the Southern heart was not true to the Constitution. [Applause.]

"If we must have war; if we cannot preserve this Constitution and constitutional government by the ballot; . . . if the war must come; . . . if inordinate love of power shall decree that America must save her Constitution by blood, let it come. I am ready. [Enthusiastic applause and cheering.] But let one thing be distinctly understood, that if another war should come, we of the South will rally under the old flag of our fathers. [Wild applause.] It always was our flag. We were never faithless to it, and our enemies were never faithful to it." [Applause.]

The reader will no doubt be at a loss to understand what relation the Presidential election of 1876 had to the Southern Historical Society, or what facts would be gathered for the enlightenment of future generations in regard to the history of the South by the abuse of the Republican Party, or by a discussion of the constitutional questions involved in reconstruction. It would seem from the ideas expressed by these two leaders that the Southern Historical Society was to take an active hand in making *modern* history as well as gathering facts in relation to *ancient* history.

Be that as it may, these speeches demonstrate the fact that, in the opinion of these gentlemen, nothing was yet definitely settled in the South, and that they proposed to summon their clans for the great political contest of 1876.

CHAPTER X

LOUISIANA IN 1873 AND 1874.

Affairs in Grant Parish—Massacre of Negroes at Colfax—Trial of the Murderers—They are Released by the U. S. Court—Statement of Rev. Dr. Hartzell, an eminent Methodist Divine—The Murderers Fêted as Heroes by the Élite of New Orleans, and sent back in Triumph to their Homes—Deplorable Condition of the Black and White Republican Witnesses—Afraid to Return to their Houses— Affairs in Red River Parish—The Coushatta Murders—The Republican Parish Officers forced to Resign and afterwards Treacherously Assassinated—Shot to Pieces and Buried in the Woods—No Attempt ever made to Arrest the Perpetrators—Assassination of M. H. Twitchell, a Republican State Senator, at Coushatta—He Escapes with the Loss of Both Arms—By his Absence the Democracy obtained Control of the State Senate.

In continuation of the story of outrage and wrong inflicted by the Democrats of Louisiana upon Republicans, a statement of what occurred in Grant and Red River parishes in 1873 and 1874 must here be recorded.

COLFAX, GRANT PARISH, MASSACRE.

In 1873 the colored people of Grant Parish in Louisiana attempted to act upon the advice so frequently given them in the Northern newspapers, which said, " If you are in the majority as you say you are, show it; assert your manhood, and, if you are attacked, defend your rights and show yourselves worthy of them." There was a contest over parish offices, and the sheriff *de facto* summoned a posse of colored men (most of them ex-Union soldiers) to take possession of the court-house and preserve the peace. The events which followed became the subject of a memorable trial in the United States courts. Judge Woods, of the U. S. Circuit Court (now Associate Judge of the Supreme Court of the United States), in his charge to the jury stated the following to be conceded facts :

"On Wednesday, the 2d of April, a small body of white men, mounted and armed, approached Colfax (the parish seat), and were met a short distance from the town by a body of armed men, most of them colored. Shots were exchanged between these two bodies of men. No one was hurt, and the white men rode off. These proceedings alarmed the colored people, and many came to Colfax for refuge, and with them a number of women and children. Many, perhaps a majority, of the men who collected in the town came armed. On Saturday, April 5, a band of armed white men, fifteen in number, as claimed to be shown by the prosecution, and three in number, as indicated by an item of evidence introduced by the defence, approached the house of one Jesse McKinney, a colored man, three miles from Colfax, on the Darrow, and found him engaged in making a fence around his lot. One of the band of white men fired upon him, shot him through the head, and killed him. His wife, assisted by another woman, got his body into a wagon and carried it to the house of her stepfather, and there left it and took refuge at the Mirabeau plantation. No evidence in the case explains the motive which led to this deed.

"This homicide increased the alarm of the colored people, who flocked into Colfax. Reports were circulated through the parish of threats made by the colored people against the whites. Most of the white families in or near Colfax, and many in more distant parts of the parish, removed from their homes and sought places of safety. On Monday, April 7, the parish court was opened and adjourned by Register, as judge, and Shaw, as sheriff. After this the alarm seemed somewhat to subside, and many of the colored people left Colfax and returned to their homes. An armed body of colored men, however, still held possession of Colfax and the court-house, and obstructed ingress to the town and court-house, and the whites maintained some sort of an armed organization outside.

"On Saturday, the 12th of April, the colored men at Colfax threw up a small earthwork in front of and in the vicinity of the court-house. At this time and on the next morning the number of colored men in the town is variously estimated at from one hundred to three hundred, more than half of whom were armed with guns. On the morning of Easter Sunday, April 13, a body of mounted and armed white men, variously estimated at from one hundred and fifty to seven hundred, approached Colfax from above. When in the vicinity they asked for a conference with the colored people, which was granted and took place (Columbus C. Nash speaking for the white men, and Levin Allen, a colored man, for his side). Nash demanded that the colored men should give up their arms and yield possession of the court-house. This demand was not acceded to by the colored men, and thirty minutes were given them to remove their women and children. The colored men took refuge behind their earthwork near the court-house, and at about ten, eleven, or twelve o'clock, as variously stated by the witnesses, the firing began. The white men had a small piece of artillery mounted on wheels, which, with their small-arms, was used against the colored men, who responded with their shot-guns and Enfield rifles ; of the latter they had about a dozen. A change in the position of their gun, made by the white men, gave them an enfilading fire on the blacks, which demoralized them, and their line broke. A portion of them, leaving their arms, fled down the Red River, in the direction of a strip of woods, at Cuny's Point, and were followed by mounted and armed whites, by whom many of them were overtaken and shot to death. The others, sixty or seventy in number, took refuge in the court-house. This was surrounded by the white men, and the small gun was brought to bear upon it, one of its shots going in one of the windows and out of the other. A rambling fire of small-arms was kept up by the whites upon the windows of the court-house, which was occasionally responded to by the blacks inside, without damage, however, to either party. The whites, after keeping up for a short time an unavailing fire upon the court-house, by approaching it upon a side which had no openings for windows or doors, set fire to the building by a torch applied to the roof. The roof was soon in flames, and the occupants of the building became alarmed. One held out the leaf of a book and the other tore off his shirt-sleeve and hung it upon a stick as a sign of capitulation, and shouted that they surrendered. They were ordered to drop their arms. At this point there is a matter of dispute between the prosecution and defence. James P. Hadnot and one Harris, on the part of the whites, approached the court-house, and, as claimed by the defence, had a white flag upon a pole. As they came near the door they fell, both mortally wounded. The defence insists that while bearing the white flag they were shot from the court-house. The prosecution and its witnesses say that when Hadnot was approaching, the blacks, having thrown down their arms, started to come out from the burning court-house and were met by a volley of shots from the whites, which, besides killing many of the colored men, struck down Hadnot and Harris. However this may be, a number of unarmed blacks who came out from the court-house were shot dead, and others were wounded. Among the killed was Alexander Tillman, one of the colored men named in the indictment. Most of those who were not killed were taken prisoners. Fifteen or sixteen of the blacks had lifted the boards and taken refuge under the floor of the court-house. They were all captured. About thirty-seven men were taken prisoners. The number is not definitely fixed. They were kept under guard until dark. They were then led out, two by two, and shot. Most of the men were shot to death. A few were wounded, not mortally, and, by pretending to be dead, were afterward during the night able to make their escape. Among them was the Levi Nelson named in the indictment.

"The dead bodies of the negroes killed in this affair were left unburied until Tuesday, April 15, when they were buried by a deputy marshal and an officer of the militia from New Orleans. These persons found fifty-nine dead bodies. They showed pistol-shots wounds, the great majority in the head, and most of them in the back of the head. In addition to the fifty-nine dead bodies found, some charred remains of dead bodies were discovered near the court-house. Six dead bodies were found under a warehouse, all shot in the head but one or two, which were shot in the breast.

"The only white men injured from the beginning of these troubles to their close were Hadnot and Harris. The court-house and its contents were entirely consumed."

On the first trial of the case in the U. S. court, before

Judge Woods, the white men arrested for these murders were convicted.   On appeal, Mr. Justice Bradley decided that the "appropriate legislation" which Congress was authorized to enact to secure the enforcement of the Fourteenth and Fifteenth Amendments did not comprehend acts of this kind, and the prisoners were released.   The manner in which their acts were regarded by leading citizens of New Orleans is thus stated by Rev. Dr. Hartzell, an eminent divine of the Methodist Episcopal Church, then stationed in New Orleans, and in no way mixed up with political matters:

"The last hope of the negroes in the South, for the present at least, for protection in their political rights, rested in the United States Government; but that too has failed.   It is utterly impossible to enforce a law in any community by any ordinary process, where the laws themselves are considered unconstitutional, and where the class the law seeks to protect is under the ban of public sentiment.   The political sentiment which now rules every Southern State pronounces United States laws which seek to superintend any election, or to protect any voter in the exercise of his franchise in any State, as an infringement upon the rights of that State, and hence unconstitutional and to be resisted.   Add to this the vicious sentiment of the South toward the negro, and it is evident that by no ordinary process of law can the United States protect him in that section in the exercise of his political rights.

"The history of the late political trials in South Carolina, Mississippi, and Louisiana proves this beyond a doubt.   A large number of arrests were made in the worst bulldozed parishes, where during the last election Republicans were whipped, and shot, and hung.   The cases susceptible of the clearest proof were selected and brought to trial before Judge Woods of the U. S. Circuit Court, a man of sterling character and a just judge. As the trials progressed the prisoners were the recipients of every possible attention from the *élite* of New Orleans. Their bills were paid at the best hotels, and every morning columns of editorials in the city papers would tell of their good characters, and of the outrage being perpetrated upon them in being dragged from their homes to answer trumped-up charges against them by 'niggers and carpet-baggers.' He also states that when the prisoners were released they were escorted to the wharf by a multitude, cannons boomed, and for three hundred miles they were greeted at every landing on the river as heroes. On the boat carrying them was what served as a cannon as to noise, and, as its roar at every landing went echoing through the villages and over plantations, is it strange that the negroes, whose friends and ·representatives these very heroes and their friends had whipped and driven from the polls, should distrust the power or willingness of even the United States to protect them? Once at home, some of these 'heroes' are installed in the principal parish offices, and others are returned to New Orleans as members of the convention to make a new constitution for the State. Look now at the negroes, who had been the victims of outrage, and their friends, who had been summoned with them to testify for the United States. Not one of them dare return to their homes unless to die. Some of them have valuable property, others are parish officers, and many are small planters and renters whose all has gone to waste by neglect. Two hundred of this class, I am told, are now in New Orleans; some I know personally to be men of means and good character."

THE COUSHATTA MURDERS.

Marshall H. Twitchell, a native of Vermont, a gallant Union soldier bearing the scars of many wounds received in battle, went to Louisiana in 1867, with his brother and other young men. They settled in Coushatta and Red River Parish, with the purpose of making their home there. They bought a number of plantations, put up cotton-gins, saw-mills, a grist-mill, a planing-mill, and a steam cotton-press. The younger Twitchell married a Louisiana lady, and was appointed postmaster. He was a Republican. The parish officers, all reputable white men and property-owners, were also Republicans. On the 27th August, 1874, the White League organization came to the determination that for the proper conduct of the coming State elections it was desirable to have no Radical office-holders in Red River. They accordingly mustered in overwhelming force, under the command of Mr. T. W. Abney, a prominent merchant of Coushatta, and demanded that all the Republican office-holders should resign. Warned by the untimely fate of the officials of Grant Parish, they did not attempt to resist an overpowering force, and sheriff, and registrar, and judge, and other officials, to the number of seven, concluded to resign.

"Hoping to appease the wrath of our people," said Abney in evidence before a committee of the Forty-third Congress, "they proposed to resign. Their proposition was accepted. They selected their own guard, and the captain of the guard; also their own route. I suggested to them the propriety of going a different route, and stated that if there was any danger it lay in the direction they had chosen. On Sunday morning, the 30th August, the prisoners were delivered to the guard. I stated to the guard 'that the responsibility of protecting the prisoners from harm now devolved on them,' and 'that I expected them to do their duty to the prisoners,' and at the same time handed the captain of the guard an order on the president of Ward Club No. 4, about thirty miles up the river, to furnish all the men that might be necessary to protect these parties to Shreveport. The prisoners and guard arrived without molestation at George Robinson's farm, about thirty miles above Coushatta, where they dined; also, sent a boy back to Mr. Walmsley, half a mile, for water-melons, which they ate, discovering no signs of pursuit or molestation. Soon it was reported that they were pursued, and a run then commenced. The prisoners, being well mounted, outrode most of the guard, who were on plough-stock. They were assassinated by parties as yet unknown to me."

Their bodies were so fearfully shot to pieces that subsequent identification was rendered impossible. They were buried in the woods, where they fell without attempt at inquest or other formality. In the course of a scathing cross-examination by Mr. (now Senator) Frye, Abney was asked:

Q. I understand that among those persons at Coushatta was a Mr. Scott?

A. Yes, sir; Henry A. Scott.

Q. I understand as a matter of fact that Henry A. Scott did not go with that crowd?

A. No, sir.

Q. I understand the reason he did not go was because you suggested to him not to go?

A. I suggested to all of them not to go.

Q. I understand that you suggested especially to him not to go?

A. No, sir; Mr. Scott appealed to me as a master-mason, and I took the responsibility upon Sunday night to take Mr. Scott out.

Q. Now let me understand you. You are a master-mason?

A. I am, sir.

Q. Mr. Scott was a master-mason?

A. Yes, sir.

Q. Those prisoners, together with Scott, had concluded to take this company as a guide to go out of the country?

A. Yes, sir.

Q. Mr. Scott, as a master-mason, appealed to you, not in the presence of the others, but to you when alone?

A. Yes, sir.

Q. You, as a master-mason, prevailed upon him not to go with this company?

A. I simply went and took him out, in the cover of the night.

Q. And the result was that his life was saved?

A. Yes, sir.

Mr. Frye. That is all.

From this and other facts the committee came to the conclusion that these six defenceless and unoffending prisoners had been deliberately murdered with the connivance of Abney, to whom they had surrendered on a promise of safe-conduct. The merciless atrocity of this outrage was too much even for the Democratic minority of the committee, and they reported (through Mr. Marshall of Illinois):

"Whether the prisoners were guilty of any crime or wrong or not, their murder, under the circumstances in which it was done, can have no excuse or palliation. It was a most dastardly murder, condemned by the entire people of Louisiana, as it must always be by the civilized world."

The statement that the deed was condemned "by the entire people of Louisiana" is curiously emphasized by the fact that no inquiry has ever been permitted by the White League into the circumstances of the murder, and no attempt at an arrest therefor has ever been made. The majority of the committee, through Mr. (now Senator) Hoar, its chairman, deduced from this and similar outrages the conclusion:

"That there has been, and is, a purpose to take possession by force and fraud of the State Government without regard to the question of who may have the numerical majority at a fair election; and that in the execution of this purpose they have refrained, and will refrain, from the use of no instruments which they think designed to accomplish it, whether those instruments be *murder, fraud, civil war,* or coercion of laborers by employers."

A few months later, Mr. M. H. Twitchell, who was absent from the parish when these events occurred, returned with the double purpose of settling some private affairs, and, if possible, obtaining some evidence as to his brother's assassins. Twitchell was a Republican State Senator. The Senate was a tie, but by the casting vote of the Lieutenant-Governor was Republican. The House had become Democratic by the award of the Wheeler compromise.

As Twitchell entered the town of Coushatta he noticed unusual commotion in the streets. At the same time a strange-looking man, wearing a heavy false beard, armed with a Henry rifle and mounted on a pony, rode up, and, dismounting on the opposite side of the river from the town, stationed himself behind a pile of cord-wood and waited. It was the custom for most of the leading citizens to visit the post-office, which overlooked the river, at noon to get their mails. The mail was all distributed, but still the people lingered and watched. As the afternoon advanced Senator Twitchell and his brother-in-law came down to the river-bank and embarked in a small skiff-ferry, rowed by a colored man, to cross the stream. When they were about in mid-stream the man with the bushy beard and the Henry rifle stepped from behind the wood-pile and fired. His first shot killed the brother-in-law; his next shattered Twitchell's right arm. Twitchell threw himself overboard, and grasped the gunwale of the skiff with his left hand. The unerring marksman put two bullets through the left arm, and then Twitchell let go his hold and sank. The colored boy shouted, "Don't shoot any more, boss; he's dead;" and satisfied that this was so, the assassin leisurely mounted his pony and rode off, in full view of the assembled townspeople. Then the colored man pulled Twitchell into the skiff and rowed with him to the camp of a detachment of United States soldiers near by, where the army surgeon amputated first one and then the other of the shattered limbs close to the shoulder.

Twitchell's absence gave the Democracy control of the State Senate.

Mr. Twitchell lives to-day, and is consul of the United States at Kingston, Canada.

It is probable that the annals of Christendom would be searched in vain for the record of a more treacherous and cold-blooded assassination than is presented in the shooting down of these unoffending citizens and defenceless prisoners at Coushatta. It is safe to say that in no other corner of the civilized world could such deeds be

done without an effort to bring the perpetrators to con-
dign punishment, or where the murderers would hold up
their heads as "our first citizens."

Meanwhile the victims sleep in their unmarked and
bloody graves. Their only offence, the only charge preferred against them, was that they were Republicans
from Northern States. They had identified themselves
with the interests of Louisiana by becoming its citizens,
by investing large sums of money in lands, houses, and
machinery, and one of them had married a wife who was
a native of the State. If they had been Democrats they
would have been safe, honored, and courted. But they
chose to be Republicans, and they were slain for their
opinions. They died martyrs to the cause of truth and
liberty, and their names should be held in enduring
honor by all who love justice and hate oppression.

CHAPTER XII.

PLAN OF THE DEMOCRATIC LEADERS TO CAPTURE REPUBLICAN STATES BY STIFLING REPUBLICAN MAJORITIES.

NOTHING comes by chance. The mighty procession of human events moves forward in strict accordance with the inexorable law of cause and effect. The opinions, passions, prejudices, and sympathies of men direct and control their actions. Behind all great acts in the human will—behind the will, stand the opinions of men. Whether the deeds are good or evil, whether they are to advance or retard the prosperity and happiness of the people, whether they are in the interest of peace or disorder, they have their origin in and may be traced to the well-settled convictions of some great leading spirit. An analysis of the facts connected with the politics of Alabama, Arkansas, Florida, Louisiana, Mississippi, North Carolina, and South Carolina, from the spring of 1873 to the time of the final result of the election of 1876, clearly indicates that a definite plan of action had been determined upon by party leaders, and that the States were to be carried for the Democratic Party at all hazards. In the light of what actually occurred it would be safe to formulate and set down their plan as follows:

1. The contest must be made upon the color line—upon the race issue.

2. The press and public speakers must pour out a torrent of denunciation against all white men who affi-

liate politically with negroes, charging them as being enemies of the white race; and social ostracism and business proscription shall be adopted by all Democrats toward white Republicans.

3. The assembling of negroes at political meetings must be regarded as conclusive evidence of their determination to "rise" and make war upon the whites; all Republican meetings must therefore be suppressed.

4. Democrats must organize and arm themselves, and be ready for any emergency. In the event of a disturbance kill the leaders and intimidate the rank and file, always alleging and proving that Republicans were the aggressors.

5. Where prominent Republicans have public meetings, demand a division of time, have a number of armed men present, and let their conduct be insulting and domineering, so as to intimidate your opponents.

6. The pressure upon all Republican office-holders must be so great as to excite apprehension of danger. Force them to resign and leave the country, if possible, and have Democrats seize the offices.

7. Use every possible means to prevent the National Government from interfering in the affairs of your State, by giving constant assurances that everything is peaceful and quiet, and by all means fill the Northern press with dispatches favorable to your side.

8. Have candidates for every office, from Governor and Congressman down, without reference to the size of the Republican majority, and after the election claim everything with arms in your hands, and yield nothing; what you lack in numbers make up in organization and aggressive energy.

We are to deal with facts. The aim is to ascertain and point out the causes which operated to revolutionize the politics of eight States, and wheel them from the Republican into the Democratic column. If Republicans, for any cause, became weary of their party, and of their own volition united with the Democracy; if the hard times, the labor question, the greenback question, or any other issue, was presented to them, and by arguments either through the press or upon the stump they became convinced that their interests would be best subserved and their rights better protected by voting the Democratic ticket—no one could complain: the elector has the right to cast his lot with whichever party best suits him. He has the right to vote the Democratic ticket if he chooses to do so. Upon the other hand, he has the right to vote the Republican ticket, and no one can be justified in depriving him of the exercise of that right by force, intimidation, or fraud.

With Democrats in the Southern States the time for legitimate discussion of public questions with their opponents, with a view of changing their opinions, seemed to have passed. Thenceforward other and more cogent reasons were to be offered in behalf of the supremacy of the Democratic Party.

CHAPTER XIII.

THE ALABAMA ELECTION OF 1874.

Decided Republican Triumph at the Election of 1872—Tone of the
Democratic Press indicates a Change of Policy—Vindictive Resolutions of the Democratic Conventions in 1874—Social Ostracism
of all Republicans declared—Inflammatory Articles in the Press
directed against the Negro and his Friends—The Republican Convention of 1874—Moderate and Conciliatory Resolutions passed—
No Abatement of Democratic Fury—General System of Intimidation Adopted—Outrages upon Negroes—A small Force of Federal
Troops sent to the State to preserve Order—Mob Violence prevails
in the Elections throughout the State—Riot in Mobile—Massacre
of Negroes at Eufaula—Shooting of Election Officers and Destruction of the Ballot-box and Ballots at Spring Hill—How Barbour
County was Carried for the Democrats—Refusal to Count Republican Votes at Opelika—The Police Force of Columbus, Ga., participate in the Election at Girard, Ala.—Other Excursionists from
Georgia come by Special Train and Vote in Alabama.

THE Republican Party carried the State of Alabama
at the election of 1872 by 10,828 majority on the Presidential vote. Six Republican Congressmen were elected
and two Democrats. In the Congressional districts
carried by the Republican Party the majorities were as
follows: First District, 2433; Second District, 3172;
Third District, 586; Fourth District, 5212. Two Republicans were elected at large by about 8000 majority.

The Democratic districts were carried by the following majorities: Fifth District, 4251; Sixth District,
4695.

Early in 1874 it became obvious from the tone of the
Democratic press that their party proposed making a

tremendous effort to carry the State at the fall election.
The campaign was evidently to be an aggressive one.
The papers inaugurated a system of wholesale abuse of
the Republican Party and its principles, and were un-
sparing in their denunciations of Republicans, both
white and black.

The declarations of the National Democratic platform
of 1872, recognizing the equality of all men before the
law, and the duty to mete out equal and exact justice
to all, and to maintain the enfranchisement of colored
men, were wholly ignored. A war of races was declared;
it was to be an issue between white men and black men.
All white men who favored the Civil Rights Bill were
denounced as enemies of the white race.

There was to be no quarter shown to those who failed
to support the Democratic Party. The teaching of
Mr. Hill, in his Atlanta speech of 1867, was approved,
and people were advised to have nothing whatever to do
with Republicans, either socially or in a business way.

The following resolution, taken from a Democratic
county platform, published in the *Troy Messenger*, shows
the spirit that animated the party:

"*Resolved*, That nothing is left to the white man's
party but social ostracism of all those who act, sympathize, or side with the negro party, or who support or
advocate the odious, unjust, and unreasonable measure
known as the Civil Rights Bill; and that from henceforth
we will hold all such persons as the enemies of our race,
and will not in the future have intercourse with them in
any of the social relations of life."

The following resolution was adopted by the Alabama
Democratic State Convention in July, 1874 :

" 1. That the Radical and dominant faction of the
Republican Party in this State persistently, by false and

fraudulent representations, have inflamed the passions and prejudices of the negroes as a race against the white people, and have thereby made it necessary for the white people to unite and act together in self-defence and for the preservation of white civilization."

The *Opelika* (Ala.) *Times* of June 29, 1874, published the following resolution of the Democratic Convention of Lee County:

"*Resolved*, That all persons, whether white or black, who are the least in sympathy with the so-called Civil Rights Bill, or who shall in any wise lend aid to those who indorse or countenance said bill, shall be regarded by the white men of Lee as the political and social enemies of the white race."

The following is from the *Mobile Register :*

" The grave question, to be settled at much cost, is, What is to be done to get rid of the negro as a voter? Sooner or later, with more or less dispatch, he will be disfranchised and thrust out of our politics.

" White men of all parties, and of every grade of religious or moral conviction, may as well come quickly to the consideration how to get the negro out of politics with the least confusion and cost.

" He must go, and there is no profit in standing long upon the order of his going. You say it is a grave question. So it is, and one that affects the moral and political welfare of the whites to such an extent that the negro must go out of the political problem by legislation on the part of the States respectively, or go to the wall in a long, bloody, and fierce struggle for his decimation. He shall own himself and be an alien citizen, with the liberty to own property, to sue as well as be sued; but he shall not attempt to do that thing impossible to him —help to govern this country through the ballot-box."

From *Opelika* (Ala.) *Times*, Aug. 22, 1874:

" If there be a colored man who is willing to recognize the necessity of putting Alabama under the rule of intelligence, he becomes our friend, and he should be preferred as tenant of our houses, cabooses on the farm, drayman upon the streets, sexton of the church, and in every way right and proper sustained and built up. Merchants, mechanics, and tradesmen of every character have a right to expect and demand support from and at the hands of those with whom they are allied in this great struggle for reform; while the Radical cannot have the effrontery to even ask a 'fish' without the rational expectation of receiving a 'stone.' Every man who sustains a scalawag individually contributes to building up Radicalism. The way to kill the party is to put upon 'short allowance' its individual members. The sea is open; the sky is beautiful; victory is ours. All of the good and prominent of Alabama are for the white-man's party. Outcasts, libellers, liars, handcuffers, and traitors to blood are for the negro party. Decide where you will place yourself in November."

This spirit of intolerance was visible on every hand. Newspapers and public speakers fanned the State into a flame of excitement against Republicans.

The Republican Convention met in August, 1874. Its members, fully recognizing the gravity of the situation, the injustice of the charges which had been preferred against them, and the entire want of foundation for any apprehension of danger on the part of Democrats from Republicans either white or black, adopted a platform, from which are quoted the following resolutions:

" 1. The Republican Party of Alabama, in State convention assembled, again declares its unshaken confidence in and its unalterable devotion to the great principles of human liberty which called it into existence, namely, the civil and political equality of all men, without distinction of race or color.

" 3. We have not made a race issue in the past, neither do we now make or tender such an issue. What we demand for one man we demand for all men, without distinction of race or color, and we point with pride and confidence to every line of our political record in proof of this declaration; and we denounce the assertion that we have ' made it necessary for the white people to unite and act together in self-defence and for the preservation of white civilization ' as untrue, and an emanation from that selfish spirit which in the past demanded everything for one race and was unwilling to concede anything to the other.

" 5. That we neither desire nor seek the invasion of the rights of the white people by the colored; we only ask equal advantages in matters of public and common right; and in order that we may be understood, and no false charges made against us, we hereby declare that the Republican Party does not desire or seek to have mixed schools or mixed accommodations for the colored people with the white people; but they ask in all of these that the advantages shall be equal. We want no social equality enforced by law; we recognize the fact that every home is sacred from intrusion, and that in a free country every one can dictate for himself the line of social exclusion; that society governs itself by laws more inexorable than statute or common law, and opens or closes its doors to whomsoever it will, and that no civil law can or should invade it."

These pacific declarations had no effect upon the Democrats; they had worked themselves up to a high pitch of excitement, which could not be allayed by any

action of the Republicans short of a total abandonment
of their right to participate in the election.   Social ostracism and business proscription against white Republicans and their families were insisted upon by the Democratic press, and were adopted by Democrats almost
throughout the State.   The carriage of the Democrats
was domineering and aggressive, insomuch that it became dangerous for Republicans to hold public meetings.   On the part of the Democratic Party it became
a campaign of murder, intimidation, and outrage.   It
seemed that the Ku Klux Klan had thrown aside its disguises, and without attempt at concealment proposed to
inaugurate a reign of terror and carry the election for
the Democratic Party by the suppression of the Republican vote.   Some prominent Republicans were murdered
and others beaten and abused.

It is difficult to enumerate the various methods
adopted to overcome the Republican majority in the
State.   Everything goes to show that there was a well-
settled purpose on the part of the Democrats to treat
the negroes with such severity as would compel many of
them to vote the Democratic ticket or else remain away
from the polls.   In some portions of the State colored
Republicans could not obtain employment on account
of their politics, although otherwise unobjectionable.
Others were discharged from employment because of
their politics.   Democratic employers held what were
called "pledge meetings," where colored men were
required to sign written pledges to vote the Democratic
ticket or be discharged from employment.   Colored speakers were threatened with death for making Republican
speeches.   In numerous instances colored men were
dragged from their homes and whipped, and otherwise
maltreated, because they belonged to the Republican

Party. These cruelties were carried to such an extent that in many instances colored men slept at night in the woods, fearing to remain in their cabins. The schools for colored children were broken up, and in a number of cases the buildings were burned. White persons who taught colored schools were ostracized and proscribed.

During the progress of the canvass the conduct of the Democrats became so outrageous, that, upon the application of the Governor of the State, President Grant ordered a body of troops, consisting of thirty-eight officers and six hundred and forty-one enlisted men, to be stationed at various points in the State to assist in preserving the peace. The orders of General McDowell, department commander, were very explicit and stringent in regard to the soldiers not being used to interfere with the election.

These six hundred and seventy-nine officers and soldiers were stationed at thirty different points, in squads and companies numbering from four to sixty persons. They, however, were encamped so far from the place of holding the election, that, with the exception of Opelika, where they probably prevented mob violence, they were of no practical benefit in restraining the conduct of the Democrats.

The turbulent and overbearing spirit of the Democracy was especially exhibited on the day of election. Mob violence prevailed in a number of places.

In Mobile a body of men, armed and mounted as cavalrymen, paraded the streets and insulted Republicans; finally, the excitement ran so high, on account of Democratic violence, that Republicans were driven from the polls, and one man was killed and others wounded.

In Barbour County, which had a Republican majority of more than two thousand, the Democrats were determined to carry the election. At Eufaula, the county-seat, colored voters in large numbers came to the polls, entirely unarmed and peaceful. About twelve o'clock, when about one third of the vote had been cast, a dispute arose as to the right of a young colored man to vote. His father alleged that he was not of sufficient age; he however was induced to and did vote the Democratic ticket.

While this discussion was going on, Deputy U. S. Marshal Williford entered the crowd and learned the facts, whereupon he advised that there should be no further dispute and that the crowd should disperse.

At this juncture, not a blow having been struck, and the colored people being entirely unarmed, commands were given, "Fall in, Company A!" "Fall in, Company B!" whereupon a large body of white Democrats instantly separated themselves from the crowd of colored people and withdrew to the opposite side of the street from the polling-places, and immediately opened fire upon the negroes, who, to the number of about one thousand, were standing in the street. Eighty-two negroes were shot, seven of whom were mortally wounded; ten or twelve white men who were standing on the sidewalk near the polling-places were also wounded. The negroes fled, and about five hundred of them returned to their homes without voting.

Captain Dagget with ten soldiers had been stationed at Eufaula; they were quartered about three hundred yards from the polling-places. Immediately after the mob opened fire Deputy-Marshal Williford called upon Captain Dagget to assist in preventing further bloodshed, but the captain declined to take any action, saying that under his orders he could render no assistance; and when appealed to that there was danger of the town being burned, he replied, " Very well, I cannot help it; I cannot give any assistance under my orders."

The Democratic Party throughout the entire country had raised so great a clamor against stationing soldiers near the polls in Southern States to keep the peace, and the Republicans in the North had yielded so much to these demands, that when soldiers were assigned to duty in those States they acted under such rigid orders, that but few officers would take the responsibility of interfering to prevent bloodshed.

Deputy-Marshal Williford, in a sworn statement in regard to this riot, said that the colored men were unarmed, and behaved themselves in a peaceable and quiet way. He expressed the opinion that at least six hundred shots were fired by the mob.

Captain Dagget, who was some distance from the scene, testified that he thought there were about five hundred shots fired.

At Spring Hill, Barbour County, about eighteen miles from Eufaula, the election proceeded without material disturbance.

The Republicans had a large majority in the precinct, and their votes were cast and the ballots properly placed in the box. As the Republicans voted, they generally left for their homes, so that when the polls closed at five o'clock there were probably not more than one hundred or one hundred and fifty persons present, Republicans and Democrats. Elias M. Keils, a native of Alabama, and a citizen of Eufaula since 1837, was the United States supervisor at Spring Hill. In his testimony before an investigating committee he stated that there were seven hundred and thirty-two (732) votes cast at Spring Hill, five sixths of which were Republican. Mr. Keils states that the reason he accepted the appoint-

ment as supervisor was to prevent the frauds which had
been perpetrated there in 1872 (when the Republicans
were only given forty-five votes in the count) from being
repeated.   Mr. Keils remained in the house with the
election officers, who were delayed in the preparation of
their tally-sheets until after dark.   The door had been
barred to keep out an excited crowd of Democrats.
After dark one of the clerks of election, who was a
Democrat, without any apparent reason unbarred the
door, when a crowd of thirty or forty Democrats forced
their way into the room.   They at once began firing
their pistols; they put out the lights, and seized the ballot-box.   The Democratic election officers rushed out of
the house, leaving Judge Keils and his son, a youth of
seventeen years, to their fate.   The judge was not injured, but young Keils was killed.   Three shots took
effect in his thigh and one in his bowels.   The ballot-
box was destroyed, the tickets were burned, and no return was made of the vote.   Barbour County was carried
for the Democratic Party.

At Opelika two ballot-boxes had been prepared by the
sheriff of the county to receive the ballots of voters in
that town.   The vote at that place was large, and the
sheriff, deeming it advisable for the convenience of
voters to have more than one box to receive the tickets,
asked the opinion of Hon. Benjamin Gardner, Attorney-
General, as to his authority to establish a second box
for the election.   In a letter, dated Montgomery, Sept.
30, 1874, the Attorney-General delivered an opinion to
the effect that, under the law as it then existed, the
whole matter of furnishing ballot-boxes was left to the
discretion of the sheriff, the law providing that "the
sheriffs of the several counties shall furnish one ballot-
box for each election precinct, and, when necessary,

more than one, but in no case more than five." The sheriff accordingly provided two ballot-boxes for the town of Opelika. Most of the Democrats voted at box No. 1 and the Republicans at box No. 2. When the Democratic Board of Supervisors counted the vote they threw out and refused to count the ballots in box No. 2. According to the sworn testimony of one of the managers, this box contained 1252 Republican votes and nine Democratic votes. It was shown that Democrats from Georgia and Mississippi voted at the election in Alabama, and repeated their votes at three or four different precincts. One of the remarkable incidents of the election was the appearance of a part of the police force of Columbus, Ga., in their uniforms, and numbering seven or eight persons, crossed the river to Girard, Ala., and, with a number of private citizens of Columbus, assisted in the intimidation of Republican voters; and thereby the usual Republican majority of four or five hundred was reduced to about one hundred and ten. It was shown that on the day of election a number of Democrats from Columbus, West Point, Brownsville, and other places in Georgia, went by railroad to Salem, Louchapoka, and other points in Alabama, and voted the Democratic ticket.

A lot of Democrats at Brownsville, Ga., engaged a special car to carry them to Salem, Ala. Upon their arrival the car was switched off the main track, and remained until they all voted the Democratic ticket.

CHAPTER XIV.

ALABAMA ELECTION OF 1874—*Continued.*

The Election investigated by a Committee of the United States House of Representatives—Extracts from the Report of the Committee—The "Race Issue" forced upon the People by the Democratic Leaders—The Bitterness of the Political Warfare waged at this Election—Murder of a leading White Republican and a leading Colored Republican—Burning of Colored Churches—Testimony of William E. Cockrell—Murder of a Negro Child by a Militia Company—Testimony of Frederick Carter—Shooting of Inoffensive Negroes at the Election in Mobile—Testimony of Reuben Selas—Testimony of Joshua McNeal—Frank Avowal of the Purposes of the Democrats—Testimony of James Brown and Richard Wright—Particulars concerning the Assassinations of James L. Ivey, Colored Mail Agent, and W. P. Billings, prominent White Republican.

UNDER the authority of a resolution passed by the House of Representatives of the United States in December, 1874, a committee was appointed to investigate the election in the State of Alabama held in November of that year.

The committee consisted of the following members:

Hon. John Coburn, of Indiana; Hon. Charles Albright, of Indiana; Hon. Jos. G. Cannon, of Illinois; Hon. A. H. Buckner, of Missouri; and Hon. J. L. Luttrell, of California.

The testimony of a large number of witnesses in every station of life was taken, including prominent persons of both political parties. This testimony covers 1306 pages of the printed report of the committee, and presents a graphic account of the tragic scenes which preceded and attended the election. The following extracts are taken from the report of the committee:

" The Democratic Party entered the contest with a determination to ' carry the election at all hazards,' and, as the testimony plainly shows, resorted to every species of intimidation, violence, and ostracism that would conduce to that result. Both white and black men in it were proscribed for the alleged reason that they were inferior, incapable, and untrustworthy by nature and essence.

" The natural consequences of such a contest were soon developed. One side assumed the attitude of superior wisdom and superior power, and undertook to intimidate and overawe the other. Intolerance of political opinion became apparent, and was soon followed by intolerance of action.

" Republicans were denounced as common enemies of the ' white race,' whose suppression was necessary to the preservation of that race. Long before the assembling of a convention of either party in the State, the Democratic newspapers were filled with appeals to the white people of the State to stand as a unit against the advance of the Republican Party. These appeals were founded upon pretended assumptions of Republican aggression, as charged by Democratic politicians, in order to inflame the white men and arouse the deadliest of human passions. The Democratic press of the State teemed with accounts of the negroes arming and drilling in order to intimidate the whites, and of negro military companies being organized for the same unlawful purpose. Careful and pointed inquiry upon this subject totally disproved every assumption of this character, and established the further fact that not a single negro military company existed or exists to-day within the borders of the State, so far as the committee were able to dis-

cover.   Published in every part of the State, their truth-
fulness vouched for by seeming good authority, these
incendiary appeals had the desired effect, and the committee is surprised that the result of this teaching did
not bring about more disastrous consequences.   And
the committee believes that, but for the timely interference of the Administration in Louisiana affairs, revolutionary measures would have been precipitated upon the
people of Alabama.

   " A ' race issue ' was thus forced upon the people of
the State—an issue in which the prejudices of the white
people were furiously aroused against the blacks and all
those who saw fit to affiliate politically with them."

   The committee stated in their report that "the Democrats began their campaign by endeavoring to break up
a Republican county convention at Clayton; by running
out of town a Republican Congressman at Tuskegee; by
pelting with rotten eggs a State judge at Greenville; by
bullying a Republican speaker and lawyer at Greens-
borough; by burning the churches of colored people in the
Wacoochee Valley; by armed raidings of whites against
their colored neighbors; by public denunciation and personal abuse of 'carpet-baggers' and 'scalawags;' by
threatening and bribing colored men, as well as by the
occasional assassination of a Republican leader."

   It was shown to the entire satisfaction of the committee that the Republicans of Alabama were for peace and
order.   The colored people were particularly desirous of
maintaining friendly relations with Democrats, many of
whom were their employers.   It was the policy of the
Democracy to create the impression that the lives of
their people were in danger by reason of the organization
and drilling of military companies of colored people.   A
most careful inquiry into this charge showed it to be

groundless, but it served the purpose of arousing the animosity of the Democrats throughout the State, and of inducing them to organize and arm themselves.

So successful was the work of the party leaders in forcing the "race issue" upon the people of the State, that the necessary evils of such a course were not slow in being developed. An era of intimidation, social ostracism, personal violence, and murder was inaugurated; and the true men that stood by the Republican principles were subjected to acts of indignity and maltreatment heretofore witnessed only in savage warfare. Just prior to the inauguration of the campaign on the part of the Republicans two of their prominent leaders were assassinated in open day, and the perpetrators of these crimes have not been prosecuted by the authorities of the State up to this time. The first instance of murder occurred in Sumter County, and was that of Walter P. Billings, a Northern man, who was shot down in the public road, as he was on his way to his home from a point at which he had addressed a Republican meeting. He had committed no offence against the laws of the State, the county, or society; was a peaceable, law-abiding citizen, following the pursuits of business; and his only offence, so far as could be ascertained, was that of being an active Republican leader.

The next instance was that of Thomas L. Ivey, a leading colored Republican, who was a route agent on the railroad running between Livingston and Meridian. In open daylight the train was "flagged" and halted, and Ivey was shot to death in the mail car.

The principal objective point, however, of the Democracy seemed to be the white Republicans. It was necessary to crush out these, to destroy their influence, and leave the colored men without wealthy, able, and intelligent leaders. To this end the new feature in American politics of "social and business" ostracism was introduced. As will be seen from the extracts taken on this point, this plan was resorted to in many portions of the State. To be called a Republican was the synonym of disgrace. Not only did the Democrats visit this ostracism upon men, but it was extended in some instances to the wives and children of Republicans. It was carried into the churches and schoolhouses and the family circle.

FROM TESTIMONY OF CHARLES SMITH.

"In regard to the white Republicans, I will say that they went through a fire of social ostracism during the last campaign; not only men, but their wives and families. It was understood amongst the white ladies that they would not speak to the wives nor to the families of any men who supported the members of the Republican Party; and it was the same way on the part of the Democrats.

"They abused, ostracized, and cursed the Republicans. I know that, and I have heard it. There never was a more bitter warfare waged politically anywhere than in Alabama during the last campaign."

Hon. W. M. Brooks, a prominent leader of the party, says: "When a man joins the Republican Party in our midst it has an effect upon his social position. And when he joins that party he must feel or realize the fact that he is giving up his social position in a great measure —not altogether so; he feels that the cold shoulder will be turned to him."

These notorious facts establish the position that the campaign of the Democratic Party in Alabama was made against the colored man as such, and his white ally.

A.. other issues were buried out of sight. The canvass on the part of the Democrats, thus inaugurated in bitterness and strife, ended in a victory won by fraud, violence, proscription, intimidation, and murder.

From the many statements of cruel outrage and murder, the following are taken as an illustration of the lawless condition of affairs in Alabama during the political campaign of 1874, and how Republicans were made to suffer for opinions' sake:

George Sharp, a colored Republican speaker in Wacoochee Valley, and candidate for justice, in his testimony shows that the political meetings of the colored men were broken up by armed Democrats; that large numbers of armed and mounted Democrats went about threatening the negroes; that they burned their churches because Republican meetings were held in them; that they then got up what they called a "peace meeting," and invited whites and negroes to rebuild the churches; that he attended and was compelled, under fear of death, to make a Democratic speech, and when the meeting adjourned, before he could get fifty yards from the church, he was fired at by two men who were at the meeting, and only escaped by dodging behind a mule, and then by sudden flight; that he had but a mile and a quarter to go to his home; that his enemies had already been there before him; that he slept in the woods that night; that the Democrats told his brother that he must leave the State, which he did, and has not since lived in the State for fear of murder, and this solely because he is a prominent Republican leader. This is uncontradicted. He is shown to be a sober, industrious, and respectable colored man. He was the only colored man who took a newspaper in that neighborhood. He says, "The Democrats knew I could read, and they cut off my papers and would not let me get them from the post-office. If I went to get the papers they said they would get me."

Wm. E. Cockrell, native of Eutaw, Greene County, testifies as follows:

Q. State whether any arms have been brought into that county by the Democrats?

A. The Democrats have a company there; there is not one Republican in it; about one hundred in number. They armed themselves with the arms of the State, which were there, and rode through the country, pretending to be quieting the negroes, pretending that they had heard that a body of negroes was stationed there for the purpose of making raids on the whites. They would go to the place where they understood such, and would find out afterward that no such body of negroes had assembled there. Their riding around through the country of course terrorized the colored people to an alarming extent. They occupied a week or two in riding around in that way. They went out generally at night.

At one time the sheriff took them out at one o'clock. They assembled at Mount Heber, in the western part of the county. They were informed that a large body of negroes had assembled at the gin-house of old Jerry Brown. There were a hundred men in the company. Two roads lead to the place; and they divided, fifty men going each way, agreeing to meet at the same time at Jerry Brown's place. They got there, and hearing a noise in the gin-house, and assuming that it was filled with negroes, fired on that house. A crowd of little negro children from four to twelve or fourteen years old, who had been sleeping in there taking care of the cotton, ran out. It was warm, and made a good bed for them. They afterward found that one child was missing. Search was made, and he was found in the gin-house, shot through the head and killed.

Frederick Carter (colored), resident of Mobile, testifies as follows:

"I was at the jail when the shooting occurred; saw a colored man, Norman Freeman, being taken to jail in a cab; there was one man in the cab with him and five or six walking behind; some were on horseback. After the negro was put in jail the men came back. A colored man was standing on the street with a gun. A. C. Danner said, 'Arrest that damned nigger with a gun.' The negro then ran, and Danner shot him. He ran a little ways and dropped his gun, and after that he shot him again, and the negro fell. Mr. McGill shot Bill Jackson, who was doing nothing. They said, 'Arrest him.' Jackson ran, and McGill shot him twice and killed him."

Reuben Selas, resident of Mobile, testifies that he "was down on Government Street the day of election, about half-past three o'clock. Allen Alexander came walking down from the Seventh Ward. I suppose there were about two hundred men in the street following him, and about twenty-five or thirty young fellows walking behind him. They came walking, laughing, and talking along, and said they supposed that there was about five hundred majority. I asked them where they were going, and they said down to the Fourth Ward to vote, saying that they were afraid of being killed if they undertook to go to the Seventh Ward. When Allen Alexander got in front of the court-house, a company of men, with A. C. Danner, Mr. McGill, and James Manette, came around from the poll and cried to arrest him; some also cried 'Kill him.' Manette got off of his horse, grabbed a colored man by the collar, and shot him. The shooting continued five or six minutes; the negroes ran off, and the white men threw up their hats and cheered. Two men were killed, to witness's knowledge; some say there were three."

Joshua McNeal, of Montgomery County, testifies that "during the canvass people were generally ostracized, and every place that I went there were difficulties about holding meetings. Those difficulties occurred until election day. I went into Montgomery once and met Mr. Jeff. Simmons, whom I had known for years. He said, 'You are canvassing again for the Radical Party.' I told him I was. He asked me what I thought the prospect was, and I told him I thought it looked very bright. He said, 'You might as well quit; we have made up our minds to carry the State or kill half of you niggers on election day.' I told him I reckoned not; that we intended to be peaceable about it. He, however, said, 'We will show you; we have begged you long enough, and have persuaded you, but you will vote for the Radical Party. If you don't come into our party by fair means, we are going to bring you by foul means.'"

James Brown (colored), of Sumter County, testifies that "I was going over to Ben Chiles's house, and going down the road, when I looked back and heard some men coming, but were not in sight then. When they began to get in sight I got disgusted, and went out to the left-hand side of the road into the woods, and they went on down a piece below me, and went out to the side of the road, and dismounted and hitched their horses. Then they came right back across the road, and went down by the side of the railway, near a little trestle. About five minutes later I heard the train coming; when I heard it I stood perfectly still, and the train passed me. I saw Mr. Ivey sitting in the car on a little round chair; and a few minutes after that I looked up and saw a colored man standing with his handkerchief waving the train down; and as the train held up I saw a man go down near a little marshy place, and I saw three guns rise, and two of them fired on the side I was on, and two fired on the left-hand side of the train. I do not know where the men from the left-hand side came from. I hadn't seen them, but I saw the guns when they fired into the car that Mr. Ivey was in, and I saw Mr. Ivey's head when it fell; it fell right against the side I was on; I saw the blood running down on the side of the track. There were about twelve men in the crowd I saw."

Richard Wright (colored), resident of Sumter County, testifies in relation to the killing of W. P. Billings as follows:

"On Saturday I was going from where I lived up to Ramsey's Station to a dinner. I started on Friday evening, and remained at Mrs. Brownrigg's place with a colored man named Andrew Brownrigg. Saturday morning, I went on toward Ramsey's Station and took my time. It was pretty late in the evening when I reached there. It was about twelve or thirteen miles from Mrs. Brownrigg's. When I got within a mile and a half or two miles of the station I met an old colored man named Nelson Doyle, who told me that he was looking for work. I told him I lived at Livingston Station and might help him get some work, and turned back. We were going home when, about one hundred yards off, we saw Mr. Billings coming. I knew him by the horse he was riding; it was my father's horse. I told the old colored man that Mr. Billings was a prominent man,— a big man,—and he said that if he was we would see him at the speaking-place. Just about the time that we got within fifty or sixty yards of Mr. Billings out stepped

Mr. Steve Renfrew, and just as Mr. Billings got up near him he drew a big pistol, and says, 'Hello, God damn you!' Mr. Billings never seemed to stop, and Renfrew fired. As he fired there were five or six more men who rose up with their guns, and all fired and shot him right down, and horse and all fell."

The election was a complete victory for the Democratic Party. In spite of intimidation and assassination the Republicans went to the polls and did their duty as best they could; but the decree had gone forth that Alabama must be carried for the Democracy, and nothing was left undone to accomplish that end. They elected the governor, the legislature, and six out of eight members of Congress.

The revolution was a success. It was now settled that Republican majorities could be overcome by violence and fraud. Majorities were no longer necessary to success. If a few thousand votes were lacking, all that was required was to prevent as many Republicans as possible from voting by the free use of the pistol and shotgun, invite Democrats from neighboring States to come over and vote the ticket, and then when the polls are closed make sure that the ballots are *properly* counted. There is nothing like having the right men to count the votes.

The most important point gained by the Democrats by the election in Alabama, however, was that Republicans in Congress and throughout the country, although satisfied that the election had been carried by violence, were indisposed to enter upon the work of correcting the evil, and therefore acquiesced in the result.

CHAPTER XV.

STATEMENTS OF ARMY OFFICERS CONCERNING THE CONDITION OF THE SOUTH SINCE THE REBELLION.

Statement of General P. H. Sheridan on Affairs in Texas in 1866—General D. E. Sickles on South Carolina in 1866—General W. D. Whipple on Mississippi, Alabama, and Georgia in 1866—General George H. Thomas on Kentucky and Tennessee in 1867—General John Pope on the Reconstruction Measures of Congress in 1867—General J. J. Reynolds on Affairs in Texas in 1867—General A. H. Terry on Georgia in 1869—General Grant's Report on the Riot at Memphis, Tenn.—Paymaster-General Rochester on Affairs in Alabama in 1874—Lieutenant-General Sheridan on Affairs in Louisiana in 1875.

GENERAL SHERIDAN, commanding Department of the Gulf, reports, under date of November 14, 1866: "My own opinion is that the trial of a white man for the murder of a freedman in Texas would be a farce; and in making this statement I make it because truth compels me, and for no other reason."

General D. E. Sickles, commanding Department of the South, reports under date of October 30, 1866, that "in some parts of Barnwell, Edgefield, Newberry, Chester, Laurens, and Richland counties in South Carolina, a freedman has little security for life, limb, or property, apart from the presence and protection of a garrison of United States troops. There are other districts in the western part of South Carolina where the same insecurity exists. Amos Wesley, a colored barber of Newberry, was killed by a party of guerillas. Some of the murderers were known to the civil authorities, but no arrests were made.

Mr. Biglow, teacher of a colored school at Aiken, was driven away under threats never to return on pain of death. Instances of the most reprehensible neglect to arrest and prosecute notorious malefactors and outlaws are frequent. Inquests in case of homicide, especially if the victim be a negro, seldom result in a verdict which points out the guilty. In an instance that occurred in Beaufort District the perpetrators of the homicide were on the coroner's jury, and joined in the verdict that the victims came to their death by means to the jury unknown. Such was also the verdict in the Wesley case, at Newberry, although the murderers were recognized on the spot and were well known to the neighborhood."

Brevet Major-General W. D. Whipple, Assistant Adjutant-General, Department of the Cumberland, reporting to Major-General George H. Thomas, commanding, the results of a tour through the States of Mississippi, Alabama, and Georgia, in the latter part of November, 1866, speaking of the necessity for keeping troops in the late insurrectionary States, says that "the bitter rebel animus of the people fully warrants it; for I found everywhere on my route, in hotels and railroad cars, the general theme of conversation to be the hated Yankee and anything representing loyalty to the Union, and the bitter state of feeling on the part of the more ignorant is fanned into a continual glow by newspaper writers. Union men were murdered in their beds in cold blood, or driven off their farms. Soldiers and Government employees were assaulted or shot at by unknown persons, and no redress could be obtained from the civil authorities. At Rome, Ga., the rebels hoisted a rebel flag."

General George H. Thomas, commanding Department of the Cumberland, in his report, dated September 30, 1867, says in regard to the administration of justice in

Kentucky and Tennessee, that "if a white man commits an outrage against the negro redress is difficult and sometimes impossible to obtain; but when the reverse complaint comes into court the utmost zeal and energy is displayed in bringing the negro offender to justice, and the efforts of the civil authorities are then worthy of the highest admiration. Murders, outrages, and robberies of all kinds existed in the country districts of Tennessee, and those who had not remained consistently disloyal to the Government were oppressed by petty law officers. Bands of 'regulators' in Kentucky scour the country, murdering and robbing."

Major-General Pope, commanding Third Military District, comprising Georgia, Alabama, and Florida, in a report to General Grant, dated July 24, 1867, relative to the enforcement of the Reconstruction acts of Congress, with which he was charged, makes the following remarks, which, in the light of subsequent events, seem almost equally sagacious and prophetic: "It is not necessary to say that, however we restrain the opposition party now, the moment reconstruction is accomplished this party will regain its activity; and we ought to know in advance whether it possesses the power to undo what we thought we had done. I do not mean to intimate that it would be possible to re-establish slavery; perhaps it would not even be practicable to take from the freedmen the right of suffrage, though this latter is doubtful. These politicians are wily and sagacious. *They will make no laws which are not equal on their face to all men. It is in the execution of these laws, which seem to bear equally on all, that wrong will be done, and a condition of things produced which bears no resemblance to free government except in name.* Social exclusion, withdrawal of business relations, open exhibitions of hostility, if not indeed actual hostile acts, interruption of or interference with the freedmen's and other schools maintained by charitable contributions from the North—these will be the weapons used against Union men and the colored race. Acts of wrong and violence will meet no sufficient redress, if indeed any redress at all, in the courts. There are acts which cannot be reached by the General Government, and yet which quietly and silently render justice impossible, and establish discrimination against classes or color odious and unbearable."

Brevet Major-General J. J. Reynolds, commanding Fifth Military District (State of Texas), under date of November 4, 1868, reports as follows: " Armed organizations, generally known as ' Ku Klux Klans,' exist, independently or in concert with other armed bands, in many parts of Texas, but are most numerous, bold, and aggressive east of Trinity River.

" The precise objects of the organizations cannot be readily explained, but seems, in this State, to be to disarm, rob, and in many cases murder Union men and negroes, and as occasion may offer, murder United States officers and soldiers; also to intimidate every one who knows anything of the organization but who will not join it. The civil law east of the Trinity River is almost a dead letter. In some counties the civil officers are all, or a portion of them, members of the Klan. In other counties where the civil officers will not join the Klan, or some other armed band, they have been compelled to leave their counties. Examples are Van Zandt, Smith, and Marion counties (the county-seat of the latter is Jefferson). In many counties where the county officers have not been driven off their influence is scarcely felt. What political end, if any, is aimed at by these bands, I cannot say; but they attend in large bodies the political meetings (barbecues) which have been and are still being held in various parts of the State under the auspices of the Democratic clubs of the different counties. The speakers encourage their attendance, and in several counties men have been indicated by name from the speakers' stand as those selected for murder. The men thus pointed out have no course left them but to leave their homes or be murdered on the first convenient opportunity. The murder of negroes is so common as to render it impossible to keep an accurate account of them.

"Many of the members of these bands of outlaws are transient persons in the State; the absence of railroads and telegraphs, and great length of time required to communicate between remote points, facilitating their devilish purposes. These organizations are evidently countenanced, or at least not discouraged, by a majority of the white people in the counties where the bands are most numerous. They could not otherwise exist. They cannot be punished by the civil courts, until some examples by military commissions show that men can be punished in Texas for murder and kindred crimes. Perpetrators of such crimes have not heretefore, except in very rare instances, been punished in this State at all.

"Free speech and a free press, as the terms are generally understood in other States, have never existed in Texas. In fact, the citizens of other States cannot appreciate the condition of affairs in Texas without actually experiencing it. The official reports of lawlessness and crime, so far from being exaggerated, do not tell the whole truth.'

Brevet Major-General A. H. Terry, commanding Department of the South, reports, under date of August 14, 1869, concerning the state of affairs in Georgia, as follows: "In many parts of the State there is practically no government. The worst of crimes are committed, and no attempt is made to punish those who commit them. Murders have been and are frequent; the abuse in various ways of the blacks is too common to excite notice. There can be no doubt of the existence of numerous insurrectionary organizations known as 'Ku Klux Klans,' who, shielded by their disguise, by the secrecy of their movements, and by the terror which they inspire, perpetrate crime with impunity. There is great reason to believe that in some cases local magistrates are in sympathy with members of these organizations. In many places they are overawed by them, and dare not attempt to punish them. To punish such offenders by civil proceedings would be a difficult task, even were magistrates in all cases disposed and had they the courage to do their duty, for the same influences that govern them equally affect juries and witnesses. A conversation which I have had with a wealthy planter, a gentleman of intelligence and education, and a political opponent of the present National Administration, will illustrate this difficulty. While deploring the lamentable condition of affairs in the county in which he lives, he frankly admitted to me that were the most worthless vagabond in the county to be charged with a crime against the person of a Republican or a negro, neither he nor any other person of property within the county would dare to refuse to give bail for the offender, nor would they dare to testify against him, whatever might be their knowledge of his guilt.

"The same difficulties which beset the prosecution of criminals are encountered by negroes who seek redress for civil injuries in the local courts. Magistrates dare not do their duty toward them, and instances are not wanting where it has even been beyond the power of a magistrate to protect a negro plaintiff from violence in his own presence while engaged in the trial of his case."

Lieutenant-General Grant transmits (July 9, 1866) the report of the commission appointed to investigate the causes and extent of the riot in Memphis, Tenn., in May, 1866, from which it appears that on May 1 (Tuesday) the first collision of any importance occurred, arising from an arrest made by the police of some disorderly negroes. " Here," General Grant says, "judging from the testimony and the relative number of whites and negroes killed, the outbreak on the part of the negroes ceased; but this massacre commenced, and until the end of Wednesday night there was a scene of murder, arson, rape, and robbery in which the victims were all helpless and unresisting negroes, stamping lasting disgrace upon the civil authorities that permitted them.

"The testimony shows that *two* whites were killed and *two* wounded, while *forty* of the blacks were killed and *fifty-four* wounded."

Major Rochester, Paymaster U. S. A. (now Paymaster-General), giving an account of affairs in Sumter County, Ala., under date of September 22, 1874, states that there appears to be a determination on the part of the whites to intimidate the negroes to such a degree that they will not dare to vote at the coming election; states at present a large number of negroes are in a swamp near Belmont, where they are not easily approached. Numbers of them have been killed, and they in defending themselves have shot several white men. Nothing is said about killing black men, but when a white man is injured the circumstances are magnified, and "another negro outrage" is heralded far and wide. The colored mail agent was killed because in a political speech he denounced the murderers of Billings (a white

Republican). Armed white men, mounted and on foot, are constantly passing to and fro, and the blacks have been so thoroughly frightened that they will not dare to vote at the coming election.

Lieutenant-General Sheridan reports to the Secretary of War, under date of January 10, 1875, from New Orleans, La., as follows: "Since the year 1866 nearly 3500 persons, a great majority of whom were colored men, have been killed and wounded in this State. In 1868 the official record shows that 1884 were killed and .wounded. From 1868 to the present time no official investigation has been made, and the civil authorities, in all but a few cases, have been unable to arrest, convict, and punish perpetrators. Consequently there are no correct records to be consulted for information. There is ample evidence, however, to show that more than 1200 persons have been killed and wounded during the time on account of their political sentiments. Frightful massacres have occurred in the parishes of Bossier, Caddo, Catahoula, Saint Bernard, Saint Landry, Grant, and Orleans. The general character of the massacres in the above-named parishes is so well known that it is unnecessary to describe them. Human life in this State is held so cheaply, that when men are killed on account of political opinions the murderers are regarded rather as heroes than as criminals in the localities where they reside, and by the White League and their supporters."

CHAPTER XVI.

HOW MISSISSIPPI WAS REVOLUTIONIZED IN 1875.

Population of Mississippi—Proportion of Colored and White Voters—
General Political Condition of the State—The Democratic Leaders
resolve to follow the Example of Alabama—Speech of Colonel Lamar—Violent Tone of the Press—The Administration of the State
and County Governments especially Attacked—More Democratic
Officers Defaulters than Republican—Warlike Preparations for
the Election—False Rumors of a Negro Rising Circulated—Organization of Democratic Military Companies under the Pretext of Self-
protection—Real Object to Intimidate Colored Voters and Control
the Election—First Outbreak of Democratic Violence at Yazoo City
—Lawless Condition of Affairs in Yazoo County—Captain Henry
M. Dixon's Company Hangs a Member of the Legislature—Violent
Opposition to Governor Ames's Proposition to Raise a Militia to
Stop these Outrages—General Plan to Break Up Republican Meet-
ings—The Election Investigated by a Committee of the U. S. Senate
—Report of the Investigating Committee—The Election in Madison
County—In Claiborne County—Murder at Clinton, in Hinds County
—Election in Lowndes County—Testimony of Robert Gleed—Tes-
timony of W. F. Connell—How "old Monroe County" gave a Thou-
sand Democratic Majority—Testimony of J. W. Lee, Sheriff of the
County and an ex-Confederate Soldier—Fears of the Interference of
Federal Soldiers—No U. S. Troops used, but the Election con-
trolled by Detachments of the Confederate Army—General Results
—Colonel Lamar Elected to the U. S. Senate, and Governor Ames
Forced to Resign—The Usurpation Complete.

THE State of Mississippi, according to the census of
1880, contained a population of 1,131,597.

Of these 479,398 are white, and 650,291 are black.
Excess of blacks, 170,893. The number of male black
persons over the age of twenty-one years was 130,278,

while the number of white persons over that age was 108,254; excess of black persons of voting age, 22,024.

The State is divided into seventy-four counties, thirty-four of which have a majority of white persons, and forty contain a majority of colored persons.

The counties bordering on the Mississippi River, those lying in the Yazoo River basin, and those along and near Pearl and Tombigbee Rivers, contain a large excess of colored population. The lands in these counties are very rich, and well suited to the growth of cotton. In slavery times extensive plantations were established there. When freedom and the ballot were conferred upon the negroes the white people found themselves in a minority.

To illustrate this difference in the white and negro population, it may be stated that Bolivar County, on the Mississippi River, has a colored population of 15,958, and a white population of 2694; Lowndes, on the Tombigbee, has a colored population of 22,656, and a white population of 5588; Hinds, on Pearl River, has a black population of 32,279, and a white population of 11,675; and Yazoo County, on the Yazoo River, has a colored population of 25,342, and a white population of 8498.

The colored voters of the State were nearly all Republicans; probably not 500 colored men adhered to the Democratic Party. There was also a considerable number of white men all over the State who belonged to the Republican Party. Many of these were men of education and influence, and some were the owners of large estates.

The Democratic Party contained the great majority of the men who tried to carry Mississippi out of the Union. Many of the old leaders were still there. The Democrats owned a very large proportion of the land and other property of the State. A large number of them were trained soldiers, having served in the Confederate army.

It is safe to say that there was not a Democrat in Mississippi who was in favor of negro suffrage. They believed in the right of white men—that is to say, white Democrats—to rule that State, and they determined to make the effort to overthrow the supremacy of the Republican Party.

The Congressional elections of 1874 had resulted in giving the Democratic Party a majority in the U. S. House of Representatives. This fact encouraged their leaders to believe that they would be able to revolutionize the State without the interference of U. S. troops.

The result in Alabama at the election of the previous year was another source of encouragement. There were certain counties in the State which were Democratic. They of course would be able to take care of themselves. It was in Republican counties where the active campaign work of the Democratic Party must be performed.

The shot-gun and revolver had proved such weighty arguments in the campaign in Alabama the previous year, and the Democracy had achieved such satisfactory results by that election, that the leaders in Mississippi determined to snatch that State from the grasp of the Republican majority. It is true that the Republican majority overcome in Alabama was less than 11,000, and that in Mississippi was almost 35,000 in an aggregate vote of 130,000, yet the Democrats were not to be deterred by so trivial a circumstance as that. The plan of operations having been decided upon, it became simply a question of organization.

The tone of the press of the State and the means used to inflame the people by leading orators may be judged by the following examples:

EXTRACTS FROM MISSISSIPPI DEMOCRATIC JOURNALS.

The *Vicksburg Herald* reports of L. Q. C. Lamar, at Aberdeen, Miss., thus:

"In his speech at Aberdeen last Saturday Colonel Lamar made an eloquent speech. A better Democratic speech we do not care to listen to, and in manly and ringing tones he declared that the contest involved the 'supremacy of the unconquered and unconquerable Saxon race.' We were glad to hear this bold and manly avowal, and it was greeted with deafening plaudits. We have never seen men more terribly in earnest, and the Democratic white-line speech made to them by Colonel Lamar aroused them to white heat."

Westville (Miss.) *News:* "Vote the negro down or knock him down. Does not the very thought boil the blood in every vein? Will you still contend that we must not have a white-man's party? Away with such false doctrines; we must and will have a white-man's party. We have tried policy long enough. We must organize on the color-line, disregarding minor considerations.

"The white man's party is the only salvation for the State. Show the negro his place and make him keep it. If we cannot vote him down, we can knock him down, and the result will be the same. Either the white man or the negro will rule this country; they cannot both do it, and it is for the white men to say who the ruler shall be. Let us have a white man's party to rule a white man's country, and do it like white men."

Okolona Southern States: "The African race can no more be absorbed and transmogrified into dignified, intelligent statesmen and responsible, self-governing citizens than the American Indians could be brought and trained to lay aside the tomahawk and live with us in peace, under an administration which promises equal rights, civil and political, to all men. Consequently we may expect these outbreaks."

Newton Democrat: "Mr. Potter and ex-Governor Brown of Hinds think the negro can be reasoned into Democracy, and they have been thinking so ever since the war; but for our part we would as soon reason with a shoal of crocodiles or a drove of Kentucky mules. And so might they, for all the convictions they have produced in the counties of Hinds and Copiah."

THE ALABAMA POLICY TRANSFERRED TO MISSISSIPPI.

From the *Meridian Mercury* report of a speech made by Colonel Taylor of Alabama, telling how the State was carried in 1874, and urging the same line of policy in Mississippi:

"At first they tried the policy of conciliation. He said he did not believe they carried one single negro vote by it. Little by little they came to try the color-line in municipal elections, and then county elections here and there, and finding it to succeed, they at last made the State canvass upon it and redeemed the State."

Yazoo Democrat: "Let unanimity of sentiment pervade the minds of men. Let invincible determination be depicted upon every countenance. Send forth from our deliberate assembly of the eighteenth the soul-stirring announcement that Mississippians shall rule Mississippi though the heavens fall. Then will woe, irretrievable woe, betide the Radical tatterdemalions. Hit them hip and thigh, everywhere, and at all times."

"CARRY THE ELECTION PEACEABLY IF WE CAN, FORCIBLY
IF WE MUST."

Jackson Clarion: "Do not submit to any of the old
'back-to-breast' arrangement—a long line of voters in
which you have hitherto had to take the rear. If that
game is tried again, break the line. After you have carried the day at the polls, submit to no throwing out of
votes or of boxes. Put your votes in the boxes, and see
that they are counted and returned properly afterward.
. . . *No difference how bold the fraud, how manifest it
may be, hang the registrar that proposes to throw out a Democratic vote or a Democratic box.*"

The press and orators of the Democratic Party also
made a violent attack upon all the officers in the State
who were Republicans, from Governor down, denouncing them as a pack of corruptionists and incompetents,
totally unworthy to fill any of the official positions in
the State. It was charged that the State was being
bankrupted by extravagance, and that the county governments were used as a means of extorting unnecessary
and very burdensome taxes from the people. Every improper or dishonest act of Republican officials was instantly taken up and full details heralded throughout
the State, while similar acts of Democratic officers
passed unnoticed. Governor Ames stated under oath
before an investigating committee of Congress, that there
were more Democratic officers who were defaulters to
the State than Republican officials, and the truth of this
statement went unchallenged. He also showed by the
official figures that the State debt was not more than
half a million dollars, and that the annual appropriations

for the support of the State Government had not been materially increased during his administration.

In regard to the affairs of the counties, it was shown that with very few exceptions their business was conducted with integrity; that the expenditures were made for rebuilding court-houses and bridges destroyed during the civil war, and the erection of schoolhouses for public schools, the system of which did not exist in former times. It also appeared that many of the officers elected by the people were native white citizens, and a few were ex-Union soldiers who had settled in Mississippi after the war was over.

These things, however, were of no weight with Democrats; they were determined to carry the election at all hazards, and to drive the Republican Party from power. In some portions of the State they commenced organizing for this purpose immediately after the Alabama election of 1874.

Breech-loading muskets with bayonets, and pistols of the most approved pattern, were purchased and brought into the State by Democrats in great numbers, with large quantities of fixed ammunition.

Rumors were constantly circulated that the negroes were gathering and organizing for the purpose of attacking and killing Democrats and burning their towns.

Military companies were organized by the Democrats in almost every county in the State, for the avowed purpose of self-protection, but for the real purpose, as it afterward turned out, of breaking up Republican meetings, raiding Republican counties, killing Republican leaders, and thereby intimidating the body of Republican voters.

The charge that colored Republicans in Republican counties wanted a collision with white Democrats is too preposterous to receive any consideration at this time. The whole history of the negro race in this country shows conclusively that they almost invariably will decline combat with white men when they can do so with safety. Where the colored men had a large majority in a county there was no occasion for them to incite a contest with the whites. All they required to carry the election was an opportunity to cast their ballots and have them properly counted.

If they wished to increase their power and influence in the State by intimidating white men, they must go into Democratic districts and organize and carry them. Mr. Lamar was a candidate for Congress; his district was Democratic by a majority much smaller than in some of the Republican districts; and yet the colored Republicans did not undertake to carry his district: he was left to make the race for Congress without a competitor, and there were no difficulties and collisions in his district. Not so in the Republican districts, no difference how great the majorities. There, there was turmoil and confusion.

In some of the counties the Democrats had as many as eight or ten military companies, armed to the teeth. When Republicans held public meetings they were attended by Democrats under arms. The first serious disturbance occurred at Yazoo City on the night of the first day of September, at a Republican meeting in the court-house, which was being addressed by the sheriff of the county, who was a candidate for re-election. There were a number of Democrats present, who came obviously for the purpose of breaking up the meeting. Taking offence at something that was said by the speaker, they opened fire with pistols and put out the lights. The deputy-sheriff was killed; the meeting was instantly broken up, and the Republicans sought safety in flight. The sheriff and other officers were driven from the county, and the court-house and county government were seized by the Democrats. A reign of terror was inaugurated against Republicans; a company numbering twenty-five men, under the command of Captain Henry M. Dixon, patrolled the county (while other strong companies were held in reserve, ready to move when needed), and killed a number of persons by hanging, shooting, and drowning. Among those who were hung was a member of the Legislature named Patterson. Just before he was killed he handed $1400 to Captain Dixon with the request that it be remitted to his two sisters, who were attending school in the State of Ohio; instead of this being done, the money was used as part of the Democratic campaign fund to carry the county.

The lawless condition of Yazoo County having been brought to the attention of Governor Ames, he undertook to raise two companies of militia to reinstate the sheriff, who had fled to the capital of the State. This proposition of the Governor met violent opposition on the part of the Democrats, and they marched with several companies of well-armed men under the command of competent officers to the railroad station, some miles from Yazoo City, at which the State militia were expected to arrive. The newspaper accounts of this affair show that Governor Ames's militia would have fared badly at the hands of this volunteer force, which had assembled in overwhelming numbers, and with a determination to put the Governor's forces to rout, if they had put in an appearance. Governor Ames, however, did not send the militia forward, and so there was no blood shed on this occasion. But the proposition on the part of Governor Ames to exercise a power conferred upon him by law to organize these companies of militia was a signal for the Democracy throughout the State to call their volunteer companies to arms. Mississippi at once became the seat of a revolutionary movement, which had for its object the subversion and overthrow of the State government then lawfully existing. The excitement ran high in all parts of the State. The Republican counties became the theatre of the active military operations of the Democratic Party. The most stout-hearted white Republicans were appalled at the danger that threatened them and their colored allies. The breaking up of Republican meetings became the order of the day. The *Raymond Gazette*, in a very vindictive editorial, insisted that every Republican meeting must be attended by a Democratic committee of at least ten persons, to observe the line of discussion, and to at once nail any statement deemed by them to be untrue. The inevitable result of such a proceeding was to compel the Republicans either to abandon their meetings, or to hold them subject to the peril of having them broken up by force.

These were the conditions under which the canvass was conducted and the election held.

The outrageous conduct of the Democracy attracted universal attention, and was brought to the notice of Congress at its ensuing session. The Senate appointed a Committee of Investigation, which was composed of the following-named Senators: Geo. S. Boutwell, of Massachusetts; Angus Cameron, of Wisconsin; Samuel J. R. McMillan, of Minnesota; Thos. F. Bayard, of Delaware; Joseph E. McDonald, of Indiana.

This committee examined witnesses in the State of Mississippi and in the city of Washington, and made a report to the Senate, which with evidence is contained in two volumes of nearly 2000 pages.

The following extracts are taken from the report of the committee, and the facts recited herein are detailed in the testimony taken by it:

EXTRACTS FROM THE REPORT OF THE INVESTIGATING COM-
MITTEE ON THE MISSISSIPPI ELECTION OF 1875.

It has been alleged that Governor Ames was an unfit person to hold the office to which he was elected in the year 1873, but, on the contrary, the committee find form the evidence, as well as from general report in Mississippi, that Governor Ames was not only not amenable to any just charge affecting his personal integrity, his character as a public officer, or his ability for the duties of chief magistrate of that State, but that his fitness in all these particulars was sustained by the testimony of those who were not in accord with him politically. The committee refer especially to the testimony of the Hon. J. A. P. Campbell, appointed by the existing government one of the Judges of the Supreme Court of the State of Mississippi.

It is also alleged in justification of the acts of intimidation, and of the crimes committed during the canvass and at the election, that Governor Ames had organized, or attempted to organize, a force termed the 'negro militia.' At the time of the riot at Clinton, on the 4th of September, 1875, which resulted in the death of at least thirty persons, there was no military organization in the State. The sum of $60,000 had been appropriated by the Legislature, at its preceding session, for the organization and support of a military force; and the event at Clinton, in connection with the fact of disturbances in other portions of the State, led Governor Ames to attempt its organization.

By the terms of the peace conference entered into by

General J. Z. George, the Chairman of the Democratic State Committee, and Governor Ames, on the 13th of October, 1875, the attempt to organize the militia was abandoned, General George on his part agreeing to secure a peaceful election and the full and free enjoyment of the elective franchise by every citizen. The stipulation on the part of the Governor was faithfully kept, but the promise made by General George was systematically disregarded by the Democrats in the larger portion of the State.

The outrages perpetrated by the white people in the canvass and on the day of election find no justification whatever in the acts or the policy of Governor Ames concerning the State militia.

The effort on his part to organize the militia for the preservation of the public peace seems to the committee to have been not only lawful, but proper; and the course of the Democrats in organizing and arming themselves to resist the Governor in his efforts to preserve the public peace was unlawful, and the proceedings should have been suppressed by the State authorities if possible, and, in case of a failure on their part, by the Government of the United States.

The constitution of the State provides that the militia shall consist of the able-bodied male citizens between the age of eighteen years and the age of forty-five years, and the Legislature provided for its organization by an act passed at its first session in the year 1870. It was the duty of the Governor to use the militia for the suppression of such riots as those of Vicksburg and Clinton; and this without regard to the question whether the white or the black race was most responsible therefor.

In the opinion of the committee, the riot at Clinton

was in harmony with the policy previously adopted by Democrats in that vicinity, and designed to intimidate and paralyze the Republican Party.

Nor do these outrages find any excuse in the statement of a number of witnesses, that the negroes were organizing or threatened or contemplated organizing themselves into military bands for the destruction of the white race. The evidence shows conclusively that there was not only no such organizations, but that the negroes were not armed generally; that those who had arms were furnished with inferior and second-hand weapons, and that their leaders, both religious and political, had discountenanced a resort to force. Many rumors were current among the whites that the negroes were arming and massing in large bodies, but in all cases these rumors had no basis.

In a sentence, it may be asserted that all the statements made that there was any justifiable cause for the recent proceedings in Mississippi are without foundation.

On the other hand, it is to be said, speaking generally, that a controlling part, and as we think a majority, of the Democratic voters of the State were engaged in a systematic effort to carry the election, and this with a purpose to resort to all means within their power, including, on the part of some of them, the murder of prominent persons in the Republican Party, both white and black.

There was a minority—how large the committee are unable to say—who were opposed to the outrages which by this report are proved to have taken place.

This minority, however, is for the time overawed, and as powerless to resist the course of events as are the members of the Republican Party. Under more favorable circumstances they may be able to co-operate with the friends of order, and redeem the State from the control of the Revolutionary element.

(1) The committee find that the young men of the State, especially those who reached manhood during the war and who have arrived at that condition since the war, constitute the nucleus and the main force of the dangerous element. As far as the testimony taken by the committee throws any light upon the subject, it tends, however, to establish the fact that the Democratic organizations, both in the counties and in the State, encouraged the young men in their course, accepted the political advantages of their conduct, and are in a large degree responsible for the criminal results.

(3) Democratic clubs were organized in all parts of the State, and the able-bodied members were also organized generally into military companies and furnished with the best arms that could be procured in the country. The fact of their existence was no secret, although persons not in sympathy with the movement were excluded from membership. Indeed, their object was more fully attained by public declarations of their organization in connection with the intention, everywhere expressed, that it was their purpose to carry the election at all hazards. In many places these organizations possessed one or more pieces of artillery. These pieces of artillery were carried over the counties, and discharged upon the roads in the neighborhood of Republican meetings and at meetings held by the Democrats. For many weeks before the election, members of this military organization traversed the various counties, menacing the voters, and discharging their guns by night as well as by day. This statement is sustained by the testimony of Captain W. A. Montgomery,

Captain E. O. Sykes, J. D. Vertner, leading Democrats in their respective counties, as well as by the testimony of a large number of trustworthy Republicans.

(4) It appears from the testimony that for some time previous to the election it was impossible, in a large number of the counties, to hold Republican meetings. In the Republican counties of Warren, Hinds, Lowndes, Monroe, Copiah, and Holmes, meetings of the Republicans were disturbed or broken up, and all attempts to engage in public discussion were abandoned by the Republicans many weeks before the election.

(5) The riots at Vicksburg on the 5th of July and at Clinton on the 4th of September were the results of a special purpose on the part of the Democrats to break up the meetings of the Republicans, to destroy the leaders, and to inaugurate an era of terror, not only in those counties, but throughout the State, which would deter Republicans, and particularly the negroes, from organizing or attending meetings, and especially deter them from the free exercise of the right to vote on the day of election. The results sought for were in a large degree attained.

(6) Following the riot at Clinton, the country for the next two days was scoured by detachments from these Democratic military organizations over a circuit of many miles, and a large number of unoffending persons were killed. The number has never been ascertained correctly, but it may be estimated fairly as between thirty and 'fifty.

Captain William A. Montgomery, a leading Democrat, and a commander of five military companies, with the designation in rank of major of battalion, testified that in some of the counties there was no military organization; that in those counties the Democrats did not try to carry the election. This appears to have been true of the two counties named ; but since the election —namely, in December and May, 1876—great outrages, attended with violence and murder, have been perpetrated, and evidently with the design of overawing the colored voters and preparing them to submit to a Democratic victory in the coming election.

The attention of the Senate is directed to the testimony concerning the events in Issaquena County, which took place in December last. A Colonel Ball, an officer in the Confederate service during the war, who at the time of the outrage was officiating as a clergyman, took command of a body of armed and mounted men, Sunday morning, December 5, and traversed the country below Rolling Ford during the day; and that night the men of his command took from their homes at least seven unoffending negroes and shot them in cold blood. Within the next two days five other leading negroes were summoned to Rolling Ford, and there compelled to sign a statement by which they became responsible for the good conduct of all the negroes in their vicinity, with the exception of fourteen, who in fact by that stipulation were made outlaws, and as a consequence fled from their homes and their families and abandoned their property. (This statement may be found in the testimony of W. D. Brown.) Reference is made to the testimony of W. D. Brown and William S. Farrish, both Democrats, and participators in the outrages, although they did not admit that they had personal knowledge of the killing of either of the seven men who were massacred on the night of the 5th of December.

(7) The committee find, especially from the testimony of Captain Montgomery, supported by numerous facts stated by other witnesses, that the military organi-

zation extended to most of the counties in the State where the Republicans were in the majority; that it embraced a proportion not much less than one half the white voters, and that in the respective counties the men could be summoned by signals given by firing cannons or anvils; and that probably in less than a week the entire force of the State could be brought out under arms.

(8) The committee find that in several of the counties the Republicans leaders were so overawed and intimidated, both white and black, that they were compelled to withdraw from the canvass those who had been nominated, and to substitute others who had been named by the Democratic leaders; and that finally they were compelled to vote for the ticket so nominated, under threats that their lives would be taken if they did not do it. This was noticeably the case in Warren County, where the Democratic nomination of one Flanigan for sheriff was ratified at the Republican county convention held in Vicksburg, the members acting under threats that if it were not done they should not leave the building alive. Similar proceedings occurred in other counties.

(9) The committee find that the candidates in some instances were compelled, by persecution or through fear of bodily harm, to withdraw their names from the ticket, and even to unite themselves ostensibly with the Democratic Party. J. W. Caradine, a colored candidate of Clay County, was compelled to withdraw his name from the Republican ticket and to make speeches in behalf of the Democratic candidates and policy. An extract from his testimony is herewith given as follows: "They told me that I would have to go around and make some speeches for them; that I had risen up a

great element or some kind of feeling in the colored men that they never could get out of them for the next ten years to come with the speeches I had made; and that I had to go around and make some speeches in behalf of them in some way, or else I might have some trouble. They told me if I could do that I could demand some respect among them, and have no further trouble with them."

"Q. What did they say would be the consequence if you did not go with them and make speeches?

"A. They did not say if I did not do it what would be done, as I remember; but they came to my house and fotched a buggy for me, and told me I had to go with them to make speeches for them. And they said, 'You know what has been said and what has been done; you have got to go along if you don't want any further trouble.' I then got in and went along with them, and they did not really appreciate my speeches at length; but I went along with them and made three speeches; and they had some fault to find with my speeches at last, but I have never had any trouble with them since."

(10) The committee find that on the day of the election, at several voting-places, armed men assembled, sometimes not organized, and in other cases organized; that they controlled the elections, intimidated Republican voters, and in fine deprived them of the opportunity of voting the Republican ticket.

The most notable instance of this form of outrage occurred at Aberdeen, the shire town of the county of Monroe. At half-past nine o'clock on the day of the election a cannon in charge of four or five cannoneers, and supported by ten or twelve men, a portion of the military company of that town, was trained upon the voting-place and kept in that position during the day while the street was traversed by a body of mounted armed men under the command of Captain E. O. Sykes. Captain Sykes testified that he did not know the men under his command, but admitted finally that they were probably from Alabama, and that they had come there upon the suggestion or the request of a Mr. Johnson, who was a member as well as also Captain Sykes of the Democratic committee of the county of Monroe.

Captain Sykes had also given orders that the fordways across the Tombigbee River, over which negroes from the east side having a right to vote at Aberdeen must pass, should be guarded by squads from the military company under his command.

During the night preceding the election the draw in the bridge crossing the river was turned, so that there was no passing from the east to the west of the Tombigbee River during the early part of the day of election.

As a matter of fact, the Republican voters who had assembled abandoned the polls between ten and eleven o'clock in the forenoon; and Captain J. W. Lee, the sheriff of the county and a leading Republican, a man who had served during the war in the Confederate army, abandoned the polls and took refuge in the jail, of which he was the custodian.

This statement in regard to Monroe County is set forth in detail by Captain Lee, and it is corroborated in all essential parts by Captain Sykes, a Democrat, and the principal actor in the events of the day. Similar outrages were perpetrated in Claiborne, Kemper, Amite, Copiah, and Clay counties.

(11) The gravity of these revolutionary proceedings is expressed in the single fact that the chairman of the Republican State Committee, General Warner, owes the preservation of his life on the day of election to the

intervention of General George, Chairman of the Democratic State Committee, as appears from a dispatch sent by General George to Messrs. Campbell and Calhoun, and a reply thereto, both of which are here given:

To Campbell and Calhoun, Canton, Miss.:

If Warner goes to Madison, see by all means that he is not hurt. We are nearly sure now, and are sure to win. Don't let us have any trouble of that sort on our hands. He will probably be at his store to-night.

(Signed)   J. Z. GEORGE.

CANTON, 2, 1875.

To General George:

Your telegram of last night saved A. Warner at Calhoun.

(Signed)   GART. A. JOHNSON.

The circumstances of this affair are given in the testimony of Chase. The testimony of General Warner gives a detailed account of his experience, showing that the fears of General Warner's friends were well founded, and that the intervention of General George was essential to his personal safety.

(12) The committee find in several cases, where intimidation and force did not result in securing a Democratic victory, that fraud was resorted to in conducting the election and in counting the votes. In Amite County the legally appointed inspectors of election, to whom in Mississippi the duty is assigned of receiving and counting the ballots, were compelled by intimidation to resign on the morning of election, in order to secure a fraudulent return. The inspector so forced to resign was a Democrat, a man of established character for probity at his precinct—Rose Hill.

"When the voting began," said General Hurst, an

eye-witness, "the Democratic club drew up in line, and demanded that Straum should not act as one of the inspectors of elections. They said, 'We don't want you, not because you are dishonest, but because you will not do what we want you to.' He said, 'If that is the case, I will go;' and they got a man by the name of Wat Haynes and appointed him inspector."

General Hurst, who was brigadier-general of the State militia in that county, thus explains what resulted :

"When it was time to close the polls, I asked one of the inspectors if he wanted a guard placed over the ballots, so that they would be unmolested while they were counting the votes. I thought that he was a very honest, high-minded man. He said, 'I am afraid to count these votes.' He had been notified by this party of Louisianians, and they told him what they were going to do with the box. Wat Haynes, when I told him I had concluded to place a guard around there that night, said, 'Don't you do it; I want to manipulate that box tonight. We want to carry this thing.' The party of Louisianians referred to were a company of outlaws, notorious in that district, whom the Democrats had invited to come into that precinct, and who fired at a crowd of colored citizens when they were in line waiting to deposit their votes. About seventy of them were thus driven into the woods."

Nor was this the only precinct at which armed invaders from adjoining States took conspicuous part in the election. It is testified to both by Republicans and Democrats that they came over from Alabama, and helped to swell the Democratic vote in the counties adjoining that State.

In Amite County the Republican sheriff, the superintendent of education, and other officers were driven into exile as soon as the polls were closed. Here the pretext that the officers were obnoxious to the people, or that the negroes and Nothern men monopolized the offices, is refuted by the facts that both Parker and Redmond, who were expelled, were offered the Democratic nomination for sheriff; that the Republican candidates for sheriff, circuit clerk, chancery clerk, treasurer, coroner, and three of the five supervisors were white men, leaving only the assessor and two supervisors to be colored, which, as Mr. Parker remarks, "as four fifths of the Republican voters were black, was the best that we could do." There were only three Northern men on the Republican ticket, and two of them had married Southern women; all the others were natives of the State.

(13) The evidence shows that the civil authorities have been unable to prevent the outrages set forth in this report, or to punish the offenders. This is true not only of the courts of the State, but also of the district courts of the United States, as appears from the report of the grand jury made at the term held in June last, when the evidence of the offences committed at the November election and during the canvass was laid before that body.

In support of this statement, reference is made to the testimony of J. W. Tucker and to the letter written by him to Colonel Frazee, as well as to the report made by the grand jury to the Hon. R. A. Hill, Judge of the District Court for the Northern District of Mississippi.

(14) The committee find that outrages of the nature set forth in this report were perpetrated in the counties of Alcorn, Amite, Chickasaw, Claiborne, Clay, Copiah, De Soto, Grenada, Hinds, Holmes, Kemper, Lee, Lowndes, Madison, Marshall, Monroe, Noxubee, Rankin,

Scott, Warren, Washington, and Yazoo, and that the Democratic victory in the State was due to the outrages so perpetrated.

(15) The committee find that if in the counties named there had been a free election Republican candidates would have been chosen, and the character of the Legislature so changed that there would have been 66 Republicans to 50 Democrats in the House, and 26 Republicans to 11 Democrats in the Senate; and that consequently the present Legislature of Mississippi is not a legal body, and that its acts are not entitled to recognition by the political department of the Government of the United States, although the President may in his discretion recognize it as a government *de facto* for the preservation of the public peace.

(16) Your committee find that the resignation of Governor Ames was effected by a body of men calling themselves the Legislature of the State of Mississippi, by measures unauthorized by law, and that he is of right the Governor of that State.

(17) The evidence shows, further, that the State of Mississippi is at present under the control of political organizations composed largely of armed men, whose common purpose is to deprive the negroes of the free exercise of the right of suffrage, and to establish and maintain the supremacy of the white-line Democracy, in violation alike of the constitution of their own State and of the Constitution of the United States.

The events which the committee were called to investigate by the order of the Senate constitute one of the darkest chapters in American history. Mississippi was a leading State in the War of the Rebellion, and an early and persistent advocate of those fatal political heresies in which the rebellion had its origin. To her, in as large degree as to any other State, may be charged justly the direful evils of the war; and when the war was ended the white inhabitants resisted those measures of equality which were essential to local and general peace and prosperity. They refused to accept the negro as their equal politically, and for ten years they have seized every fresh opportunity for a fresh denial of his rights. At last they have gained supremacy in the State by acts of violence, fraud, and murder, fraught with more than all the horrors of open war, without its honor, dignity, generosity, or justice.

By them the negro is not regarded as a citizen, and whenever he finds a friend and ally in his efforts to advance himself in political knowledge or intellectual culture, that friend and ally, whether a native of the State or an immigrant from the North, is treated as a public enemy. The evil consequences of this policy touch and paralyze every branch of industry and the movements of business in every channel.

Mississippi, with its fertile soil, immense natural resources, and favorable commercial position, is in fact more completely excluded from the influence of the civilization and capital of the more wealthy and advanced States of the Union than are the distant coasts of China and Japan. Men who possess capital are anxious to escape from a State in which freedom of opinion is not tolerated, where active participation in public affairs is punished often with social ostracism, always with business losses, and not infrequently, as the record shows, with exile and the abandonment of property through fear of death.

This tendency cannot be arrested by the unaided efforts of the peaceful, patriotic, and law-abiding citizens. There is a small body of native white persons who with heroic courage are maintaining the principles of justice and equality. There is also a small body of men from the North who with equal courage are endeavoring to save the State from anarchy and degradation. If left to themselves, the negroes would co-operate with these two classes.

But arrayed against them all are a majority of the white people who possess the larger part of the property; who uniformly command leisure, whether individually they possess property or not; who look with contempt upon the black race, and with hatred upon the white men who are their political allies; who are habituated to the use of arms in war and in peace; who in former times were accustomed to the exclusive enjoyment of political power, and who now consider themselves degraded by the elevation of the negro to the rank of equality in political affairs.

They have secured power by fraud and force, and if left to themselves they will by fraud and force retain it. Indeed, the memory of the bloody events of the campaign of 1875, with the knowledge that their opponents can command on the instant the presence of organized bodies of armed men at every polling-place, will deter the Republican Party from any general effort to regain the power wrested from them. These disorders exist also in the neighboring States, and the spirit and ideas which give rise to the disorders are even more general.

The power of the National Government will be invoked, and honor and duty will alike require its exercise. The Nation cannot witness with indifference the dominion of lawlessness and anarchy in a State, with their incidental evils and a knowledge of the inevitable consequences. It owes a duty to the citizens of the United States residing in Mississippi, and this duty it must perform. It has guaranteed to the State of Mississippi a republican form of government, and this guarantee must be made good.

The plan of the Democrats was to have such an array of military force in most of the large Republican counties as to create consternation amongst their opponents, and to add to this fear from day to day by threats, the breaking up of Republican meetings, and the occasional killing of leading Republicans, white and black. Prominent white Republicans were constantly being waited upon and directed or advised to leave the State to save their lives. Murders in one county would be used in another to excite the fears of Republicans. The military companies of one county would visit adjoining counties and aid in the work of intimidation and murder.

MADISON COUNTY.

In Madison County the Democrats expended $4000 in the purchase of breech-loading guns. A number of companies were organized and armed. The Republicans had a majority of about 1500 votes; but the peril of the leaders was so great that they finally held a conference with prominent Democrats, and agreed to withdraw half of their candidates for the Legislature and county offices, and substitute Democrats in their stead. The terms of the agreement and the reasons for making it were reduced to writing by a Mr. Jeffrey. One of the paragraphs in the agreement is as follows: "This arrangement was entered into by us solely in the interest of peace, to prevent scenes of riot and bloodshed which are taking place in other counties of this State."

Mr. E. S. Jeffrey, testifying in regard to this matter, stated that "about a week before the election there was a compromise effected at the suggestion of some leading Democrats, who thought that, as they expressed it, 'they could not keep the young men down,' and that they thought it best to have a compromise effected, to have a good feeling existing between both parties during the election. Some of them said that bloodshed could not be avoided, and it was under that state of feeling that the compromise was brought about."

He also stated that it was a general apprehension among the Republicans of that county that riot and bloodshed would result if the compromise was not entered into, and that the compromise would not have been entered into by the Republicans if it had not been for that apprehension, and that the Republicans had a majority of 1800 or 2000 in the county.

CLAIBORNE COUNTY.

In Claiborne County the Republicans held a public meeting and barbecue close to the town of Port Gibson; while the procession was marching through the town it was set upon by Democrats, and many were struck with sticks. After the procession reached the grounds and the meeting was called to order and speaking began, about two hundred and fifty or three hundred horsemen, and about one hundred and fifty or two hundred men on foot, armed with breech-loading muskets, Spencer rifles, and Smith & Wesson revolvers, marched to the meeting. These were all Democrats; their conduct was insulting and threatening; they were evidently determined to break up the meeting. One of their prominent leaders was appealed to for God's sake to help keep the peace, and to allow the Republicans the privilege which all American citizens have of making speeches.   He replied, "Well, I did not come here with a view of keeping the peace.   The time for keeping the peace is past.   I cannot keep the peace, and there is no use in talking about it.   I cannot do anything even if I had ever so much disposition to do so.   The best thing you can do now is to just disperse this meeting; it is the only way to prevent a row."

It becoming evident that the Democrats were determined that the meeting should not proceed, to avoid being attacked the Republicans broke up the meeting and went home.   That night the Democrats patrolled the town, and the next day (Sunday) parties of armed Democrats marched through the county, hunting leading Republicans.   This was continued during the next day, and on the following (Tuesday) morning the election was to be held.   The Republican candidate for assessor was induced to sign a card in which he declined to be a candidate.

During the election at Port Gibson the excitement ran high on the part of the Democrats; finally, the white Democrats opened fire with pistols upon colored voters, killing one and wounding six others.   The colored people broke and ran just as soon as the shooting commenced.   At this juncture a horn was blown, and the Democrats with their guns formed a line across the street, commanding the place where the election was held.

The colored people were advised by leading Republicans and Democrats that any further attempt to vote would probably cause a repetition of the shooting, and so a large number of them returned to their homes without voting.

At Grand Gulf, in the same county, on election-day, the Democrats attempted the intimidation of colored voters, but a large number of the negroes were armed, and this prevented a disturbance. Failing to overcome the will of the majority by intimidation, the Democrats stuffed the ballot-box, and although the Democratic inspector protested against the fraud, the ballots were counted.

At Bethel Precinct, after the polls were closed, the Democrats burst open the door of the room in which the votes were being counted, rushed in, put out the lights, knocked the clerk over, seized the ballot-box, carried it some distance from the polls, and burned the ballots.

At Patona, some days before the election, the Democrats dug a rifle-pit commanding the place where the election was to be held. On the day of election they appeared there armed, as they did at nearly every precinct in the county. By these means the Democrats carried the county by a large majority. After the election the Democrats held a jollification meeting; upon one of their banners they had inscribed, "If they contest, send for the Modocs." The "Modocs" were a Democratic club at Vicksburg.

HINDS COUNTY.

Jackson, the capital of Mississippi, is situated in Hinds County. The Democratic State Central Committee had its headquarters there, and directed and watched the course of the campaign throughout the State. The Republicans had an overwhelming majority in this county, and it was important for the success of the Democrats that it should be overcome. Military companies armed with guns and pistols were formed at the capital and other points in the county. On the 4th of September the Republicans had a large public meeting and barbecue at Clinton; a number of public speakers had been invited ; the attendance was large, and the people came in from different parts of the county in processions including women and children. The Republicans were well-behaved and orderly.

In compliance with the demands of the Democrats, the Republicans consented to a joint discussion, and Judge Johnson spoke for the Democrats without interruption. At the close of his speech Mr. Fisher, of Jackson, arose to speak on behalf of the Republicans. He commenced his speech by congratulating his audience upon the peaceful character of the meeting and the friendly intercourse of the two parties, and expressed the wish and hope that that state of things might continue. This remark was answered by one of the Democrats by saying, "It would be so if you would stop telling your damned lies."

This created considerable commotion; the Democrats were very demonstrative. One of them shot and killed a colored man; this resulted in a serious affray, in which pistols were used on both sides, and three white men and three or four negroes were killed.

Great preparations had been made for the meeting: a bountiful barbecue had been prepared; the meats had been cooked, and every arrangement had been made for the comfort of the audience. It was a good-tempered crowd, people having come there with their wives and children with the expectation of enjoying themselves.

The meeting was at once broken up, and the people dispersed and returned to their homes, apprehensions being felt that the Democratic military companies would turn out and attack the crowd. The indignation of the Democrats was so great at the resistance offered by the Republicans to the disturbance of their meeting that the next day Democratic companies patrolled the country round about Clinton and killed a number of negroes. The number was never definitely ascertained, the testimony of witnesses not agreeing upon this point, but enough is known to justify fixing the number killed at from thirty to fifty persons. Governor Ames was appealed to for protection. He issued a proclamation requiring all unauthorized military companies to disband. No attention whatever was given to this proclamation, the Democrats maintaining their military organizations and continuing their work of intimidation. Republicans, white and black, were killed in various parts of the county. Defenceless and unoffending citizens were ruthlessly murdered without excuse or provocation. A reign of terror prevailed against Republicans. The Democratic leaders at Jackson did not attempt to prevent these outrageous proceedings. Their motto was that the election must be carried at all hazards. The election came off, and a Republican majority of 2500 was converted into a Democratic majority of 1500.

LOWNDES COUNTY.

The usual Republican majority in Lowndes County was from two thousand to twenty-five hundred prior to the election of 1875. The Democrats decided, however, to carry the county, not through the means of public discussion, but by the regular Democratic methods of that year—intimidation, murder, and fraud; and for this purpose strong military companies were organized in all parts of the county, and well armed with guns and pistols.

Robert Gleed, testifying in regard to the intimidation, stated:

"You can imagine yourself—a whole race of people,

twenty or thirty thousand, lying out of doors for a month every night, men, women, and children—you can imagine yourself the state of affairs there. Men, women, and children just went right out into the woods, and felt that they were only safe in that way."

On the day before the election a body of armed Democrats from Alabama rode into the town of Columbus. These men were employed as policemen, and the city council paid their expenses for being present on election-day.

Mr. W. F. Connell testified that about supper-time he was informed that there would be some men from Alabama in town, and there would be " hell to pay." Shortly after dark an old warehouse, worth probably two or three hundred dollars, and occupying a somewhat isolated position, was discovered to be on fire, and an alarm was sounded. Immediately the town was overrun with armed men, the Alabamians parading the streets on horseback. The fire companies turned out, but they were told to put up their engine and go to killing " niggers." Firing occurred all over the town, and persons passing up and down the streets were halted. The firing was continued during the night. They also sent to New Orleans and procured a cannon. Arrangements were also made with military companies in Alabama to come over and help carry the county for the Democratic Party. For some time prior to the election the Democrats held meetings in the county. The Democratic companies attended these meetings heavily armed, and the cannon was also taken along. All persons were invited to attend. It was openly announced at these meetings that Republicans should not vote unless they voted the Democratic ticket, and if they did not vote that ticket they should not vote at all.

Robert Gleed, a prominent colored Republican, testifying upon this subject, stated:

"We had a meeting. We had so many threats of violence, we wanted to avoid any difficulty if possible, and we had a meeting at the court-house. Dr. Lipscomb and Judge Simms, the candidate on the Democratic side, were invited to speak, to see if they could suggest some plan to avoid any collision on the day of election. He and Dr. Lipscomb spoke, and I had a few words to say myself; and, as the whole objection seemed to be against me, I made a statement to the meeting that if by forbearing to exercise the elective franchise or hold office in any way would be the means of reconciling the white and black men, so that we could have a peaceable election, or be at peace afterward, I would forbear to hold office, or forbear to run for office, or even vote as an individual, if by that means I could secure the peace and harmony of the two races in our county. He [the Democratic candidate] spoke afterward, and said that was the only way. I asked what we could do?—was there any concession that we could make that would secure peace and a quiet election? and he said the way we could have it was by abstaining from voting altogether. Of course I could not concede that for others than myself, but I was willing to undergo and sacrifice as far as I was individually concerned, but I could not do anything for other persons; and I believe I told him in the speech I made that we were now simply asking,—we used to ask for life and liberty,—but now, if we could be just spared our lives, so as we could go peacefully along and be permitted to enjoy our lives as men and as human beings, we would be satisfied with that."

Mr. Connell, testifying in regard to the scenes that

came under his observation during that night and the next day at Columbus, stated:

"About one o'clock I went to bed; I heard considerable firing all over the town during the night. On the next day, which was Tuesday, the election-day, it looked like Sunday more than it did an election-day in the town of Columbus. There were no colored men about town at all—very few to what ought to have been there or usually are at such places on days of the election."

Mr. Connell testified that the number of registered voters at Columbus was about 1400, of which between 900 and 1000 were colored. He also testified as follows:

"I walked up to Worrell's corner and I found Mr. David Blair there and Mr. McDonald; and we three were standing talking, and there was a man ordered to halt right behind us, right across the street, and he did not halt. Some little conversation and pretty quick words passed between them, and one was shot. There were two guards, and one ran down east about thirty or forty yards, and the other one told me to halt, and I said 'Why,' and asked him what his name was, and he told me that his name was Winfield."

Q. Were those men black or white?

A. I suppose they were white men.

Q. The man that was shot?

A. He was a black man; his name was John Gordon.

Q. Was he killed?

A. Yes, sir. I examined him about half an hour after he was shot. He was shot just under the nipple on the left side. That occurred on Monday night.

Q. Do you know how many votes were cast in that beat that day?

A. My recollection is about 700.

Q. Do you know what proportion Republicans and what Democrats?

A. I don't think the Republicans got to exceed forty. I have got a list of the votes at home and a statement of the election. I don't think, though, that we got over forty at that beat.

Q. Were there many Republicans present in the village?

A. No, sir; very few.

Q. How many colored men would you say?

A. Very few, sir. I saw a squad of colored men, and Captain W. W. Humphrey and myself went to them and tried to get them to vote, and told them that they should not be intimidated or interfered with in any manner, shape, or form; that they should vote for just for whom they pleased; but they came to the court-house gate and turned away and went back, and never came back to vote.

Q. Was Mr. Humphrey, who was with you, a Democrat or Republican?

A. A Democrat.

Q. Did you see any other colored men that day?

A. Yes, sir; I did. Two or three came to me and asked me to fix their tickets for them, and I did so; and they voted without any trouble or molestation whatever.

Q. How do you explain the absence of the colored men from the polls at that time?

A. I imagine it was done from the scare that they had got the night before. There was some six killed, I think, all told, that night, and the negroes all ran out of town and went to the swamp, as I understand, and none of them made their appearance, but very few, except those who voted the Democratic ticket. There was a good many of them—nine tenths—that voted there that day; voted the Democratic ticket. They were just led up to the ballot-boxes by Democrats and deposited their tickets. I stood by and saw them go and get them to go up and vote.

Q. Did you see any person shot except the one whose death you have mentioned?

A. I did not, sir.

Q. Did you observe any conduct on his part or hear any remarks made by him which might have led to his killing?

A. No, sir; none in the world. As he came out of the brick house the guards came up. As they came north he came out of the house near the corner, and met a white man named Winfield, a Dutchman, who had a lamp in one hand and a pistol in the other. They ordered the negro to halt, and the negro halted and turned around, as I suppose toward them, from the position he was lying in when I met him. He was shot in the breast. He was ordered to halt and give up his pistol, and he said, "I have not got a pistol." He asked him where he was going, and the negro remarked something about Judge Orr,—he called Orr's name,—and the man fired. That was our circuit judge, and I suppose he intended to say something about going to see Judge Orr, or something of that sort. They then halted Winfield and asked him where he was going, and he said he was going home; and Winfield went on about his business, and they turned around and went to where the station was that they were to guard that night. On Tuesday I ate dinner with some gentlemen that said they were from Alabama, and they said they were going to Butler's brick church to regulate affairs there. That was at the precinct six miles south of Columbus. I understood after that there were one or two men shot down there. Colonel Meek was at dinner at the same time, and the Alabamian spoke to Meek as though he recognized him, and Meek did not seem to take much notice of him, and the Alabamian remarked, "God damn you, colonel, you don't know me to-day; you knew me very well last night!" Meek said, "Oh, yes, I know you very well," and kept on eating his oysters. I did not let on who I was, but I saw the fellow was half drunk, and I thought I would draw him out. He said he was going down there to kill the God-damned niggers, and when he had done that he was coming back up here in town to clean out these God-damned white Radicals here in town. I said, "These white Radicals are a pretty nice set of fellows, and if you do not believe it ask Colonel Meek; he can vouch for them." I hunted up Judge Simms, the candidate for State senator, and told him that these men were going down to this brick church, and said to him, "You and Meek can stop it if you are a mind to. Meek is down to the restaurant now eating his dinner, and you can go down there, and you and him can keep them from going there." I said, "Those are country negroes that vote down there, and they ought not to be disturbed, as they have had nothing to do with the trouble here in town." Simms replied to me that when such things as firing and burning had taken place, and it had been set by niggers, the Anglo-Saxon race would rise; there was no controlling them. I said to him that did not make any difference; that I did not think that innocent parties should suffer for what guilty ones had done. Whether Simms stopped them or not I don't know; I did not follow him up to see.

By these means Lowndes County, which usually gave, as has been shown, a Republican majority of 2500, was carried by the Democratic Party; their county officers, one senator, and three members of the Legislature were elected. In 1874 large numbers of the citizens of Mississippi assisted their Democratic brethren of Alabama in carrying the election, and now in 1875 the Democrats of Alabama, gun in hand, reciprocate the favor.

MONROE COUNTY.

The Democratic organization in Monroe County, with its headquarters at Aberdeen, the county-seat, was quite equal to anything of the kind in the State. The military companies were armed with needle-guns, shot-guns, pistols, and a twenty-four-pound cannon, properly mounted, with a caisson and ammunition. They were quite as determined "to carry the election at all hazards" as were their Democratic brethren in other portions of the State. They canvassed their county thoroughly in due military style, terrorizing Republicans wherever they went. In October the Republicans concluded to hold a number of meetings, and they put up notices fixing the times and places. Their first meeting was at the town of Cotton Gin. The Republicans of the precinct turned out in a body. A large number of Democrats also assembled at the meeting. What occurred at that and other meetings is graphically told in the testimony of J. W. Lee, a native of Alabama, who had served four years in the Confederate army, had been mayor of the town of Aberdeen, and was then sheriff of the county. His statement is as follows:

J. W. Lee, sworn and examined:

"The Republican nominees had their printed announcements, and they started out. On the first occasion I was one of the number that was to speak at

Cotton Gin, in our county. I do not remember precisely the date, but I think it was about the middle of October. There were, however, in advance of that a good many things that were aggressive, and calculated to get up a great deal of difficulty; but this little town I speak of I was in, and know all about what occurred there. We went to Cotton Gin to fill the appointment, and when I got there I found the Republicans strongly represented for the precinct, which was a small one. They were mostly colored people; in fact, nearly all. I found a large number of Democrats there too, not only from the precinct there, but from other parts of the county; in addition I found quite a number from Aberdeen that had gone up ahead of me. I also found an artillery company that had recently been organized in Aberdeen. They had a twenty-four-pound cannon, a caisson, and several kegs of powder and several bags of buckshot. I saw from the temper of the crowd that they were not in a very good humor about something, and one of their speakers who lived in Aberdeen came to me and said, 'We want a division of time here to-day.'"

Q. What crowd do you speak of?

A. The Democrats.

Q. And when you speak of one of their speakers, whom do you mean?

A. Captain E. O. Sykes came to me and said they wanted a division of time. I told him to make his application in writing and I would submit it to my friends. He did so, and I submitted it to my friends, and we discussed the matter. They were opposed to any division of time, because the Democrats had canvassed the county before us, and we had never asked them for any division of time. To show something of the temper of the crowd: some colored men would perhaps come up and want to talk to me, and as soon as three or four of them would assemble around me quite a number of young men who belonged to the artillery organization would come right up and stand around, and would not permit us to say anything unless they could hear what was said. They continued to follow us around that way, and I became satisfied from their actions and everything of the kind, and I told my friends—there were only two of them: no colored speakers were with us—they knew it would not do; that it was not safe, in other words, for any of the colored speakers to go with us on the east side of the Tombigbee River; and there were but three of us—all white men and Republicans. When I submitted the proposition to them in regard to a division of time they opposed it. I told them there was one thing about it—there were a great many men armed with double-barrelled shot-guns and pistols. They openly and grossly insulted one of my friends, a Mr. Coleman, and I said, "I see very clearly that we will not be permitted to leave here without speaking, and we cannot speak here without a division of time, that will not be permitted; and the only way is to grant the desired division of time, and make the best of it we can." In the mean time the cannon was being fired just as fast as they could load it up and shoot. They scared the colored people nearly to death. Our next appointment was at Smithville. I told the gentleman who had invited me out to stop with him that he had been abused because of the invitation, and that we would go on to Smithville and stop at the hotel. We went there, and after considerable persuasion we got in and stayed all night. The next day we had the speaking in Smithville, and we got a few Republicans,—only a few,—and the few that came out said they were afraid; but they did come. We met there very nearly the same crowd that we had spoken to the day before at Cotton Gin.

Q. A crowd of Democrats?

A. Yes, sir; pretty much the same crowd of Democrats, for I know every one, having been a merchant and a sheriff of the county. And we had to submit to much the same thing next day. When we were speaking they did not hesitate to interrupt us; and occasionally they would call one of the speakers a liar or something of the kind. We were subject to all manner of insults and indignities.

Q. Can you state any of them?

A. I do not remember the names now.

Q. But the indignities and insults,—what was done,— state any of them you can recall?

A. They would insult them and tell them they were damned scoundrels and damned rascals, and while speaking they would get up there and pronounce any statement a lie. The next place we went to was Quincy. The white men were so insulting that we just withdrew; we did not attempt to speak at all. I did get up and talk a few minutes, and one man came up and was so insulting that I said to the audience we did not come there to raise any disturbance, did not come to be insulted or to insult any one, and we would withdraw; and we did withdraw from the meeting.

Q. When you say a man came up, whom do you mean —a Democrat or Republican?

A. He was a Democrat, and came in the audience while I was speaking, and seemed to have been drinking.

Q. Did he come near you?

A. He came right up to me.

Q. Was he armed?

A. I did not see any arms. However, there was no

effort to quiet him, and I withdrew. Those who seemed to be kindly disposed followed me, and begged me to come back; but I told them I did not want to have anything further to say. Mr. Coleman, who was with me, got up to speak, but they were so insulting that he withdrew, and we got in our buggy and went home. It was a long ways home, sixteen miles, but we had no place to stay that night; we had also another appointment down for the next day. There was one day we had an appointment where there was no meeting. They did not meet, and then the day following we had a meeting at Sulphur Springs. Four of us went down there, and I think one colored man went with us. It was rather a strong Republican precinct—the strongest on the east side of the river. Notwithstanding all these were Republican meetings, we had to give them the organization, and we yielded rather than to have any trouble.

Q. You say you had to give them the organization; what was said or done that you had to give them the organization?

A. The temper of the crowd that made the demand. I saw very clearly that it was a demand. We would dissent from their views, but it did no good. They insisted, and said they were going to have it that way, and we just yielded without any trouble. We saw it was impossible to organize our own meeting and attempt to have speaking.

Q. Do you mean to say that they chose the chairman?

A. Yes, sir. When we came to this place, Sulphur Springs, a gentleman from the southern part of the county, an old citizen, formerly sheriff of the county, Colonel J. H. Anderson—I suggested to some of the Democratic speakers that we take him for chairman of the meeting, and they said no.

Q. Is he a Democrat?

A. A Republican; a moderate man. They said no; that they proposed to organize the meeting themselves. There was a very large crowd there, about one hundred and sixty Republicans, and there must have been three hundred Democrats. There was a large church there where we held the meeting, and it was a large crowd for country speaking. We delayed a long time any effort at organization. We saw there was no hope after we had submitted the proposition that we had; and after considerable delay they organized the meeting, and notified us that we could have a chance to speak. I was the first speaker; no, the first speaker was theirs—Captain Sykes; he spoke an hour, and then they allowed me an hour; I had the floor, and they had the chairman, the sergeant-at-arms, and everything. The colored people organized themselves in clubs, and they had a fife and drum generally to call their members together, and to use in marching. They had I remember two clubs there that day, and two drums—two sets of drums. When they came in and took their seats very often they took their drums with them. They had done it on that occasion. I got up to speak, and soon after I did so there were four men who marched right up the aisle in front of me, and I saw one of them put his hand behind him and take out a pistol and slip it into the inside pocket of his coat, and they stood there. I stopped, and told them that I did not propose to speak while men were standing blocking up the aisle. Finally, some one one asked them to sit down, and they sat down, and only sat down for a few minutes and then got up again; and I stopped again and asked them if they would be seated, and they took their seats. When I would say anything that would bring the colored men down by way of applause, it seemed to arouse the Democrats fearfully. The colored people when attending these meetings with their drums had the habit of tapping their drums when they wanted to applaud the speaker. On several occasions when this was done I saw a man rise up in front of me and pull out his revolver and level it at the man who tapped the drum, and say, "You cannot beat that drum here; this is a white-man's country, and we don't allow that." The demonstration was so hostile that I stopped speaking. I was followed by another of the Republican speakers, and he by a third—who was so insulted that he asked them to excuse him, and said that he would take his hat and go; and he started out. In the mean time I had gone to one of the speakers to see if he could not stop the thing. I had seen boys go off that morning, and in a few minutes we would see the same boys return with shot-guns on their shoulders, white boys, the sons of Democrats. A large body of the Democrats had assembled from different parts of the county, many of them armed with guns and pistols. I did not like the demonstration, and really felt very uneasy all the time. I was afraid something would be done that would cause a riot. When this man—a colored man—withdrew the colored people attempted to withdraw; and as they attempted to withdraw, and as they attempted to come out of the doors, armed Democrats flew to the doors and blocked each of the three or four doors to the house. They told the negroes that they should not leave—that they should sit down and hear the truth, and struck several on the head with revolvers and sticks. Then the colored people, becoming frightened, commenced leaping out of the windows, and some one in the crowd, I don't know who, shouted, "Shoot them! shoot them!" I was then in the outskirts

of the town. I had gone out to eat something—I had
my dinner with me—after leaving Captain Sykes, and
appealing to him to quiet the Democrats, or do something
to prevent the difficulty that appeared inevitable. The
colored men came running out—men, women, and children—closely pursued by the Democrats. They overtook them, and just took a knife and cut the head out
of the drum, and they stamped on the kettle-drum and
burst it all to pieces. There was a great deal of trouble
and confusion. You would see the crowd running after
a negro, and I would expect to see him killed as soon
as they overtook him. They did not kill him, but after
knocking him around, would turn him loose and go
after another; the leading negroes, I suppose, they were
generally after. This condition of things continued for
about half an hour or more; and as soon as we could
conveniently do so we got into our hack and went
away, abandoning the whole thing. This was just after
the agreement between Governor Ames and the chairman of the Democratic State Executive Committee here,
General George. We submitted the whole matter to
Governor Ames, who reported it to General George, and
they of course denied the whole thing. We had other
appointments then announced for the west side of the
river. The first after that was on Saturday, at Paine's
Chapel. As we came back from Sulphur Springs I said
to my friends, "If you are disposed to keep up this
speaking and submit to this abuse, I am not. I am
going to stop my part of it." We held a little caucus
that night, and we decided to revoke our announcements that had been made to speak. We employed
some couriers, and sent them to notify the people not to
go to any more of our appointments; that there was not
going to be any speaking, as it would result in the kill-

ing of a great many people, etc. But the Democrats, the next day after that occurred, went out to Paine's Chapel in style, with their cannon, ammunition, and speakers, and to the place where we were to have our meeting. When they got there, however, and found no one there, they came back in the afternoon, and it would not have been safe for any leading Republicans to have been seen by them, I assure you. There was a colored policeman, New Williams, on the street, and one of them ran up to him with a pistol, and told him that he was the cause of all this thing, and that they were going to kill him.

Another colored man, Osborn Ward, was shot at on the streets of Aberdeen that evening, and the condition of things was perfectly fearful, so far as I could learn. I was not on the streets at all, as I knew it would not do for me to be seen; but I was receiving messages constantly, first from one way then from another, about certain threats that certain parties had made that I should be killed, and that others should be killed, and of course I had to keep out of the way of the crowd. The feeling displayed was perfectly fearful during the campaign. The Democrat speakers in advance of the election did not hesitate to say openly that there was a revolution, that they intended to overturn the State Government of Mississippi.

Captain E. O. Sykes said on several occasions that it was a revolution, and two or three other Democrat speakers said so. They did not hesitate about saying it; and they said furthermore that they intended to carry the election in Monroe County; that its twelve hundred Republican majority did not amount to anything; that they intended to show us how to carry elections; that they would have fifteen hundred armed men from Alabama to assist them in carrying the election.

They said that in their public speeches. This condition of affairs existed from the time the campaign opened, in fact, from 1874 up to the election in November, 1875.

On the morning of the election I had considerable difficulty in having tickets distributed; but I got them distributed, however, early that morning at the court-house.

Before the election I had advised all colored men to come to the election unarmed—to be there, and to come unarmed; I did not know but that there might be trouble if they came armed or made any demonstration; and I advised them particularly to come unarmed, and also advised them, as far as possible, to vote at their own precincts. The colored men on the east side of the river had been told before the election by the Democrats that they would not be permitted to vote there, and they were afraid to attempt it; yet I did not think it would be any better anywhere else. I advised them especially to try to vote at their own precincts. Under the law they could vote from any part of the county at the county-seat, the court-house; but to avoid a large crowd centring there I told them as far as possible to vote at the voting-places where they were registered. When I went to the court-house on the morning of the election I found between twelve and fifteen hundred men on the ground; it was very early.

Q. Who were these men?

A. Republicans, all colored men nearly. Very soon quite a number of leading Democrats came. They seemed to be very much excited. One of them came to me and said, "I think you are going to have trouble here to-day." Said he, "Well, I am informed that you have advised the colored men to concentrate here from the different parts of the county and vote here." I said,

"You are mistaken; on the contrary, I have advised them as far as possible to vote at their own boxes; and I have advised the people of this beat to go to the other box in this beat, and keep away from Aberdeen." Looking around he said, "You have men enough here to elect every man on your ticket, but we are determined that not a man shall vote here to-day unless he votes the Democratic ticket; and," said he, "that is the programme that will be carried out all over the whole State to-day."

Q. What was his name?

A. His name is Thomas P. Sykes, the present mayor of Aberdeen.

Q. Was he the speaker you referred to before?

A. No, sir; his brother, Captain E. O. Sykes. The colored people were very uneasy and afraid. They came to me repeatedly and told me that they were satisfied that they would not be allowed to vote. I told them, however, to wait and we would see.

Very soon the young white men commenced congregating, and they all took occasion to wear their pistols so they could be plainly seen. They were thoroughly and completely armed when they came to the court-house.

Q. Were they Democrats?

A. Yes, sir; I saw them myself pull out their pistols and force colored men to show their registration papers and tickets they had to vote, and then they would tear them up and throw them down. They were insulting and abusive in all their movements and demonstrations. A gentleman told me that he had bade his wife and children good-by that morning; that he never expected to see them again unless they (Democrats) carried the election that day in Monroe County; that they meant business, and intended to carry the election. He was a Democrat; and he said that they would show us that they intended to carry the election before the day was over, or die.

Having been informed that General Gholson, who is also a Democrat, was opposed to the policy they were pursuing in the county, and being personally friendly with him, I went to hunt him up, as he is an old man of influence, to see if he could do something with the mob that was gathering around the court-house. I failed to find him, however, and failed to get back to the court house any more. I started for the court-house, and when I got near there I found a company of infantry marching up a right-shoulder shift, with their needle-guns; and I moved around through the jail-yard and went into the jailer's house just in front of the east end of the court-house, and just across the street; and I could not get away from there any more until everything was disposed of.

While I was sitting in the window, however, I saw everything that was done on the east side of the court-house, which was next to me. I saw this infantry company march up into the court-house square near the east door, which was a voting box. In the mean time I saw a company of cavalry move around between the jail and the court-house very near to me. As they advanced they were hollering for me, though they did not know where I was, and asked them to bring me out, they wanted to see me. I was sitting near by and knew a good many. Quite a number I did not know; they were from Alabama, as I was informed afterward. They moved around near the south corner of the court-house square. There was about three hundred men waiting there for the polls to be opened. This cavalry company moved right around and told these colored men to just leave within three minutes. Said they, "Not one of you shall cast your vote here to-day. We give you three minutes in which to leave here, and if you don't, you have got to take the consequences." In the mean time the infantry company moved up in front of the east door of the court-house, and one of them got up on the stone steps and waved a stick over his head,—one of the Democrats,—and said, "If you don't leave here within three minutes the last one of you shall be shot down." The twenty-four-pound cannon was brought up and placed in position at short range, bearing on, I suppose, three or four hundred colored people who had assembled at the west entrance to the court-house, and one of the officers of the militia said, "If there are any Democratic colored men in this crowd let them get out; we are going to fire." And they all got out.

Several colored men were knocked down during the time with pistols and sticks; and they fled in wild disorder and confusion from the court-house in every direction. Under that kind of treatment they went away, and out of 1400 Republican votes we ought to have polled there, we polled about 90. I am simply approximating now, but the Republican vote of the beat (precinct) was 1400 from the best information that I have. I never attempted to rally the colored men, because I had been informed time and again that it would not be safe for me to attempt to go into the mob, and I certainly knew when it was safe. A man would know from the temper of the men whether it was safe to risk himself there or not, and I did not attempt to go among them.

Q. Were the colored men armed or otherwise?

A. They were unarmed. I never saw a pistol or gun displayed by one of them during the day. A large crowd of voters were dispersed very early in the morning, and they never returned. The crowd had been dispersed, driven away in every direction, after having been notified that they would not be permitted to vote there on that day unless they voted the Democratic ticket.

Q. That announcement was publicly made?

A. That announcement was publicly made by several men on different occasions. I heard the announcement made myself frequently. They said that if they did not leave within three minutes they would be shot down. I saw the guns, the armed men, the artillery, the cannon, and heard what they said to the extent I have mentioned.

Thirteen hundred colored men, I think, were driven away in this manner. I have got in my possession the names of that many who will swear that they were driven away from the polls. After the crowd were driven away a committee of gentlemen, with whom I had always been very friendly, came over to the jail, and asked if I was in the jailer's house. The jailer told them that I was sitting in his room. They said they wanted to see me. They were all Democrats. They came and told me that they had come to offer any assistance that I desired; that they came, in other words, to assure me that they would either protect me there or escort me to my residence. After they had remained there a few minutes I told them I had sent for my horse already, and that I should ride home as soon as he came. About the time they left my horse was brought, and I got on him and went home. I had nothing further to do with it; I did not vote. I am satisfied that if I had attempted to vote there, especially early in the morning before the crowd was dispersed, that I should have been killed.

I will state, furthermore, that one of these gentlemen

who came over to wait on me told me that he had no doubt but I had saved myself just by coming here to the jail. Said he, "I believe some of these strangers would have picked you off"—having reference, I presume, to the Alabamians.

Q. Did any of those military companies belong in Aberdeen?

A. The infantry and the militia company belonged in Aberdeen. The cavalry company were mostly strangers. I was informed that they came from Alabama.

Q. State the number of those infantry, cavalry, and militia companies?

A. I don't know the number of the infantry company, but I will say about sixty, armed with needle-guns and pistols. There must have been from 50 to 100 cavalry. There were, I suppose, from 40 to 60 artillery, and they were all armed with revolvers—these large army pistols, new. And I will state further that all the Democrats, as far as I could see, were armed outside of the organization, unless it was a few old men.

After this narrative of a Confederate soldier, the reader will fully appreciate the contents of the following telegram forwarded by citizens of "old Monroe" to General J. Z. George, Chairman of the Democratic State Committee:

ABERDEEN, MISS.

J. Z. George:

I am instructed by the Democratic and conservative citizens of old Monroe, who have rolled up a majority of over a thousand, to request that you will, in their name, appoint a day of thanksgiving and prayer for the victory the God of hosts has given. The whole State will respond.　　　　　　　　　　S. A. JOMAS.

How they rolled up a Democratic majority of over a thousand in "old Monroe," where there was a legitimate Republican majority of about twelve hundred, sufficiently appears from Mr. Lee's story. It was indeed a "famous victory," for which the God of hosts was to be impiously thanked by the law-breakers.

Space cannot here be given for all the bloody details of this monstrous outrage upon free government. It would be mockery to call what occurred in the State of Mississippi on the 2d day of November, 1875, an election. It was a revolution. Everything went forward according to a well-matured plan. The Republican majority of 35,000 was to be overborne by military array.

For this purpose large sums of money were expended for arms and ammunition. A majority of the Democrats were organized into military companies. They marched through the country by day and by night, firing their pieces, threatening the lives of Republicans, breaking up Republican meetings, announcing that they intended carrying the State for the Democratic Party at all hazards, and declaring that Republicans could not vote unless they voted the Democratic ticket. They drove Republican county officers from their homes and seized the county government; they killed hundreds of Republicans and terrorized half the people of the State.

General George, chairman of the Democratic State Committee, Mr. Lamar, Mr. Singleton, and other Democratic candidates for Congress, did not raise their voices to allay the excitement of the hour.

Such law-abiding Democrats as opposed the methods adopted were drawn into the current and swept forward without the power of resistance.

The Democrats held the power of the State government in utter contempt, and were determined to resist by force any effort on the part of Governor Ames to protect the people in their lives and rights. When he proposed to raise a few companies of militia under the laws of the State, for the purpose of suppressing violence, his action created intense opposition and excitement throughout the State amongst the Democracy.

Desirous of allaying all excitement and securing a fair election, the Governor listened to overtures from General George and other prominent Democrats, who proposed that if the Governor would forbear to organize militia companies they would guarantee a peaceful and fair election. Finally, a "Treaty of Peace" was made, which was kept by the Governor and never observed for a moment by the Democratic military companies.

The Democrats, however, constantly labored under the apprehension that their hellish work would be put an end to by the interference of the National Government.

The following dispatches indicate the feeling on this point:

YAZOO CITY, Sept. 4, 1875.

General J. Z. George or Marion Smith:

Are troops to be sent here? What sort and when? Everything quiet.

J. C. PREWITT.

JACKSON, MISS., Sept. 4, 1875.

To J. C. Prewitt, Yazoo City:

Don't think troops of any sort will be sent.

J. Z. GEORGE.

JACKSON, MISS., Sept. 6, 1875.

S. M. Shelton, Clinton, Miss.:

Be prudent in all you do. Allow no advantage to the enemy. Use as much forbearance as possible. The Federal authority will be invoked against you.

J. Z. GEORGE.

CLINTON, Sept. 6, 1875.

General J. Z. George :

There can be no peace in Hinds County while the Radical leaders are at large. We are fully prepared to meet the issue, and accept no terms which do not embrace the surrender or removal of those leaders from the county. We do not recognize the Ames government, but will have no conflict with the Federal authorities.

S. M. SHELTON,

For the Executive Committee of the County.

To prevent the sending of troops, representations were made to the Government at Washington that everything was quiet in Mississippi, and that peace reigned throughout the border, as will be seen by the following telegrams :

JACKSON, Sept. (10), 1875.

To Hon. Edwards Pierrepont, Attorney-General United States :

There are no disturbances in this State now, and no obstructions to the execution of the laws. There has been an unexpected conflict at a political meeting, and some subsequent disturbances, but everything is quiet now. The Governor's call for United States troops does not even pretend there is any insurrection against the State government, as required by the revision of the U. S. Statutes of 1875, p. 1034. Peace prevails throughout the State, and the employment of United States troops would but increase the distrust of the people in the good faith of the present State government.

J. Z. GEORGE,

Chairman Democratic State Executive Committee.

Sept. 11, 1875.

*To Hon. Edwards Pierrepont, Attorney-General United
States, Washington:*

Offers are freely made to the Governor of assistance
to preserve the peace should disturbance occur. The
people of Mississippi claim the right of American citizens to be heard before they are condemned. I reassert
that perfect peace prevails throughout the State, and
there is no danger of disturbance unless initiated by the
State authorities, which I hope they will not do.

J. Z. GEORGE,
*Chairman Democratic and Conservative
State Executive Committee.*

The clamor against stationing U. S. troops at the polls
had its effect: United States troops were not sent to
Mississippi. But detachments of the late Confederate
army, by intimidation, murder, and fraud, carried the
State for the Democratic Party.

The net result of this so-called election was:

MEMBERS OF CONGRESS.

Democrats 4.   Republicans 2.

STATE LEGISLATURE.

Senate.	*House of Representatives.*
Democrats............... 26	Democrats............... 97
Republicans............. 11	Republicans............. 20
Dem. Maj........ 15	Dem. Maj............: 77

At an honest election the case would have stood:

CONGRESS.

Republicans 5.   Democrat 1.

STATE LEGISLATURE.

Senate.	*House of Representatives.*
Republicans............... 26	Republicans............... 66
Democrats................ 11	Democrats................ 50

Upon the meeting of the Legislature two important events occurred.

Mr. Lamar was elected to the Senate of the United States, and Governor Ames was forced to resign.

The usurpation thereby became complete, and the Democratic Party was established in power in the State of Mississippi by the suppression of the voice of the majority of the people, by fraud, intimidation, and murder.

CHAPTER XVII.

THE ELECTION OF 1876 IN ALABAMA AND LOUISIANA.

Alabama—Increase of the Democratic Majorities—The Victory of 1874, won by Force and Fraud, improved upon—Helplessness of the Republicans in the Hands of a hostile State Government—How the State went for Tilden—Louisiana—Secret Circular of the Democratic State Committee—Tacit Avowal of their Intention to Carry the State by Violence—The Mounted Rifle Companies Organized for the Work—Outrages in Ouachita Parish—Murder of Dr. B. H. Dinkgrave, a Leading White Republican—Testimony of Captain Hale, 16th Infantry—Written Protection furnished to Negroes who Vote the Democratic Ticket—Shocking Outrages on Negroes—The Eliza Pinkston Case—Testimony of Lieutenant Henry M. McCawley, 13th Infantry—Outrages in East and West Feliciana Parishes—Murder of Don A. Weber, Supervisor of Registration—The Republican Majority in the State—General Plan of the Democratic Campaign—Counties Selected to be "Bulldozed"—Suppression of the Republican Vote—Senator Sherman's Report to President Grant—Origin of the Term "Bulldozing"—Final Result of the Election in the State—Action of the Returning Board.

ALABAMA.

THE signal success of the "shot-gun policy" in the Alabama election of 1874 and in the Mississippi election of 1875, supplemented as it was by ballot-box stuffing, fraudulent counting, and various other devices for overcoming Republican majorities, placed the Democrats of Alabama in such a position that it was only necessary for them to maintain the advantages they had gained to hold permanent control of the State. They regarded the Presidential election of 1876 as of paramount interest to the Southern cause, and were determined to roll up such a majority for Tilden and Hendricks as would place Alabama in the lead of Democratic States. They abated nothing in organization, and conducted the campaign in the most aggressive and vindictive manner. Their efforts were directed especially against the strong Republican counties, and every means was taken to deter Republican voters from exercising the elective franchise. In fact this was the purpose of the Democrats throughout the entire State, and to accomplish this they bent every energy.

As an illustration of what was accomplished in this way the vote in the following counties is taken—Barbour, Bullock, Dallas, Macon, Russell, and Sumter Republican counties, and Pickens a Democratic county:

In 1874 these counties cast 36,073 votes, while in 1876 they cast 24,854 votes, being a reduction in the total vote of 11,219; but the reduction of the Republican vote in these same counties in 1876, as compared with the vote of 1874, was 12,845. So it appears that the entire number of 11,219 persons who remained from the polls were Republicans. A comparison of the Republican vote of 1874 with that of 1876, in these counties, shows how successful the Democrats were in reducing the Republican vote.

COUNTIES.	Republican Vote, 1874.	Republican Vote, 1876.
Barbour	2,671	162
Bullock	2,503	959
Dallas	6,819	3,930
Macon	2,076	881
Pickens	1,177	48
Russell	2,625	1,002
Sumter	3,305	1,370
Total	21,177	8,352

The loss of the Republicans at the election in 1876, as compared with the vote of 1874, was 25,691.

It cannot be said that these electors voted the Democratic ticket, for Mr. Tilden received 5116 votes less in 1876 than the Democratic candidate for Governor received in 1874.

The colored Republicans of Alabama had had forced into their brain, as with a red-hot iron, the fact that the Democratic Party had reached the determination to rule that State; that they were organized and armed, and had control of the State government; and further, that the United States Government would not interfere in their behalf and protect them in the free exercise of the right of suffrage.

An examination of the record of the vote is all that seems required to satisfy any reasonable mind that extraordinary causes were operating in that State in 1876, when a great Presidential contest was arousing the interest of the people—to cause nearly 26,000 Republican voters to abstain from voting LOUISIANA.

It became apparent early in the year 1876 that the Democratic Party had determined to eliminate the Republican vote in some of the larger Republican parishes of Louisiana by organized violence and bloodshed, trusting to carry some of the close parishes by other means, and relying upon previous terrorism, which had to a great extent demoralized the Republican organizations in portions of the Red River country,—in such parishes, for instance, as Natchitoches, De Soto, and Rapides, where the Republicans had previously cast heavy votes,—to keep those parishes in check. In this way they expected to obtain control of the Legislature and the State. A secret circular was issued by the Democratic State Central Committee to prominent Democrats in the parishes selected, giving advice as follows' (Sherman report, p. 37):

"We recommend that in conversation with each other no gloomy forebodings shall be indulged in, and that the result of the coming election shall be spoken of as a foregone conclusion, as *we have the means of carrying the election and intend to use them.*"

It is further recommended, in order to "produce harmony" as well as to "impress the negroes with a sense of your united strength," that "occasionally the ward clubs should form at their several places of meeting and proceed thence on horseback to the central rendezvous," and that Democrats should be detailed to attend every Republican meeting to take note of the proceedings. The Democracy of Ouachita improved on the instructions of their committee. In the Sherman report (p. 24), where reference is made to the organization of mounted rifle companies in Ouachita Parish as adjuncts to the Democratic clubs of the different wards, it is said:

"The organization of these companies began about the 1st of July last, about the time the registration of voters began. It appears at the time these companies began to form there was comparative peace and quiet in the parish. After they formed and traversed the parish, confusion, violence, whipping, bloodshed, murder, and shameless brutality commenced, and continued until the election, and some instances since. There were eight of these rifle companies, or what were known among the Republican negroes as 'bulldozers.' They were supplied with membership from the different wards and voting-places in the parish. They were armed with guns and pistols, mounted, had regular officers, all the appointments of military organizations, and frequent meetings. They existed by virtue of no law of the State, but sprang up as aids and missionaries to re-enforce the Democratic clubs. Democrats alone composed them. Armed, they rode over the parish in the day and night time—more frequently at night. They would fire off their arms, guns and pistols, to create alarm and terror among the negroes. They would halt before and enter at unseasonable hours of the night the houses of the negroes; often commit violence upon the men and women by shooting and whipping, with the accompaniment of profane and abusive language. The assurance would be given if the party assailed would vote the Democratic tieket all would be well; if not, they would be left without protection."

The leading white Republican of Ouachita Parish was Dr. B. H. Dinkgrave, a native Louisianian, son-in-law of the chief-justice of the State, and a man of spotless character and fearless courage. He was notified that if he did not desist from organizing Republican clubs harm would happen to him. He disregarded the warning. On the 30th of August, on the highway, at noon, on his way to dinner, he was shot dead by a disguised assassin, who rode off unmolested and unpursued, protected by the sympathies of the Democrats at Ouachita. From this time forward the disintegration of the Republican Party in the parish of Ouachita proceeded apace. Republican meetings were broken up by the Democrats sent there in pursuance of the circular letter of instructions of the Democratic State Central Committee above quoted. Disorder and violence became so rife that at last Major-General Emory, commanding the United States forces in that State, upon representations made to him which he could not disregard, sent a detachment of United States troops, under the command of Captain and Brevet Lieutenant-Colonel Clayton Hale, of the Sixteenth Infantry, to Monroe, the parish seat of Ouachita, where they remained until some time after the election.

In a deposition sworn to December 1, 1876, found at pages 330 to 336, inclusive, of the Sherman report, Captain Hale says that he was stationed in command of Company H, Sixteenth Infantry, at Monroe, in Ouachita Parish, Louisiana, and that he assumed command of the post on the 24th of September, 1876.

He says:

"The condition of affairs in Ouachita Parish was very much unsettled. A strong feeling of political bitterness and intolerance was apparent among a large class of white persons, residents of it. Complaints were made to me daily by negroes of being driven from their homes, of being threatened, whipped, and treated with other acts of violence; of their houses invaded at night by masked and armed white men; of visits by committees from Democratic clubs, and of notifications from such committees to join Democratic clubs within stated periods, under penalty of death. So intense was the manifestation of intolerance, and so determined was the threatening attitude of this lawless class of white men, that the colored population of the parish seemed to have been reduced to the most abject condition of terror and helplessness. Mounted and armed organizations of white men were formed in different parts of the parish, and the acts and influence of these armed and mounted organizations seemed to have effectually repressed whatever law-abiding sentiment may have heretofore existed in the parish. In consideration of this state of affairs, I deemed it a measure of prudence to send detachments of troops to every Republican meeting appointed to be held in remote parts of the parish, to preserve the peace and prevent rioting and bloodshed."

He states further that he sent—

"A detachment of eight men and a non-commissioned officer, under command of Lieutenant McCawley, to accompany Mr. Hardy, the district-attorney *pro tempore* of Ouachita Parish, to the residence of Eaton Logwood, on the night of October 10, ultimo. A murder had been committed on the morning of that day at that place. Primus Johnson (colored) had been shot and killed, and Eaton Logwood, another colored man, had been shot and dangerously wounded. Information of the murder of Johnson, the wounding of Logwood, and that the roads leading to the place were picketed and patrolled by armed men, was communicated to me, and, on District-Attorney Hardy announcing his intention to proceed to the place to obtain the declarations of Logwood and other evidence concerning the murder of Johnson and the wounding of Logwood, I considered it my duty to send a detachment with him in order that he might do so in safety.

"A number of colored persons residing near the place where Primus Johnson was killed and Eaton Logwood wounded did call upon me after the shooting, and sought my advice and protection. They seemed almost paralyzed with terror, and announced, many of them, their intention to leave the country and find some place where they could live with some assurance of not being shot down at any moment. Very many applications were made to me by colored people for protection. I cannot enumerate the number of such applications, nor by whom nor when made. They were made almost daily. They asked protection by reason of threats of violence having been made, by reason of many murders of colored people having been committed, and by reason of the general feeling of insecurity which seemed to prevail in every part of the parish."

Coming down to occurrences immediately preceding the election, Captain Hale says:

"I do know that an armed body of mounted men marching as cavalry was on the roads on the island on the 3d day of November. I was informed at the time that it was a Democratic rifle company, commanded by one William T. Theobalds (pronounced Tibbles). This armed body of men was in attendance at a Republican meeting at Saint James Chapel on that date. Lieutenant Henry M. McCawley, Thirteenth United States Infantry, reported officially to me that the same body of armed men was on the road and in attendance at a Republican meeting held at Grody's schoolhouse on the island on the 1st of November. It has also been reported to me by many colored people residing on the island, that the same body of mounted and armed men has frequently, during the month of October and in the first days of November, been on different roads in the various portions of the island, and has attacked the houses of many colored people at different times and places, committing acts of murder, violence, and intimidation upon their occupants. It has also been reported to me at various times that other armed and mounted companies have patrolled the roads in the different sections of the parish for the purpose of raiding and intimidating negroes. It has also been officially reported to me by non-commissioned officers of my command having charge of detachments on duty in the town of Monroe, that bodies of armed men, mounted and on foot, had at different times before the election patrolled the streets of that town during the hours of night.

"I do most certainly believe that the organization of these armed bodies of men, the patrolling by them of the roads in the different sections of the parish of Ouachita, did have a very decided influence in preventing a fair and free election in that parish on the 7th day of November, 1876.

"My conclusions are based upon observations of effect produced upon colored people by the presence of W. T. Theobald's armed body of men at the Republican meeting at Saint James Chapel, and by the statements of many colored people made to me, that they were afraid of these armed bodies of men, and by the many acts of violence and murder charged to have been committed by them, and by the hostile attitude assumed by them toward men professing to be adherents of the Republican Party.

"I was present at a Republican meeting held at Saint James Chapel, on the island, in Ouachita Parish, on the 3d day of November, 1876. Attempt was made on that occasion by armed white men belonging to Theobald's Democratic rifle company to disturb and break up that meeting and intimidate the persons attending it. The attitude of these men was menacing toward the speakers and toward the colored people in attendance. I was present, accompanied by an orderly, and had a detachment of United States troops with their arms in stack about one hundred yards distant from the place of meeting. I was standing on the outskirts of the crowd in attendance, composed largely of colored people, men and women. Mr. Astwood, the first speaker, had just commenced his address, when these persons made a rush for the wagon from which he was speaking, several of them attempting to draw their revolvers while doing so, and all or most of them denouncing his statements as 'damned lies' and calling him a 'damned liar.' The colored people, men and women, were much alarmed at these hostile demonstrations, the most of them turning to flee from the ground.

"I did interfere to preserve order on the occasion referred to. When I saw the crowd of colored people swaying back from the stand of the speaker, and heard the angry denunciation by these men of the speaker's statements as 'damned lies' and he as a 'damned liar,' I rushed through the flying crowd of negroes. Springing in front of these men, I pushed them back with my sword from the wagon in which the speaker was standing, admonishing them to discontinue their unlawful attempt at violence; that their language and acts were calculated to produce a breach of the peace, and that I would, if necessary, use the detachment of troops to preserve order and prevent acts of violence on their part. The aspect of affairs was for a few moments very threatening; but quiet was fully restored, these men assuring me that they would refrain from further acts of violence, and that they would not again attempt to interrupt the speaker. After this the meeting was reasonably quiet, these men contenting themselves with denouncing in undertones the statements of the speakers as 'damned lies,' and conversing with each other. After the close of the meeting these men mounted their horses, marching in military formation as cavalry from the ground. From frequent observations of columns of cavalry, I should judge that there were of these men present on that occasion about sixty in number, all of them armed with revolvers belted around their waists, underneath their coats."

Mark, this is not the volunteered testimony of a political partisan. It is the calm, dispassionate statement of an officer of the United States army, describing scenes which passed under his own observation, and relating

events as they were told to him by the parties partici-
pant when all the facts were fresh in memory; which
statement is called out by official interrogatories propounded to him.   His reports to his superior officers
recite substantially the same facts, but in a more con-
densed form.   He goes on to narrate:

"Charles Williams, William Burrell, and Elisha Moore,
all colored, complained to me on the 5th of November
that on the 4th they started to Columbia, in Caldwell
Parish, to carry there a quantity of Republican National,
State, Congressional, and parish tickets, for the use of
that party in said parish; that at Cuba, in southern
part of Ouachita Parish, they were apprehended by a
large party of white men, questioned, threatened with
violence, and finally compelled to burn and destroy the
said Republican tickets in their possession.   After promising to join the Democratic Party and vote the Democratic ticket, they were permitted to return to Monroe, a
pass being furnished them by a Mr. Gacy, living near
Cuba, in said parish, of which the following is a true
copy:

"'CUBA, LA., November 5, 1876.

"'DEAR COLONEL : The three men say they desire the protection of the Democratic Party, and ask that you see they have
the opportunity to vote as they desire.

"'Very respectfully,

"'LOGTOWN CLUB.'"

On the back of this paper was addressed, "Col. R.
Richardson, Monroe, La.," who was chairman of the
Democratic parish committee, and who has since been
rewarded for his services by "election" to the State Sen-
ate on the Democratic ticket from this overwhelmingly
Republican district.

"With this paper as their guarantee, they were enabled to return to Monroe, though several times stopped and questioned by armed parties of white men while *en route*. They stated that they saw large numbers of negroes trying to make their way to Monroe by travelling through woods and country remote from the public highways. They also stated to me that they were desirous of voting the Republican ticket at the election then to occur, but that after the threats made to them and the promise they had given they were afraid to do so; that they were certain of being watched, and to vote the Republican ticket under the circumstances would be to imperil their lives.

"Henry Gull and Alex. Williams (colored), living near Saint James Chapel, on the island, in Ouachita Parish, on Mr. Charles Tidwell's place, stated to me, November 6, that on the night of Saturday, the 4th, and Sunday morning, the 5th of November, Theobald's men, thirty or forty in number, raided the houses of colored people in the vicinity of their (the witnesses') houses; that they killed Henry Pinkston and his infant daughter, and dangerously wounded Eliza Pinkston, his wife (all colored); that as late as one o'clock P.M. Sunday, the 5th, the body of Henry Pinkston was lying where killed, naked and unburied; that the armed raiders broke into and entered the houses of Ronald Driver, Eldridge Larkspur, and Solomon Matthews (all colored), living on the Lyle place; that Driver was taken out, stripped, and badly beaten by them; that Larkspur was not at home, and Matthews escaped and was pursued across a field, a number of shots being fired at him as he fled; that on the Ruth place, now occupied by a Mr. Davidson, they broke open the house of William Logwood (colored), but he was away from home.

"These witnesses stated that they were only enabled

to reach Monroe by travelling through the woods remote from the highways by stealth; that all of the roads on the island leading to Monroe were patrolled by mounted and armed white men, and that the Chauvan bridge across the bayou of that name was strongly picketed; that these patrols and pickets were stopping all colored people on the road.

"Lebrun Roberson (colored) stated to me, on the same day, that he lived on James F. Pace's place, near and below Saint James Chapel. That on Saturday, October 21, he was told by Dr. William P. Young that if he (Roberson) did not join the Democratic club there would be shooting done near his (Roberson's) house on the following week; that being afraid of losing his life he abandoned his home, going to Monroe; that on the night of October 23 his house was broken open by a body of men and search made for him. Ronald Driver (an old colored man) stated to me that he lived on the Lyle place; that about midnight of Saturday, November 4, his house was broken open and entered by a large body of armed men, among whom were William T. Theobalds, the three Logan boys (James, Robert, and Walter), and Dr. Young (white men), Frank Dorham and Tom Lyons (colored). That he was seized, taken from his bed and house, blindfolded, thrown and stretched upon the ground, his shirt and drawers stripped off, leaving him entirely naked, men holding him by feet and arms, in which condition he was beaten by these men upon his naked body with a leather surcingle; that he thinks he received at the hands of these men at that time over four hundred lashes; that one of these men struck him on his head with the handle of a pistol, and that others gathered handfuls of dirt and forced it into his mouth; that after the beating Theobalds said to him, 'If you do not join us at the Grody schoolhouse, at the ballot-box, on election-day, I will kill you.' This man Driver (who was very much crippled and badly bruised from the beating inflicted upon him) further stated that he started from home early Sunday morning, the 5th, travelling by stealth through the woods, and reached Monroe (a distance of about eighteen miles) about noon of the 6th.

"James Henry Coleman (colored) stated to me that he was working on Mr. Charles Tidwell's place, near Saint James Chapel, on the island, in Ouachita Parish, Louisiana. That he boarded and lodged in the house of Henry Pinkston, on said place. That about midnight of November 4, while sleeping there, laying on the floor in front of the fire, he heard a large body of mounted men approaching the house. That he raised and jumped out of a rear window, and crept under the house and remained there concealed. That the mounted men referred to, he thought about thirty or forty in number, surrounded the house, broke open the door. That he heard a struggle inside the house, and saw Henry Pinkston dragged outside by his feet, and shot to death near the corner of his house. That afterward he heard another struggle inside the house; also heard shots fired and outcries of Eliza Pinkston. Saw her dragged outside by her feet, and saw her cut and stabbed while laying on the ground, and that she was left lying there naked, and, as he thought, dead. That the moon was shining brightly, and he saw and recognized among those engaged in the murder, Buck Boker, Dr. Young, Joe Swan, John Collins, and Dave Tidwell, the son of Charles Tidwell. He also stated that about ten days previous to the occurrences above mentioned, that Mr. Charles Tidwell caused him to be seized, stripped, stretched, and tied across a cotton-bale, in which condition and position he was whipped in obedience to Mr. Tidwell's order, and in his presence, by the colored foreman or boss, and that he was then given about one hundred lashes, because of his unwillingness to join the Democratic club."

At this point something should be said of the conduct of some so-called Republican papers at that time in speaking derisively of this poor woman, Eliza Pinkston, of coupling feeble jokes with her name, and of referring with a contemptuous sneer to the story of her sufferings and wrongs. From newspapers and orators of the political party which upholds such methods of carrying elections nothing better could be expected. Attempted ridicule is the only answer to be made to facts which cannot be disproved.

It is true that the full story of this woman's wrongs strains human belief almost to its utmost capacity. If this were an isolated case, if there were no well-authenticated instances of similar crimes, differing only in degree of atrocity, perpetrated about the same time and for the same purpose, if her statement rested on her own uncorroborated evidence, the gibes and jeers directed at this poor, miserable creature might have some excuse, though even then the taste which could frame a joke on such a theme would be more than questionable. But here are two witnesses named by this disinterested army officer, who report seeing the dead body of her husband lying naked and unburied where killed, as late as one o'clock in the afternoon of the Sunday following the murder; and here is another named witness who actually heard the shots and the struggle, and saw the man dragged out and shot to death and the woman cut and stabbed as she lay on the ground in the moonlight. Pinkston is dead, his child is dead, its throat cut from ear to ear. The ghastly, unhealed wounds, with which the wretched woman herself found her way to New Orleans, gave silent evidence of brutality without a parallel. Senator Sherman and other members of the committee examined the fearful wounds which had been inflicted on this poor woman.

The deposition of Lieutenant Henry M. McCawley, Thirteenth Infantry, also stationed at Monroe, published at pages 336 to 340 of the Sherman report, confirms in many important particulars the statements of Captain Hale. In answer to the interrogatory "Do you or not know of the killing of Primus Johnson and wounding of Eaton Logwood, on the 'island,' in Ouachita Parish? If yes, state how you know it, and when and where it was done," he replies:

"I do know of the killing of Primus Johnson and wounding of Eaton Logwood on the 'island' in Ouachita Parish, Louisiana. It was on or about the 11th day of October, at a place known as Logwood's, on the island in said parish. I did escort District-Attorney *pro tempore* W. R. Hardy, of said parish, to the island, and by order of my commanding officer, Captain Hale, Sixteenth Infantry. It was on or about the 11th October. I was sent with Mr. Hardy to see that he arrived safely at Logwood's, as it was then feared that persons going in that direction might be shot down by some assassin. My command consisted of eight men and non-commissioned officer. It was about ten o'clock P.M. when we arrived at Logwood's house. After innumerable stoppages in Chuville swamp, it being very dark at the time, we were compelled to carry a lantern to see through the swamp or woods. Upon arriving at Logwood's the sight was indeed appalling, and one which will never be erased from my memory—helpless women, frightened men, and children, all huddled together in groups, looking terror-stricken, as though about being led out to be slaughtered; a few more surrounding a camp-fire which was burning to enable them to keep warm. In the passage-way of the front house was Primus Johnson, who lay there with the blood oozing from his wounds, which caused his death. In the rear of the house, or kitchen, Logwood was in bed, with at least eight or ten men and women surrounding his then supposed death-bed. The district-attorney, Mr. Hardy, took his declaration, and, from all I could learn, two white men, who were blackened, committed this atrocious deed, and were supposed to be then on the lookout to return and finish their fiendish work, which had only been partly accomplished. I have seen many sad, sad sights, but the expression upon the faces of those helpless ones that night portrayed all that fright could possibly do; and when we had finished our business and about leaving, the supplication of those poor creatures was heart-rending, fearing they, as well as Logwood, would be murdered. I therefore left a detail of three men and a corporal of my own company to protect Eaton Logwood, his wife, and Mrs. Primus Johnson, at all hazards, and not to permit any one to enter the premises without permission from Logwood's wife or Mrs. Primus Johnson. The detail remained there for one week or more, and returned to the camp when Logwood was removed to the city of Monroe for safety.

" I did have conversations with colored persons after the killing and wounding of these men. My impression was and is that the colored people thought they were killed and shot for their political opinions, both being known as strong Republicans—particularly Logwood, who was a property-owner and who had great influence with those of his own color. The effect, therefore, upon them (those colored people) was to drive those who were

Republicans into joining Democratic clubs, for the purpose of avoiding a like calamity befalling them."

Under military protection Logwood was enabled to reach New Orleans. He recovered sufficiently to give his evidence before one of the investigating committees, and then relapsed and died of his wounds.

With regard to the parishes of East and West Feliciana, bordering on the Mississippi line, the testimony taken by committees of the Senate and of the House of Representatives teems with proofs of murders by hanging, by shooting, by drowning, of whippings and maimings and burnings and woundings perpetrated for political purposes, in pursuance of a preconceived plan and to obtain a predetermined end. The assassination of John Gair, for instance. He was a leading colored man of courage and ability, and represented the district in the State Senate in 1874. His sister was nurse-maid in the family of a Dr. Saunders, a prominent Democrat of East Feliciana. One warm day the doctor was taken suddenly sick with violent pains in his bowels after drinking cold water. The cry was at once raised that the family well must have been poisoned, and that John Gair's sister must have done it by John Gair's instructions. On no evidence but this surmise a warrant was sworn out for Gair. He was arrested in a neighboring parish, and while in charge of the sheriff was riddled with buckshot and buried in the woods. A crowd of the " best citizens" of East Feliciana took his sister, this sixteen-year-old nurse-girl, and in broad daylight hanged her to a tree in the court-house square, she protesting her innocence to the last. Dr. Saunders recovered, is alive and well to-day, and subsequent investigation disclosed the fact that the well had not been poisoned at all. However, a troublesome and influential Republican had been put out of the way, which was more than sufficient compensation for the little mistake committed.   Next in influence to John Gair in this Senatorial district was John Law, another colored man. He was assassinated without going through the formality of trumping up a charge against him and having him arrested and genteelly murdered in the sheriff's hands.   The fate which befell Don A. Weber, the Supervisor of Registration of West Feliciana, who dared to file his protest against these and other outrages, will not be forgotten.   Shortly after the election, while walking peacefully from his newspaper office to his house to his noon-day dinner, as he passed the court-house, where the Democratic sheriff and coroner and clerk of court held their offices, half a dozen shot-guns were thrust out of the windows and he dropped dead in his tracks, leaving a young widow (like himself, a native of the parish) and an infant child desolate.   No effort was made by the Nicholls government to bring the murderers of D. A. Weber to justice.

There were in the State of Louisiana on the day of election 92,996 registered white voters, and 115,310 registered colored voters—a clear majority of 22,314 colored voters.   It was well known that if left free to vote, unaffected by violence or intimidation, the blacks would be almost unanimously Republican, and that with the white Republican vote the Republican majority would be about equal to that above indicated, or about 20,000 in round numbers.

The plan of the "bulldozers" appears to have been to select for purposes of intimidation and violence parishes in which the colored vote was largely predominant ; for in so doing, although the majorities thus unlawfully secured by them might be rejected, they would in any event succeed in suppressing a large Republican vote.

In pursuance of this plan five of the parishes selected in which the greatest violence and intimidation were practised were East and West Feliciana, which border upon that portion of Mississippi in which murder and outrage so prevailed during and preceding the election of 1875 as substantially to prevent any Republican vote; East Baton Rouge, which borders upon the southern portion of East Feliciana; Morehouse, which adjoins the State of Arkansas; and Ouachita, which adjoins and lies directly south of Morehouse.

These parishes contained 5134 white voters and 13,244 colored—over one third of the colored majority of the State. Instead of a majority of six or seven thousand which the Republicans should have had in those parishes, there was actually returned to the canvassing board a Democratic majority for the parishes of East and West Feliciana, Morehouse, and Ouachita of 3878, *and in East Feliciana, where the registered colored voters numbered 2127, not a Republican vote for President was cast.*

How this result was accomplished has, perhaps, been sufficiently indicated by the foregoing testimony taken chiefly from the lips of army officers. Senator Sherman in a report to President Grant says in regard to it: "A result so suggestive of violence and intimidation was obtained by means the most terrible and revolting. Organized clubs of masked armed men, formed as recommended by the Central Democratic Committee, rode through the country at night, marking their course by the whipping, shooting, wounding, maiming, mutilation, and murder of women, children, and defenceless men, whose houses were forcibly entered while they slept, and as their inmates fled through fear, the pistol, the knife, and the rope were employed to do their horrid work."

It may here be noted, as has been before stated, that

these bodies of armed men were called by the negroes of Louisiana "bulldozers." This term had its origin in this campaign, and now the noun "bulldozer" and the verb "to bulldoze" have passed into our common speech, and bid fair to secure a permanent place in the language. The etymology of the word is uncertain, but it is undoubtedly of negro origin.

The final result of the election throughout the State was that, on the face of the returns, the Tilden electors had a majority ranging from 3459 to 6405. But under the election laws of the State of Louisiana the Returning Board was authorized to exclude from the returns the votes of any poll or voting-place where they were satisfied upon evidence "that there had been any riot, tumult, acts of violence, intimidation, armed disturbance, bribery, or corrupt influences which prevented or tended to prevent a fair, free, and peaceable vote of all qualified electors." After a careful hearing of the evidence, the votes of many polling-places were rejected for these reasons, two of the worst bulldozed parishes being entirely excluded upon the ground that there had been no legal election within their borders. The count of the Returning Board gave the Hayes electors a majority ranging from 3437 to 4800. The same count also returned the Republican Governor Packard as elected by about three thousand majority. His accession to the Governorship was, however, opposed by an army of White Leaguers about six thousand strong, fully equipped and under military discipline, which encamped in the city of New Orleans. The support of United States troops being withdrawn from the lawful government, it was unable to sustain itself against the formidable army arrayed against it, and a usurping government, headed by the Democratic candidate for Governor, Nicholls, took its place. And so was fastened upon this Republican State a Democratic yoke as yet unlifted.

The action of the Louisiana Returning Board has been much criticised for partisan purposes; but there can be no doubt that the impartial historian will record that its action was strictly legal and wholly just. It was, however, only a partial measure of redress that it could apply to the great wrong which the Republicans of the State had suffered. It was authorized to reject illegal votes only; it could not count the lawful Republican votes which would have been cast except for Democratic violence. And so the twenty thousand Republican majority existing in that State largely disappeared when it made its returns.

It was in the power of no earthly tribunal to redress those other terrible wrongs—the whippings, the woundings, the murders, and the nameless outrages to which the Republican voters of the State and their families had been subjected during that Democratic saturnalia of crime which preceded this election; but as sure as there is justice in Heaven they will not always remain unavenged.

CHAPTER XVIII.

THE ELECTION OF 1876 IN MISSISSIPPI AND SOUTH CAROLINA.

Mississippi—How Issaquena County was Changed from Republican to Democratic—Shocking Murder of Seven Negroes—Intimidation of the County Supervisors—Atrocious Assassination of a Colored State Senator and his Brother at Clinton, Hinds County—The Fatal Christmas Drink—Shameful Treatment of the Dead Bodies by Vicksburg "Modocs"—Redistricting the State for Congress—The Famous "Shoe string" District—Oppressive Execution of the Registration Laws so as to Disfranchise Republican Voters—Military Organization of the Democrats still continued—Republican Leaders generally Killed or Driven from the State—Dangerous Canvass of J. W. Lee, Republican Candidate in the First Congressional District, and of J. R. Lynch in the Sixth Congressional District—General Change of Large Republican Majorities to Democratic ones—How the State was Counted in for Tilden—South Carolina—Population of the State—Large Majority of Colored Voters—Attitude of the Colored Voters toward the Democratic Party—Testimony of Governor Orr—Policy of the Democratic Leaders—High Character of Governor Chamberlain—Final Resolve to Overcome the Republican Majority at all Hazards—Wade Hampton Nominated for Governor—Organization of the Red Shirt Rifle Clubs—Their Work in Disturbing and Intimidating Republican Meetings—The Hamburg Massacre—Correspondence between Governor Chamberlain and President Grant—The Ellenton Riots—General Results of the Election—Great Increase of the Democratic Vote—Tilden fails to Carry the State—But Wade Hampton is Counted in, and the State is Lost to the Republicans—Falsity of the Democratic Fraud Issue on the Election of 1876—Alabama and Mississippi should rightfully have been Counted for the Republicans as well as Louisiana, South Carolina, and Florida—The Potter Investigating Committee and the Cipher Dispatches.

MISSISSIPPI.

THE political campaign of 1876 in Mississippi was opened by the Democracy in December, 1875. There was certain political work of importance which had been left undone prior to the November election, which it was now thought advisable to complete.

In Issaquena, a county always largely Republican, the election of 1875 was held without disturbance, and the usual Republican majority was given. After the election the Democrats declared that it was no use for them to vote, that they never could rul~ Issaquena County or do anything with the Republicans; they said that they would go to work and kill out the leading men and get control.

In December a white man was arrested upon a warrant for stabbing two colored men. While under arrest he attempted to escape, and was fired upon and killed. This circumstance was made the occasion of an extensive raid through the county by three hundred or four hundred armed Democrats. They captured Moses Johnson, a constable, who however had nothing to do with the arrest above mentioned; he with five other colored men were confined in a store-house for twenty-four hours, and were then taken out and shot to death, and left where they fell. These men were unarmed, offered no resistance, and there were no charges preferred against them. A negro man named Cornelius Washington was also killed about the same time.

This lawless act was soon followed by another, quite in keeping with it. When the supervisors of the county assembled in January to qualify and proceed with the transaction of the county business, they were met by a band of armed Democrats, who demanded that certain men named by them should be appointed upon the Levee Board. At first the supervisors concluded not to organize the meeting while such demonstrations were made against them. General Wade Hampton, however, exercised his influence with the supervisors, and induced them to proceed with business, giving them an assurance that if they did so they would not be molested. They accordingly qualified, and organized the board and proceeded to business. The Democrats, with their pistols buckled about them, filled the room, and demanded the appointment of certain persons, whom they named, upon the Levee Board. One of the supervisors testified under oath that these men were appointed by the supervisors to avoid assassination.

At Clinton, in Hinds County, the thirst of the Democrats for Republican blood was not slaked by the murders which occurred in September during the previous canvass. Then they killed forty or fifty obscure men. It was the Republican leaders they were after; and so plans were laid for the assassination of Hon. Charles Caldwell, a colored man of influence and property, and a State Senator. After sundown on the evening of December 30, 1875, while on the street in Clinton, Mr. Caldwell was invited to take a Christmas drink by a Mr. Cabell, a white man. He at first declined, but at last consented and entered a saloon, Cabell having taken his arm. They touched and jingled their glasses, when some one from the outside fired and shot Caldwell in the back. Caldwell fell mortally wounded and called for help, addressing several prominent citizens, but none of them went to his relief. A number of persons had assembled outside with their guns, and finally he called for Preacher Nelson, requesting him to take him out, that he wanted to die in the open air. He asked Mr. Nelson to take him home and let him see his wife before he died. The armed men objected to his being taken home, and when taken to the middle of the street he fell upon the ground. The men said, "We will save

him while we have got him. Dead men tell no tales."
When his enemies refused to allow Caldwell to see his
wife before he died, he drew the skirts of his coat about
him and said, "Remember, when you kill me you kill a
gentleman and a brave man. Never say you killed a
coward. I want you to remember it when I am gone."
While he was lying in the street, mortally wounded, a
number of men marched around his body and riddled it
by firing thirty or forty shots into him. Mr. Caldwell's
brother was also killed in the street that evening as he
rode into town.

What followed is best told by the widow of Senator
Caldwell, who testified before Senator Boutwell's committee. She stated that—

"After the bodies were brought to my house, Pro-
fessors Hillman and Martin stayed until one o'clock, and
then at one o'clock the train came from Vicksburg with
the 'Modocs.' They all marched up to my house and
went in to where the two dead bodies laid, and they
cursed them, those dead bodies there, and they danced
and threw open the window, and sung all their songs,
and challenged the dead bodies to get up and meet
them, and they carried on there like a parcel of wild
Indians over those dead bodies, these Vicksburg
'Modocs.'"

These atrocious acts had the effect of giving emphasis
to the oft-repeated declaration of the Democrats, that
they proposed at all hazards to control the State.

The Democratic Legislature of Mississippi, chosen by
the revolutionary measures of 1875, passed two laws
which were to have an important bearing upon the election of 1876. One was to redistrict the State into six
Congressional districts. The celebrated "Shoe-string"
district, which extended almost from the Tennessee line

along the frontage of the State on the Mississippi River to the Louisiana line, was created. It contained a Republican majority of about 15,000. This arrangement threw about one half of the Republican majority of the State into one district. The other five districts covered the balance of the State.

The other measure was an act for the registration of the voters of the State, by which the election machinery was placed in the hands of the Democratic Party, and the provisions of the law were such that in the hands of unscrupulous men qualified electors could easily be prevented from registering as voters. In Claiborne and Warren counties alone fully four thousand Republicans were refused registration for one cause or another.

In Warren County the Democratic vote was confined mainly to the city of Vicksburg. There registration went on without any obstruction; but in the country—on the plantations, where the Republican voters lived, under a provision of the registration act which required the elector to state in what portion of the voting precinct he resided, the registrars required the voters to give a description of the lands upon which they lived according to the Congressional surveys; and failing in this, white men and colored men were refused registration, although no question was raised as to their being qualified electors under the constitution and laws of the State. Fully 2500 voters were cheated out of their votes by this device in Warren County.

The Democratic Party maintained their military organizations of 1875, and many of them donned the red shirt as the insignia of Democracy. Elated with the success of the previous year, and now well versed in the art of overcoming Republican majorities, the Democratic

Party entered the campaign with enthusiasm and confidence. Not so with the Republicans. Many of their leaders had been killed or driven from the State, and the rank and file found themselves unable to make head in politics against their well-organized and armed opponents. They were disorganized and dispirited; but they believed in the Republican Party, were anxious to vote its ticket, and were ready so to do if they could be protected in the rights which the laws gave them.

In the First Congressional District James W. Lee, of Aberdeen, was the Republican candidate for Congress. As has been stated in a former chapter, he was a native of the State and had served in the Confederate army. He made all the necessary arrangements for canvassing his district and advertising for meetings to be held at various points. At every appointment he was met by large bodies of armed Democrats. In Oktibbeha and Lowndes, two of the strongest Republican counties in the district, he was not permitted to speak at all. Republican processions were not allowed to march through the towns or villages. At Palo Alto the Democratic rifle club intercepted and prevented the Republican procession from going to the place of speaking. The Democrats took pieces of artillery to the meetings, and would fire them so as to disturb the meetings. At Astoria the Democrats fired into the Republican crowd and wounded six negroes. Judge Acker, the Democratic candidate for elector, against Frazee, the Republican elector, on one occasion asked Mr. Lee, "Lee, did it ever occur to you that I could have had you and Frazee both killed by just saying the word at any one of our appointments?" Lee replied, "Yes, it has occurred to me."

In the Sixth District John R. Lynch was the Republican candidate for Congress. Mr. Lynch gave his testimony before Senator Boutwell's committee in regard to the canvass and the election in the State, and especially in his district. He swore that the election was characterized by intimidation throughout the State. That in Claiborne and Jefferson counties the opposition of the armed companies of Democrats was so violent, that he did not attempt to speak, for fear of causing bloodshed. The sheriff of Claiborne County admitted his inability to keep the peace at Mr. Lynch's meeting at Port Gibson. The meeting was dismissed, and no speeches were made.

In Jefferson County Mr. Lynch was prevented from speaking both at Rodney and Fayette. At the latter place armed Democrats assembled to the number of 1200 or 1500, bringing three pieces of artillery with them. They marched in from various points, some of them arriving at Fayette before daylight on the morning of the meeting. It was not possible to hold a meeting without incurring the risk of bloodshed.

The negroes quietly adjourned the meeting to a point eight miles in the country. Here they were addressed by Mr. Lynch, but they were not safe even at that remote point. Armed Democrats were soon upon them, and it was with difficulty that some prominent peaceable citizens were able to prevent an assault being made upon the unarmed Republicans and their families.

The result was, that in a district in which every county was Republican the Republican majority of 15,000 was overcome, and the Democrats carried the district by nearly 4000 majority.

It was shown that on the day of the election the Democrats refused to get into line and take their proper turn at voting, but crowded the polls so as to prevent Republicans from voting. Democratic newspapers had advised Democrats not to get into line. The judges so conducted the election as to allow the Democrats to vote promptly, but delayed the voting of Republicans.

At Tinniers' Monument, Hinds County, 437 Republican voters were thus prevented from casting their ballots.

As the result of the intimidation and murders of 1875, carried on by the Democrats with a high hand, and continued during the campaign of 1876, wherever it seemed necessary to success, and which was at the election of the latter year supplemented by gross frauds, the State of Mississippi cast its electoral vote for Tilden and Hendricks by a majority of 49,568.

An examination into the history of the events connected with the elections of 1875 and 1876 in Mississippi shows that in every county where the Democrats had large military companies, and killed a number of Republicans and terrorized the rest, that the Republican vote fell off, and the Democrats were enabled to carry the election.

A few counties will be taken as an illustration, and a comparison instituted between the vote of 1872 and 1876.

NAMES OF COUNTIES.	1876		1872	
	Hayes.	Tilden.	Grant.	Greeley.
Lowndes..................	2	2,073	3,217	698
Madison..................	13	1,473	2,512	765
Tallahatchee..............	1	1,144	891	328
Yazoo......	2	3,672	2,433	922
	18	8,362	9,063	2,713

In these four counties Hayes received only eighteen votes in 1876, while Grant received 9063 in 1872.

Take another group of counties:

	Hayes.	Tilden.	Grant.	Greeley.
Amite......................	73	1,471	995	578
Claiborne..................	423	1,504	2,240	439
Monroe....................	1,897	2,791	2,598	1,394
Montgomery..............	451	1,514	901	764
Hinds.....................	1,474	4.503	4,015	1,539
Warren...................	623	2,036	4,709	1,284
Washington....	1,598	2,901	2,969	195
	6,539	16,720	18,427	5,193

The vote received by Mr. Hayes in 1876 in the before-named eleven counties was 6557, while the vote received by General Grant in 1872 in the same counties was 27,490.

The Republican vote in the four counties first named for a series of years was as follows:

	1869.	1872.	1875.	1876.
Lowndes.................	4,082	2,725	2,021	2
Madison........	2,508	2,512	2,587	13
Tallahatchee..............	756	891	969	1
Yazoo....................	2,642	2,433	7	2

The evidence is overwhelming that the arguments offered to Republicans to induce them to vote the Democratic ticket, or not to vote at all, were the rifle, the shot-gun, the pistol, and the halter. It is therefore simply preposterous to assume that the Republicans in these counties voluntarily remained from the polls or willingly voted the Democratic ticket. As an admirable illustration of the effect the Democratic system of electioneering has upon the result of an election, the county of Issaquena, heretofore alluded to, may be cited. In 1875 there were no outrages committed in that county by Democrats upon Republicans; the result was that Mr. Buchanan, the Republican candidate for State Treasurer, received 2044 votes, while the Democratic candidate received 266 votes.

In December after the election the Democrats raided the county and killed seven negroes, and in January they intimidated the board of supervisors. At the November election 1876 Hayes received 909 votes and Tilden 788 votes. The census of 1880 shows that this county has a colored population of 9174 and a white population of 826.

It is obvious that the so-called election of 1876 was not a free expression of the voice of the people of Mississippi. That voice was stifled. The majority of the people of the State were prevented from giving expression to their sentiments and will through the ballot-box by force of arms and fraud.

The State government, legislative and executive, was brought into power by the same means the year before, and was pledged in advance to the subjugation and suppression of the Republican vote. A fair election would have given the State to Hayes and Wheeler, and would have elected five Republicans out of the six members of Congress.

SOUTH CAROLINA.

The State of South Carolina has a population, according to the census of 1880, of 995,577; of these 391,105 are white and 604,333 are colored. The number of colored persons of voting age was 118,889, and the number of white persons of voting age was 86,900, giving a majority of 31,989 colored persons of voting age.

The State is divided into thirty-three counties, eight of which contain a majority of white persons. The Democrats in fact, prior to 1876, made no nominations of candidates for Governor. Knowing that the contest was hopeless, they undertook to distract the Republican Party by divisions in 1870, 1872, and 1874, and coalesced with Independent Republicans, contenting themselves by placing a Democrat on the ticket for the office of Lieutenant-Governor. These plans, however, failed. The Republicans maintained their ascendency in 1874 by electing a Governor, a large majority in the Legislature, and a full delegation to the United States Congress, consisting of five members. Hon. D. H. Chamberlain was elected Governor. His administration proved satisfactory to both parties. He had shown himself to be a man of excellent ability, free from partisan bias in conducting the business of the State, and honest and faithful in the performance of every duty.

The *News and Courier* of Charleston, the leading Democratic paper of the State, favored the re-election of Mr. Chamberlain, and most of the country papers followed suit. It seemed for a time that the Democrats would make no nomination, but would indorse Governor Chamberlain and help elect him.

From the date of the reorganization of the State under the reconstruction laws the Republican majority at all the elections prior to 1876 was about 30,000 votes.

The attitude of the colored voters of the State to the Democratic Party was well stated by Governor Orr in his testimony before a Congressional Committee in 1871. He said:

"It was supposed by the whites, when the Presidential election of 1868 came on, that they could have some influence with the colored vote. Great pains was taken. The whole State was stumped by leading gentlemen who were supporting the nominee of the Democratic Party. And of course the other party were represented by their orators, yet I do not suppose there were five hundred colored men in the whole State who voted for Seymour and Blair. That was very much the case last year, when the reform party was organized. A Republican was nominated for the position of Governor by the reform party, and they nominated a Democrat for Lieutenant-Governor. They made a very active canvass in the State, and yet I do not suppose they received five hundred colored votes.

"The tendency has been to solidify the colored element. I think that a great many of those who would otherwise be expected to control the State in its affairs have desponded of their ever being able to relieve themselves from the incubus, as they regard it, upon them, of so great a majority of colored voters in the State. The colored majority in the whole State is about 30,000; while there may be differences of opinion, I have a very decided one as to the mistakes the white element made in trying to control the colored population. A mistake has been made, and I myself think it will be some time before they will be able to control the colored element."

Their State convention met in May, 1876. General M. C. Butler and General Gary opposed the indorsement of Governor Chamberlain. While Mr. Conner, afterwards Attorney-General, and Mr. Hagood, afterwards Governor, were in favor of indorsing him, no agreement was reached, and the convention adjourned for about a month. At its second meeting it was decided in a secret session to nominate a full ticket for State offices and for Congress.

General Wade Hampton was selected as the Democratic candidate for Governor. It was a bold undertaking on the part of the Democratic Party to overcome the great Republican majority in the State. They decided to set themselves that task, and having done so they were not slow in adapting the means to the end.

The first thing to be done was to impress upon the minds of the colored voters of the State the important fact that the time had come when the Democratic Party proposed to establish its supremacy in the State by force of arms.

THE HAMBURG MASSACRE.

On the 4th day of July, 1876, Company A, Ninth Regiment National Guards (colored) of the State of South Carolina, celebrated the day by drilling on one of the public streets in the town of Hamburg, where many of the members lived. The street on which they drilled was not often used, and was between one hundred and one hundred and fifty feet wide. While the company was thus drilling, Thomas Butler and Henry Getsen (whites) drove along in a carriage, and demanded that the company should make way for them. The captain halted the company, called the attention of these gentlemen to the fact that there was plenty of room on each side of the company to pass, and remonstrated with them for seeking to interfere with the company. Finding them unwilling to turn out of their course, Adams, the captain of the company, opened ranks and they drove through. This incident angered Butler and Getsen, who made complaint against Captain Adams for obstructing the highway, and on the 5th of July a warrant was issued against him, and he was arrested that day. After the arrest of Adams the case was continued until four o'clock Saturday afternoon, July 8th. At that time General M. C. Butler appeared as the attorney of the prosecutors. After ascertaining the nature of the charge, General

Butler stated that he thought the case might be arranged, and at his suggestion time was given him to
see the parties. In the mean time some two hundred
armed white men had assembled in Hamburg, and a demand had been made that the militia should surrender
their arms. This large force of armed Democrats were
from Barnwell and Aiken counties, and assembled at
Hamburg at the request and upon the notice of some
very influential person; their coming was not by acci-
dent. The presence of so large an armed force created
alarm amongst the citizens of the town, and many of the
members of the militia company repaired to their
drill-room. Upon the suggestion of General Butler the
trial-justice went to the drill-room of the company, and
advised them to surrender the arms. This they refused
to do, upon the ground that General Butler had no authority to require them to surrender their guns. The
trial-justice proposed to both sides that he would receive
and box the arms and send them to the Governor of the
State. This was refused on the part of the white men,
who insisted that the arms should be given up to them;
and upon the refusal of the company to do so, fire was
opened upon them in their drill-room.

The firing was kept up for about half an hour, and
was returned by the company. One of the attacking
party was killed. After this the white men sent over
to Augusta, Ga, for a cannon, which was brought
loaded with grape and canister, and they fired three or
four times at the armory. Before the cannon was fired
the negroes escaped from the building by means of lad-
ders, and hid under floors of adjacent buildings or
wherever else they could find shelter. The town marshal, James Cook, who was not a member of the company, came out of the armory building into the street,

and was instantly fired upon and killed. Search was then made by the white men for the colored men who had fled from the armory. Twenty-seven persons were captured. The arrests were not confined to members of the militia company, some of whom had made good their escape in the darkness. These arrested men were kept under guard until two o'clock A.M., when a colored man by the name of Attaway was taken out from the rest of the company, and although he and his mother pleaded for his life, he was fired upon and killed. Soon afterward David Phillips was taken out, and was also killed.

Other men were taken out of the ring where the prisoners were kept, and were told to run, and were then fired upon and either killed or wounded.

As some of these colored men were taken out of the crowd they recognized white men with whom they were acquainted, and pleaded with them to interpose and save their lives; this they refused to do. In one instance where a negro had been wounded two white men interfered, and saved him from being killed, and sent him to Augusta, Ga.

Extract from a letter of Governor Chamberlain of South Carolina, to President Grant, dated Columbia, S. C., July 22, 1876, in regard to the Hamburg massacre:

"In respect to the Hamburg massacre, as I have said, the fact is unquestionable that it has resulted in great immediate alarm among the colored people and all Republicans in that section of the State. Judging from past experience, they see in this occurrence a new evidence of a purpose to subject a majority of the voters of that vicinity to such a degree of fear as to keep them from the polls on election-day, and thus reverse or stifle the true political voice of the majority of the people.

"But the Hamburg massacre has produced another

effect. It has, as a matter of fact, caused a firm belief on the part of most Republicans here that this affair at Hamburg is only the beginning of a series of similar race and party collisions in our State, the deliberate aim of which is believed by them to be the political subjugation and control of this State. They see therefore in this event what foreshadows a campaign conducted on the 'Mississippi plan.'

"From what I have now said it will not be difficult to understand the feeling of the majority of the citizens in a considerable part of the State. It is one of intense solicitude for their lives and liberties. It is one of fear that, in the passion and excitement of the current political campaign, physical violence is to be used to overcome the political will of the people."

Extract from President Grant's letter dated July 26, 1876, in reply to Governor Chamberlain of South Carolina.

"The scene at Hamburg, as cruel, bloodthirsty, wanton, unprovoked, and as uncalled for as it was, is only a repetition of the course that has been pursued in other Southern States within the last few years, notably in Mississippi and Louisiana. Mississippi is governed to-day by officials chosen through fraud and violence, such as would scarcely be accredited to savages, much less to a civilized Christian people. How long these things are to continue, or what is to be the final remedy, the Great Ruler of the Universe only knows. But I have an abiding faith that the remedy will come, and come speedily, and earnestly hope that it will come peacefully."

THE ELLENTON RIOT.

After the butchery at Hamburg, the leaders of these lawless organizations, the Red Shirt Rifle Clubs, were

anxious for an excuse to make such a raid through a few
Republican counties as would strike terror to colored
Republicans throughout the State.   In September a circumstance occurred, trivial in itself, but exactly suited
to their purpose.

It appears that some negroes called at the house of a
Mr. Harley and asked for something to eat. One or two
men entered the house.   Presently Mrs. Harley detected
one of them pulling at a lot of clothing in a wardrobe,
and at once ordered him to desist.   The man started
to leave the house.   As he passed out he pushed or
struck Mrs. Harley and her son, a boy of nine or ten
years.

This assault upon his wife and child justly excited the
indignation of Mr. Harley, but instead of seeking redress
at the hands of the law, he called to his aid a body of
armed Democrats.   On Friday, the 14th of September,
1876, these men arrested, without a warrant, one Peter
Williams, a young colored man, and took him from the
house of another colored man where he was staying.
They told him he had to go to a trial-justice to answer a
charge of assaulting Mrs. Harley and her son.   The negro was taken to the road, where Mr. Harley struck him
three times in the face.   The negro then endeavored to run
from his captors; he was pursued, and shot and severely
wounded, from the effects of which he died several days
afterward.   After he was shot he was put on a wagon
and taken to Harley's house.   Mrs. Harley was called
out to see him; she said he was not the man who struck
her.

While lying in the wagon, one of the white men put a
pistol to his heel and shot him, the ball coming out at
the calf of the leg.   He was taken a short distance up
the road, thrown into a fence corner, and a white man

stood guard over him, declaring that he should not be moved until he died.

After Williams was mortally wounded and was in the custody of his tormentors they procured a warrant for his arrest, and also for the arrest of a negro named Pope, for the alleged assault upon Mrs. Harley. Angus P. Brown was deputed as a special constable to serve the warrant.

By Saturday morning two hundred mounted men, well armed, had assembled near Harley's place. Other companies from adjoining counties, and one company from Augusta, Ga., marched toward Ellenton. Fully eight hundred men rose in arms to quell a pretended mob. Colonel A. P. Butler assumed command of this force and directed its movements. It was divided into several detachments, and they marched up and down the country, threatening to kill and occasionally killing negroes wherever they went. These terror-stricken people gathered in squads at their preaching-places and other points for consultation. Many of them decided that their only plan for safety was to take shelter in the woods and swamps, and sleep away from their homes. Their coming together became a new cause of danger; the rifle-clubs, anxious to put the whole community in the wrong, now alleged that the blacks were organizing to resist lawful authority.

On Sunday Colonel Butler's command shot and killed three negroes as they were endeavoring to get away, none of whom offered resistance to their slayers.

The colored men sent a messenger to Aiken, the county-seat, who reported on Sunday afternoon to the Democratic sheriff that the whites were shooting negroes, and asked him to go down and protect them from further violence. He did not conclude to go until Monday morning, when he started, and reached the neighborhood of the disturbance Monday afternoon. While the sheriff delayed at Aiken to go to the relief of the colored people, the Aiken Rifle Club marched from that town Sunday evening to re-enforce Colonel Butler's command, and joined him Sunday night.

The sheriff on his arrival took no steps whatever to cause these bands of armed men to disperse and go to their homes.

On Monday Senator Coker, a colored man of respectability and influence, having learned of these difficulties, went to Ellenton to consult with the colored people. He met seventy-five or one hundred persons and advised them to go home, as he did not think the white people would trouble them. They took his advice and left in the direction of their homes. On the same day, as Colonel Butler advanced upon Jackson Station he threw out skirmishers, and an unarmed negro was shot to death there. Colonel Butler marched toward Ellenton, crossing at Union Bridges. A portion of the column was sent to the house of a colored woman named Joanna Bailey; two men entered the house and found there Joanna's nephew, who had been wounded in the leg the night before. He was unarmed, and offered no resistance. Five pistol-balls were shot into him by these two men, in the presence of his aunt, killing him instantly. The squad rejoined the main column, and marched with it to Ellenton.

When near the station, John Kelsey, a colored man, was killed while trying to elude Colonel Butler's men. The column then turned and went to the house of some colored people also named Kelsey; David Bush and Sam Brown, a deaf and dumb boy, were killed in the field near the house, and Warren Kelsey was killed in his yard, in the presence of his wife and family, while begging for his life and promising to vote the Democratic ticket.

That night the main body of Colonel Butler's command encamped at Ellenton. Tuesday morning Colonel Butler moved in the direction of Rouse's Bridge, near which about a hundred colored people, men, women, and children, had fled to a swamp for safety. At this critical juncture Captain Lloyd and Lieutenant Hinton, in command of a detachment of United States troops, who had marched from Aiken, pursuant to orders from General Ruger to see what was going on, halted near Rouse's Bridge. The negroes were overjoyed at the arrival of these troops, and fell upon their knees, praying, and saying, " Thank God the Yankees have come." Firing was heard toward the swamp, and the officers were told that the whites had shot a colored man. Presently the cry was raised, " Here they come!" and Captain Lloyd and Lieutenant Hinton looked down the road and saw a body of armed white men approaching. These officers walked down the road to meet them. Colonel Butler came forward and asked Captain Lloyd and Lieutenant Hinton what they proposed. They replied that they had nothing to propose, and their orders were simply to preserve the peace. They were asked if they would disperse the negroes, should the whites leave for home. They replied that they would advise them to go home, and they had no doubt they would do so. In about half an hour afterward Colonel Butler and his command rode off in the direction of Meyers and Augusta. The United States officers estimated the number of Colonel Butler's command at between three hundred and four hundred men, all well armed and mounted.

Colonel A. P. Butler left at Ellenton a company of

men under the command of O. N. Butler, of Augusta. About the time of the conference above spoken of, Senator Coker, who lived at Robbins Station, went to the depot unarmed, carrying his satchel, and intended taking the train for Yemassee. Some of Butler's men took him prisoner. The train backed up to Ellenton, six miles, and Coker was taken out of the car. He did not seem to realize that he was in danger. O. N. Butler being consulted as to what should be done with Senator Coker, replied, "Kill him; all we want to do is to kill the leaders and then we can rule the others." Coker was taken out about two hundred and fifty yards from the station, about twelve o'clock M., and was shot to death by O. N. Butler's command, and left to lie where he fell.

After Colonel Butler separated from Captain Lloyd, instead of having his command disperse and go peacefully to their homes as he had agreed, when they came to a field by the roadside, about three miles from Ellenton, they found William Goodwin and his son Charles, and Robert Turner and his son George, all colored, picking cotton. Robert Turner, testifying under oath, thus describes what followed :

" They flung open the big gate and all poured in like a storm, and went down to William Goodwin's and took him and carried him outside of the fence, and enlisted him with the horse company; and my son had gone outside in the wood whilst they were tangling about, and he came back in the house and got in the house and sat down. They hunted all about in the cribs and in the fodder loft, and everywhere else; they spied him, I suppose, when he went off out of the field. They couldn't find him. After a while two of them went into the house. They took him out of the house. His wife beckoned to me. I went to them and begged them not to kill my son; he was sick, and I knew he never would go out in any riot. I asked them, 'Please not to kill him; he is a poor sickly creature, and he never got in any disturbance.' Then they carried him off in the woods, him and William, to a thicket by the side of the branch, and killed him. I took my little wagon and went and found him dead, and hauled him, and fixed him and buried him."

William Goodwin's body was found the next day, with nine bullet-holes through it, in the swamp, about one hundred yards from where George Turner had been killed. On the following Thursday a body of armed men, part of whom had been under the command of A. P. Butler, captured two colored men, named Thompson and Bush, a few miles from Rouse's Bridge. They were taken out of the house and down a lane. Thompson was finally allowed to go back. Bush was taken to the foot of the lane, where three white men each fired two shots into him, killing him instantly. Bush's wife was at the house with three young children when her husband was taken out. The children called to the men, "Don't kill papa.'

The facts connected with the whole of this awful tragedy, which began on the 14th of September and was continued for a period of seven days, and in which thirteen negroes were killed, against whom there was no accusation of crime, were brought out upon the trial of A. P. Butler and others in the United States Circuit Court, District of South Carolina, April Term, 1877. This case will be found in Volume I. United States Court Reports, Fourth Circuit.

In the course of the trial it was proved that during the progress of the riot Colonel A. P. Butler and others spoke of their proceedings as intended to carry the election for the Democratic Party. It was stated that the whites intended to adopt the Mississippi plan—kill a few of the "niggers" and scare the balance. George W. Bush, one of the defendants, said that the riot was not started altogether in behalf of Mrs. Harley, but to win the election. The two colored men who were sent to Aiken on Sunday for the sheriff were captured by the Aiken company of armed Democrats, and were compelled on their knees to swear that they would vote the Democratic ticket. Colonel A. P. Butler inquired of one of his prisoners what his politics were, and told him to fall in line. Other men were heard to say that the whites were going to carry the election on the Mississippi plan—the shot-gun policy. It was shown that H. J. Miller stated a week after the Hamburg massacre that the Democrats intended to carry the election if they had to kill every negro in the whole country. Miller testified as a witness, and did not deny this fact.

It was shown that one of the rioters, some time before the riot took place, stated that the plan was to kill eight or ten leading Republican negroes, and they could manage the balance. Negroes were told that if they voted the Republican ticket they would die; that the Democrats intended to carry the election if they had to wade to their saddle-skirts in blood. These lawless and bloody proceedings seemed to be the signal for the organization and arming of a great many Democratic military companies in the State; most of them were formed in about twenty counties which had large Republican majorities. They became famous that year as the Red Shirt Rifle Clubs of South Carolina. The Democratic Party relied upon these clubs to do the necessary work to carry the election. It was made their business to attend all the political meetings in the State, both Democratic and Republican. They performed this duty well.

Republican meetings were constantly disturbed and broken up by them. Governor Chamberlain held several meetings; he was insulted in the grossest possible manner, and every indignity heaped upon him short of actual personal injury. At one place, in addition to abusing him roundly, his hat was knocked from his head. At Winnsboro', while he and several friends were taking dinner at a restaurant after his meeting, a large body of Democrats assembled in front of the house and serenaded him with tin horns, tin pans, and cow-bells. They actually marched up the street, following close after him to his hotel, making the air discordant with their horrid sounds.

These rifle clubs would march up to Republican meetings and force their way on horseback through the audience to the speaker's stand, and there offer every possible insult to the speakers and to the crowd. They would endeavor to force a quarrel upon the people assembled so as to have an excuse for killing some one. If any person who happened to be run over or pushed aside by their horses undertook to defend himself, they would instantly open fire upon him with their guns and pistols.

The Democrats made it a point to have such a force of well-armed men assembled at the Republican meetings as would be able to overpower any crowd that might come together. They had worked themselves up into a frenzy against Republicans—against colored men who proposed to vote the Republican ticket, and were prepared to go any length to overcome the Republican majority of the State. They waged a crusade against free speech and a free ballot, and would not agree to the peaceful exercise of either right unless the speech and ballot were for the Democratic Party.

Taking the census of 1880 as a basis of calculation, the voting population of South Carolina in 1876 was about as follows: White voters, 81,000; colored voters, 107,000.

The Presidential vote in 1876 was reported as follows: Hayes, 91,786; Tilden, 90,896.

By this count Tilden received nearly 10,000 votes more than there were white voters, and Hayes received 15,000 less than the number of colored voters.

The history of all the elections in the State since 1868, and the undisputed facts as to the manner in which the Democrats conducted the campaign of 1876, are totally inconsistent with the idea that any voluntary accessions were made from the Republican to the Democratic Party. The Democrats did not argue, they commanded; they did not solicit, they drove. With them it was not a canvass of discussion, but of angry denunciation. They did not organize clubs with banners and music and torches and good-cheer, but companies of armed men, whose mission was rather that of war than of peace.

The distinctive feature of their campaign was violent opposition to the right of the negro to vote; the "white line" was the division they attempted to force upon the people, and white men who failed to respond to their demand that the negro should be eliminated as a voter met with their fiercest denunciations. The Democrats of South Carolina introduced into their State the methods which had been so successfully used in Alabama and Mississippi, and it is not to be supposed that they adopted the terrible expedient of murder and omitted to use the milder and equally effective remedy of fraud. It is therefore safe to say that the vote of the Republican candidate was wrongfully cut down

15,000, while the Democratic vote was wrongfully enlarged at least 10,000.

It is not the purpose of these pages to discuss the merits of the controversy which was ended by President Hayes recognizing General Wade Hampton as Governor of the State of South Carolina. Whether the votes certified as having been cast gave General Hampton a majority or not, it is perfectly clear that he was not chosen Governor as the result of a free and fair expression of the will of the electors of the State.

It was claimed that General Hampton was elected Governor by a majority of 1134. This count included Edgefield and Laurens counties, where the Democratic vote had been increased about 7000.

Hamburg and Ellenton had done their perfect work.

Whatever of success the Democratic Party attained in 1876 in South Carolina was secured by a shameless invasion of the rights and liberties of a majority of the people, and is simply a usurpation.

Although the Presidential election of 1876 was settled by the most august tribunal ever created in this country, after hearing the case discussed by the most learned lawyers in the land, yet the Democratic Party never tires of alleging that Tilden and Hendricks were cheated out of the election.

No grave charge was ever made that possessed less merit than this. An examination of the question shows that not only were Hayes and Wheeler entitled to the electoral votes of the States that were counted for them, but that a free and fair election would also have given them the States of Alabama and Mississippi. The votes of those two States should not, according to equity and good conscience, have been counted for Tilden and Hendricks. The same diabolical means which secured Alabama and

Mississippi for the Democratic Party were used in Florida, Louisiana, and South Carolina; and because the Democracy were by lawful measures prevented from capturing those States by force and fraud, and from seizing the Government of the United States by the "Mississippi plan," the "fraud issue" is raised, and an abortive attempt made to have it control the Presidential election of 1884.   The people of the United States have not forgotten the results of the Potter investigation of 1878, when a Democratic committee of Congress went in search of Republican frauds in the election of 1876, and to their amazement were presented with a translation of the cipher dispatches which had been sent from and received at Mr. Tilden's house in New York City, being the correspondence with a number of prominent Democrats to whom were entrusted the buying with money a sufficient number of Hayes and Wheeler electors to secure the election of Tilden and Hendricks.   And thus to the Democratic campaign of 1876 of bulldozing, murder, and fraud was added an attempt at bribery.

CHAPTER XIX.

THE CHISOLM MASSACRE IN KEMPER COUNTY, MISS.
1877.

Origin of the Chisolm Family—Judge Chisolm a Successful Merchant, Kind-hearted and Generous—A Zealous Republican, and frequently Elected to Office—He is the One Obstacle to the Democrats retaining their Stolen Power in Kemper County—He becomes the Special Object of Democratic Hate—Prevented from Speaking at Scooba in 1876 by an Armed Mob of Democrats—Mobbed at his own House in De Kalb—Gully, who led this Mob, the Leader of the Mob in 1877—John W. Gully Killed by an Unknown Assassin—Judge Chisolm, J. P. Gilmer, and three other White Men arrested on False Charges as Accessories to the Crime—Judge Chisolm thrown into Jail, and is accompanied by his Wife and Children—Angus McLellan, a faithful Scotchman, follows him to Jail, carrying a Shot-gun with him—J. P. Gilmer gives himself up to Answer the Charges, and is Cruelly and Treacherously Assassinated—Two Colored Men Hung until nearly Dead in the Endeavor to extort False Statements from them Incriminating Judge Chisolm, but it fails—A Mob surrounds the Jail—Angus McLellan shot in the Back as he leaves the Jail—Terrible Scenes in and around the Jail—Judge Chisolm's Little Boy is Killed—The Judge is Mortally Wounded, after bravely defending himself—His Heroic Daughter Cornelia shares her Father's Fate—All this happened on Sunday, in Christian Mississippi.

To the tragic chapter of political murders in Mississippi must now be added a brief account of the Chisolm Massacre in Kemper County April 29, 1877.

William W. Chisolm was born in the State of Georgia December, 1830. In 1846 he removed with his father's family to Kemper County, Miss., where he lived the remainder of his life.

He married, and had an interesting family of four children, the eldest a daughter, Cornelia, nineteen years of age, the youngest John, thirteen years old.

Judge Chisolm was a merchant, and had been very successful in business.   He was a kind-hearted, generous man, who made friends wherever he went.   He zealously espoused the cause of the Republican Party, had been elected to a number of offices from time to time, and in 1876 was the Republican candidate for Congress in his district.   He was an active Republican during the stormy canvass of 1875, and was a witness before the Congressional Committee which investigated the outrages of that election.

A man of wealth, of influence, and of courage, he was regarded as the one obstacle necessary to be removed to break down forever the Republican Party in Kemper County.   This county was largely Republican on a fair vote, but had been captured by the Democrats in 1875 by the same tactics that prevailed throughout the State. During the canvass of 1875 his life was frequently threatened, and for a time, acting upon the advice of friends, he deemed it prudent to absent himself from his home.   In 1876 as a candidate for Congress he became the special object of Democratic hate.   His meetings were broken up by armed bodies of Democrats, and every possible indignity was heaped upon him.

Just before the election he was to speak at Scooba, but was advised not to attend the meeting, as his life had been threatened, and there were assembled there three hundred armed Democrats ready to prevent his speaking. Instead of going to Scooba he went to De Kalb, his home, where he was to speak the next day.   The Democrats at Scooba learning his movements, at once marched across the county, taking a cannon with them.   About the time Judge Chisolm's family were retiring for the night, the

Democrats assembled at his house and opened fire with their pistols, guns, and the cannon, knocking the glass from the windows. This was accompanied by a band of music and the yells of the crowd, and was continued for some time and repeated about midnight. The next day the disturbance was so great that it was deemed useless to attempt to hold the Republican meeting, although many prominent white Republicans had come to town and large numbers of negroes. The Democrats marched through the town, and made it a point to frequently pass Judge Chisolm's house, where they would fire the contents of their loaded guns and pistols at his house, striking it in many places.

The man Gully, who afterward led the mob in April 1877, was the leader of these lawless armed Democrats in November, 1876. Various plots were laid by Gully and his crowd to get Judge Chisolm into their power so they might murder him, but so far he had managed to evade them.

On April 26, 1877, John W. Gully, one of the numerous family of that name, while returning from De Kalb to his home in the country about one mile and a half distant, was waylaid by some unknown person and killed.

Two days afterward a warrant was issued for the arrest of one B. F. Rush, charged with the killing, and against Judge Chisolm, J. P. Gilmer, Alex. Hopper, Newt. Hopper, and Charlie Rosenbaum, all white men, charging them with being accessories to the crime. There was no pretence that either of the white men were near the place of the killing, and it turned out that Rush had left the State a month before the murder of Gully. Chisolm was arrested early Sunday morning, the 29th of April, the warrant fixing the time of trial for the next day. Judge Chisolm was at once thrown into jail, and was accompanied by his wife and four children, who insisted upon going with him.

Angus McLellan, a Scotchman and a great friend of Judge Chisolm, followed them into the jail, carrying a shot-gun with him.

Mr. Gilmer, who was a native of Georgia, a merchant, and had also been a State Senator, lived in Scooba, having been informed that a warrant had been issued for his arrest, at once, with another one of the accused, started on Sunday morning for De Kalb.

When about half-way to De Kalb Mr. Gilmer met a deputy-sheriff who had been directed to arrest him. This officer did not make the arrest, but advised Mr. Gilmer not to go to De Kalb that day; but he preferred to meet the charge at once, and proceeded on his journey to De Kalb, at which place he arrived about twelve o'clock on Sunday.

On his arrival he at once reported to the sheriff, who directed one of his deputies to take him to jail. This officer took him by the wrist and was leading him toward the jail when one of the Gullys fired a charge of buckshot into his back. Gilmer broke loose and attempted to escape through an alley, but was met by a body of armed men, who shot him down and riddled his prostrate body with bullets. That evening, while Mr. Gilmer's wife was preparing to follow her husband, his dead body was brought home.

At the time of the killing of Gilmer there were about three hundred armed Democrats at De Kalb. After the killing of Gilmer the mob captured two colored men, and took them to the woods and hung them until they were almost dead, for the purpose of extorting from them a statement incriminating Judge Chisolm in the murder of John W. Gully. No such statement was made by the

negroes. After this the sheriff required McLellan to
leave the jail, where he had remained with several men
charged with the duty of guarding the prisoners. As he
left the jail in the direction of his own house and family
one of the Gullys shot him in the back and killed him.
His body was seen a few minutes after by Mrs. Chisolm
as she returned to the jail from her house, whither she
had gone for a short time. As Cornelia looked out upon
the dead body of McLellan she appealed to the men below to have mercy on her father. Her appeal was
answered by oaths, and a volley of shot at the window.
The mob now rushed into the jail and up the stairs to the
place where the prisoners were confined. This room contained iron cages in the centre, with a corridor running
around them on the outside. It was in this corridor that
Judge Chisolm and his children were, with two guards.
As the mob ascended the stairs Mrs. Chisolm, with super-
human strength, pushed her way up the stairs to the
jail door, which was fastened. Rosser and the Gullys
led the way, and, failing to gain admittance, obtained an
axe and soon chopped the wooden door so they could
get at the lock. Cornelia and Johnny Chisolm stood
against the door to keep the people out. Mrs. Chisolm
seizing Rosser by the arm as he was wielding the axe,
appealed to him in the name of his own wife and children
to desist, but he answered by thrusting her aside. The
guard begged the mob to retire, but refused to fire upon
them, fearing that his own life would pay the penalty.
At the request of the Judge, Cornelia carried to her
father several guns which had been left in the corridor
by the guard. She then returned to the door just as
some one fired; the shot struck some iron, and glancing
wounded Cornelia in the face in many places. The door
began to give way. Rosser now placed his gun in the

crack and fired.   This shot tore off Johnny's right arm at the wrist and set his clothing afire; his brother Clay carried him behind one of the cages, but the little fellow immediately returned to the door to aid his sister to keep the ruffians out.

Finally the door flew open, and Rosser stood there, gun in hand.   Johnny rushed into his father's arms, crying, " Oh, don't shoot my father !" while Cornelia seized Rosser's gun and endeavored to keep him out.   Rosser pushed her aside and fired at Chisolm.   The balls pierced Johnny's heart, killing him instantly.

Judge Chisolm in desperation seized a gun, and firing at Rosser shot him in the head, scattering his brains against the wall.

Mrs. Chisolm now forced her way into the jail, to find Cornelia wounded and Johnny dead.   The mob, appalled at the death of Rosser, remained outside the door and opened fire into the corridor.   They at last entered, seized Rosser's body, and dragged it down-stairs and out of the jail.   An alarm of fire was now raised, and the mob cried out, " Run them out; the jail is on fire !" Judge Chisolm and his family decided to leave the jail and take their chances with the howling mob rather than be burned to death.

They started down-stairs, Mrs. Chisolm and Clay bearing the dead body of Johnny, while the Judge, with Cornelia clinging to his neck, descended the stairs.   Mrs. Chisolm reached the landing below without interference, but the Judge was met by Henry Gully.   Cornelia appealed to him, saying, " If you must have blood, I pray you to take my life and spare my darling papa, who has never done you a wrong."

His answer was a charge of shot, which crushed into her arm, shattering the bone from the wrist nearly to the elbow.   One shot carried away a piece of the Judge's nose.   The Judge and Cornelia struggled down the stairs.

Bill Gully twice attempted to shoot Mrs. Chisolm, and she defended herself with a gun which proved to have been loaded for a guard with a blank cartridge.   When the Judge reached the foot of the stairs he attempted to gain the shelter of a pile of goods in the lower room, but was fired upon from front and rear, and fell mortally wounded at the moment when Phil Gully was about to strike him with a heavy stick.

Judge Chisolm begged his wife to be carried home so that he might not die a felon in jail.   Cornelia, although dreadfully wounded, went to the door and begged for help to carry her father and dead brother home.   This appeal was answered by some one firing sixteen large duck-shots into her leg and foot.   Her hip was struck, and the bonnet-strings almost severed at the neck; thirty bullet-holes were in her clothing, and she was bloody from her head to her feet.

Finally two men volunteered to help carry Judge Chisolm to his home, about one hundred yards distant.   Cornelia, though mortally wounded, went without help, while an old gentleman, Dr. McClanahan, assisted by two negroes, carried the dead boy to his father's house.   Upon reaching the house it was found locked and abandoned by the servants through fear.

A window was broken open, and the Judge, helpless and bleeding, was dragged through it.   He and his daughter were at last placed in bed, and every attention possible was rendered by Dr. McClanahan, who, however, was a feeble old man.   The greatest difficulty was experienced in obtaining suitable surgical attention.

All this happened on *Sunday*, in Christian Mississippi.

These unhappy people bore up against these weighty misfortunes with true Christian fortitude. Letters of sympathy and encouragement from prominent people in various parts of the Union poured in upon them. These were of course highly appreciated, and constituted the silver lining to the dark cloud which hung over them.

The Judge and Cornelia suffered and lingered from the effects of their wounds for some time. He died on the 13th and she on the 15th of May, 1877. From Wells's history of the massacre the following extract is taken in respect to the burial of the Judge and his daughter:

"Thus, within sight of three Christian churches, one after another the victims sank and died, and not a minister of the gospel nor a member of the congregation with which the mother and murdered daughter worshipped ever offered to cross the threshold of the house of mourning. One after another the mangled forms were carried out and buried, with just enough hands to perform the manual labor incident thereto, and not a requiem was sung nor a benediction offered, save only the prayers which came silently and spontaneously from the hearts of the faithful few who stood around."

A crime more atrocious and cruel has never stained the annals of mankind. Gilmer, unarmed, defenceless, in the hands of the law, was shot like a wild beast, and when bleeding and wounded cried out, " O Lord, don't shoot any more ! I gave myself up and you promised to protect me." No mercy was shown him; he was shot down and his body filled with bullets.

McLellan, unaccused of crime, unarmed, and quietly returning to his home, was ruthlessly slain, simply be- cause he dared to be a friend of Judge Chisolm.

But what shall be said when hatred and passion are turned loose upon an innocent boy and upon a beautiful, accomplished, and heroic girl, and they shot to death or mortally wounded. Words are powerless to convey the sense of horror which must fill every humane and Christian breast at the recital of such deeds. Chisolm is dead; his daughter and his son are dead; McLellan is dead; Gilmer is dead; and their families surviving them weep for their untimely taking off. But the assassins live, and for their cruel deeds have the plaudits of their fellow-citizens.

CHAPTER XX.

INCIDENTS OF THE ELECTIONS OF 1878-79 IN SOUTH
CAROLINA, MISSISSIPPI, AND LOUISIANA.

South Carolina—Continuation of the Red Shirt Rifle Club Organi-
zations of 1876—Some of the strong Republican Counties not suffi-
ciently Terrorized—Sumter County taken in Hand—Republican
Meeting at Goodhope—Outrage on Sam Lee—Governor Hampton
promises Protection to Republican Meetings, but fails to give it—
Action of the U. S. Attorney-General—Republican Meeting at
Sumter, S. C.—It is broken up by a Democratic Mob with
Artillery—Universal Frauds at the Elections—Use of Tissue
Ballots—Mississippi—The Murder of Captain Henry M. Dixon at
Yazoo City—The Danger of being an " Independent" in Missis-
sippi—Louisiana—Outrages upon an Election Officer in St. Mary's
Parish.

IN 1878 the Democrats of South Carolina entered
upon the political contest with confidence; the rifle-club
organizations of 1876 had been continued, and constituted the chief reliance of the Democratic Party for
carrying the election.

Some of the strongest Republican counties had not
sufficiently yielded to the influences brought to bear in
1876, and now it was determined that they should be
fully apprised of the weight of responsibility and danger
they incurred by continuing their opposition to the
Democracy.

Sumter was one of these counties. In 1876 the Republicans rolled up 1500 majority for their ticket.

The Republicans called a convention to meet at Goodhope, about twenty-one miles from Sumter, in the latter
part of September, 1878, to elect delegates to the county

convention. Ex-Senator Coghlan, a venerable gentleman of seventy-seven years of age, and Samuel Lee, a
colored man and probate judge of the county, were appointed to address the meeting. They drove out from
Sumter in buggies, and reached the place of meeting
about eleven o'clock. A large crowd of Republicans
had already reached the ground. They were not alone:
four or five hundred Democrats were also there; most of
them were armed, and many wore red shirts—the recognized uniform of the Democratic Party.

When Senator Coghlan and Mr. Lee drove in sight
they were greeted with the "rebel yell" from their opponents.

Upon reaching the grounds a prominent Democrat
cried out, "You are caught at last at your old game of
making speeches to the negroes: we intend to make you
deliver your speeches in our presence, and we will
divide time with you; so get out and begin." Some of
them objected to allowing the Republicans to speak at
all. Senator Coghlan insisted that the Republicans
should be allowed to hold their meeting undisturbed.
A number of the Democrats surrounded Mr. Coghlan
while others surrounded Mr. Lee. They were both
grossly insulted and abused. The crowd demanded of
Lee that he should announce to the audience his determination to take no further part in politics, and that he
would not attend a meeting outside of the town of Sumter.

Lee positively refused to comply with this request.
He was then forcibly placed in a wagon and told to
make the declaration; he again refused, and was then
assaulted and slapped in the face by one of Governor
Hampton's aids, who seemed to have control of the
Democratic crowd. Lee and his assailant fell from the

wagon, where a scuffle ensued. Lee was choked and kicked, and a number of Democrats drew their guns and pistols upon him. An influential Democrat interposed and prevented his being shot. The Democrats seized the president of the Republican precinct club and forced him to declare that he would take no further interest in politics. Lee was thrown into a buggy and driven off, surrounded by about three hundred armed men, he being unarmed.

When they reached a point about a mile from the place of meeting, Lee was taken into a thicket, where the Democrats declared they would kill him unless he made the required declaration. A number of persons drew their pistols upon him; amongst these was Governor Hampton's aid, and a gentleman who has since been made solicitor of a judicial circuit of the State. Lee again refused. He was again placed in the buggy and driven about a mile farther, when he was taken from the buggy and a rope put about his neck. Lee declared it as his fixed determination not to comply with their request. The two prominent gentlemen spoken of then stated to Lee that they intended to leave him, and would not be responsible for him any longer. Lee declared that they might kill him, but he would not surrender his rights as a citizen; and with the rope about his neck he declined to comply with their request. He was again placed in the buggy and driven to the town of Sumter, the parties from time to time drawing their fire-arms upon him and threatening him. Upon reaching town Lee jumped from the buggy and endeavored to get away. The horsemen ran over him, trampled him down, and bruised him severely. He was again placed in the buggy and taken to the court-house steps, where this body of armed Democrats warned him not to be caught out of town. The police of the town interfered for Lee's protection, but were overpowered by the rifle-club. That night Lee's house was visited and searched by disguised men. Lee was away, fearing to remain at home during the night. His wife was abused and threatened by them.

Senator Coghlan was seized, and a red shirt was placed upon him. The Democrats drew their guns upon him and threatened him. He got away without injury. The fact that he was a white man and extremely old probably saved him from actual harm. Mr. Lee appealed to the civil authorities for redress, without effect. He then visited Governor Hampton and laid the matter before him. The Governor promised to inform his aid and citizens generally that Republican meetings were not to be interfered with. He also stated that he would soon be at Sumter to address a meeting, where he would publicly request Democrats not to disturb Republican meetings. In a few days Governor Hampton visited Sumter to attend a Democratic meeting. It was a grand military and red-shirt display. Governor Hampton addressed the meeting, but made no allusion to the subject of Republicans being allowed to hold their meetings without disturbance. At the close of his speech Mr. Lee rose and requested permission of Governor Hampton to ask him a respectful question. The Governor consented that he might do so if it would not cause a controversy. Before Lee could propound the question he was seized by a number of red-shirters and borne from the meeting. They almost tore him limbless. A crowd of mounted men demanded that he should be given to them. Governor Hampton rushed out and called upon his aids to assist him, and they prevented Lee from being killed.

That night Lee started for Washington, and upon his arrival laid the matter before the President and Attorney-General. Attorney-General Devens at once issued a circular to United States marshals, calling attention to the law for the protection of the people in the right to advocate the election of candidates for members of Congress, and required them to see to its enforcement. Upon the advice of the Attorney-General a meeting was appointed for the town of Sumter, for the advocacy of the election of the Republican candidate for Congress for that district. After notice was given of this meeting, the Democrats also called a meeting for the same time and place, and the military companies of the five neighboring counties were invited to be present. They selected their place of meeting about one hundred yards distant from the Republican stand. On the day appointed large crowds of people, unarmed and peaceable, came to attend the Republican meeting. Large bodies of armed Democrats marched in to attend the Democratic meeting, bringing with them three pieces of artillery, which were brought from the capital of the State for the occasion. These guns were put in position, pointing in the direction of the Republican stand. At twelve o'clock the Republican meeting was called to order by Senator Coghlan. Immediately the Democrats commenced firing their cannon over the heads of the Republicans, and kept it up for an hour or more, making it impossible for the meeting to proceed. The Democrats did not pretend to have speaking. Finding that they could not hold their meeting at that point, the Republicans formed a procession for the purpose of marching to another place to hold their meeting, whereupon the Democrats. also formed a procession, placing their cannon in advance. They intercepted the Republican column, and their conduct was so offensive that a serious row occurred. The Democrats at once loaded their cannon with nails obtained from a neighboring store, and then ordered the streets to be cleared. The Republican meeting was broken up, and the crowd dispersed to their homes. Mr. Coghlan was seized, but was released upon the application of the mayor, who guarded him home.

On the day of election acts of violence occurred in various parts of the State, and in some places Republicans were forcibly kept from the polls. But this was not actually essential to the success of the Democratic Party. A novel feature was introduced into this election—that is, the use of tissue-ballots. They had been carefully prepared, well distributed, and every necessary arrangement made for their introduction into the ballot-boxes. At some polling-places the Democratic judges would add to the regular list of voters a sufficient number of names to cover the fraudulent tickets placed in the box. This was done at precinct No. 2 in Sumter County, where Samuel Lee was supervisor. Two hundred and eleven fraudulent Democratic tissue-ballots were thus counted. At other places and generally one of the judges or clerks of election would be blindfolded for the purpose of drawing out the excessive ballots in the box.

This proceeding was in compliance with a provision of the election laws. The Democratic tickets were printed on thin paper, and were distinguishable from Republican tickets by the touch; the result was that while the Democrats could lose nothing if some of their tickets happened to be drawn out, the Republican vote was greatly reduced by this fraudulent device.

THE MURDER OF DIXON IN MISSISSIPPI.

The spirit of intolerance toward Republicans is unhesitatingly turned upon a Democrat if he presumes to abandon the party and seek its defeat. A tragic illustration of this fact occurred at Yazoo City, Miss., in 1879. Captain Henry M. Dixon, who, as has been shown, figured conspicuously in the campaign of 1875 as commander of a company of scouts, concluded to become an independent candidate for sheriff. He was encouraged to make the race by a number of influential planters.

The negroes had decided to support him, believing that he would be able, as he had promised, to secure them in the exercise of the right of suffrage. The prospect of Democratic success began to fade rapidly. The leaders, however, decided to settle the question in a prompt and summary manner. An armed mob numbering several hundred men was brought together, and they waited upon Dixon at his residence in Yazoo City. They demanded that he should withdraw as a candidate for sheriff, threatening to kill him upon his refusal. He signed a paper withdrawing as a candidate.

After the mob disbanded he declared that the paper was obtained while he was under duress, and he would not be bound by it.

So he again declared himself as a candidate. His action created considerable excitement, and his wife and friends had great apprehension for his safety.

August 19, 1879, a day or so after this, as Dixon was crossing the street, his competitor for sheriff, Mr. Barksdale, fired upon Dixon from behind, mortally wounding him in the back. He was shot at 9 A.M. and died at 12 M. the same day. Dixon had made no attack upon Barksdale, nor did he have arms in his hands; nevertheless

Mr. Barksdale was held to have performed this act of killing his opponent in his necessary self-defence. It seems needless to say that Mr. Barksdale met with no further opposition in his canvass, and was duly elected.

OUTRAGES ON AN ELECTION OFFICER IN LOUISIANA.

In St. Mary Parish, La., the election of 1878 gave the entire Republican ticket large majorities. The parish officers elected were all Republicans.

After the returns of the election had been received by the parish clerk, duplicate abstracts of the result were made, according to law. One was delivered to the sheriff and the other retained by the clerk, Mr. G. R. M. Newman.

On the night of the 8th of November Newman was informed that a raid was about to be made upon the court-house for the purpose of obtaining the returns. He hastened to his office and took the set of returns of which he had custody to his home. That night the clerk's office was broken open and all the election-papers found there were destroyed. The next day, however, the raiders discovered that the sheriff's set of returns alone had been destroyed, and that that of the clerk of the court was still in existence. This much having been accomplished, it was determined to complete the enterprise, and to demand the returns of Newman personally. With this object in view, W. K. Wilson, parish attorney *pro tem.*, called at Newman's house at about eleven o'clock on the night of the 9th. He knocked on the door, and Newman, who had just finished making a new tally-sheet for the sheriff and was in bed, demanded who was at the door. No answer was given, but the knocking continued. Newman now becoming alarmed, armed himself with a pistol and dirk, suddenly appeared at the ʼɹoor, and with presented weapons confronted Wilson.

Wilson stated that he had just received a telegram from the attorney-general, instructing him to call on Newman and get the returns of election. He said further that Newman must go to the court-house with him and deliver the returns.

Newman refused to comply with the demand, telling Wilson that midnight was not the proper hour for transacting official business. With this, Wilson warned Newman not to speak of the visit paid him, and retired without having accomplished his purpose.

On the following day, however, Newman failed to pay any attention to the warning, and soon all the town were acquainted with the facts, although not with the name of the visitor. Everything moved smoothly, however, and nothing more was said to Newman on the subject. In the mean time, on the morning following the visit of Wilson, the tally-sheet and returns of Newman were privately sent to New Orleans, and the next day a telegram from the city announced to the people of Franklin that they had arrived safely.

The following night Newman was warned that it would be unsafe for him to remain at home. Accordingly he and his wife left home, going different ways. That night and during the two days following his house was visited by men in search of him.

On the 19th, at night, Newman and his wife were awakened by the report of a rifle discharged at the foot of the bed in which they were. On being thus suddenly alarmed, Newman saw by the light of the mosquito-bar, which had caught fire from the discharge of the rifle, that he was surrounded by enemies, one of whom was pulling his wife from the bed by her hair, another was shooting at him from the foot of the bed, and another, who stood between the bed and the front door, was also shooting at him.

He was so closely wrapped in blankets, for the night was a cold one, that, although one or two of the balls struck the bedclothes, none penetrated sufficiently to wound him. Slipping and rolling over in bed, he found himself between the bedstead and the wall. There his hand encountered his shot-gun, loaded with bird-shot. Seizing this timely aid, he crept beneath the bed and emerged upon the other side. Seeing a man standing near the door he levelled his gun and fired. The man at the door and the man who previously had hold of New-man's wife now ran out of the front door, while New-man, anxious only to escape, pushed for the door lead-ing to the back yard. At the foot of the bed his foot caught upon something and he stumbled. Looking down, he saw a black-looking object, which he rightly conjectured to be a man, lying prone upon the floor. Instinctively raising his gun perpendicularly in the air, he discharged the remaining load of the gun into the man's body.

Opening the back door he sprang into the yard. As he did so he heard a gun or pistol shot behind him, and fled only the faster, leaping fences and clearing garden patches until he at length found refuge in the house of a friend. Here he hid away for some days and then fled to New Orleans.

The evidence shows that W. K. Wilson was the leader of the attack, and that he was assisted by his brother, T. P. Wilson, and another young man. The last shot was fired by one of the two raiders who retreated out of the door. These two after getting out of the house missed their companion, and pushing open the door, which

Mrs. Newman had in the mean time slammed to, they rushed in, firing the shot which Newman heard while escaping. Mrs. Newman, concealed behind the door, watched while the two men entered, lifted their wounded companion, and carried him away. The next morning at daylight T. P. Wilson was found lying upon the front gallery of his father's house, two miles distant from the scene of the night attack. He died the next day.

The object in securing these returns was to destroy them, thus removing the evidence that Republicans had been elected to the parish offices, and in this way, upon the expiration of the term of office of the incumbents, to place the offices within the appointing power of the Governor of the State, who, it was hoped by those who participated in the raid, would appoint Democrats, although he had knowledge of the true results of the election.

CHAPTER XXI.

THE ELECTION OF 1880.

Wade Hampton Promises the National Democratic Convention the Electoral Vote of the Solid South for Hancock and English—The Promise Fulfilled—South Carolina having 30,000 Republican Majority, gives Hancock 54,000 Majority—How it was Accomplished —Objections to the Presence of U. S. Supervisors at the Polls— Brutal Treatment of some of them — Stuffing the Ballot-boxes with Tissue-ballots by Democrats—Drawing out Excessive Ballots from the Boxes—Preternatural Dexterity of the Democratic Managers in Drawing out Republican Ballots without seeing them— Falsification of Poll Lists—Polls opened by Democrats at Obscure Places and Unusual Hours—In certain Strong Republican Localities not opened at all—Action of the Boards of County and State Canvassers in Furthering and Supporting the Frauds—Intimidation and Violence used toward Republican Voters.

THE Democracy were so well established in the control of the Southern States in 1880, that at their National Convention held at Cincinnati Governor Hampton gave an assurance that the South would cast a solid vote for Hancock and English. He was well versed in the actual political condition of the Southern States, and knew that they had been subjected to the "Thorough" political processes of the then Bourbon Democracy. No massacres to shock the sensibilities of the North preceded this election. The Democrats were organized, disciplined, and armed, and if need be were prepared for any work required to insure success. The improved methods introduced into the business of holding elections rendered it quite as easy and more humane to secure favorable results by *counting* rather than by *killing;*

and so, to all outward seeming, the election of 1880 was *very quiet.*

The majorities given in some of the States to General Hancock must have been very gratifying to him. In Alabama his majority was 34,509, in Louisiana 33,419, in Mississippi 30,896, and in South Carolina, which was pledged in advance by Governor Hampton, General Hancock received 54,241 majority. It would be an interesting study to go into the history of the election in all these States, so as to learn how these great Democratic majorities were obtained in Republican States; but time and space will only be given for a brief examination into the election in South Carolina.

It must be stated in the first place that the managers (or judges) of election in all the counties except five were Democrats. In Beaufort County there was one Republican manager at each poll; and in Lexington, Oconee, Pickens, and Greenville counties at some of the polls Republicans who could not read and write, and Democrats who personated Republicans, were appointed as managers. In many places the opposition to U. S. supervisors was so great that it was difficult to find men who were willing to serve.

In the county of Laurens such was the violent conduct of the Democrats for days preceding the election, and so loud were their threats, that no Republican could be found willing to risk his life by undertaking the duties of supervisor.

For similar reasons no Republican could be found willing to incur the danger of serving as supervisor either at Millet's or Robbins precincts in Barnwell County, and hence from neither of those polls was a single Republican vote returned.

In Aiken County the Republican supervisors appointed

for Miles' Mill and Vaucluse went to a Republican meeting at Ellenton three days before the election, and while there were assaulted and badly beaten by Democrats, who, armed with guns and pistols, broke up the meeting and chased the two supervisors into the woods, through which they had to travel a distance of forty miles to reach home, One of them was pursued with dogs, and only escaped by taking the swamp and swimming the creek near by. Owing to the treatment these two men received and the threats made against their lives, they did not go on the day of election to the polls for which they had been appointed. At Kneece's Mill, Creed's Store, and Low-Town Well so great was the violence of the Democrats and so numerous their threats against the supervisors that the latter were compelled to abandon the polls, from which the Republican voters had been previously driven away by the armed bands of Democrats who had taken possession of them early in the day.

At every precinct in the county of Edgefield the Republican supervisors were prevented from witnessing the voting and the count, and at many of them they were brutally assaulted with clubs, pistols, and other weapons, and driven away. Such was the case at Meeting Street Precinct, where the supervisor was beaten with a club and his papers taken away from him ; at Red Hill, where the supervisor was assaulted and ordered to leave, and his instructions snatched from his hands; and at Johnston's Depot, where the supervisor was also assaulted and ordered to leave. Feeling that their lives were in danger, the supervisors at the three places named, and at several others, left when ordered to do so by the armed bands of Democrats who had congregated around the polls.

In Newberry County the supervisor for Pomaria Precinct was arrested by a State constable on the morning of the election just before the opening of the poll and carried to the court-house, a distance of about sixteen miles, where he was released by the trial-justice who had issued the warrant. Two nights after the election his home was visited by a band of armed Democrats, who, upon being refused admittance, proceeded to break in, and he escaped by jumping out the window and taking to the woods. This supervisor dares not return to his home. At Jalapa Precinct, in the same county, because the Republican supervisor persisted in keeping a poll-list, he was told that if he did not stop, his d——d head would be shot off, and during the day he was assaulted and his coat-sleeve cut and torn into pieces. Owing to the treatment he received and the threats made against him, he was advised by friends to leave the poll, which he did about two o'clock in the day.

At Ware's Precinct in Greenville County and Lawtonville in Hampton County the supervisors were also forced to abandon their posts because of the threats made against their lives and the violence exhibited toward them by the Democrats.

At Scranton in Williamsburg County the Republican supervisor was threatened with arrest if he persisted in acting, and in order to avoid arrest by the State authorities he left the polling-place.

In addition to the instances cited above, in which supervisors were forcibly driven away or compelled to leave the polls, instances are almost universal in which they were obstructed and prevented from discharging their duties by compelling them to remain outside of the polling-places, or having one of the managers to stand between them and the ballot-boxes, or having the room crowded with red-shirt Democrats so as to completely prevent them from seeing or hearing what was going on around and about the ballot-boxes. In many places one of the methods adopted to prevent supervisors from scrutinizing the conduct of the election was that of holding the poll in a private house or building, and forbiding the entrance of the Republican supervisor, on the ground that it was private property and no Republican supervisor would be allowed to enter. Such was the case at Talbert Precinct in Edgefield County and Stafford's Cross Roads in Hampton County.

At the close of the election, when the boxes were opened, the number of ballots in them was found to be largely in excess of the number of names on the poll-lists, which of course compelled the managers to return the ballots to the boxes and draw therefrom and destroy a number of votes equivalent to the excess, in order to make the number of votes correspond with the number of voters on the poll-lists. By this operation every Republican vote drawn out was a loss of one to the Republicans and a gain of one to the Democrats. The drawing out of a Democratic ticket occasioned no loss to the Democrats, because the excess was created either by the Democratic managers stuffing the boxes or by the Democratic voters voting two or more ballots; but nevertheless, in order that the number of Republican ballots drawn out might be as large as possible, the Democratic ballots were so devised that the person drawing out the excess could easily distinguish them, even when blindfolded, from the Republican ballots by the difference in the feeling. Two kinds of ballots were generally used at every poll by the Democrats, one larger than the other, so that a number of the smaller ballots might be enclosed within the folds of the larger ballot. The small ballots were usually printed on tissue-paper, though in many places both the large and small ballots were printed on that kind of paper. In some parts of Charleston County paste-board ballots capable of concealing a large number of tissue-ballots were used. In Newberry County, in addition to the small tissue-ballots, paste-board ballots with seriated edges were voted by the Democrats. The character of the Democratic ballots used at every poll clearly showed that the entire excess in each ballot-box was created by the Democrats for the purpose of compelling the drawing out and destruction of a large number of votes, by which they knew the Democratic candidates would profit.

Notwithstanding the obstructions thrown in the way of supervisors generally at those polls where they had not been forced to leave by threats and violence, they were permitted, after the ballot-boxes had been stuffed, to witness to a limited extent the count and canvass of the votes. From the reports made by them to the chief supervisor a table was prepared, which exhibits the number of names on the poll-list, the number of ballots found in the box, the amount of the excess and the number of Republican ballots destroyed in drawing out that excess, at one hundred and twenty-three polls in twenty-three counties out of the thirty-three counties in the State.

To show how easily the parties could and did distinguish Republican from Democratic tickets, the following facts are presented:

At twenty-one polls, containing an aggregate excess of 593 ballots, not a single Democratic ticket was drawn out, although from one box as many as 135 tickets were drawn and from another 73. At eight other polls only one Democratic ticket was drawn out at each poll, and at nine other polls only two Democratic tickets were drawn out at each poll. It is true, on the other hand, that at some polls more Democratic than Republican tickets were drawn out, but this generally arose from the fact that at such polls more Democratic ballots had been stuffed into the boxes than were necessary to accomplish the purpose intended, and consequently the excess was almost equal to, and sometimes even greater than, the number of Republican tickets in those boxes: as at Killian's in Richland County, where there were only 92 Republican tickets in the box, while the excess was 126; and at Davis's in the same county, where there were only 57 Republican tickets in the box, while the excess was 71. At Privateer in Sumter County there were only 17 Republican tickets in the box, while the excess was 120; and at Brunson's in Hampton County there were only 75 Republican tickets cast, while the excess was 232. Under no circumstances therefore could the managers at these two polls have avoided drawing out a majority of Democratic tickets even if they had drawn out every Republican ticket in those boxes. They did not, however, go quite so far, but contented themselves with drawing out 10 of the 17 Republican tickets at Privateer and 56 of the 75 at Brunson's. This, however, was not quite as bad as the action of the managers at the Hope Engine House in the city of Charleston, where the excess was 1071, while the number of Republican tickets in the box was only 597, and before drawing out a single Democratic ticket the managers drew out all but five of the 597 Republican ballots voted at that poll.

No better evidence could be adduced of a conspiracy on the part of the Democratic leaders to perpetrate this fraud than the almost universal use of tissue-ballots throughout the State.

At fourteen precincts in Orangeburg County and at twenty precincts in Charleston County these fraudulent tickets were used. In Charleston County alone 3871 fraudulent tickets were put into the boxes. This county had since reconstruction always given large Republican majorities. In 1876 Hayes received 15,086 votes and Tilden received 8778 votes, but at the election in 1880 under the new system Hancock received 11,440 votes and Garfield received 8162 votes. Thus a Republican majority of 6308 in one county was converted into a Democratic majority of 3288.

The gain to the Democrats by ballot-box stuffing was not limited to the drawing out and destruction of Republican ballots, but was still further increased by the insertion of fictitious names on the poll-lists at many precincts and by counting for such names a corresponding number of the Democratic ballots which had been stuffed into the boxes. Such was the case at Calhoun in Clarendon County, where 110 false names were inserted on the poll-list kept by the managers and a corresponding number of ballots counted therefor; but at the Stonewall Engine House in city of Charleston, where 161 names were fraudulently inserted on the poll-list, only 138 ballots were counted therefor; as some of the ballots stuffed into the box did not drop out of the folds of the tickets in which they were voted, and being found in that condition were destroyed by the managers on the first count before it had been discovered that by so doing they would not have quite enough ballots to cover the names on their poll-list.

In addition to the two polls mentioned above, the poll-lists are known to have been falsified by the insertion of fictitious names thereon to the number of 65 at Walterboro' and 148 at Ridgeville, Colleton County ; 15 at Montmorenci and 80 at Graniteville, Aiken County; and 116 at Cheraw, Chesterfield County. At each of the places named the Republican supervisor reports that he kept a correct list, which he is positive contains the name of every person who voted, and at two of those polls, Graniteville and Cheraw, the ballots in the boxes fell short of the number of names on the poll-lists, showing that the poll-lists had been falsified to a greater extent than the ballot-boxes had been stuffed.

The full extent to which the Democratic vote was increased by the falsifying of poll-lists is not fully known, because of the measures resorted to by the Democrats to prevent the supervisors from keeping poll-lists, which they had been instructed to do by the chief supervisor as a check upon that kept at each poll by the Democratic clerk of the managers. So great was the Democratic opposition to the keeping of poll-lists by the Republican supervisors, that not only were they at many places compelled to desist from so doing, but at some polls their poll-lists were forcibly taken away and destroyed ; and instances are known where in order to prevent the supervisors from obtaining the names of the persons voting, the names were handed to the Managers by Democratic voters on slips of paper, or given to the managers in such a low tone as to be inaudible to the supervisors, to whom such names were refused when demanded. It can be safely asserted that at more than one half of the polling-places in the State the Democratic supervisors neglected to obey the instructions of the chief supervisor in regard to the keeping of poll-lists, and the Republican supervisors were either prevented from keeping them or obstructed in such ways as to prevent them from keeping correct lists. Occasionally the blundering manner in which a ballot-box was stuffed led to the disclosure that the poll-list had been falsified. For instance, at Greenville C. H. the keeping of a poll-list by the Republican supervisor was at first strenuously objected to by the managers, who positively refused to allow him to continue keeping the one he had commenced, and upon his undertaking then to keep a tally of the persons voting, he was ordered to stop, as the clerk objected "to being watched;" but after the voting had gone on for about two hours the managers consented to a poll-list being kept by the supervisor, informing him that 399 names had been, up to that time, recorded on their list. At the close of the poll, when the box was opened, and during the progress of the count, large numbers of Democratic tickets were found folded in rolls or bundles. The first two packages taken out were destroyed after one out of each package had been counted; but the managers, seeing the large number in the ballot-box that from some cause would not unfold and separate, began to apprehend that if they continued to pursue that course the ballots might probably fall short of the number of names on the poll-list; so they decided, after considerable controversy, to lay aside all tickets found folded together until after they had counted all the single ballots. Under this arrangement forty-five packages of Democratic tickets, containing some four or five hundred ballots, according to the estimate of the supervisor, were laid aside. Although numerous ballots were counted which were shaken out of other ballots, yet upon the completion of the count it was found that the number counted was 105 less than the number of names on the poll-list, and 105 Democratic ballots were then taken to make up the deficiency from the packages which had been laid aside, and the balance destroyed.

At Camden, the county-seat of Kershaw County, only 2066 ballots were found in the box while 2390 names were recorded on the poll-list kept by the managers—conclusive proof that at least 324 names had been fraudulently placed on the poll-list. How many more names were added and to what extent the box was stuffed it is impossible to tell, because a few minutes before the hour for opening the poll the Democratic county chairman requested the two supervisors to step out a moment as he wanted to see them; which they did, and upon the return of the Republican supervisor he found the door locked and no attention was paid to his repeated knocks until after the managers had declared the poll opened and received several votes. By this trick the supervisor was prevented from inspecting the ballot-box so as to see if it was empty before the voting began, and in the course of the day his poll-list was stolen from him, so that in the absence of any check upon them the Democratic managers had full scope to insert all the names they desired on the poll-list and to stuff as many ballots into the box as they deemed necessary to overcome the large Republican majority which had always been given at that place.

The system of stuffing the ballot-boxes by creating in them an excess of ballots over the voters on the poll-list and thereby compelling the drawing out of a number of ballots equal to the excess, prevailed to such an extent throughout the State that it at once gives rise to the inference that it was not the result of local manipulation, but of a well defined and matured plan emanating from some central authority. The chairman of the State Democratic Executive Committee issued the following circular to the chairman of the Democratic Party in each county, which clearly indicates that the Democratic Executive Committee of the State were aware that the ballot-boxes were to be stuffed, and knowing upon which party the loss was to fall by the process of drawing out and destroying ballots, were exceedingly anxious to prevent the evidence from being obtained of the extent to which the Democratic Party profited by that process:

"ROOMS OF THE
"STATE DEMOCRATIC EXECUTIVE COMMITTEE,
"COLUMBIA, S. C., October 27, 1880.
"To...............................

"*County Chairman:*

"DEAR SIR : The attention of the State Executive Committee has been called to the instructions issued by Chief Supervisor Poinier to the supervisors of election in this State.   These supervisors are directed to report 'the number of ballots drawn out of the ballot-box and destroyed by the managers of election because of the excess of votes over names on the poll-list ;' also the number of such ballots that '*bore the names of the Republican candidates*' and the number which bore the names of the Democratic candidates and Greenback candidates.

"The instruction to report *the character* of the ballots drawn out and destroyed is unauthorized and illegal. The State Election Law, by which alone you are governed, requires (see compilation of Election Law, Section 12) that 'if more ballots shall be found on opening the box than there are names on the poll-lists, . . . one of the managers or the clerk, *without seeing the ballots,* shall draw therefrom and *immediately destroy* as many ballots as there are in excess of the number of names on the poll-list.'   You will, therefore, instruct the managers of election throughout your county at once, that they *must not allow the supervisors to see or inspect* any ballots drawn from the box in excess of the number of names on the poll-list, in order to ascertain for whom such ballots were cast. The ballots must be drawn *without being seen* and must be *immediately destroyed* as the law directs.

"By order of the Committee.

"JOHN BRATTON,
"*Chairman.*"

The positive language in which the chairman of the Democratic Party of each county is commanded by the chairman of the State Committee to *instruct* the managers of election in their respective counties, shows how completely the managers of election were under the control of the Democratic Executive Committee of the State; and the conduct of these officers throughout the State in the general management of the election and the counting of the votes indicates that they regarded themselves more as agents of the Democratic Party than as sworn officers of the election. Indeed, it is safe to conclude that generally the work of stuffing the ballot-boxes was performed by them; and when not by them, by others with their knowledge and through the facilities by them furnished.

In many precincts the managers, instead of opening the polls at the usual places, removed them to remote and obscure points, without notice to the Republican supervisor or the Republican voters; and even in some instances took steps to deceive the Republican supervisors and Republican voters so that none of them might have the opportunity of inspecting the ballot-boxes to see that nothing was in them before the polling of votes began.

Such was the case at Mount Pleasant, in Charleston

County, where the managers opened the poll on the piazza of a private house nearly a half mile distant from the place where the night previous they had informed the Republican supervisor that the poll would be held; and at George's Station, Colleton County, where one manager was sent to the usual polling-place with a ballot-box, and finding the Republican supervisor and many Republican voters present, remained with them until some time after the hour fixed by law for the opening of the polls, when, the other two managers not appearing, he coolly informed the supervisor that he supposed the other managers had opened the poll somewhere else, and thereupon conducted him to a place distant about one quarter of a mile, where they found the voting going on, with none but Democrats present. In Clarendon and the adjacent counties of Williamsburg and Sumter this trick was resorted to at so many polling-places as to establish the fact that it was the result of a general understanding among the Democrats, and one of the methods devised for the purpose of enabling the managers to stuff the ballot-boxes.

With the same object in view the polls in many precincts were opened before six o'clock, the hour fixed by law, and it was a very common occurrence for a Republican supervisor to be told upon his arrival at a poll that the poll had just been opened. It made no difference what hour the Republican supervisor arrived, for in some instances where they went to polls nearly an hour before the time they found them opened. In the city of Columbia, the capital of the State, where the hours of the day are struck on an alarm-bell by a man employed by the city authorities for that purpose, material assistance was rendered the managers in the scheme of opening the polls before the regular time by the action of that bellman, who on the morning of the election at half-past five o'clock struck the hour of six. Immediately thereupon the managers of election, who were all conveniently present at that early hour, declared the polls opened and proceeded to receive votes, and when the Republican supervisors arrived, they found the election going on, and after the polls had been opened thirty minutes, the bell again rung six o'clock—the second time that morning.

In certain strong Republican localities, in order perhaps to save themselves the trouble of stuffing the ballot-boxes, the Democrats did not open any polls. This was the case at Summerville, Delemar's, and Gloversville in the county of Colleton; at Grier's in Georgetown County; and at Statesburg in Sumter County.

The frauds did not stop with the election managers.

The boards of county canvassers lent a hand to make certain a Democratic majority. In Charleston County the vote returned by the managers was, Garfield 12,824; Hancock, 10,905. The majority heretofore stated in favor of Hancock was produced by throwing out the votes from certain precincts.

In Sumter County, at the court-house, there were two polling-places, one known as Box No. 1 and the other as Box No. 2. The Democrats took forcible possession of the latter poll, which was held in the second story of a building, in a room at the end of a long, narrow passage-way, and by remaining in the passage-way after they had voted they blocked up all access to the box, thereby preventing the Republicans from voting at that poll, and compelling them to confine their voting to Box No. 1. The Republican vote being very heavy, at two o'clock in the day the ballot-box at the latter poll became too full to admit any more, while there were still over four hundred Republicans awaiting their opportunity to vote. Under these circumstances the managers of the election, acting under the advice of the Democratic county chairman, who is also a leading lawyer of the county, sealed the ballot-box and sent to the board of commissioners of elections for another box to receive the votes of those who had not then already voted. On the arrival of the box the voting proceeded until the close of the poll, when on counting the votes it was found that the two boxes contained a total of 1419 Republican and 9 Democratic votes. The managers of the election made up and certified their returns to the county board in the usual form. Not a single objection was then urged against the proceedings. Nobody charged any irregularity, and not a single word of complaint was heard, until it had been ascertained that in spite of the efforts of the Democrats to cheat the Republicans out of the election by fraud and violence and intimidation the Republicans still had on the face of the returns, as made by the managers of election, a majority in the county of 1327 votes. Bent upon the consummation of their plan to defeat the will of the people of the country, a protest was submitted to the board of county canvassers by certain Democrats against the counting of any of the votes cast at Box No. 1, on the novel ground that not only were the votes deposited in the box used after two o'clock illegal, but that the votes cast prior to that hour and deposited in the original box were also illegal, because the box, although too full to receive any more votes, should not have been sealed before the close of the polls at six in the evening. And, strange to say, the attorney for the protestants who appeared and argued in support of this novel doctrine was the same Democratic county chairman under whose advice and counsel the managers had acted. The result was that although it was not pretended that any irregularities had taken place at that poll, or that a single vote had been received which ought not to have been received, or a single ballot had been counted which ought not to have been counted, or a single ballot not received or not counted which should have been received and counted, the entire vote at that poll was thrown out by the board of county canvassers, who also rejected the returns from two other Republican precincts, which had cast 720 Republican and 80 Democratic votes. By these means the Republican majority of 1327 in Sumter County was transformed into a Democratic majority of 723.

In Orangeburg County, according to the returns of the managers of election, the Garfield electors received 4169 votes and the Hancock electors 4058—a Republican majority of 111. By rejecting the returns from four Republican precincts, which had cast in the aggregate 1445 Republican and 433 Democratic votes, the board of county canvassers transformed the Republican majority of 111 into a Democratic majority of 901.

Williamsburg County was carried by the Republicans by a small majority. Owing to apprehensions felt that the board of county canvassers would throw out votes enough to give the county to the Democrats, the Republican candidates on the local ticket employed an attorney to be present during the canvassing of the votes, but the board declined to admit him or any other person, on the ground that the law did not require the canvassing to be done in public. Thereupon application was made to one of the judges of the State, then in Williamsburg, for a mandamus to compel the county canvassers to permit the attorney employed by the Republican candidates to be present and witness the canvassing, but the judge held that a mandamus would not lie. Undisturbed, therefore, by the presence of any outsider, the board manipulated the returns so as to give the Democrats 1178 and the Republicans 993 votes—a Democratic majority of 785. This result it was afterwards learned was partially obtained by throwing out three Republican boxes, aggregating 799 Republican and 151 Democratic votes; but for some time it was impossible for the Republicans to ascertain what boxes had been thrown out, for the county canvassers not only declined to give them that information, but even refused to send to the State board of canvassers the returns of the managers of those polls which they did count, and upon which their return was based. From the action of the county canvassers the Republicans appealed to the State board of canvassers, and, although the latter in rendering their decision admitted that the failure to send up the managers' returns was "a grave irregularity" and that the refusal to permit the presence of the candidates or their attorneys during the canvass was "unwarranted by law," yet they decided to adhere to the declaration of the vote made by the county canvassers. From this decision one of their number dissented, because "so many and so serious irregularities had been established that, in his opinion, no legal election had been shown to have been had in that county."

With one exception every poll in Georgetown County was carried by the Republicans, the Garfield electors receiving, according to the returns of the managers, 2613 votes and the Hancock electors 757—a Republican majority of 1856. When the board of county canvassers met, five out of the six Republican boxes were thrown out, although before doing so they threw out the only

poll which gave a Democratic majority, thinking perhaps that this action might create the impression that
they had performed their duties with a spirit of fairness.
Only one poll was left to be canvassed, and, as that had
given a Republican majority, the vote of the county for
electors was declared to be 622 Republican, 161 Democratic, and 143 Greenback.

In Beaufort County alone did the Democrats make
no attempt to subvert the will of the majority, but the
failure to do so, if we may judge from the following
article taken from the *Beaufort Crescent*, the Democratic
organ of that county, is in no wise due to a spirit of
fairness and honesty on the part of the Democracy of
the State, but rather to an unwillingness on the part of
the local Democratic managers of that county to achieve
success by following the teachings and practices of their
associates throughout the State—presenting the only instance of political virtue to be found in the current
history of the Democratic Party of South Carolina:

" There is one thing to be said of the Democracy of
Beaufort County that unfortunately cannot be said of
some others, and that is, they have not as yet learned
*to make one Democratic vote count as five and five Republican
votes as none.* Nor have we yet adopted the system by
which ballots are substituted in the boxes for those
which were originally placed there. Upon these little
matters we are sadly deficient, which will account for
the small showing we are able to make with 300 votes.

" For ourselves, we had rather be afflicted with years
of Republican misrule, trusting to the justice of our
cause finally asserting itself, than *to steal an election.*"

In certain sections of the State the general plan for
preventing Republicans from voting seems to have been
to keep up a constant discharge of fire-arms during the

night preceding the election and to congregate around the polls hours before the same were opened, and to remain there in solid mass, blocking up all avenues of approach, until the Republican voters, after waiting for hours and seeing no prospect of being able to vote, would get discouraged and go away. In case some Republican more determined than others attempted to force his way to the box through the crowd of Democratic voters, who were always armed with guns, pistols, or clubs, he invariably received such treatment as to deter others from making a similar attempt. In some places cannons were placed in front of the polls to intimidate the Republicans from endeavoring to force their way to the ballot-boxes, and at other places large numbers of guns were deposited by the Democrats in houses opposite the polling-places and rifle-clubs kept on duty throughout the day.

At Darlington Court-House a constant discharge of fire-arms was kept up throughout the night preceding the election and during the day of election. The poll was opened at the regular polling-place, but was immediately removed to the court-house, and the box placed in position there. To reach it the voters had to ascend the steps of the court-house, which were crowded with Democrats, among them two companies of Red Shirts, armed, who after voting kept the steps blocked so as to prevent the Republicans from getting an opportunity to vote. Several Republicans, who attempted to force their way up the steps, had their clothes nearly torn off, and several others, who did succeed in getting up, were compelled to vote the Democratic ticket against their will. Finally one Republican, who made an effort to go up the steps to the box, was knocked down and ten or twelve pistols drawn on him by Democrats. After waiting nearly four hours to see if the Democrats would clear the steps, the Republicans were advised by their leaders to go home in order to prevent a collision, which seemed to be getting imminent. At least 800 Republican voters were thus forced to return to their homes; and this poll, which gave Hayes 892 votes in 1876, gave Garfield at the recent election less than a dozen. The intimidation and violence in Darlington County was not confined to the court-house poll, but extended all over the county, and by such means—together with repeating and ballot-box stuffing—the majority of 840 obtained by the Republicans in 1876 has been transformed this year into a Democratic majority of 2550.

At Abbeville Court-House the poll was held in the grand-jury room. A table with the box thereon was placed across the door of the room which opens into the hallway of the court-house. There was but one entrance to the poll, which was through the front door of the hallway. The door, which was but partly open, was blockaded by the Democrats, who stood before it all day in a solid mass. Fire-arms were constantly discharged during the day, and the colored men were prevented from approaching the poll, unless they yielded to the demands of the Democrats that they should vote the Democratic ticket. Such was the intimidation and violence of the Democrats that at least 800 Republican voters had to retire from the poll and return to their homes without voting.

At Edgefield Court-House the polling-place was taken possession of by about one hundred and fifty Red Shirts, the night before the election, and with the re-enforcements received the next day, they kept possession of it until the election was over. Every window opening on the public square, on which the court-house building stands, where the poll was held, was crowded with Democrats, armed with shot-guns and rifles, as if awaiting an attack, and any attempt of the Republicans to force their way to the box in any considerable number, through the crowd of Democrats, who with guns and pistols in hand blocked all access to the poll, would have been so regarded. Red-Shirt companies paraded the streets, and all the stores in the town were closed, whilst most of the merchants and their clerks, armed with shot-guns and rifles, could be seen marching about the streets. For nearly five hours the Republicans waited to see if they were going to be allowed an opportunity to vote. Several had tried it, and in making the attempt one had his coat cut to pieces. Believing that the Democrats would continue to block the poll as long as they remained, they finally retired to their homes, knowing that any effort on their part to force a passage to the ballot-box would have led to bloodshed. A few remained behind, and to these the Democrats *kindly* offered an opportunity to vote, thinking perhaps that it would be just as well to have one or two Republican votes in the box. When the poll closed and the votes were counted, it was announced that 701 votes had been cast for Hancock and English and only 14 for Garfield and Arthur at Edgefield Court-House, where in 1876, in spite of the most fearful scenes of violence and intimidation, 826 votes had been cast for Hayes and Wheeler. Had the Republicans been allowed to vote at Edgefield Court-House a much larger vote would been cast by them at that place at the recent election than at that of 1876, because, believing that there would be less danger in voting at the court-house, many of them had come from country precincts, where they could not vote without running great risks, so that the number assembled at the court-house was not less than two thousand.

At Aiken Court-House a barricade ten feet high and twelve feet long was placed in front of the poll, leaving a passage-way only two feet wide. Colored voters were required to enter at one end and white voters at the other. The latter passed through freely, while the former were obstructed and delayed in various ways. Throughout the day the Democrats, with pistols exposed, were turbulent and overbearing. Guns were stored near by, and a cannon was placed in the middle of the street, opposite the polling-place. During the excitement ensuing upon three colored men being cut and stabbed, the cannon was manned for action, and the guns were brought out and distributed among the Democrats. A conflict seemed imminent, and was only prevented by the forbearance of the Republicans, who generally kept their places in the line and seemed more bent on voting than on fighting. All sorts of measures were resorted to for the purpose of preventing Republicans from voting, and even red pepper was thrown amongst them and in their eyes to make them scatter. The result of all this was, that when the poll closed 600 Republicans were still waiting an opportunity to vote, many of them having been forced to come to the court-house, because at their own polls the violence was so great that they did not dare attempt to vote at them.

The details of the violence and intimidation which prevailed at the court-houses in Union and Laurens would be simply a repetition of the facts recited about Abbeville, Darlington, Edgefield, and Aiken. The extent of the violence and intimidation at the two former places can be judged best by its effect in suppressing the Republican vote. At Union Court-House 497 Republican votes were cast in 1876 and only 15 in 1880. At Laurens Court-House 1097 Republican votes were cast in 1876 and only 91 in 1880.

Violence and intimidation were not confined to the polls located at the court-houses, but in some counties prevailed at almost every poll, especially in the counties of Aiken, Edgefield, Darlington, Hampton, Barnwell, Laurens, Union, Newberry, and Fairfield.

In Aiken and Edgefield counties the violence which forced the Republican supervisors to leave most of the polling-places has already been described. Throughout those two counties the polls were generally taken possession of by bands of Democrats, dressed in red shirts and armed with shot-guns, rifles, and pistols. In Edgefield County they seemed to regard the polling-places as so many forts, to be occupied and defended by them against the attempt of Republicans to vote. In Edgefield County so great was the violence and intimidation that three fourths of the Republican voters in the county failed to secure an opportunity to vote, although they made every effort to do so. In Aiken County the intimidation and violence at many of the polls compelled the Republicans to abandon them entirely. For instance, at Low-Town Well the house in which the poll was held was crowded with Democrats, who, armed with guns and pistols, amused themselves by firing from the building into the Republicans standing around. About nine o'clock in the day another crowd on horseback, armed as the others, came yelling and whooping toward the polling-place, and with a general discharge of fire-arms drove the Republicans away. At Page & Hankerson's Store, one of the polls in Aiken County, the Republican ticket-distributor was carried into the woods by the Democrats, stripped naked, severely whipped, and his tickets taken away from him and destroyed. The Republican who undertook to carry the tickets to Silverton Academy met with similar treatment. On his way to the polls he was captured by the Democrats, carried into the woods, stripped naked, and whipped. The Republican tickets were taken away from him and destroyed, in consequence of which not a single Republican vote was cast at that poll, although in 1876 the Republicans cast 232 votes there, and had a majority of 50.

The seizure and destruction of the Republican tickets appears to have been one of the methods adopted for suppressing the Republican vote. In pursuance of this policy, the parties who were carrying the Republican tickets to Beach Branch, in Hampton County, were met on the road on the morning of the election by a band of nine Democrats, who threatened to blow their brains out if they did not surrender them. Of course the tickets were given up, and at that poll no Republican vote was cast.

To such mild forms of violence the Democrats did not entirely confine themselves in Hampton County. At Brunson's they kept up a steady fire of musketry during the night previous to the election, and in the morning the poll was opened in the back room of an old storehouse. In order to reach the box voters had to pass through the main hall of the building, the entrance to which was guarded by State constables, who would admit only one Republican at a time. After being admitted every Republican had to pass through the ordeal of being cursed and abused, and sometimes assaulted, by the crowd of drunken Democrats who were allowed to remain in the hall all day. As a consequence of this state of affairs less than one fourth of the usual Repub-

lican vote was cast at Brunson's, and three fourths of
that one fourth were afterward destroyed by the managers in drawing out the excess. At Lawtonville, in the
same county, the red-shirt cavalry rode up to the poll
in the afternoon and made an attack upon the colored
men, shooting five, one of whom has since died, and
cutting seven.

At Johnston's Depot, in Edgefield County, a colored
man named Anthony Miles was killed, and for hours his
body was allowed to remain where he fell, because no
colored man dared to remove it, and because no Democrat cared to have it removed, as it served as a warning
to other colored men not to attempt to vote at that poll.
Another colored man was shot and killed near the polling-place at Dry Creek, Lancaster County; and at Cro-
mer's, in Newberry County, a party of Democrats rode
up to the poll, and in a disturbance which they raised
one colored man was killed. For these three murders on
the day of election no arrests have been made by the
Democratic State authorities, for whom the murderers
voted.

In Laurens County the violence and intimidation
exceeded that of 1876, and those who are familiar with
the history of that election in South Carolina will
remember that Laurens and Edgefield were the two
counties in which the State board of canvassers declared
that there had been no lawful or valid election. As great
as was the terrorism during that election, out of 3000
Republicans in the county, 1814 succeeded in obtaining
a chance to vote, but at the recent election only 493 were
allowed to exercise that privilege. Armed bodies of
Democrats crowded the polls. Democratic guards were
stationed at the cross-roads to interrupt colored men
going to vote. At no poll in the county could a Repub-

lican be found willing to act as supervisor. Fear of physical violence deterred Republicans, even when clothed with the authority of the United States, from undertaking the hazardous duty of watching Democrats conduct an election in Laurens County.

The foregoing facts in regard to the election of 1880 in South Carolina, fully attested by supervisors and other eye-witnesses, were presented to the American people in an address by the Republican Executive Committee of that State, in which they conclude as follows:

"The Republicans of South Carolina, through scenes of violence, bloodshed, and intimidation, have voted on the side of Nationality against Sectionalism, in favor of Human Rights against Intolerance and Oppression. Their rights have been ruthlessly trampled under foot, whilst they are powerless to protect themselves from injury. They can only wait with patience to see whether the Government of the United States is alike powerless to redress these wrongs and to render impossible in the future similar attempts to destroy its peace by wholesale and systematic pollution of the ballot-box."

CHAPTER XXII.

DANVILLE, VA. MASSACRE, 1883.

Rise of the Readjuster Party in Virginia under General Mahone, Cameron, Riddleburger, Wise and others—The Alliance with the Republicans—It Triumphs at the Elections—The "Solid South" Menaced—Determination of the Bourbon Leaders to Raise the Race Issue—Inflammatory Circular Issued by the Democrats—The Richmond *Dispatch* (Democratic) urges the Drawing of the "Color Line"—Origin of the Riot at Danville, Saturday, November 3—It is evidently Preconcerted—Opening of a General Fusillade on Unarmed Negro Men, Women, and Children while doing their Marketing—Four Negroes Killed and others Wounded—Investigation by a Committee of United States Senate—What the Testimony Disclosed—Unprovoked and Unjustifiable Character of the Outrage—Incendiary Dispatches and Posters Issued—False Charges of a Negro Rising—All for the Purpose of Influencing the Election on Tuesday, November 6—It has the desired Effect—Outrages on Negroes after the Election—Appeal to Virginians.

In Virginia there had been a division in the Democratic Party, and many of the most prominent men in the State, with a following of about 33,000 white men, under the leadership of General Mahone, Cameron, Riddleburger, Wise and others, broke away from the Democratic Party, and organized the Readjuster Party. They formulated a plan for the settlement of the debt of the State. Upon this issue they went before the people in 1879, and with the aid of Republican votes chose a majority to the State Legislature. General Mahone was elected to the United States Senate.

The cause that induced Republican support for this new party was that it declared in favor of a free ballot, general education, and the abolition of the poll-tax and whipping-post.

In 1881 these political allies nominated a strong ticket for State officers, and were again triumphant before the people. The financial measures for the State, which had been urged by the Readjuster Party, and denounced by the Bourbon Democracy as repudiation, were enacted into law. This Legislature elected Mr. Riddleberger, a Readjuster, to the United States Senate.

At the election in 1882 the Readjuster Republican Party elected six out of the ten members of Congress. This was a complete political change for Virginia. The legislative, executive, and judicial branches of the State government, the two Senators, and six members of Congress were anti-Bourbon, and were in close alliance with the Republican National Administration.

It seemed that the solid South was about to be broken, and that Virginia, the mother of States and of Presidents, under the leadership of some of her most gifted and gallant sons, was to take the initiative in the struggle. The Democratic leaders saw the danger to their party in the success of this movement, and determined to make a great effort to defeat it.

In their State nominating convention, while they abandoned their former position upon the debt question, and accepted and indorsed the measures advocated and enacted by the Readjusters, the Democrats were totally wanting in respect for the party whose measures they indorsed, but denounced them quite as earnestly as though they had not adopted their platform on finance. The Democrats selected some of their most able leaders to manage their campaign. The race issue was brought out, dressed in its most appalling robes, and presented to the people as the only thing that was worthy their consideration, and every effort was made to excite a race conflict. As the time for the election approached it became evident that the main reliance of the Democrats for success was upon stirring up the passions and prejudices of white men against the negro.

An inflammatory circular, entitled "Coalition Rule in Danville," was prepared by Democrats at Danville for circulation in the Shenandoah Valley and the south-western portion of the State, where the white people were in the majority. This circular was full of exaggerations and misrepresentations as to the effect the negro vote and a few negro officers had upon the affairs of Danville.

The circular was intended to arouse the prejudices of the white people against the negroes of the State, and to draw the "color-line" in politics at the next election if possible. This was in accordance with the settled purpose of many Democrats in the State. The Richmond *Dispatch*, a Democratic paper, in its issue of July 25, 1883, contained the following in an editorial:

"Before another issue of the *Dispatch* reaches the public the Lynchburg Convention will in all probability have finished its work. . . . The only matter of difference, developed by a canvass of the delegations, is regarding the advisability of drawing the color-line. The Richmond delegation remain practically unanimous in the opinion that it should be drawn, and are, it will be seen, sustained by some of the strongest men in the party."

This circular was not distributed at Danville, but was scattered broadcast over the western part of the State, and was followed by letters and affidavits affirming its truth. It created a considerable sensation, and prepared the minds of the people for what was soon to follow.

The Democrats at Danville provided themselves with arms, and on Saturday, November 3, 1883, three days

before the election, they had a club meeting, the members
of which attending had their arms with them.   On that
day, while the streets of that flourishing tobacco-manu-
facturing town were full of negroes, men, women, and
children, doing their marketing, a white man assaulted
and beat a negro without cause, while two white men
stood by with revolvers and prevented both police
officers and citizens from interfering to restore the
peace.   In a few moments white men from a Democratic
meeting assembled on the sidewalk in line, and opened
fire upon the defenceless and fleeing crowd.   The fire-
bell was rung, when there was no fire, as a signal to arms,
and in a few minutes armed Democrats had possession
of the town.   The men who raised the riot and did the
killing were not arrested as murderers, as should have
been done, but were accorded prominence in a volunteer
organization for the avowed purpose of defending the
town against the negroes.

In this unprovoked and unjustifiable affair four negroes
were killed and a number of others wounded.

The Committee on Privileges and Elections of the
United States Senate, under a resolution of the Senate,
investigated the facts in connection with this wanton
outrage.

The testimony of a number of witnesses was taken,
amongst them that of Hon. John D. Blackwell, Judge of
the Corporation Court of Danville, and Mr. Daniel Dugger, two prominent citizens of Danville.

It happened that they were together in the second
story of a building across the street from where the riot
occurred.   Upon hearing the noise incident to the assault
and battery upon the negro these gentlemen threw up
the window, and were enabled to and did witness the
whole affair.   Mr. Dugger stated that he saw no colored

people with arms, nor did he hear any shots from them.

The testimony of both of these witnesses shows that while the white man was pommelling the negro with his fist two white men stood by with pistols to prevent any one interfering; that presently a number of men rushed down from the Democratic meeting at the Opera House, and in a few moments a dozen or twenty persons opened fire with their pistols upon the crowd of negroes, men, women, and children as they were in the street and running off. The evidence shows that there were no grounds for apprehension of danger from the blacks; that they were unarmed and peacefully engaged in marketing in the street on the Saturday evening of this occurrence.

News of this riot was immediately telegraphed all over the State by the Democrats, in terms intended to show that the negroes were waging a war of extermination upon the white people, who stood at bay, defending their homes, their families, and their civilization. Dispatches like the following were distributed by riders and Democratic clubs throughout the State:

"DANVILLE, November 5, 1883.

"For God's sake help us with your votes to-morrow. We are standing in our doors, shot-gun in hand, trying to *protect our families !*

"If you only knew our suffering here on account of negro rule you would vote different. We are standing in our doors with guns protecting our families.

"Post this up at the court-house door."

"RIOT IN DANVILLE.

"Mahoneism has worked its legitimate result in Danville. Riot and bloodshed have come to pass. Inflamed and crazed by the diabolical speeches which have been addressed to them by the Mahone nihilists, the negroes have precipitated the bloody issue. . . . People of the Valley and Southwest, the East calls upon you to come to its rescue; to help beat back the black wave which threatens to roll over us. Arouse ye, and to the polls!"

In some localities it was reported that from one hundred to one hundred and fifty persons were killed at Danville.

On Sunday evening an "enormous mass meeting of white citizens was held in Armory Hall," at Richmond, Va.

The object of the meeting was to express sympathy with the white people of Danville. The following is part of the preamble:

"Whereas reliable information did reach this city on Saturday night that a conflict between the white and black races took place at Danville yesterday, the result, as we believe, of a conspiracy to force the race issue upon the white people in the present political canvass:

"*Resolved,* . . . That in the conflict which took place in Danville on yesterday the white men of this city sympathize fully and cordially with their own race.

"That whenever or wherever this conflict shall take place in Virginia all white men are affectionately, earnestly, and solemnly entreated to take the part of their own race."

The Democrats also held a public meeting at Lynchburg, on Monday, for the same purpose, and passed earnest resolutions of sympathy.

Nothing can better show how wholly unjustifiable these dispatches and resolutions were than the statement of the committee, taken from the evidence, of the condition of things in Danville that Saturday afternoon after the riot. The committee says:

"What, then, it is pertinent to inquire, was the condition of affairs in the city of Danville after the massacre, and at the time these telegrams and reports were sent out? The Democrats came from the Opera House, shouting and hallooing as they ran. They kept it up on their way up Main Street until they reached the Arlington Hotel. They yelled in exultation 'Hurrah for us Democrats!' The signal-bell for the people to fly to arms was sounded. The ringleaders in the massacre were placed on guard to patrol the city, as the mayor states, without his authority and without being sworn. Every white Democrat and even boys were armed, some with guns, others with pistols, and still others with bowie-knives. The white mob ruled the town."

As usual, the murderers were the heroes of the hour, and the innocent victims of their wrath were denounced as instigators of strife.

This riot, like Hamburg and Ellenton, was wholly without justification or excuse. Judge Blackwell stated before the Senate Committee of Investigation that the blacks turned to flee before the firing began. The committee states that "Upon all the evidence it is clearly established it was a wanton, wicked, and groundless attack upon unoffending men, women, and children."

In this case, as at Hamburg and Ellenton, the Democrats availed themselves of a trifling difference between a white and a colored person as a pretext for an indiscriminate assault upon the negroes.

And, like Hamburg and Ellenton, it was a preconcerted outbreak by Democrats against colored Republicans for the sole purpose of political effect. The result at Danville was that, out of twelve hundred colored voters registered, less than thirty cast their votes at the election.

The effect of this riot and the gross misrepresentations made of it by the Democrats was to excite race prejudice throughout the State, and the result was a victory of the Bourbon Democracy.

At this point it is proper to say that the pledges made by the Readjuster Party to the Republicans to secure their support have been amply redeemed, wherever their power extended, in protecting the rights of the people, supporting the cause of popular education, and advancing the material interests of the State.

No one has been punished for the perpetration of these atrocious crimes. These Danville murderers, instead of being held up to public scorn as criminals, have been rather regarded as benefactors of their race by the leading spirits of the Democratic Party. The natural result of this state of things has been to render less secure the lives of the colored people. Since the massacre in November, 1883, six or seven negroes have been shot and otherwise seriously injured at and in the vicinity of Danville by white men, without provocation or justification. In one case a colored man just recovering from a spell of sickness was sitting in front of his door when he was shot with a pistol by a white man who happened to be passing in a wagon. No reason was assigned for the act except that the assassin wanted to try his pistol. In another case a negro was arrested by two constables because he playfully struck his wife as they were walking home. These officers declined to accept the explanation of both husband and wife, but hurried the man toward the station-house, leaving the wife in the street. In a few moments she heard a pistol-shot, and, running in the direction of the sound, found her husband in an alley, where he had been taken by the two constables and shot by one of them.

These and other acts quite as lawless show that the spirit of murder is abroad in that portion of Virginia, and that the lives of negroes may be taken with impunity.

Are such things to be tolerated in a civilized community? Do the good citizens of the old Commonwealth of Virginia propose to support a political party that resorts to murder as a means of carrying an election?

Would Washington, and Jefferson, and Madison, and Monroe, and Patrick Henry, and Marshall justify such conduct as this? Have the people of Virginia degenerated since the days of the fathers? Are they no longer in favor of protecting every citizen in his right of " life, liberty, and the pursuit of happiness"? Are they, for the purpose of gaining a party advantage, in favor of exciting in the breasts of white men a prejudice and hatred against colored men?

The laws of the country have made the negro free, and have conferred upon him all the rights of citizenship.

The conduct of the colored people since these rights have been cast upon, has been such as to fully justify the course that was pursued toward them. They have been peaceful, law-abiding, and industrious. They have aspired to better the condition of themselves and their families. They have striven to acquire homes and to educate their children. They have been patient and long-suffering, looking forward to the time when, under the influences of a just and benignant public opinion, they would be permitted to enjoy in full fruition the rights of American citizenship.

Why shall not Virginia take the lead in this great movement? The Bourbon spirit of prejudice, intolerance, and oppression should be cast out. Virginia should take her position in the front rank of the great States of this Union in favor of giving to every citizen an equal chance in the race of life, of protecting every citizen with equal and just laws, of providing from the property of the State a generous fund for the education of the children of the State.

What Virginia needs to rapidly advance her in population and wealth is the development of those great natural resources which have to this time been allowed practically to lie dormant. Before this can be accomplished it must be the recognized and well-known policy of the people of the State to yield to all persons, without reference to race or political opinions, the same rights, privileges, and protection that they claim for themselves. It seems obvious that before this point can be reached it will be necessary to sweep out of the way the great obstacle to the progress of the State—the Bourbon Democratic Party.

CHAPTER XXIII.

THE ELECTION OUTRAGES IN COPIAH COUNTY, MISS., 1883.

Report of the Committee on Privileges and Elections of the United States Senate—Character of Copiah County—Preparing for the Election—Proceedings of the Armed Company—Murder of Tom Wallis—The Band at Ainsworth's Store—Tactics at Political Meetings—Escape of Independent Leaders—Purpose and Result of the Offences—The Murder of J. P. Matthews—Matthews' Character—Determination to Murder Matthews unless he kept out of Politics—The Armed Band at Hazelhurst—Matthews Warned not to Vote—Matthews Murdered—How the News of Matthews' Murder was Received—Resolutions of the Mass Meeting—Honoring the Murderer—Shooting of A. W. Burnett—Effect on the Election—Responsibility of the Local Authorities—Attempts to Palliate the Outrages—Why Matthews was Killed—Spirit of the Southern Press.

AFTER the election of 1883 it gradually became known to the country that during its progress election outrages of peculiar atrocity had been perpetrated in Copiah County, Miss. This latest development of the "Mississippi plan" was at first regarded with the languid indifference which constantly recurring reports of kindred crimes, coming from the same source, had bred in the public mind. There was something, however, so tragic in the story of Matthews, shot down as he was depositing his ballot, something so cold-blooded in the "deep damnation of his taking off," that the slumbering indignation of the people was partially roused. This led the United States Senate to order an investigation through its Committee on Privileges and Elections, which was made, and a report submitted to the Senate by Mr. Hoar, the chairman, on May 6, 1884 (Report 512). This report, which is extremely able and deeply interesting, is signed by Senators George F. Hoar, Angus Cameron, John Sherman, William P. Frye, and E. G. Lapham.

From this shameful story so powerfully told by the committee, the following copious extracts are presented. In reading it it is difficult to believe that these are the annals of the people of a Christian State in the latter part of the nineteenth century. Rather does it seem that this must have happened in some heathen land, or in one of the darkest periods of the Christian era. And when it is known that the red-handed murderer, Wheeler, was honored for his crime by election to office, amid the acclamations of his fellows, it may well be wondered, What impudent band of assassins has thus leagued itself together and presumed to call itself a civil government?

CHARACTER OF COPIAH COUNTY.

Copiah is a county of a little less than 35 by 40 miles in extent. It contained in 1880 a total population of 27,552, of which 13,101 were whites and 14,442 colored. Its county-seat was Hazlehurst, a little town containing 463 inhabitants. It is divided for election purposes into five precincts, called beats, whose population, according to the census of 1880, was as follows:

BEAT.	White.	Colored.	Indians.	Total.
1	3,414	4,104	....	7,518
2	4,120	1,403	....	5,523
3	1,536	2,338	8	3,882
4	1,294	2,876	1	4,171
5	2,737	3,721	....	6,458
Total	13,101	14,442	9	27,552

The population is chiefly farmers and planters of cotton. The whites were shown by the testimony of many Democratic witnesses to stand high in character and intelligence, as compared with the people of their race throughout the State. No question was made that the colored people were quiet, orderly, industrious, and law-abiding. The superintendent of schools testified that there were sixty-five colored schools in 1883, which number increased in 1884, with an average of thirty to thirty-five scholars. He further testified that the teachers of these schools were all colored, generally, perhaps altogether, Republicans in politics, coming up to a high and strict standard of moral character and of literary attainment, and of great influence with their race.

The county had been Republican since the readmission of the State until 1875. In that year the State was carried by the Democrats by the processes which have been made familiar by the report of the special committee of the Senate who investigated the election [see Chapter XVI. of this volume]. Since then the vote has been close. The majority of the county officers have been Democrats ; but the Republicans had chosen a majority of the supervisors—a board invested with the power of assessing taxes, directing the county expenditure, and selecting grand jurors.

PREPARING FOR THE ELECTION.

November 6, 1883, an election was held for county officers, including sheriff, district attorney, supervisors, and clerk of the courts, and for members of the State Legislature. The Republicans made no nominations of their own for these offices, but all the opponents of the Democratic Party united under the name of Independents, and placed in nomination a ticket composed entirely of white men, who were conceded by the Democratic witnesses before the committee to be excellent men, unexceptionable in point of character and ability. The Democratic candidate for district attorney stated in his campaign speech that "there could be no objections made against the Independent ticket, and if the county affairs fell into their hands, they could rest assured they were in safe and good hands." All were natives of the county, belonging to respectable families. As the canvass went on it became known that some five to seven hundred white men, who had previously acted with the Democratic Party, had joined the Independents, and that this was likely to render certain the defeat of the Democrats. To prevent this result, and maintain Democratic ascendency, was unquestionably the motive for the crimes which it becomes our duty to detail.

PROCEEDINGS OF THE ARMED COMPANY.

A company, consisting of about one hundred and fifty persons, was organized under the command of Erastus Wheeler, who had the title of major. These men were mounted, ninety of them armed with guns, the remainder with pistols buckled round them, army style, or hanging on the horns of their saddles. Of this company, Mr. Barksdale, the member of Congress from that district, testified: "The procession, so far as I knew, the citizens who composed it, were among the best in the county, a good many of them planters and men of various professions, living in the country." This opinion is abundantly supported by that of many other witnesses, and controverted by none.

This company began its operations about the time

when the debate closed, some fourteen days before the election. It does not appear that any Republican speech was made in the county after the Democratic "procession," to use the euphemism of their member of Congres, began to move.

Beat 3 had been a Republican stronghold. The population consisted of 2338 colored persons and 1536 whites. But parties in this precinct were by no means divided by a color-line. A considerable number of white men, formerly Democrats, were enlisted in the Independent movement. About two weeks before the election, the armed company above named began riding about the country, taking with them a cannon. They began operations at the lower end of Beat 3, but for twelve days ranged over the county. Their operations were very largely conducted at night. They kept up a constant firing with their guns and cannon. The cannon was burst, but was replaced by another. These disturbances, which are compared by several witnesses who had been soldiers to the firing in a hotly contested battle, were committed in the dead of night in the localities where the colored people dwelt in large numbers. They killed, wounded, whipped, and otherwise outraged a large number of persons. In two or three cases it is claimed that the person injured had a personal enemy who had joined the Democratic mob, and under the cover of their society had gratified his own hatred. In one instance, and perhaps in two, this may be true, but in every case proved before the committee the persons committing the crimes avowed it as their purpose to carry the election for the Democrats. In every instance the person committing the offence was a Democrat and the victim a Republican or Independent.

MURDER OF TOM WALLIS.

Between one and two o'clock of Thursday night, ten days before the election, Tom Wallis, a respectable colored man, was in bed in his own house with his wife; their baby and a little son were with them at that end of the house; two sons occupied the other part of the dwelling. He was a Republican and had taken a good deal of interest in politics. The mob broke into his house, took him from his bed, and attempted to throw a rope over his neck. As he threw up his arm to prevent them he was shot, five guns being fired, and instantly killed, falling upon the skirt of his wife's dress. One ball went through the neck of the husband and the arm of the wife. There were about twenty persons armed and mounted who came to the house. The road for thirty yards from the gate was full of armed horsemen. They left at the house a rope, and a leather strap made of a piece which looked like a gin-belt, with a handle about eighteen inches long. They subsequently passed resolutions, which were sent to Mr. Erastus Matthews by five or six men "with guns at their hips," that if "Frank Thompson, Marion McCree, Joel East, or Tom Wharton," who were four of the principals in the transaction, "was injured in any way, they would hold the Matthews brothers responsible." The Matthews brothers, as will hereafter appear, were prominent Republicans. The newspapers state that Mrs. Wallis has died of her wounds since her examination by the committee.

On the Friday night before the election they came to the Isham Gilmore house again, firing off their guns about it; some of the shot struck the house. At the same time they burst open the door of Isham Gilmore, a colored man in the neighborhood. There were twenty or thirty of them. Wheeler, who was in command, took a light and said (we give Gilmore's narrative):

"'Hello, Isham, come out and set down, and let us talk about politics.' I wouldn't go out. The reason I wouldn't go out, I thought of old man Wallis, and thought if I got out there, while I was talking with him some of them might come and throw a rope over my head, and so I told them, 'No, I didn't want to talk about politics; I had no politics to talk about.' He says, 'Well, by God, what is you gwine to vote?' I said, 'I don't know what I'm gwine to vote.' He answered me back, and says, 'By God, if you are going to vote the Radical ticket you needn't come on the ground, but if you are going to vote the Democratic ticket you can come; by God, we are going to kill out the whole God-damn seed and generation of Radicalism.' . . . When they went out the gate that night I went out the back door, and I never went back, but strayed out and only went in the day, and lay around in the fields. . . . The day I went there, Mr. Matthews there gave me the ticket, and I simply thought to myself, now I have got the ticket in my hand, and rather than to take the ticket and go back home I am going to vote the ticket. If they don't kill me here to-day they won't see me till the thing will be done."

Gilmore voted, but he stayed in the woods for three weeks. He testified that nearly the whole settlement, a large settlement of colored people, did the same.

Other outrages of this armed company upon white and black Republicans described by the committee, as gathered from the testimony, are too numerous to be given in detail here. It is a terrible story, including arson, the most brutal whippings, shooting negroes in their beds or dragging them out of their cabins in the dead of night and compelling them to swear to vote the Democratic ticket, with every variety of outrage that the ingenuity of devils could invent.

THE BAND AT AINSWORTH'S STORE.

J. W. Bondurant is an active Republican, a white man, dwelling in Beat 3. On Friday night before the election he saw this armed and mounted band, about 150 in number, at Ainsworth's store, a neighborhood where many colored people live. The mob shot off their pistols and cannon, and "hollered and whooped and yelled around." Ormond had made a Republican speech, and it was reported that they were trying to get hold of him. Bondurant and Ormond, and Erastus Matthews, a brother of Print Matthews, who was afterward murdered, went up to Erastus Matthews's store. The Democratic band came round the store shouting, "Somebody had better get away from here." They turned their cannon toward the store and shot it, one of them crying, "Put a log-chain in it and shoot the damn thing." Wheeler was in command. They rode away and rode back and fired their guns into the store, first two pistols or guns, and then a continual firing. Two balls passed between Erastus Matthews and Bondurant, who were about a foot apart. There were also cries, "Bring them out and swing them up to a limb." This was between nine and ten o'clock Friday night before the election.

The next Monday Bondurant saw a young man named Higdon, whom he knew, who belonged to the company, and told him of the alarm felt by his sisters and other female relatives in his house. The reply was that ."no Democratic women were scared." Dr. Jones asked young Higdon what his father thought of it. He replied, "He told me to go ahead and carry the election."

TACTICS AT POLITICAL MEETINGS.

Burnet, the chairman of the Independent executive committee, was advertised to speak at White Oak Church. When he got there he found Hargraves, the Democratic sheriff, Meade, the chairman of the Democratic executive committee, and Dodds, a prominent Democratic lawyer, and Fulgum, Democratic candidate for supervisor in Beat 4. The Democrats came in whooping and yelling in crowds. Fulgum accosted Burnet and told him, "We are having peace and quiet down here, and we don't want any speaking." Burnet replied, "Mr. Fulgum, I want you to understand that I didn't come here to break up your peace and quiet; I did not come here to make any incendiary speeches or anything of that kind, but I came here to exercise a right that is guaranteed by the Constitution." "Well," he said, "I have come to you to tell you that we don't want any speaking, and you had better not speak." Burnet replied, "I came here to speak, and I am going to speak, and you men here can murder me if you feel so disposed; but I will guarantee to you one thing, that I am going to kill some of you whenever you attempt to do it; I am going to speak right here on this ground. It is my meeting; you were not invited here, and you are trying to intimidate me and keep me from speaking." The ruffians seem to have been somewhat daunted, but demanded a division of time, to which Burnet consented. But, in violation of the agreement, Meade made a violent and abusive speech after the close of the meeting.

The meeting of the Independent executive committee, held at Hazlehurst the day before election, was broken up by the approach of the armed mob. Enochs, the Independent candidate for chancery clerk, was advised by a Democratic friend to leave town the day before election, which he did.

ESCAPE OF INDEPENDENT LEADERS.

Joseph P. Jones, the president of the board of supervisors, who had lived in the county from infancy, was warned that three men had been elected to kill him on the first opportunity. On Tuesday evening, about two weeks before the election, he rode up to a place by the road-side where about forty Democrats were in consultation. A proposition was made to take him off his horse and hang him, but the majority, fortunately, were against it. After the election forty or fifty men went to his house armed, for the purpose of hanging him, but he had received warning and made his escape from the county.

At a political meeting held some time before election, near Erastus Matthews's store, Charles Allen, then and now clerk of the Democratic executive committee, moved that they " go into Matthews's store and buy a rope and take Bufkin out and hang him." Bufkin was an influential Independent, served in the Confederate army, had been treasurer of the county, and was then supervisor in Beat 3.

PURPOSE AND RESULT OF THESE OFFENCES.

As a result of all these proceedings the Republican meetings ceased a fortnight before the election. There was a reign of terror all through the county. The negroes fled to the woods. There was no desire to conceal the purpose of these crimes by the men who committed them. Williamson, the mayor of Hazlehurst, a Democrat, testified that their purpose was to carry the election.

Bufkin, a Democrat, testified that he asked Higdon, one of the leaders, if they were going to kill anybody, and he said yes. As he passed a mounted crowd, Womack, a Democrat, asked him if he didn't know what was up; said they were going to clean out Beat 3; going to clean it out by Monday night; going to be ready by Tuesday morning to carry their beat

A Democratic newspaper said, " The Crystal Springs cannon is doing good work for us in Beat 3."

The Republicans sat in their houses every night expecting to be taken out and killed. The crowd were heard to say they would carry the election or kill every Republican in Beat 3.

Wheeler made several speeches. In one he said they had spent a good deal of time trying to persuade the negro to vote their way, and now they had set out to undertake to make him. In another he said:

" They were out electioneering; that they didn't expect to coax these colored people any longer to vote; they expected them to vote the Democratic ticket, and if they did not he would kill them outright; that he had pulled several of them out and made them say they would do it, and that that election had to be carried at all hazards."

The audience " cheered him terribly." At the same or another speech he said, " They were going to carry Beat 3. If they could not persuade the negroes, they were going to kill out the leaders."

A conversation was overheard between Thompson and Beacham, two leading Democrats, shortly before election. One said to the other, " We must carry this election at all hazards, and the only way to do it is to kill the ringleaders." The other replied, " Yes, and the quicker it is done the better."

The Democratic newspapers seem to have carefully

suppressed any mention of the crimes which would call attention from the rest of the country. The Copiah *Signal*, edited by Meade, chairman of the Democratic county committee, said on the 18th October:

"The Independents out in Beat 3 imagine they are entitled to full possession of the affairs in that locality, but they are laboring under a grave mistake. The Democrats are not going to be ruled or dictated to by them any longer. The negroes had as well understand this now. If they will not vote with the Democrats it would be best for them and the country that they refuse to participate in the election. The weather might be warm that day, and they might possibly get sunstruck."

THE MURDER OF J. P. MATTHEWS.

But the most conspicuous crime is yet to be reported. J. P. Matthews was a merchant about forty-five or six years of age, of great capacity and energy, and of large property. He and his wife belonged to old and respectable Mississippi families. He was a native of Copiah County, as was his father before him. He had been a Union man through the war. He had two sons in college and two daughters aged about nineteen and sixteen years. The wife and children all testified before the committee. It would be difficult to find anywhere a family whose impression as they appeared before the committee could be more attractive. There is no member of the Senate who might not be proud to introduce anywhere as his own the four children who came to tell us the story of the murder of their father for no other offence but that of being a Republican.

MATTHEWS'S CHARACTER.

Mr. Matthews was one of the wealthiest and most successful business men in Copiah County. His dealings were largely with Democrats. He had been sheriff of the county six years by appointment from the Governor and once or twice by popular election. He was alderman of the city of Hazlehurst year before last. He was extremely public-spirited, taking a great interest in schools and a liberal benefactor to churches. Persons in trouble and distress were wont to resort to him for sympathy and aid. The man who killed him was his debtor, and had been hospitably entertained beneath his roof a fortnight before the murder. There never was a charge against him of dishonorable conduct, or of an offence against the law. He was extremely hospitable, entertaining much company. He had more influence with both whites and blacks than any other man in the county. Many Democrats would vote for him who would vote for no other Republican. Wheeler, who killed him, had solicited his support for the office of mayor, for which he proposed to be a candidate, and had said, "I had rather vote for him than for any man that is running for office, from the simple fact that I never went to him in my life to get an accommodation that I didn't get it." His wife said, "He always helped anybody who was in distress, no matter who it was. They never came to him and went off without anything." Mr. Millsaps, a Democratic clergyman who had known Matthews since he was a boy and to whom he went to school, testified:

"He was a very pleasant, peaceable, quiet, good man, very charitable, generous, and social in his disposition. I can say generally that he was as good a man as was in Hazlehurst, leaving out all idea of religion."

Mitchell, editor of the Copiah *Signal*, the Democratic paper, testified:

"J. P. Matthews, personally, was a very clever, social man, but the people there regarded him as an agitator."

Judge Bridewell, an intelligent and able lawyer, who had been an officer on General Hardee's staff, testified:

"I can express his character in three words: He was a man who had the courage of his convictions. He was perfectly honest. I never heard his integrity called in question. He was a very generous man. He possessed beyond contradiction the qualities which are described by the word 'manly.'"

Williamson, the Mayor of Hazlehurst, a Democrat, testified:

"He was a man who was regarded as a very clever man, personally and socially. He was generous; a man who had a good many friends belonging to the different parties in the county. Outside of his politics Mr. Matthews was very well liked. Of course they didn't like his politics."

He was of small stature; he weighed only one hundred and thirty pounds, and was quite lame.

There was a little evidence from Mr. Matthews's political opponents that he was regarded as overbearing and violent in speech and had made threats of violence. There was no evidence to sustain this charge other than mere hearsay, and very little of that, except the statement from two or three witnesses that Matthews, in expectation of being killed on account of his political opinions, had declared he would not die unavenged, and had instructed his family to hold leading Democrats responsible if he were murdered. If there be any truth in these statements we believe them greatly exaggerated.

Whether exaggerated or not, few persons who consider the provocation will be disposed to blame him severely.

DETERMINATION TO MURDER MATTHEWS UNLESS HE KEPT OUT OF POLITICS.

The Democratic minority of Copiah County regarded Mr. Matthews as the leader of their opponents and the great obstacle to their taking possession of the offices in spite of the will of the majority. They determined to kill him unless he would abandon politics, and so to strike terror into his supporters.

As the election approached this purpose became well known. The conversation between two active Democrats, to the effect that the leaders of the Republicans must be killed, has been already related. The night before the election, Woods, the Democratic candidate for coroner and ranger, said that Matthews would be killed. Hartley, one of the Democratic procession, said, after the death of Matthews, that he knew he was to be killed on that day for a week beforehand. At the polls at Tailholt, early in the morning of election, in a crowd of Democrats, who were swearing and firing their pistols, one was heard to say:

" Oh, yes, by God, we will get some of them to-day. We would have got Print Matthews yesterday, God damn him, if he hadn't crawled into his hole."

The armed crowd who broke into Wallace Gilmore's house in Beat 3 told him they were going to kill Print Matthews to-morrow. William P. Ware, a highly respectable Democratic merchant, testified that he heard before the election that the crowd had passed a resolution to kill Matthews, and that the sheriff had been notified and had said it was out of his power to stop it.

Ware warned Matthews, who told him the sheriff had promised him protection if he would stay in town. Williamson, the Democratic mayor, heard Matthews say he expected to be killed. Myers, the Democratic Secretary of State, met young Matthews the day of the murder, as he was taking the train at Oxford. He asked Matthews what he was going home for; and being told, said,

He knew it would be done, though he hadn't heard of it; he knew it would be done that day."

THE ARMED BAND AT HAZLEHURST.

The armed band we have described came into Hazlehurst with their guns and cannon on Monday, the day before election. The statement that they passed a resolution to kill Matthews before they entered the town rests upon hearsay only. But as they approached the town one of them was heard to say, as he rode along the line, "If I can get ten men to go with me we will wind matters up." The reply was, "You can get as many backers as you want." After they disbanded in the evening they were heard cursing one another for cowardice, and saying, "We knew you would not do it after you promised." Both these declarations probably related to the purpose to kill Matthews that day. When they were within a short distance of the town a colored man came to Matthews, who was in his house, and told him he had just overheard a plot between Meade, the chairman of the Democratic committee, and several others, to deputize Matthews to quell the mob, and to have it arranged that he should be killed on his way to meet them. A few minutes after this notice, Sheriff Hargraves and Meade arrived at the house. Hargraves said:

" He had tried to get somebody to go out and make the arrest, and that he would deputize him to go out and arrest the mob; he was an old sheriff, and a suitable person."

MATTHEWS WARNED NOT TO VOTE.

Matthews had received three letters, one signed " 150," threatening his life. He told Hargraves, pointing to Meade, that not half an hour before he had been informed that Meade and others had made a plot to assassinate him. If they were going to murder him they might just as well come there and murder him as to get him off there and assassinate him. Matthews had a daughter sick in his house. He had previously demanded protection from the sheriff and from the city marshal. The city marshal had reported this request to Meade, who had said he believed there was no danger, and had called at Matthews's store to assure him he would aid in protecting his family. Matthews's brother said they would protect themselves. Meade told him he "would play hell at that." As the crowd came into town Meade went out and met them and guided them away from Matthews's house, telling them of the pledge he had made in their behalf. They went to the court-house and were addressed, as they sat on their horses, by Mr. Barksdale, the Democratic Member of Congress for that district. After the speech they passed directly by Matthews's house, saying as they passed, "Somebody had better get away from here." After passing the house they halted and passed the following resolution, which was handed by Meade to one McLemore, and by him brought to Matthews's house:

"Whereas it is thought that the public interest will be

subserved by Print Matthews absenting himself from the polls on election: Therefore,

"*Be it resolved*, That Print Matthews be ordered to keep within his own inclosure to-morrow.

"Adopted by citizens of Copiah County, this the 5th day of November, 1883."

Matthews replied:

"This is a very strange proceeding in a Republican government. I think I have as much right to vote as any one of you. I have never done any of you any harm. I have tried to be useful to society in every way that I could. Now, John, *you have got it in your power to murder me, I admit. But I am going to vote to-morrow, unless you do kill me.*"

This message was delivered to Matthews in his own house in the presence of his wife and daughter.

MATTHEWS MURDERED.

The hour of his doom approached. After breakfast, not far from nine in the morning, the election officers opened the polls just across the street from his house. By the custom of Mississippi no persons are admitted to remain in the room where the election is held but three inspectors, the clerk, and a challenger representing each party. Into their presence the voters are admitted, who deposit their ballots and depart. A double-barrelled shotgun had been secretly conveyed beforehand into the room and concealed in a wood-box. There were some Democrats with shot-guns, friends of Wheeler, at the door. Wheeler had been constituted the Democratic challenger. Matthews was selected by the Republicans present when the polls opened to act as their representative. He said he had to go home, that his daughter was sick, but he would vote before he went. Wheeler and

he sat down together on a bench and talked pleasantly
in an ordinary tone.   What they said was not overheard.
But Wheeler himself afterward said that he ˙said to
Matthews, " Print, I would not vote to-day if I were
you."   Matthews went to the table and handed his vote,
open, to the election officer.   The officer handed it back
to him and asked him to fold it.   He took the ballot in
both hands, when Wheeler, who stood at a distance of
eighteen feet, shot him with both barrels in the breast.
Twenty-four buckshot lodged in him, one charge just
below the throat, the other between the breasts.   He
fell instantly dead to the floor, an American citizen, on
his native soil, within earshot of his home, in the act of
casting his ballot.   A man braver or kinder never conse-
crated battle-field with his blood.

Wheeler's son-in-law and other young men with arms
instantly pressed into the polling - room, by the back
door, through which the voters were to go out.   The
front door was at once locked.

Matthews's daughter Mary, a girl of nineteen, heard
the sound of the gun as she sat on her father's porch.
She says in her testimony:

" I did not know he had gone until I went through the
house to look for him, and I went back and asked ma
if he had gone; she said she reckoned so.   I looked all
through the house, and could not see him anywhere, and
then I went out on the front porch and sat down, and
directly I heard a gun fire, and I knew what it was as
soon as I heard it.   I told ma I heard the gun, and I
knew what they had done; and I went up-town where
he was, and they had the front door locked.   Mr.
Coggswell, one of the inspectors, was on the outside,
with the door locked.   He told me I could not come in
there, and I told him I was coming in any way.   He

said I had no business in there, and could not come in. I told him I knew pa was in there, and that they had murdered him, and that I was going in. Mr. Groome came along and caught hold of me, and carried me half way to the store, and I turned round and went back, and Mr. Coggswell told me he thought I had better go home, and stay there. I told him I didn't care what he thought, that I was going in there; that it was none of his business. The door was still locked, and my uncle Leon came in a few minutes and they broke the door open then, and we went in and found my father dead."

Wheeler sat unmolested in the room for some time, quietly reloading his gun, until one of his friends suggested he had better go to the sheriff and deliver himself up. He went to the sheriff accordingly; was taken before Lowe, a Democratic magistrate, then a candidate for re-election and re-elected, who afterward united in electing him city marshal. Lowe went through some form of holding him to bail in the sum of $5000, which was promptly furnished by three leading citizens, although murder is not bailable in Mississippi, and the whole transaction was unlawful. The sheriff suffered Wheeler all the time to retain his gun. Twenty minutes after the murder he was seen sitting at a grocery store with Meade, the chairman of the Democratic committee, each with a double-barrelled gun in his lap. He remained about the streets of the town during the day; stood with the sheriff for an hour on the street corner with his gun in his hand, "for fear," as the sheriff said, "that he might be attacked;" attended a public meeting in Hazlehurst the next day, and was in New Orleans during the sessions of the committee there. He has remained wholly unmolested in Copiah County from that day to this.

The tidings of Matthews's death was received by the Democrats throughout Copiah County with extravagant demonstrations of joy. Meade, the Democratic chairman, at once telegraphed the news to other voting-places. It was received at Crystal Springs at about a quarter-past nine. A gun was then fired, and the band ordered out, who played martial music for an hour. At Martinsville when the news came there was a proposition for a salute, but a man, who had been a leading Democrat, told them if there was a salute fired he would kill the first man who did it. At Tailholt, in Beat 3, a note came bringing the news. It was received with great rejoicing, shouting and yelling for joy. They waved their hats and formed a procession. In the language of one witness:

"Old men and leading men, that you would think would shudder at murder and be horror-struck, just yelled and fairly shouted."

In Hazlehurst, the scene of the murder, a cannon was at once fired. Mr. Ware, a Democratic merchant, testifies that Meade told him that the cannon was fired in consequence of an understanding that if Matthews was killed they were to fire the cannon. Meade denies this; but on careful re-examination of his testimony, recalling his manner and appearance on the stand, and the evidence which seems to connect him with these transactions almost at every step, we are constrained to withhold credit from his denial. At any rate, the demonstrations of joy were abundant. The band was kept playing on the streets. Crowds, excited and jubilant, thronged into Matthews's yard, and about his house, where his dead body had been carried. One band, in some sort of military array, marched to his house, where they were halted by their commander, and poured forth a flood of profane and indecent language in the hearing of the family. A crowd of 150 presented arms to Matthews's brother as he rode into Hazlehurst with his family after the murder.

RESOLUTIONS OF THE MASS MEETING.

On the next day a large and enthusiastic public meeting was held in the court-house at Hazlehurst, at which Meade presided, and Allen, secretary of the Democratic committee, was secretary. The following resolutions were passed, which were copied in the handwriting of Dodds, an eminent Democratic lawyer, chairman of the Democratic committee in the absence of Meade, who sat by the side of the minority of the Senate Committee at the hearing as their adviser in the conduct of the case. The reputed author of the resolutions was Mr. Miller, the district attorney. Mr. Dodds, who copied them, refused to tell who was their author, and refused to say that Miller was not their author.

"Whereas certain rumors are current that the relatives of the late J. P. Matthews have threatened the peace of society, in order to avenge his death, by killing Democrats and destroying their property: Now, therefore,

"*Be it resolved by the people of Copiah County in mass-meeting assembled this day, at the court-house of said county,* That if any person shall be injured, or an attempt made to injure him, either in person or in property, in any manner, by the said relatives or friends of said J. P. Matthews, that we hereby declare that we will hold his said relatives and friends who participate, accountable for the same, and that we will regard them as without the pale and protection of the law and common enemies of society, and that we will visit upon them certain, swift retribution.

"*Be it further resolved*, That so long as the friends and relatives of the said J. P. Matthews obey the laws and become good citizens, we hereby pledge them the protection of the law.

"*Resolved further*, That in the opinion of this meeting it is necessary to the safety of society and the welfare of all races and classes in this county, that the Matthews family shall keep out of politics in Copiah County.

"*Resolved further*, That from henceforth no man or set of men shall organize the negro race against the whites in this county, and if it shall be attempted in the future, we hereby give notice that it shall be at the peril of the person or persons attempting so to do.

"*Resolved*, That we do hereby pledge ourselves, each to the other, our lives and fortunes and our sacred honor, that we will, all and individually, from henceforth, hold ourselves in readiness to enforce the foregoing resolutions, and to meet at any time upon the call of the chairman of this meeting.

"*Resolved*, That a committee of twenty-four from each supervisor's district be appointed by the chair to present a copy of these resolutions to the brothers and sons of the late J. P. Matthews, and that the same be published in the Copiah *Signal* and the Crystal Springs *Meteor*.

"*Resolved by the citizens of Copiah County in mass-meeting assembled*, That the honors heretofore worn, and worthily so, by Beat No. 2, be, and the same are hereby, awarded to Beat No. 3.

"*Be it further resolved*, That this resolution is by no means intended to reflect upon the past and present services of Beat No. 2, but to show our appreciation of the result of the election of the ticket in Beat No. 3.

" *It is also resolved*, That the clubs continue their organizations, and consider themselves not disbanded. subject to the call of the chairman of the Democratic executive committee.

" *Resolved*, That the thanks of this meeting be extended to the Hazlehurst brass band for their services on this occasion. J. L. MEADE,
Chairman.

" JESSE THOMPSON, JR.,
" C. J. ALLEN,
" *Secretaries.*"

These resolutions were served on the family of Mr. Matthews as they returned from the funeral. They need no comment.

Yazoo, with which Copiah desired to shake hands, is the county with whose history of crime and blood the country is familiar; the county where Dixon was shot in the back, the county whose " best citizens " celebrated last Christmas eve by murdering the United States collector of internal revenue with three other colored citizens.

At this meeting Bailey, the lawyer, and captain of the company of which Wheeler was major, made a speech. He was received with tumultuous applause, and said,

" My friends, you have won a great victory. Democrats we were and Democrats we are. We have got a Democratic stock of officers. By the next election we hope to have a Democratic Congress."

Some one called out, " Tell us about Beat 3." He went on:

" Now, I will tell you something about Beat 3. I went down in Beat 3, me and my friend Wheeler. I had thought to stump the beat, but after I got down there in a portion of that country, we came to the conclusion that I could do more in the saddle than I could on the stump. Therefore, we went round to electioneer, and I tell you when we started out we took along with us something like this [pulling out a pistol]. I tell you, my friends, it is the best method of electioneering I have ever seen. My friend Wheeler is a noble hand to electioneer. We would come to a house, and my friend Wheeler would get right down and go right in and take a seat right by the fire with those persons. He would electioneer a few minutes, and they most invariably agreed to vote the ticket before we left. Oh, we didn't hurt anybody."

He continued:

"It would be well for some persons to go around and see those people who affiliate with the opposite party and are voting different to us, and encourage them to come together and vote with us. If they agree to come back and vote with us, grant them all courtesy and be peaceable with them, but in the event that that should fail, then what shall we do? [Loud cries, 'Kill them out, kill them out;' cheering, and after the cheering subsided, 'a loud voice, 'Kill them out!'] No; I would not advise you to kill them out; *but I believe you will do it without advice.*"

The resolution "that the clubs continue their organizations, and consider themselves not disbanded, subject to the call of the Democratic executive committee," preserves these associations for future use as the regular Democratic organization of Copiah County.

There was no coroner's inquest; Dodds and other lawyers advised that officer that, as Wheeler said he did it, such a proceeding was unnecessary.

HONORING THE MURDERER.

Wheeler was elected city marshal of Hazlehurst, about three weeks after the murder, by the mayor and aldermen. The board who elected him consisted of the mayor, J. M. Norman, chancery clerk; I. N. Ellis, cashier of the Merchants' and Planters' Bank; D. S. Burch, a school-teacher, now appointed by the Governor superintendent of education for the county; and Mr. Lowe, justice of the peace, chosen to that office by the people of Beat 1: these were all eminent Democrats. Wheeler was also, on the 6th of February, 1884, elected a delegate by the temperance people of Copiah County to appear before the Legislature with a memorial in their behalf.

Jordan, the city marshal of Crystal Springs, met young Matthews on the cars as he was on his way home on the day of his father's murder, and said to him, "Well, by God, you need not kick; you can't do a damned thing now."

SHOOTING OF A. W. BURNET.

On the 6th of September, just two months before the election, Burnet, the chairman of the Independent executive committee, learned that an ignorant Democratic negro had been recommended to the Governor as Republican inspector by the Democratic committee. He waited on Governor Lowrie and remonstrated against the transaction. He was waylaid on his return and shot by Charles Hart, an active Democrat, afterward conspicuous in the armed mob. Burnet was active in politics. An attempt was made to impeach his character. But it was abundantly shown, even from the most hostile sources, that his character stood high, except as affected by political prejudice. He was the only lawyer at Hazle-hurst who was not a Democrat, and had a large and growing practice. He had made some political speeches, and on one occasion met Góvernor Lowrie in debate and divided with him the time. Hart was in company with eight Democrats, among them Bailey, who made the principal speech at the meeting of November 7, and who acted under Wheeler as captain of the Democratic company. As Burnet passed them, near the corner of the hotel, in the street, Hart said, "I understand you say you didn't make sport of Bailey the other night." Burnet replied that he had not and could prove that he had not mentioned Bailey's name. Hart replied, "You are a God-damned liar," and began to draw his pistol. The weapon caught in his pocket, when Burnet drew a knife and struck at Hart, cutting his clothes in the shoulder, but not wounding him. Burnet then ran, and had got about twenty feet and was entering the hotel when Hart shot him through the groin. The men who were with Hart separated in different directions, as if to surround and head off Burnet in whichever direction he might attempt to escape. He lay several weeks in great danger of his life, but recovered.

EFFECT ON THE ELECTION.

The effect on the election it is hardly necessary to state. Instead of the anticipated Independent majority of 300 to 500, the Democrats carried the county by 2000. They went to many of the polling-places armed with guns, and frightened the Independents from the polls. At Spencer's Mills there was an Independent majority of 70 at noon, but the returns indicated a total Independent vote of only about 23 votes when the polls closed. From one poll the Independent election-officer was driven away. At another the Democrats had their guns concealed in large quantities in a house near by. One prominent Democrat remarked at Spencer's Mills, when the news of Matthews's death was received, "All we have to do hereafter is just to appoint our men and let them take their seats." At several polling-places the negroes either refrained from voting or voted the Democratic ticket on compulsion. At one the Democrats present put it to vote whether individual negroes might put in their ballots, and admitted only such as voted their way. Wheeler himself was one of a squad of armed men who after the murder led up negroes to the ballot-box.

RESPONSIBILITY OF THE LOCAL AUTHORITIES.

The crimes were going on for weeks, and there was never an exercise of authority for their suppression. Arms were sent from the Governor to the sheriff on the afternoon of election, by him delivered to Meade, and from him went into the hands of the mob. The sheriff's house was the resort of active members of the mob when they came to Hazlehurst. Application was made to the sheriff, and, after repeated shifts and evasions, he consented, on warrants being obtained, to arrest some of the mob, but they were promptly discharged without bail or legal recognizance on their promise to appear after the election. The warrants were issued by a magistrate who had no jurisdiction, never returned to him, and no others were issued. The sheriff testified that he applied to many white Democrats to act as a posse to put down the mob, but could not get a man to go. The grand jury found no bills. No officer of

justice made any attempt to discover the murderers of
Wallis or the men who committed arson on the dwelling of Crump or outraged Fortner.   There was a complaint before a magistrate of the shooting of Burnet.
When it was inquired who appeared for the criminal,
the answer was "The Hazlehurst bar."   The grand jury
found no bill.   Every Democratic officer has accepted,
without scruple, the office fruit of the double crime of
murder and fraud.

ATTEMPTS TO PALLIATE THE OUTRAGES.

There has been some attempt to find a feeble palliation for the murder of Matthews by representing that
he was a violent man, a desperado, and that his death
was not due to political causes.   This, at least, is to be
said to the credit of the murderer, that he himself dis-
dained this contemptible pretext.   Wheeler declared
that—

"It fell to his lot to kill him; . . . that he had nothing against Matthews, but that he had pledged himself
to Beat 3 to kill him, and he had done it and was not
ashamed of it."

On the 13th or 14th of February, 1884, Wheeler said
in a street-car in Jackson—

"I killed Print Matthews.   I told him not to vote and
he voted, and I killed him.   It was not me that killed
him; it was the party.   If I had not been a Democrat
I would not have killed him.   It was not me, but the
Democratic Party; and now if the party is a mind to
throw me off, damn such a party."

He also said "It was my lot."

Nothing appeared in the evidence indicating a purpose to throw Wheeler off.   He has been decorated

with such honors as that community had to bestow. Few of the numerous Democratic witnesses who were called before the committee would consent to speak of Wheeler's band as a mob, or the killing of Matthews as murder. Meade, while he admitted there was no fear of the Independents getting the offices except by having a majority of the votes at a fair election, frankly stated that rather than give up the government into the hands "of that ignorant crowd" he would be willing to use violence. Of the resolution ordering Matthews not to vote he declined to say whether he approved it. He thought it "a little ill-advised." He approved the resolutions passed after Matthews's murder; said the crowd who rode about the county were generally tax-payers, bore a good character, and were some as good citizens as were to be found anywhere. It would depend upon circumstances whether he approved their going after midnight to the houses of colored people and threatening them with personal injury if they did not vote the Democratic ticket.

Dodds said that if General Grant should come into Copiah County and undertake to organize the negro race against the whites he would be killed quicker than anybody else. He further emphatically affirmed his belief in the right and duty of the Democrats of Copiah County, even if a minority, to use force if need be to prevent such persons as he represented the other party there to be from obtaining political power, even if a majority, in a fair election. In short, the whole tone of approving with faint condemnation the crimes we have related cannot be mistaken.

The mayor of Hazlehurst issued a proclamation calling upon the citizens to restore order, but not till after the election, although he knew of the offences long before. He testified that he thought the majority of Democrats there were in favor of law and order, but he refused to say that he thought a majority of them were in favor of bringing these offenders to trial and punishment.

The sheriff said before the election that he didn't think there would be much peace while Matthews lived.

Mr. Birdsong, a Democratic witness called to prove that the better class of Democrats disapproved the outrages, was asked " which he thought would be the greater calamity to Copiah County, to have the Independents carry the county or to have these outrages happen," replied:

" It is very hard to tell which, in the long-run. I am free to confess that the necessities of the case required such desperate remedies."

There was little abatement of the spirit of ferocity and intolerance after the election. Robinson, the workman who prepared the vault for the interment of Matthews, left the county for fear the Democrats would kill him. The laborers on the land of James M. Matthews, some of whom had lived with him seventeen years, were ordered to leave, and the house of one who did not leave when ordered was fired into. The laborers all departed. For seven or eight of the families Mr. Matthews paid the expense of transportation to Kansas.

A young man who inquired if Wheeler had any hard feeling against Matthews, being answered " No," then said he thought it a cold-blooded murder, had three pistols presented at his head, and was compelled to retract his statement.

With few honorable exceptions the Democratic press of Mississippi, both before and since the election, has given its warm encouragement and support to the political crimes we have set forth. We subjoin some extracts, which show both the exception and the rule.

WHY MATTHEWS WAS KILLED.

Matthews was slain solely because he was an eminent and influential Republican, that his death might strike terror into the opponents of the Democratic Party, and enable that party, being in a minority of legal votes, to take possession of Copiah County. He was not murdered for any intemperance of speech. He was not murdered for any personal quality of character. He was not murdered because he advised the negro to vote. If, every fault imputed to him being intensified tenfold, he had advised the negro to vote the Democratic ticket, the minority now calling itself Mississippi would have been ready to clothe him with office and honor. He was murdered that the Democratic Party, though a minority, might possess the government of the county of Copiah and the State of Mississippi, and might send Representatives and Senators to the National Congress without constitutional right.

No national election was pending, except an election of a legislature authorized to elect a Senator of the United States in case of a vacancy. But these crimes, if successful, render a fair national election impossible. They enabled the minority to appoint the officers of justice who should protect the citizen in his franchise. We believe that the result of the next election in Mississippi will have no relation whatever to the will of a majority of her people.

They say in defence of these practices that they are necessary to preserve their civilization. We do not see the necessity. The sooner a civilization perishes which is founded on cheating and murder the better.   Better that the waters of the great river should again cover the land, which in ages it has formed, than that it should be occupied by a State which breeds her youth to fraud and assassination.

The census shows nine Indians in Copiah County. We are happy to report that there was no evidence implicating any of them, or which tended to induce the belief that any one of them was capable of the barbarities which are disclosed.

Spirit of the Southern Press.

WHY THE MURDER OF MATTHEWS WAS A VIRTUE.

Nobody knows yet what Print Matthews suffered the extreme for.   It was not because he was voting the Republican ticket, nor that in a fair and honorable way he had persuaded negroes to do it.   No, it was not for that.   It was not on account of politics in any way.   He had organized the negroes in a frenzied spirit of hate to antagonize the white people: that made him a perpetual danger to the white people.   He had put himself outside the protection of the civilized white men of Copiah, and made it a virtue for any one of them to slay him, for the benefit of the community.   The slaying of such a man under such circumstances is not murder;   however it may appear technically, it is justifiable homicide.—*Meridian Mercury* (Democrat).

TRUE SOUTHERN SENTIMENT.

Instead of being tortured by his inquisitors, Mr. Barksdale should have prized the opportunity to hurl in their faces the truth about the sentiments of the white citizens of Copiah, of the State, and of all the Southern States.   The truth is, that they will not submit to negro leaders. *Rather than do it they will kill them.* This is the simple, valuable truth, and the sooner the whole country is prepared to accept it, that the two races may adjust their own relations, the better for all.—*Vicksburg Herald* (Democrat).

FAITHFUL BULLETS AND EARNEST BUCKSHOT.

Pinchback presiding over a convention to nominate a governor of Louisiana reminds one of reconstruction times. If such a character could preside over a Republican convention in John Sherman's State, or Hoar's State, it would help them very much to understand and appreciate what the white people of the South had to contend with. We have faith that it would satiate their appetite to investigate every case where a negro leader stops a faithful bullet or a few earnest buckshot.— *Vicksburg Herald* (Democrat).

AN INDEPENDENT VIEW.

We have repeatedly defied those who are disposed to condemn the *Post* for its utterances in regard to the Matthews killing to name a single word or sentence of ours that would or could be used by the Republicans of the North. We renew the defiance. . . . The killing of Matthews has been shown beyond the possibility of doubt by the most skeptical to be a cold-blooded, predetermined, heinous assassination, instigated by the Democrats of Copiah County, and, since the perpetration of the cowardly, inhuman act, condoned and defended by them, to an extent next in shame and disgrace to the shocking deed itself. Matthews, unwarned of his life, was shot down like a dog because he had exercised the fundamental right of free government of casting a free ballot; shot by the calmly appointed tool of an intolerant and bloodthirsty mob. . . . Then, such things being true, who, knowing any distinction whatever between honor and dishonor, and cowardice and courage, brutality and humanity, will refuse to denounce and condemn them? We are not of those who muzzle their conscience that the iniquities and villany of any man or party may go unbranded and unpunished. . . . The killing of Matthews was a bloody, brutal murder, and the arrogant defence of the ugly crime by pretended Democrats cannot free it from the fatal stain. By what code of moral or political ethics are men who defend such crime governed ?—*Vicksburg Post* (Independent Democrat).

THE QUESTION OF REMEDY.

The Sherman committee bodes no good to us. He is a cold-blooded statesman, and does nothing except in pursuance of a very definite idea. The injection of 7,000,000 freedmen into the social economy of the South has given our section almost the power of choosing a Government for the great North and a nation of 50,000,000 people. If it can be shown that we, who were so lately warring on the Government, are about to assume power through seizing by violence on the electoral votes of this extraneous population, the question of remedy will be presented to the so-called loyal States.—*Greenville* (Miss.) *Review* (Democrat).

WHAT ARE YOU GOING TO DO ABOUT IT?

Suppose it should turn out that the Danville and Copiah affairs are all that the fancies of the organs have painted them—what do the organs propose to do about it ?—*Atlanta* (Ga.) *Constitution* (Democrat).

CHAPTER XXIV.

REVIEW OF THE PRESENT POLITICAL CONDITION OF SEVERAL OF THE RECONSTRUCTED STATES.

Alabama —Wilcox County Captured by Fraud—Hopelessness of any Opposition to Democracy under the Present Régime—Letter of Hon. Chas. P. Lane giving an Account of the Present Condition of Political Affairs in that State—Arkansas—How Phillips County was Changed from Republican to Democratic by Force and Fraud —Georgia—Flagrant Outrage upon the Right of Suffrage in Chatham County—Meagreness of the Vote in Georgia and in other Southern States—Louisiana—The General Election of 1884—Gross Frauds throughout the State—Proclamation of W. J. Behan, Mayor—Indignant Editorials of the New Orleans *Picayune* denouncing the Frauds—Notice of Contest by W. J. Behan, claiming Election as Mayor—North Carolina—Unjust Election Laws—Unrepublican Character of the County Governments Exposed—Democratic Officials Governing Republican Counties—South Carolina—The Election Laws of 1882—Disfranchisement of Negroes by Conviction for Petty Crimes—Provisions for Registration—How Republican Voters are Left Off the Lists—Particularity in Size, Paper, and Print of the Ballot to be used—The Infamous Six Ballot-box Law—These Provisions made with Intent to Stifle the Negro Vote—Drawing out Excessive Ballots by the Democratic Managers—Separation of the State and Presidential Polls—The County and State Boards of Canvassers—Certain to return Democratic Majorities.

ALABAMA.

The spirit of the rebel Democracy is so aggressive that they cannot tolerate the idea of the Republicans having control even of any of the important counties in a State. The county of Wilcox, Ala., is a strong Republican county, and many of the most intelligent and able men in it belong to the party. In 1874 they were able to resist all efforts of the Democrats, and the county gave its usual Republican majority. But after the Democrats got hold of the election machinery they notified the Republicans that unless they divided the county offices with them, and ran a fusion ticket, that they would beat them. Relying upon their two thousand majority to take them safely through, the Republicans refused to make a fusion ticket.

The Democrats carried their threats into execution, and by fraudulent counting elected in 1880 a full com-plement of Democratic county officials.

As an evidence of the hopelessness of any opposition to the Democratic Party in Alabama, attention is called to the fact that at the August election of this year (1884) for members of the Legislature the Republicans had but five candidates throughout the entire State.

The following letter from Hon. Charles P. Lane will give a distinct idea of the condition of political affairs in that State:

HUNTSVILLE, ALA., July 10, 1884.

J. M. Whitehead, Chairman People's Anti-Bourbon Party of Alabama.

DEAR SIR: After mature consideration I have determined to decline making the race for the high position of Governor of Alabama. My reasons for so doing are obvious. In the first place, there is no regard whatever paid to the voice of the people as expressed at the ballot-box in this State. In 1876 the right of self-government was taken from the people. In 1878, by a Democratic Legislature, the robbery of the ballot-boxes and violations of the fundamental principles of government were ratified, indorsed, and encouraged by the most villanous legis-lation that was ever conceived or enacted in political viciousness and depravity. Since the acts of 1878, repealing the election law that had been in force since Alabama was a State, the people of Alabama have had no chance, no hope, no future. We have been but puppets in the hands of political tricksters and ballot-box stuffers. I hardly need refer to the fact in support of my assertion that North Alabama, where the whites are largely in majority and have the courage to closely and jealously guard the ballot-box, that they elect Independents and Republicans from Congressmen down. But this is not the case with the intimidated and ignorant colored voters of the black belt, except in the case of Smith *v.* Shelley, and Craig *v.* Shelley, from the Fourth Congressional District, where Congress has been twice absolutely shocked at the indecency of Shelley's pretended claim and certificate, and twice sends him home and seats his Republican opponent. With the light of these circumstances before me, the ridiculous and overwhelming Democratic majorities counted in the negro belts, the majorities alone often exceeding the entire voting population, when the truth, as shown by census and otherwise, indicates ten Republican votes to one Democrat, force me with a keen sense of shame to admit that I am even a citizen of the United States, and a voter in a State that has no form of government. There is no help for us, no power that can stop the outrage at the negro boxes. We are bound hand and foot at the mercy of the ballot-box stuffers. We can only look to the Nation for aid; with this end in view, although I cast my maiden vote for Tilden and Hendricks, my second Presidential vote for Hancock and English, I at the same time severed my connection with the reckless Democracy while a member of the Legislature of 1880 and 1881, when I cast my vote with the only Republican in the Legislature, J. M. Long, of Walker, to repeal this infamous election law, that tends only to destruction and rebellion.

My next vote for President I unhesitatingly say will be: For President, James G. Blaine, of Maine; for Vice-President, John A. Logan, of Illinois; and I further assert that our hopes for peace and prosperity in the South depend upon their election. Pledging my support to any measure that may tend to extricate Alabamians from the political thraldom that surrounds them, and at the same time thanking the Anti-Bourbon Party for the honor conferred upon me by the nomination as their candidate for Governor, for the reasons given, I respectfully decline making the race, and remain, with very great respect, your servant,

CHARLES P. LANE.

ARKANSAS.

Space cannot be given for a detailed account of Democratic outrages upon the right of a free ballot in Arkansas. The same spirit has prevailed there which has characterized that party in Mississippi and other States; but the suppression of the Republican majority in Phillips County in 1882 is too recent and was too outrageous to be passed without notice. That county has for years been strongly Republican. In 1880 General Garfield received 2257 and General Hancock 924 votes.

In 1882, however, the Democracy organized and armed themselves, and by force and violence and by fraud suppressed and overcame the 1300 Republican majority. In that election the Democrats counted for themselves 2818 votes and for the Republicans 1127 votes.

GEORGIA.

The most flagrant outrage upon the right of suffrage inflicted under the forms of law in the South is in Chatham County, Ga. That county had a population in 1880 of 45,009; of these, 30,709 were in the city of Savannah and 14,300 in the body of the county.

The number of colored people in the county was 27,515, the number of white persons, 17,494; the total voting population, 11,269; of these 6565 are colored.

To enable the Democrats to obtain control of this county and of the Congressional district in which it is situated, the Legislature passed an act authorizing the county commissioners of Chatham County to abolish election precincts.

This act was approved February 21, 1873, and will be found in the acts of Georgia for 1873, page 238, sec. 15.

Under this authority all election precincts outside of the city of Savannah were abolished, and the voting-place for the entire county was established in that city at the court-house, in the hall of which building the elections are now held. The county is of sufficient size to make it necessary for electors to travel twenty-five miles to reach the polls.

Thus it will be seen that in this county, containing over 11,000 voters, this large number of men is required by law to go to the court-house in Savannah and take their chances, on one day and in one building, of reaching the polls. The inevitable effect of this arrangement is to discourage voting. The vote cast in that county at three important elections is as follows:

```
1874: total vote cast..................................4,783
1876:   "    "    "  ..................................3,774
1880:   "    "    "  ..................................5,552
```

At all elections the Democrats get possession of the polls; this does not require a large number of men, as the hall, the space to be filled and held, is not large.

They are thus enabled to work in their own voters and keep out the Republican voters.

In fact, elections in the State of Georgia are travesties upon a free expression of the will of the electors.

In 1880, by the census returns of that year, the number of persons of voting age in that State was 321,438, while the number of voters for President was 155,170, leaving the number of persons not voting 166,268.

It seems obvious that some extraordinary influence is exerted upon the voting population of a State when more than one half of the electors remain from the polls and do not vote at the most important election in the State. This lethargy of electors is shown by the votes cast for candidates for Congress. Take the following districts as an illustration of the paucity of the votes given to elect Democrats to Congress.

1st District Ga.: votes cast for member elected						4,384
3d " " " " "						4,131
4th " " " " "						5,583
6th " " " " "						3,514

A striking contrast will be observed in the votes cast for successful candidates in other States, taking those cases where the fewest votes were cast.

2d District Indiana: votes cast for members elected						16,339
15th " Ohio: " " "						13,739
2d " Illinois: " " "						9,360
7th " Iowa: " " "						13,632

A more complete illustration if possible of the unnatural political condition of the Southern States is shown by an examination of the total vote cast in a number of those States at the Congressional election of 1882 as compared with a Northern State.

At the election of 1882 for Congressmen there were cast in the twenty Congressional districts of Illinois, 525,270 votes, while in the thirty-eight Congressional districts of Alabama, Georgia, Louisiana, Mississippi, and South Carolina, including one member elected at large, there were cast 498,973.

Although the Republicans are in the majority in many counties in the State of Georgia they virtually have no voice in public affairs.

The last Legislature consisted of 44 Senators, all of whom were Democrats, and 175 members of the lower house, only five of whom were Republicans.

LOUISIANA.

On the 22d day of April, 1884, a general election was held in the State of Louisiana for Governor and other officers, and also for Mayor in the city of New Orleans.

There was a serious division in the Democratic ranks. The Independent Democrats united with the Republicans in supporting Mr. Stephenson on The People's ticket for Governor against Governor McEnery, who was the Democratic candidate for re-election.

The result of the election was to give McEnery 88,794 votes and Stephenson 43,502 votes—a Democratic majority of 45,292.

It is alleged that great frauds were perpetrated in twenty-nine parishes, and that the vote should have stood as follows:

For John A. Stephenson	71,738
For S. D. McEnery	54,988
Stevenson's majority	16,750

The frauds at this election show that the Bourbon Democracy are no respecters of persons. They propose to retain control, and will cheat any one who may oppose.

The following address from the Mayor of New Orleans sets forth the line of conduct pursued by Ring Democrats at the election:

ADDRESS OF THE MAYOR,

MAYORALTY OF NEW ORLEANS,
CITY HALL, April 24, 1884.

To the People of New Orleans:

The occurrences in the general election held in the city of New Orleans to-day have been such that I deem it proper, and to be due her citizens to express to them a condemnation of the course of proceedings and the manner in which the election has been conducted, and therefore, at this hour, before the returns have been made and any information in the shape of alleged results received, to address you upon the present grave situation.

The representation by a commissioner of election required by law has not been accorded to the largest embodied opposition to the Ring party, and though laboring under this disadvantage, it was hoped that some degree of fairness could be attained.

At and before the hour of beginning the election, the ninety-one (91) polls in the city were taken possession of by an organized band of men commissioned as deputy-sheriffs, and numbering, according to the best information, from eight hundred to twelve hundred men, who, usurping entire control of the election, inaugurated such a system of intimidation as to destroy for the entire day all prospect of a fair and free expression of the popular will. The inspectors of election, authorized by law, were in most instances denied admission into the polling-places, and in some cases by violence driven from the polls.

The very act of exclusion of such officers was equivalent to a declaration of a determination to suppress a free vote and a fair count, and to obstruct the detection of fraud in the balloting.

The conduct of this army of deputy-sheriffs, who were by no law clothed with any authority to interfere, was such as to indicate early in the day that a real election by the people was altogether hopeless, and resulted in only a partial vote being actually cast.

Although myself a candidate, any personal interest I have as such is not to be considered in view of the enormity of this proceeding, which has disgraced our city.

Such a condition of affairs does not and cannot prevail in any other city of our country.

Such an election as this has been is but a mere mockery, a defiance of the people, and is in law and justice but a *sham election.*

The New Orleans *Picayune* of the 23d of April, 1884, contained the following editorial comment on the election:

IF YOU BE MEN, ARISE.

Yesterday the people of New Orleans repaired to the polls to declare their choice for State, parish, and city officials. It was an occasion that had aroused the utmost popular interest. The people had, after freely counselling together, put up a carefully selected list of names for the several offices to be filled, and yesterday they closed their places of business and devoted themselves to the duty of free citizens by going to the polls and presenting their ballots peaceably and in due form of law. But they are now met by the fact that their votes were cast in vain. The election was a mockery, the popular will was nullified, the popular voice was stifled, and free citizens were robbed of their dearest rights.

At an early hour the polling-places were seized by the minions of the Ring Democracy, and the inspectors, who had been appointed in accordance with law by the mayor, were ejected and excluded from the polls. An army of State officers was distributed at the voting precincts, but they made no attempt to prevent this violation of law. On the contrary, they encouraged it; and when the mayor used his authority to attempt an execution of the law he was resisted, and a greater number of the ninety-one polling-places of the city were left hopelessly in the hands of the Ring interested in maintaining their hold on public place. The people cast the ballots, but the Ring counts them; thus there was no election.

The result is the most gigantic wrong ever perpetrated on a people. They can no longer speak through the ballot-box. They have no longer a voice in the affairs of government. It is not alone the people of the city, but of the whole State who must suffer, for the Ring machinery will embrace them all. The real election commenced at the closing of the polls, and it will not cease until the Ring ticket is fully provided for.

A people robbed of the elective franchise are slaves. They

are chattels bought and sold by their masters. This is a desperate situation, but to it the people of this city and State have been brought. They are slaves if they submit.

Fellow-citizens, will you submit? Can you consent to this degradation? You have complied with every requirement of law. You have done all peaceable and well-ordered citizens could do to exercise your constitutional right to choose your public officials; but does duty require you to consent to this iniquity? Does it not rather command you to resist, not with blood and violence, but with courage and firmness as freemen?

The mayor has issued his official proclamation reciting the facts of the infamous wrong put upon our city, and he has declared the election a shameful mockery and an outrageous fraud. What will you do then? You must act as becomes men.

Whatever is to be done, let the people call at once a mass meeting and deliberate on their proper course in the face of such a formidable evil. They have all along acted peacefully and justly, but real justice is demanded. Then let the people rise in their might and show that it is a crime most grave to defraud free citizens of their liberty and dearest rights. They cannot consent to submit to this crime without becoming participants in its guilt.

The following appeared in the editorial columns of the same paper on April 24:

LET THE PEOPLE ACT.

As the returns from the city precincts come in they bear such obvious evidences of manipulation that they proclaim fraud upon their faces. The manipulation has not in many cases been done with any sort of skill, but is crude and bungling, as only the most barefaced and reckless rascality could have executed. Sometimes whole boxes full of tickets read straight for the Ring candidates without a scratch or variation, while the tally-sheets are a mass of badly executed erasures and alterations. There was plainly the most obvious juggling with the people's ballots and a thorough thwarting of the popular will.

This is not the first time that this nefarious work has been carried on in this city. Elections have been stolen before, and they will be again if the people quietly submit. The People's Party has made a fair test in this case. Why should the people be taxed for the expenses of election if they are to have no real voice in the affair, but are simply expected to accept the dictation of a few Ring managers enforced by a corps of ballot-box stuffers?

We do not believe that the people of this city will submit longer to such an outrage. Long suffering and patient as they have been in the past, more than once their forbearance has been trusted to in vain, and the men who have sought to throttle the people's will have been overwhelmed and destroyed by the storm they raised.

We deprecate violence, but the transactions which have nullified the will of the people of this city and have converted a solemn election into a miserable farce must be stopped, and if there be no other way to overthrow such a gigantic evil, then let force be invoked.

We fully believe, however, that there are other means, peaceful means, by which a remedy can be reached ; but prompt action must be taken. The city should not be given over to the possession of usurpers until at least resort shall have been had to the proper judicial measures for the public protection. The courts remain and they have not yet ceased to be the bulwark of the popular rights. There is at least rallying-ground for the citizens before they are driven to enforce their rights by a last resort to sterner measures, and there is time to act. Then let the wisest and bravest of our people take in hand the work of protecting popular rights. Let them formulate their plans, and then, if necessary, call on the people to ratify them.

We do not believe it is the disposition of the people to submit to the terrible wrong that has just been inflicted upon them. A simple protest is not enough. A mere reproof is nothing to evil-doers who have been encouraged in their acts by past immunity. Action alone will meet the necessities of the case if the people consult their own interests. Delay may be fatal to the most just cause of a deeply wronged community.

The following editorial appeared in the same paper April 25:

A QUIET ELECTION (?).

"It was an unusually peaceable election," cry the Ring press with one accord, and they doubtless congratulate themselves that they have been able to speak at least that much about what was one of the most shameful outrages ever put upon a free people.

It was indeed a peaceable election where everybody was permitted to vote. The ancient practices of insulting and bullying and beating voters at the polls always produced disturbances and violent acts which defeated the objects they were intended to promote. People are ready enough to meet force with force, and there is no certainty in being able to control the results of an election riot.

This was certainly a new spectacle in New Orleans in late years, and no doubt not a few timid persons, having in mind the violence and bloodshed that had been the almost invariable attendant of previous elections, kept away from the polls. Their caution was needless. There was no intimidation of voters. Anybody who chose could vote. It is not the people that vote who determine the result of the election. This portion of the business is entrusted to other parties. It was therefore necessary to get possession of the ballot-boxes. This was easily done. An army of deputy-sheriffs, stated in the Mayor's proclamation to be somewhere about one thousand men, were on hand to maintain order at the polls and to prevent Mayor Behan's election inspectors from inspecting anything. No such inspection was desired by the managers. It was indeed of the utmost importance that there should be no such scrutiny or inspection, consequently there was none. The majority of the ballot-boxes were thus given up to those who knew best how to handle them in the interests of a quiet election, and they made the most of the opportunity and without trouble. The election was then allowed to be proceeded with, and it was an unusually quiet one; far too quiet in fact, for by it, under the protection of a host of State officers, the liberties of the people were stolen away.

It was a quiet election. Can the people remain quiet under the outrages it has inflicted upon them?

The following notice of contest of General W. J. Behan for the office of mayor, for which he was a candidate for re-election, will give a clear idea of the nature of the frauds complained of:

NEW ORLEANS, May 2, 1884.

Mr. J. Valsin Guillotte.

SIR: You will take notice that I intend to contest your right to the office of Mayor of the city of New Orleans, on the grounds following:

The protest of Wm. J. Behan, a citizen of this parish and State, respectfully represents that at a general election held in this city and parish for State, municipal, and parochial officers on the 22d of April, 1884, your petitioner was a candidate for the office of Mayor of the city of New Orleans on the Citizens' and Parish Democratic ticket, and also on the Republican ticket for the same office, to be voted for by the qualified voters of this parish at said election; that at said election your petitioner received over and above you, his competitor for the same office, running on the "Regular Democratic ticket," a majority of fully 7000 votes, and was fairly elected to said office, and would have been so returned had it not been for the high-handed, outrageous, illegal, and fraudulent action of the commissioners, clerks, and deputy-sheriffs who officiated at said election in the interest of the Regular Democratic ticket aforesaid. Your petitioner further represents that there are ninety-one voting precincts in this parish; that at all of said precincts—with the exception of Poll 6, Seventh Ward; Polls 2, 3, 4, and 5, Tenth Ward; Poll 4, Eleventh Ward; Poll 3, Twelfth Ward; Polls 1 and 2, Thirteenth Ward; Poll 2, Sixteenth Ward; Polls 1 and 2, Seventeenth Ward—the said commissioners and deputy sheriffs aforesaid, in the interest of said Regular Democratic ticket, did threaten, overawe, and intimidate the commissioners and inspectors representing the Citizens' and Parish Democratic ticket, and Republican ticket, in violation of law; and did furthermore, at all of said precincts, in wards one to seventeen inclusive, in the First, Second, Third, Fourth, Fifth, Sixth, and Seventh Districts of this city, save and except at the polls above enumerated, by a system of ballot-box stuffing, false counting, false tallying, and swearing to false, incorrect, and improper returns, change and alter the true result of said election, and substituted their will for that of the people; that by said improper and fraudulent practices, your petitioner was defrauded out of fully 7000 votes, which were counted for his said competitor; that of the total votes cast in the parish at said election, your petitioner received fully 16,000, and his said competitor less than 9000 votes; that your petitioner is the real choice of the people for said office, was elected to same by a large majority of votes cast as above set forth, as will be shown upon the trial of this cause, but owing to said fraudulent, illegal, and improper practices, your petitioner was defrauded of the said office.

That the ejection of the commissioners and inspectors as aforesaid of the Citizens' and Parish Democratic ticket and the Republican ticket was done to enable the commissioners, clerks, and deputy-sheriffs aforesaid of the regular Democratic ticket an opportunity of reversing the will of the people as expressed at said election; that had the votes been counted, returned, and promulgated as cast, petitioner would have received over his competitor fully 7000 votes.

Respectfully,   W. J. Behan.

This account of the latest "election" in Louisiana may fitly conclude with the following powerful and thoughtful editorial from the New Orleans *Picayune* reviewing the whole situation in a masterly manner.

THE LAST RESORT.

The supreme issue in American politics just now is the protection of the ballot-box. To find a due expression for its immense importance we must say that it is an essentially *vital* issue; for, very clearly, it involves nothing less than the life of free institutions in this country. We have only to specify a few of the more fatal consequences inevitable upon the contemptuous disregard and open reversal of the edicts of popular suffrage in order to realize the truth of this proposition.

In the first place, the defeat of the people by the politicians establishes a government by the minority which in itself amounts to the complete destruction of the foundation upon which alone a democratic republic can repose.

But, in the second place, the oligarchic government thus violently or fraudulently imposed upon the people will be controlled by the most objectionable influences in politics, for it is evident that only bad men, sustained by ignorance and lawlessness, would consent to assume office by criminal procedure. It is quite possible that the majority may be sometimes in error, and it is probable that the rule of a wise and virtuous minority might occasionally prove a salutary consummation. But what could be more deplorable than a government of the many by a few, and for a few, of the worst men in the State or in the country?

The saddest feature in a situation of this sort is its tendency to perpetuate itself. Government falling into the hands of expert tricksters becomes a specialty. Ordinary people, unversed in the arts of the professionals, find themselves powerless to deal with the wily demagogues, whom it is their interest and their duty to oppose. A trained and disciplined class of officeholders and their retainers become in time as all-powerful over the decision of public questions as were the Pretorian Guards at Rome or the Janizaries at Constantinople. On the other hand, the better elements of society, becoming more and more disgusted and hopeless, gradually retire from the struggle, and end by virtually surrendering their rights as freemen and as citizens. When it comes to that, of course, our boasted liberty is but a name, and the progressive emancipation of mankind is everywhere discouraged.

These are but the general outlines of the picture. Consider the consequences of the death of ambition in all generous minds, the rapid growth of corruption in every department of government, the demoralization of society and the loss of confidence in business, and it will be seen that anarchy is not far in the background. The vast extent and wonderful resources of this country enable it to stand a great deal of misgovernment. If it were of the size of Greece, in the days of its ancient prosperity, life would even now be well-nigh intolerable within its limits. But as population increases the pressure of misrule will every year be more sorely felt, and the breadth of the national territory will confer continually less of immunity in the face of suffrage violated and laws despised. Think what will be the condition of New York, Philadelphia, and New Orleans, with four times their present population, and still governed as they are to-day!

Well, it may be said, it is easy enough to describe the disease, but who will prescribe the remedy? In New Orleans an attempt will be made to secure vindication through the courts. Wherever there are written laws and constitutions, a learned, wise, and upright judiciary is the bulwark of liberty and of justice. So long as the judiciary stands firmly upon its authority in support of the rights of the people, the cause of free institutions can never be overwhelmed with disaster and disgrace. It will stand like a rock amid the storms of public tumult. The last citadel of the world's hope for freedom and progress, neither force nor fraud shall capture it. To the judge, then, we appeal from the demagogue. To the seat of justice we bring the desecrated ballot-box, and from the constituted interpreter of the law we implore the law's redress.

And if that resource fails what other will remain? The answer must be given. When the people can no longer make themselves effectually heard either at the polls or in the courts, their indignation finds expression at the cannon's mouth. The right of revolution rests upon the universal law of self-preservation. It is exercised when the evidence is all in, and then the sentence and its execution are not far apart, A few bold, bad men are summarily punished on the spot or are driven into exile, and when the popular wrath has subsided, society reconstitutes itself upon an equitable basis. Not only New Orleans, but Louisiana as a whole, is drifting toward that conclusion. The State is under the oppression of machines and the despotism of rings, and it is for the courts to say whether the people shall find relief through the written or the unwritten law.

NORTH CAROLINA.

When the Democrats obtained control of the State of North Carolina they found in existence a most admirable system of self-government which had been established by the Republicans. The people of each county and of each town were invested with the authority of electing all their officers, and by this means of exercising a salutary influence in respect to their local affairs.

This system, so full of promise for educating and training the entire body of the people of the State in the principles and practice of self-government, became the immediate point of attack.

In order to subjugate the Republican Party it was necessary that the Democrats should control all the county governments, and have possession of the election machinery.

This system of free county government stood in the way, and the Democrats determined to get rid of it. They called a convention in 1875 to amend the constitution, and got control of that convention by excluding two Republican members from Robeson County, who according to the returns were duly elected, and giving the seats to the Democratic candidates.

By the insidious provisions of the seventh article of the new constitution the power was conferred upon the Legislature of providing by law the method by which the counties shall be governed.

At the next session of the Legislature a law was passed abolishing the plan of local self-government, under which the people selected their own officers, and a system of government was adopted through officers selected by the Legislature.

Under this system of county government the people

are deprived of the power of exercising any salutary control over the officers who levy the taxes, manage the schools, erect the public buildings, build bridges, etc.

Under existing laws the following system is now in force:

1st. The Legislature elects all the magistrates for each county.

2d. The magistrates meet and elect the county commissioners for their respective counties.

3d. The county commissioners in turn appoint the registers of election for each election precinct, and also the judges or inspectors of election.

4th. The inspectors of election also appoint one of their number to carry the returns to the county commissioners. These inspectors and the commissioners constitute a board of county canvassers, and are almost invariably all Democrats.

The election law provides for the use of seven ballot-boxes at each voting precinct, to receive the ballots of the different classes of officers to be voted for.

There is no provision of law requiring the ballots to be preserved, and the custom has been established by Democratic election officers of destroying the ballots as soon as they have been counted. This is a most extraordinary and mischievous arrangement. The immediate destruction of the ballot obliterates all trace of fraud in case a ballot cast for the candidates of one party is counted for the candidates of the other party.

It is obvious that a successful contest of an election under such circumstances would be almost hopeless.

When it is seen that the Legislature elects the magistrates, the magistrates select the commissioners, the commissioners choose the election officers, and the election officers manage the election for choosing the Legislature, it is quite clear that the people have very little to do with this business. It is in the hands of a ring of Democratic officials who run everything so as to maintain the supremacy of their political party.

As an illustration of how officers are foisted upon the people who are not in accord with the political sentiments of a majority of the voters, the following-named Republican counties are given, with the number of magistrates, county commissioners, and tax-listers or assessors, with their political sentiments:

NAMES OF COUNTIES.	MAGISTRATES.		COUNTY COM'RS.		TAX-LISTERS.	
	Dem.	Rep.	Dem.	Rep.	Dem.	Rep.
Forsyth	42	17	2	1	9	4
Cumberland	49	1	5	....	13	....
Gaston	21	....	5	....	6	....
Bladen	68	3	5	....	14	..
New Hanover	40	3	5	....	5	....
Yadkin	32	12	3	....	9	....
Pender	44	....	3	....	9	....
Polk	12	8	2	....	4	2
Chowan	10	....	5	....	4	....
Wake	97	13	5	....	18	....
Craven	39	9	5	....	8	....
	454	66	45	1	99	6

In these eleven Republican counties there are 454 Democratic and 66 Republican magistrates, the Democrats having a majority in every county. There are 45 Democratic and 1 Republican county commissioner, and 99 Democratic and 6 Republican tax-listers.

Comment seems to be unnecessary. It is obvious that this system was expressly devised to deprive Republicans of their just power and influence in the management of their own affairs.

The constant tendency in this country is for the people to take more and more interest in public affairs, and to become more and more closely identified with every important interest in government. As a result of this, in almost every instance where State constitutions are changed the people retain to themselves more power in respect to the choosing of public officers and grant less and less authority to the legislative and executive departments of the government in this regard.

But such is not the case in North Carolina. There a great backward step has been taken. This movement rests solely upon the proposition that the best interests of the people will be promoted by restricting them in the exercise of the fewest number of duties in connection with the affairs of county government. They are treated as incapables. They are held up to the world as a people who cannot be trusted to take care of their own interests.

Ye men of North Carolina, is it true that you are unfitted to exercise the powers and duties of freemen? Are the people of North Carolina incapable of self-government that they should tamely submit to this system, so utterly repugnant to every idea of government by the people?

No. Their ancestors when few in numbers dared the perils of war to throw off the British yoke and establish for themselves and their posterity a government founded upon the will of the majority.

And now that the wisdom of a hundred years of experience in civil government in that State is possessed by the people of this generation, no argument will long induce them to give up the fundamental right of choosing through the ballot-box the officers in whose hands are to be placed the management of their local concerns. The majority of the people will not long continue to allow themselves to be made the buttress of the falling fortunes of the Democratic Party, which has done so little during the past twenty-five years to advance the interests of the people, but upon the other hand has done so much to bring turmoil, confusion, and strife upon them.

SOUTH CAROLINA.

On the 9th of February, 1882, South Carolina, under the control of its usurping State government, enacted a new code of laws regulating elections. This code contains some extraordinary features which it will be interesting to point out.

The first section of these laws, after defining the general qualification of voters, has the following proviso:

"Provided, that no person while kept in any almshouse or asylum, or of unsound mind, or confined in any public prison, or who shall have been convicted of treason, murder, *robbery of the goods or chattels of another with or without violence,* whether taken from the person or otherwise, or of duelling, shall be allowed to vote."

This exclusion of paupers, criminals, etc., from the elective franchise may seem at first view to be wholesome legislation, but it is capable of being made, and has been made, an instrument for the permanent disfranchisement of large numbers of colored people in South Carolina. Negroes are frequently arraigned before petty magistrates on the most trivial charges of larceny, and a conviction in these petty courts is sufficient to disfranchise them forever. This conviction is readily obtained, and the whole proceedings clearly indicate, in many cases, that the prosecution is merely a pretext to deprive the negro of his vote.

Sections 2 to 18 inclusive provide machinery for the registration of voters which was to be completed on the 1st of July next succeeding the passage of the law, and the lists closed until after the next general election. Section 6 provides that "after the said next general election the books shall be reopened for registration of *such persons as shall thereafter become entitled to register*, on the first Monday in each month, to and until the first Monday of July, inclusive, preceding the following general election, upon which last-named day the same shall be closed, and not reopened for registration, until after the said general election;" and so on ever after. Under this provision it has been held that only persons becoming *thereafter entitled* to registration can register subsequent to July 1, 1882. Persons who were at that time *entitled* and failed to get registered are forever after without remedy, and consequently many colored citizens, who through insufficient notice or other causes failed to be registered in May and June, 1882, are permanently disfranchised.

The voting machinery is provided by sections 20 to 39 inclusive. It is proper to observe here that the registration officers are appointed by the Governor, who also appoints the commissioners of elections for each county, who in turn appoint the managers of elections for each election precinct. The Governor is a Democrat, and it is needless to say that with few exceptions all these appointments are also Democrats. The whole machinery of registration and voting are therefore in the hands of that party, whose determination to perpetuate its power by any means, however foul, is not only manifest, but openly avowed.

The election of 1880, as has heretofore been shown, was carried by frauds of every imaginable kind, and was

probably one of the grossest outrages and farces ever
perpetrated in the name of a free and fair election.
Stuffing the ballot-boxes, and substitution of Democratic ballots for Republican ballots during the count
were the principal means resorted to to defeat the will
of the people. Tissue-ballots, false poll-lists, and other
fraudulent devices were freely used, while violence and
intimidation lent their clumsier aid. By these crimes a
legitimate majority of 30,000 for Garfield was converted
into 54,000 majority for Hancock.

These frauds, so open, gross, and palpable, somewhat
disgusted even the perpetrators themselves, and feeling
the necessity for some further legal devices to aid them
in stifling the negro vote, they invented the following
ingenious system, to which particular attention is invited:

Sec. 28. The voting shall be by ballot, which ballot shall be
of plain white paper, of two and a half inches wide by five
inches long, clear and even cut, without *ornament, designation,
mutilation, symbol, or any mark of any kind whatsoever*, except
the name or names of the person or persons voted for, and the
office to which such person or persons are intended to be
chosen, which name or names and office or offices shall be written or printed, or partly written and partly printed, thereon, in
black ink ; and such ballot shall be so folded as to conceal the
name or names thereon, and so folded shall be deposited in a
box to be constructed, kept, and disposed of as hereafter provided ; *and no ballot of any other description found in any election box shall be counted.*
Sec. 29. There shall be separate and distinct ballots for the
following officers, to wit: 1. Governor and Lieutenant-Governor. 2. Other State officers. 3. Circuit Solicitor. 4. State
Senator. 5. Members of the House of Representatives. 6.
County officers. 7. Representatives in Congress. 8. Presidential electors; on which shall be the name or names of the
person or persons voted for as such officers respectively, and

the office for which they are voted. *Provided,* That whenever a vote is to be taken on any special question or questions a box shall be provided and properly labelled for that purpose, and the ballots therefor shall be deposited therein.

Sec. 30. The commissioners of election shall provide for each election precinct a sufficient number of boxes to meet the requirements of the foregoing section. An opening shall be made in the lid of each box not larger than sufficient for a single ballot to be inserted therein at one time, through which *each ballot received proper to be placed in such box shall be inserted by the person voting, and by no other.* Each box shall be provided with a sufficient lock, and each box shall be publicly opened and inspected to show that it is empty and secure, and locked, just before the opening of the poll, and the keys returned to the managers, and shall not be opened during the election. Each box shall be labelled in plain and distinct Roman letters with the office or officers voted for, and the managers, on the demand of the voter, shall be required to read to him the names on the boxes, *and no vote for any office other than that for which such box shall be designated and labelled shall be counted.* At each precinct a space or enclosure such as the managers of election shall deem fit and sufficient shall be railed off, or otherwise provided, with an opening at one end or side for the entrance of the voter and an opening at the other for his exit, as a polling-place in which to hold the election for the State, circuit, and county officers. A similar but separate and distinct space and enclosure shall be railed off, or otherwise provided, as a polling-place for the election of Congressmen and Presidential electors, at such a distance from the polling-place for State officers as the commissioners of election for each county shall determine and appoint for each election precinct. *But one voter shall be allowed to enter any polling-place at a time, and no one except the managers shall be allowed to speak to the voter while in the polling-place casting his vote.*

Sec. 31. Each clerk of the poll shall keep a poll-list, which shall contain one column headed "Names of Voters;" and the name of each elector voting shall be entered by the clerk in such column.

Sec. 32. At the close of the election the managers and clerk shall immediately proceed publicly to open the ballot-box and count the ballots therein, and continue such count, without adjournment or interruption, until the same is completed, and make such statement of the result thereof, and sign the same, as the nature of the election shall require. If, in counting, two or more like ballots shall be found folded together compactly, only one shall be counted and the others destroyed ; but if they bear different names, the same shall be destroyed and not counted. If more ballots shall be found on opening the box than there are names on the poll-list, all the ballots shall be returned to the box and thoroughly mixed together, and one of the managers or the clerk shall, without seeing the ballots, draw therefrom, and immediately destroy as many ballots as there are in excess of the number of names on the poll-list. . . .

It will be seen that section 28 provides that voting shall be by a ballot printed on a certain paper and of a certain size, " *clear and even cut, without ornament, designation, mutilation, symbol, or any mark of any kind,*" or it will not be counted. It may be imagined how easy it would be to throw out a Republican ballot when subjected to the tests described above, and how difficult it would be to prepare and vote a ballot which could not be objected to for some of these reasons. When we remember that the law is to be administered by Democrats in the interest of Democrats, it may be taken for granted that all opportunities of this kind are to be improved to the fullest extent.

But the diabolical ingenuity of these attempts to nullify the negro vote is probably exhibited in the fullest degree in the provisions of the next two sections (29 and 30). In brief, they provide in the case of vote for State officers that there shall be six separate ballots, to be placed in six separate ballot-boxes, and no ballot found in a wrong box shall be counted.   Now, an educated person would find that it required great care and strict attention to place his ballots unaided in the right boxes.   We can imagine, then, the perplexity of the poor ignorant freed-man, who can neither read his ballots nor the labels on the boxes.   The law provides that he must enter the en-closure where the boxes are placed *alone*, and must *himself* insert the ballots in the openings of the proper boxes.   It is true that it is made the duty of the manager of the election to read to him the labels on the boxes, but this can do him no good unless he also knows the proper ballots to be put into them.   No symbol or " *designation*" on the ballot is allowed to aid him in this, however, and the result can easily be seen.   When the Republicans attempted to foil this plan by giving the freedmen their ballots arranged in an order to correspond with the order of the boxes, the Democratic managers of elections changed the order of the boxes, and of course every ballot went in the wrong box.

Section 32 has the provision, retained from former laws, " that if more ballots shall be found on opening the box than there are names on the poll-list all the bal-lots shall be returned to the box and thoroughly mixed together, and one of the managers or the clerk shall, without seeing the ballots, withdraw therefrom and im-mediately destroy as many ballots as there are in excess of the number of names on the poll-list."   As the ballot-boxes are almost sure to be stuffed by Democrats, the number of ballots and the number of names on the poll-list will seldom agree unless the managers have been in-dustrious enough to make a fraudulent poll-list at the same time.   But when it becomes necessary to withdraw the excessive ballots the preternatural dexterity of the Democratic managers in distinguishing and drawing out

Republican ballots can never be sufficiently admired. It is proved that at the election of 1880 the managers at a precinct in the city of Charleston, where the excess was 1071, while the number of Republican tickets in the box was only 597, before drawing out a single Democratic ticket drew out all but five of the 597 Republican ballots voted at that poll.

An important feature of these laws is the separation of the polls at which candidates for Presidential electors and Congressmen are voted for, from the polls at which candidates for Governor and other State officers are voted for. The obvious intent of this legislation is to prevent United States supervisors of election from having any possible influence in the detection and prevention of frauds at the election for State officers.

The Democrats of South Carolina are determined that whatever may betide their candidate for President, they will retain control of their State government.

The remaining sections of these laws relate to the county and State boards of canvassers, which, it is hardly necessary to say, are "ironclad" in their certainty to return Democratic majorities.

With all these weapons, legal and illegal, at the command of the usurping State government, it is safe to say that South Carolina can be counted as "solid" for the Democratic Party. Indeed, with this machinery so thoroughly perfected, any resort hereafter to the shotgun and the revolver must be regarded as the mere wantonness of cruelty and race hatred.

CHAPTER XXV.

DISCUSSION OF REMEDIES.

Effect of the Suppression of the Negro Vote upon the Representation
in Congress and the Electoral College—The Violation of Section 2,
Fourteenth Amendment of the Constitution—Partial Remedy to be
obtained by Reducing Representation—Remedy by Refusing to
Seat Members of Congress Fraudulently Elected—Section 4, Article
IV. of the Constitution—Power of Congress to secure to each State
a Republican Form of Government—The Best Remedy a Reforma-
tion of the Public Sentiment Supporting the Evil—This can be
Accomplished by Leading Democrats throughout the Country—
They are now Reponsible for the Continuance of the Mis-Govern-
ment—An Appeal to Democrats in Favor of Fair Elections.

ASIDE from the question of the right of the colored
people to a voice in the affairs of the States in which
they are citizens—in the enactment and enforcement of
laws by which they are to be governed, arises the question of the increased power given to the Southern States
in the Electoral College and in Congress by reason of
the presence of the negro. Under the Constitution as
originally framed three fifths of the slave population
was added to the white and free colored population, as
an aggregate upon which to calculate the representation
in Congress and the Electoral College to which the
Slave States were entitled.

The emancipation of the slaves gave these States the
right to have the entire number of negroes counted in
making such an apportionment.

In the eleven States that went into the Rebellion the

colored population by the census of 1880 was 5,360,298. Upon the present basis of representation in Congress, viz., 154,325 population for each member, these States made a gain by the emancipation of the slaves of fourteen members of Congress and fourteen electoral votes for President.

These States now have thirty-five members of Congress and votes for President, based exclusively upon colored population.

It would seem that it needs no argument to establish the proposition that these Southern States are not·justly entitled to this increase of power in the affairs of the Nation, based upon the colored population, unless they secure to colored voters the free exercise of the elective franchise. In fact, sec. 2 of the Fourteenth Amendment to the Constitution was designed to provide against such contingency. It is as follows:

"Sec. 2. Representatives shall be apportioned among the several States according to their respective numbers, counting the whole number of persons in each State, excluding Indians not taxed. But when the right to vote at any election for the choice of electors for President and Vice-President of the United States, Representatives in Congress, the executive and judicial officers of a State, or the members of the legislature thereof, is denied to any of the male inhabitants of such State, being twenty-one years of age, and citizens of the United States, or in any way abridged, except for participation in rebellion or other crime, the basis of representation therein shall be reduced in the proportion which the number of such male citizens shall bear to the whole number of male citizens twenty-one years of age in such State."

While this section of the Constitution is a warrant for the correction of the evil complained of, it is not self-enforcing, but is simply a delegation of power to Congress to enact the necessary law in the premises.

Here, then, is a lawful mode by which a partial remedy can be obtained. Not by *directly* securing to electors the exercise of the franchise, but by reducing the representation of the States where the right is denied, a sentiment favorable to free and fair elections may be *indirectly* aroused, as the means whereby the State so reduced can have its normal representation restored.

Another remedy often suggested, and which is entirely within the power of the two Houses of Congress, is to deny seats to senators and members who have been elected by the instrumentalities heretofore stated. This involves a long, tedious, and expensive contest upon the part of the person cheated out of the election. The proceeding is upon the principle that the member holding the certificate of election from the Governor has *prima facie* the right to the seat.

This rule cannot be changed as long as the State governments are, under the laws of Congress, recognized as valid,—that is, Republican in form,—and not in the hands of usurpers.

The Democratic beneficiaries of these fraudulent elections have therefore an immense advantage over the Republican contestants.

During the past ten years many notable contests have occurred, and in some cases the Republican contestants, after immense trouble and long delay, have been given their seats. But the sitting members as a rule, even when certified to have been elected from Republican districts of 10,000 majority, were so well fortified by the action of the State officers that they have been able to hold their seats. In these contests much evidence has been taken in regard to intimidation of Republican voters, preventing them from voting: the stuffing ballot-boxes with tissue and other ballots; the use of false poll-lists; the throwing out of Republican ballots; neglecting to open the polls at precincts containing large Republican majorities; the throwing out of the returns from Republican precincts and counties: in fact, of the use of almost every conceivable fraudulent device to reduce the Republican vote so as to give to the minority the appearance of having carried the election.

And upon these returns thus made up the State officers would base their action in giving their certificate.

In connection with these numerous contests this remarkable fact has been demonstrated, that however much murder, intimidation, bulldozing, ballot-box stuffing, destruction of ballot-boxes and their contents, false election returns, and fraudulent throwing out of returns of Republican majorities whereby Democratic majorities have been fraudulently manufactured, no Governor has yet because of these frauds refused to grant a certificate of election to the Democrat, nor has any Democrat been found who declined on account of such frauds to accept the certificate of election and claim a seat thereunder.

The relief which would be afforded by the adoption of either or both of the remedies above suggested would as respects a number of the States be entirely partial in its nature. The great wrong of the deprivation of the right to vote would still continue, but its unjust effect upon the people of other States would be prevented. The States would be deprived of their increased power in the National Government, but the usurpers would be left in their unlawful control of the State governments which they had seized.

Where the election machinery of a State is seized by a revolutionary faction, and by force and fraud is used to suppress the rightful voice of the majority and to give the color of law to the usurpation of the government by a minority, it would seem that Congress should possess the power to correct such an evil.

Where the minority by force prevents a fair election and deprives the majority of their rightful control, the act is a usurpation, and is a direct and palpable violation of the republican principle that majorities shall rule. If there is no remedy in the National Government to correct such an evil, the citizens deprived of their lawful rights would be compelled to submit, or else resort to force to regain them.

The elections would degenerate into a trial of physical strength between the contending parties, and would necessarily be decided in favor of the party which brought the most formidable military array into the campaign and to the election.

A State government conducted upon such a system cannot be a republican government: it is an oligarchy.

It seems clear that under such a state of facts Congress would have ample power, under the fourth section of the fourth article of the Constitution, to afford by appropriate legislation the required relief. That section provides that "the United States shall guarantee to every State in this Union a republican form of government."

Whatever may be said in regard to the remedies above discussed, there can be no doubt of the constitutional power of Congress to pass all needful laws for the prevention of fraud and corruption in all elections at which members of Congress and Presidential Electors are voted for, and for the protection of all voters in their right of advocating the election of the candidates of their choice, and of casting a free ballot and having it honestly counted. This power results as a necessary incident from those provisions of the Constitution which create the Government and establish the principle of the suffrage as the means by which its Legislative and Chief Executive officers are from time to time to be chosen. There seems to be no reason to doubt that Congress possesses the power of providing by law for holding the elections at which Presidential Electors and Congressmen are voted for. These elections may be taken entirely from the control of State laws and State officers, and placed under the management of such officers as Congress may determine.

Moreover, Congress no doubt has power to enact such laws as will provide for a suitable force of officers for maintaining peace and order, and for the prevention of intimidation and fraud at the election.

This subject has recently been discussed by the Supreme Court of the United States in the case *Ex parte* Jasper Yarborough and others, decided at the October Term, 1883.

In discussing the constitutionality of sections 5508 and 5520, U. S. R. S., the court said:

"That a government whose essential character is republican, whose executive head and legislative body are both elective, whose most numerous and powerful branch of the legislature is elected by the people directly, has no power by appropriate laws to secure this election from the influence of violence, of corruption, and of fraud, is a proposition so startling as to arrest attention and demand the gravest consideration. If this government is anything more than a mere aggregation of delegated agents of other States and governments, it must have the power to protect the elections on which its existence depends from violence and corruption."

Democrats in Congress have done everything possible to repeal all laws which in any manner provide for the supervision of these elections by United States supervisors and marshals.

These efforts were evidently in the interest of their Southern friends who have so successfully suppressed the Republican vote.

The Republican Party should now demand the energetic enforcement of such laws as are now on the statute-book, and the enactment of others if required.

The most wholesome and effective remedy that could be applied for the correction of these evils in government would be a radical change in the conduct of the leading Democrats of the Northern States upon this subject. It is within their power to put an end to lawlessness and fraud in connection with elections in the Southern States. If they choose to do so, they can bring such influences to bear upon their party friends in the South as will work a complete change in the public sentiment in regard to conducting elections.

The Democrats in the South will give the country fair elections whenever their party friends North demand that they shall do so.

It is of no avail for Northern Democrats to profess to be in favor of honest elections while they give countenance to the most atrocious outrages upon the ballot, by excusing and covering up the crimes, and struggling to secure for their party the fruits of a political victory gained by murder and fraud. Is not the time at hand when every good citizen, without reference to party ties, should throw the weight of his influence in favor of having the whole business of electing public officers conducted in an orderly and peaceful manner, and with perfect fairness and integrity?

Let the Democratic and Republican National Committees and Democratic and Republican Senators, Members of Congress, and other prominent citizens unite in an effort to secure an election this year, where every voter shall be permitted to cast a free ballot, and be protected in that right, and when it is cast, that it shall be honestly counted and certified. What is now needed in these States to insure fair elections is for the Democrats to concede to their political opponents—

1st. Free speech.

2d. The right of party managers to organize their party friends into political clubs and holds meetings without disturbance.

3d. The Republicans should be given one judge and one clerk (where there are two of each) at every voting precinct; these officers to be appointed upon the recommendation of the Republican committees.

4th. Republican ticket-holders and challengers should be accorded the same privileges at the polls that are claimed by Democrats.

5th. Armed men of both parties should be kept from the polls, and no intimidation should be allowed.

6th. One party should not be allowed to take possession of the polls and exclude the voters of the other party.

7th. The election officers should in good faith seek to allow every legal voter to cast his ballot, and not prevent Republicans from voting by wasting the time by propounding frivolous questions.

8th. The United States supervisors should not be interfered with, but should be aided in the performance of the duties imposed upon them by law so they can detect and prevent frauds.

In the States of Louisiana, Mississippi, and South Carolina the whole authority for conducting the elections centres in the Governors. All the election officers are appointed by them and by their appointees. These Governors can cause free and fair elections to be held in November, 1884, in their respective States if they wish to do so. It is well known that the Republicans there are seriously apprehensive that the Democrats will carry the elections in those States by intimidation and fraud. It is well known that the Republicans are confident of being able to cast a majority of legal votes in those States if they can have a free and fair election. Is it not just and right that the Republicans shall have an equal opportunity with Democrats in Louisiana, Mississippi, and South Carolina in every political contest? Will leading Democrats in the North decline to assist in securing fair elections in those States? Gentlemen, it is too late to deny that your party friends in the South have resorted to means the most foul to suppress and subdue the Republican vote, and now stand ready to continue the same game in 1884. You set yourselves up as the special champions of reform in government. Is there anything in this country that cries louder for reform than the existing Democratic system of conducting elections in the Southern States?

They are indeed a gross reflection upon free government, a mockery of the expression of the public voice, a scandal upon the American name, and constitute a menace to the prosperity and progress of those States, and to the repose of the country.

Here is an opportunity for the Democrats both North and South to show their sincerity in respect to the reforms which they demand, by aiding promptly and earnestly in securing this greatest of all reforms—the establishment of the purity of elections. Louisiana, Mississippi, and South Carolina have, as before stated, placed the election machinery in the hands of their Governors. Those officers will no doubt pay respectful heed to all reasonable requests that may be made to them upon this subject by prominent citizens throughout the country.

Fair elections in those States will pave the way to fair elections in all the other Southern States. The elimination from elections in those States of bulldozing, preventing voters from registering, intimidating and driving voters from the polls, ballot-box stuffing, controlling the polls by bands of armed men, importing voters from neighboring States, preventing United States supervisors and marshals from performing their duties, false counting and fraudulent returns, " is a consummation devoutly to be wished." If the Democratic Party through its National Committee and its public men will take this subject in hand they can bring about this great reform. Will they do it? That is the question.

Can the people afford to entrust to the Democratic Party the weighty affairs of this country if that party neglects and refuses to perform its duty upon this great and paramount question?

Louisiana, Mississippi, and South Carolina are as surely Republican States with a fair election as is the State of Vermont. The people of the Northern States should demand that the Democratic Party shall give to the citizens of those States "a free ballot, an honest count, and correct returns" in November.

If the leaders of the Democracy are unwilling to meet this issue by immediately demanding that there shall be free and fair elections in all the Southern States, especially in South Carolina, Mississippi, and Louisiana, where the Governors have control, then the conclusion will be irresistible that the Democratic Party is content to allow the wrongs against the ballot to go unredressed, and is willing to accept success by the means shown to be in use by the Democracy in the Southern States.

It will then remain to be seen whether the people of the Northern States will become a party to these outrages by bringing the Democracy into power.

CHAPTER XXVI.

CONCLUSION.

Settled Purpose of the Southern Leaders to Suppress the Colored Vote—Cruel and Unrelenting Course pursued by them to that End —Recapitulation of their Acts—Reward of Colonel A. P. Butler, of the Ellenton Massacre—Alabama, Mississippi, Louisiana, and South Carolina indisputably Republican on a Fair Vote—Effect on the Pending Presidential Election—The Southern Republicans, Black and White—Their Claim on the Esteem and Support of Northern Republicans—Appeal to the People to Right these Great Wrongs.

THE political phenomenon now under consideration is the outward, visible expression of the deep-seated opinions and sentiments of the people engaged in these extraordinary proceedings.

The ordinary differences of political opinion do not lead the members of one party into a settled purpose of cutting the throats of their antagonists. The divisions of opinion in this case are not ordinary. They involve the very foundation principles of our system of government.

The motives that prompted men to action for the extension and perpetuation of slavery are still regnant.

It was assumed that slavery was right; that the natural relation between the white and black races was the servitude of the blacks. Upon this foundation the whole superstructure of government and society in the South was built. Slavery has been abolished; the negro has been made free. And while in this country the inexorable logic of freedom is equal rights and the ballot, the Southern Democracy has not accepted that fundamental doctrine. They profess to be in favor of freedom, but it is the freedom of the white man and not of the negro. They profess to be in favor of equal rights, but the negro is not included in their scheme of equality. They profess to be in favor of a government founded upon the will of the people as expressed by majorities at the ballot-bot, but they deny the wisdom and justice of giving force and effect to the lawfully expressed will of colored majorities.

The issue, then, is, Shall colored men be admitted to a share in government in the Southern States?

It may be answered that such an issue cannot arise, for the reason that freedom and the suffrage are secured to colored men by both National and State constitutions and laws. The answer is, that constitutions and laws are not self-executing; their enforcement is dependent upon the action of officers, and if they conspire to defeat the laws of course they will not be enforced.

The Southern Democracy believed in slavery; its extirpation did not change their opinions. They believed that the negro was not entitled to the ballot; giving him the ballot did not convince them that they were in error. They profess to believe that bringing the negro in as a part of the governing force was intended to humiliate them, and that it is a direct assault upon the foundations of society and good government.

They therefore claim to be acting in their necessary self-defence when they adopt means which they deem to be necessary to wrest from the hands of these *black intruders* the powers of the State. These men seek justification in their own bosoms for the perpetration of deeds which to others seem specially atrocious.

They have unquestionably adopted the theory that the

end to be attained *justifies* the means, whether lawful or unlawful.

Upon these motives they have acted. These opinions constitute the force which has driven them forward in their desperate contest with the fundamental principles of self-government.

It would be unjust to say that they are animated simply by a spirit of diabolism.

This great reactionary movement was not set on foot and carried to a final consummation by a few "young men." The leaders of public opinion organized and directed it, and most of them have reaped the reward of their efforts by attaining to high official positions.

A common error into which not a few have fallen, and by which the consciences of the Northern people have been quieted, is, that these crimes against our republican form of government are sporadic; that they are disapproved by the best people of the South, and that they are dying out.

No greater mistake could be made. There has been absolute continuity of purpose on the part of the Southern Democracy upon this subject, from the close of the civil war to the present hour.

Before the war, believing in the divine origin of slavery, they fought for its extension and perpetuation.

After the war they endeavored to re-enslave the negro by a system of labor and vagrancy laws shocking to every sense of justice and humanity.

Foiled in this attempt, they opposed making him a citizen of the United States and of the States wherein he resides. They opposed giving him the equal protection of the laws. They opposed granting him equal civil rights with white men. They opposed giving him the right to testify in the courts against white men.

They opposed giving him the right to hold office. They opposed giving him the right to vote.

When all these rights were secured to him by law, and the Southern States were to be reconstructed under acts of Congress, they refused to take part at the ballot-box in that proceeding, but allowed the whole matter, as far as they were concerned, to go by default. When negroes were elected to office the Democracy, instead of aiding to make their administration of public affairs a success, threw the weight of their influence to make their government odious and if possible a failure.

The leaders advised the adoption of an unrelenting system of social ostracism and business proscription against their opponents. This policy was adopted and carried out with rigor.

The Democratic press teemed with the grossest abuse of their opponents, and in many cases suggested acts of violence and a disregard of their rights.

The Ku Klux Klan, probably 500,000 strong, was a political organization whose cruel and inhuman acts for four or five years were directed against Republicans for the purpose of suppressing the Republican vote.

The long and bloody list of political massacres and riots, commencing with that at Mechanics' Institute in New Orleans in July, 1866, and including St. Landry Parish, Vicksburg, Clinton, Colfax, Coushatta, Hamburg, and Ellenton ; the killing of Chisolm and his daughter in Kemper County, Miss., in 1877; the wanton and cruel murder of J. P. Matthews at the ballot-box in Copiah County, Miss., in 1883, for voting the Republican ticket;

The prearranged and unprovoked riot at Danville, Va., in November, 1883, just before the election, in which four negroes were murdered and a number of others wounded, and the false dispatches sent throughout the State to precipitate the " race issue;"

The thousands of cases where men were driven from their homes, were beaten and abused, were killed singly or in numbers;

The wholesale intimidation of voters;

The widespread and systematic arrangements for driving electors from the polls;

The stuffing of ballot-boxes;

The voting of fraudulent tissue-ballots and having them counted;

The making of false poll-lists, and of fraudulent returns, as has been done in South Carolina and other States;

Depriving Republicans of the right to vote by refusing them registration, as has been done in Mississippi;

Abolishing convenient voting-places and requiring 11,000 voters in a large county to assemble at the courthouse to cast their ballots, as in the case in Chatham County, Ga.;

The systematic suppression of free speech all over the South;

The placing of the election machinery almost exclusively in the hands of Democrats, and when Republicans are chosen as election officers the selection of the most ignorant, as has been done in South Carolina, Mississippi, and other States;

The adoption of a system of county government which deprives Republicans in counties where they have a majority of votes from electing their magistrates, county commissioners, tax assessors, and election officers, as is the case in North Carolina;

The acceptance by the most prominent Democrats all over the South of offices to which they have been chosen by means the most foul, including intimidation, murder, and fraud;—all go to show that there is a well-settled purpose on the part of the Southern Democracy to control their States without reference to whether they have a legal majority of electors or not.

It has been shown how the Democrats of Alabama, Mississippi, Louisiana, and South Carolina seized those States in 1874, 1875, and 1876. There has been no abatement in their energy and determination to hold them. The leaders in those campaigns are leaders still; when their work is well done they are not forgotten. For example, Colonel A. P. Butler, of Ellenton-riot fame, is now Commissioner of Agriculture for his State, and has held the office for several years.

The legislative, executive, and judicial officers of the States, and the county officers in nearly all the counties in those States, are directly interested in the suppression of the Republican vote. Their places would be immediately filled by Republicans if a free, fair, and honest election were held.

And so with the Representatives in Congress: a fair election would give every district, except probably two in Mississippi and South Carolina, and a majority of the districts in Alabama and Louisiana, to the Republican Party. The Legislatures of all these States would after a fair election be Republican, and they in turn would elect Republicans to the Senate of the United States. This would be the inevitable result of honest elections in Alabama, Mississippi, Louisiana, and South Carolina.

It therefore will be seen that the Democratic Senators and Members of Congress, the Governors and other State officers, the Democratic members of the Legislature, the Democratic judiciary, and the whole corps of

Democratic county officers are directly interested in maintaining the ascendancy of the Democratic Party in those States by suppressing the Republican vote. Besides this, the election of a Democratic President is directly involved. If it was positively assured that there would be a free and fair election in Louisiana, Alabama, Mississippi, and South Carolina in November, 1884, the Presidential contest would be ended. There would be no doubt of the election of Blaine and Logan, the Republican candidates.

But how stands the case at present. The Democratic Party enters the contest with the expectation of carrying the Southern vote of 153 electors solid for Cleveland and Hendricks. No questions will be asked as to how this result is accomplished, although it is well known that Mississippi and South Carolina with a free and fair election would be as certain for the Republican candidates as Kansas and Iowa.

In the eleven States which went into the Rebellion there are probably one million and a quarter of Republican voters. These men have adhered to the party under circumstances the most trying. Every influence that Democratic ingenuity could devise has been brought to bear upon white Republicans to induce them to abandon the party of their choice. The war waged upon Republicans born in the Northern States has been so fierce, that the great majority of them have abandoned their new homes in the South, and have settled in States and Territories where men are not persecuted because of their political opinions. A few Northern men have held their ground, determined to aid in fighting out this battle for freedom of thought and action. The great majority of the white Republicans in those States are native and to the manner born. They have been made the special objects of denunciation and persecution by Southern Democrats. Characterized as "scalawags," they have been held up to scorn as enemies of the white race, and consigned to social outlawry. There has been a disposition on the part of some Republicans in the .North to disparage these men, and to look upon them as persons who held on to the party simply for the purpose of securing the Federal offices in their States. This is a monstrous injustice. No men ever assumed a party name with more earnest devotion to party principles than has been done by Southern white Republicans. Believing in the principles of the Republican Party, and believing that its mission was to conserve the rights and interests of the whole people of this country, they have maintained their political integrity through ostracism and intimidation, and are still willing to struggle to restore the supremacy of the party in their States.

It is scarcely necessary to speak of the Republicanism of the colored men of the South. They have looked upon the Republican Party and its great leaders with a reverence amounting almost to religion. Their emancipation and enfranchisement—the greatest political events of the century—they know were the work of that party. They know that the Republican Party has been their friend, and has sought to lift them up and advance their interests. Gratitude and self-interest combine in causing them to adhere to its fortunes. To-day ninety-nine out of every hundred colored electors are ready to vote the Republican ticket.

These Republicans, white and black, feel that they have not been in the past, and are not now, as well sustained by the Republicans of the North, in their fierce political struggle with the Democratic Party, as their numbers and cause entitle them to be.

Their political contest has been conducted in those States which were the theatre of the great Rebellion. And while thousands of the men who served in the Confederate army are now earnest adherents of the Republican Party, the great majority of the old leaders are not with them, and so they have to contend with men who had acquired national reputations in *ante-bellum* days. In many of the States they have found themselves unequally matched in leadership, yet they have gone forward relying upon the justice of their cause and the sympathy and support of liberty-loving people throughout the country.

Upon a survey of the facts and a consideration of the mighty principles involved in this contest the question forces itself upon the mind, Will the majority of the people of the United States quietly submit to the overthrow of the republican principle in a number of the States of this Union by the subjugation of the majorities by force and fraud?

The vital principle in a government by the people is the right of majorities to rule through the ballot-box. This is the distinctive feature of our system, and constitutes not only its form, but its very substance.

When this principle is ignored, is overthrown, and the oligarchic system of minority rule is substituted in any portion of the country, an immediate alarm should be sounded, and for the time, laying aside every other issue, the people should demand that the powers of every department of the Government shall be invoked to their fullest extent for the correction of so monstrous an evil. Is it so that the people whose rights are secure have no care for those whose rights are overborne?

The Democratic Party in its platform of 1876, speaking "for the Democracy of the whole country," declared their "devotion to the Constitution of the United States, with its amendments, universally accepted as a final settlement of the controversies that engendered civil war," and also their "absolute acquiescence in the will of the majority—the vital principle of republics."

Were these idle, empty words? Have they no meaning, are they without force, with the body of Democrats in the Northern States? Not so; thousands of Democrats in the North, yea in the South also, accept these doctrines, and earnestly desire that they shall prevail.

The Democratic leaders have put a political yoke not only upon Republicans, but also upon the necks of Democrats. The one is to be deprived of his equal rights as a citizen, while the other is required to perform the unworthy task of despoilment, or close his eyes upon and acquiesce in the outrage. It cannot be that the hearts and consciences of all good men in the Democratic ranks are hardened against justice and right. There must be many men who are willing to concede to others an equal chance in the race of life—who object to ostracism and proscription, who condemn violence, and who revolt at fraud.

Is it not time to break the chain of political tyranny, and yield to the voice of reason and humanity? Is it not time that the rights of a common manhood be respected and maintained? Is it not time that the spirit of the progressive civilization of this century, and especially of this people, should fill the hearts and minds of the citizens of every State, and animate and inspire them to demand that every citizen shall be protected in all his rights, so that he may exercise them without fear?

There should be an awakening of the people upon this subject. No mere party advantage should induce any man to close his eyes and stop his ears against the overwhelming evidence of the wrongs inflicted upon the right of suffrage.

Democrats and Republicans alike should take this subject up as a public wrong to be redressed, as a wrong against white men as well as black men; as a wrong against the principles of the three great amendments to the Constitution, which were forged and welded in the heat of the mighty struggle between Freedom and Slavery

As proper exercise of the body gives strength to the physical man, so the lawful and free exercise of political rights gives strength to the intellectual man. The enjoyment of free speech and a free ballot is a great educator of the people. For a man to learn to vote correctly he must be allowed to vote freely. The question with Republicans is not that colored men shall vote their ticket, but that they shall be allowed to vote without fear, and have their votes counted without fraud. If Democrats can by fair arguments convince colored men that it is for their interest to vote with them, no objection can or will be made. But as long as the shot-gun, the revolver, the rope, and the scourge are the real Democratic arguments, Republicans will raise their voices in indignant protest.

Let no one underrate the character and magnitude of this conflict. Let no one conclude that the party which has its grip upon the governments of the South will release its hold without a terrible struggle.

Immigration from our own States and from foreign lands has planted the Republican principle in the great West and Northwest; little, however, can be expected from the influx of a new population for the disinthralment of the majorities in the South. People seeking new homes prefer to settle where their right to speak and act will not be questioned because of their political opinions.

The Existing Conflict upon the issue joined between Republican Government and the Oligarchy in the Southern States must therefore be settled with the people now there resident. It involves the rights of white men, but more largely does it involve the rights of the negro.

If freedom for the negro is not right, then nothing is right.

If giving him the equal protection of the laws is not just, then the scales of justice are broken and thrown aside.

If giving him the ballot was wrong, then the boasted principle that governments derive their just powers from the consent of the governed is a myth and a dream.

If freedom, equal rights, and the ballot are to be overborne by intimidation, murder, and fraud, then the laws which confer these rights are a delusion and a snare.

If the State governments are in tacit league with the people who perpetrate these wrongs, and neglect to protect the people in their lives and liberties, then are the just powers of the State abdicated, and the people must look to other and higher authority for relief.

If the United States Government possesses no power to correct these evils, or if, possessing the power, it refuses to exercise it, then is our system of free government for the protection of the rights of these people a failure.

There can be no backward step by the American people upon this issue. They have advanced to the position of putting into the laws, Freedom, Equal Rights, and the Ballot for all men, irrespective of color. And they will yet move forward to that more lofty and sublime position of requiring the observance and enforcement of those laws.

" To this complexion must we come at last," that from Ocean to Ocean, from the Lakes to the Gulf, every citizen shall be protected—by the States if they will, by the Nation if it must,—in the rights of free assemblage, free speech, free press, free ballot, and an honest count, and that minorities shall peacefully submit to the result of elections.

THE END.